Behavior-Based Assessment in Psychology

About the Editors

Tuulia M. Ortner, PhD, has been head of the Department of Psychological Assessment at the University of Salzburg, Austria, since 2012. She started working on objective personality tests more than 15 years ago at the University of Vienna, Austria, and continued her research at the Free University of Berlin, Germany. She is a member of the Executive Committee of the European Association of Psychological Assessment. Her current research includes examining the validity of behavior-based tests and their convergence with other measures.

Fons J. R. van de Vijver, PhD, is professor of Cross-Cultural Psychology at Tilburg University, The Netherlands, and holds honorary positions at North-West University, South Africa, and the University of Queensland, Australia. He has published widely on assessment issues, notably in the area of cross-cultural psychology, and also serves on the Executive Committee of the European Association of Psychological Assessment.

Psychological Assessment – Science and Practice

Each volume in the series *Psychological Assessment – Science and Practice* presents the state-of-the-art of assessment in a particular domain of psychology, with regard to theory, research, and practical applications. Editors and contributors are leading authorities in their respective fields. Each volume discusses, in a reader-friendly manner, critical issues and developments in assessment, as well as well-known and novel assessment tools. The series is an ideal educational resource for researchers, teachers, and students of assessment, as well as practitioners.

Psychological Assessment – Science and Practice is edited with the support of the European Association of Psychological Assessment (EAPA).

Editor-in-Chief: Anastasia Efklides, Greece
Editorial Board: Itziar Alonso-Arbiol, Spain; Tuulia M. Ortner, Austria; Willibald Ruch, Switzerland; Fons J. R. van de Vijver, The Netherlands

Psychological Assessment – Science and Practice, Vol. 1

Behavior-Based Assessment in Psychology

Going Beyond Self-Report in the Personality, Affective, Motivation, and Social Domains

Edited by
Tuulia M. Ortner and Fons J. R. van de Vijver

hogrefe

Library of Congress Cataloging in Publication information for the print version of this book is available via the Library of Congress Marc Database under the LC Control Number 2015936493

Library and Archives Canada Cataloguing in Publication

Behavior-based assessment in psychology : going beyond self-report in the personality, affective, motivation, and social domains / edited by Tuulia M. Ortner and Fons J.R. van de Vijver.

(Psychological assessment--science and practice ; vol. 1)
Includes bibliographical references and index.
Issued in print and electronic formats.
ISBN 978-0-88937-437-9 (paperback).--ISBN 978-1-61676-437-1 (pdf).--
ISBN 978-1-61334-437-8 (html)

1. Behavioral assessment. I. Ortner, Tuulia M., author, editor II. Vijver, Fons J. R. van de, author, editor III. Series: Psychological assessment--science and practice ; vol. 1

BF176.5.B44 2015   155.2'8   C2015-902319-X
                                  C2015-902320-3

2015 © by Hogrefe Publishing
http://www.hogrefe.com

PUBLISHING OFFICES
USA: Hogrefe Publishing Corporation, 38 Chauncy Street, Suite 1002, Boston, MA 02111
           Phone (866) 823-4726, Fax (617) 354-6875; E-mail customerservice@hogrefe.com
EUROPE: Hogrefe Publishing GmbH, Merkelstr. 3, 37085 Göttingen, Germany
           Phone +49 551 99950-0, Fax +49 551 99950-111; E-mail publishing@hogrefe.com
SALES & DISTRIBUTION
USA: Hogrefe Publishing, Customer Services Department,
           30 Amberwood Parkway, Ashland, OH 44805
           Phone (800) 228-3749, Fax (419) 281-6883; E-mail customerservice@hogrefe.com
UK: Hogrefe Publishing, c/o Marston Book Services Ltd., 160 Eastern Ave., Milton Park,
           Abingdon, OX14 4SB, UK
           Phone +44 1235 465577, Fax +44 1235 465556; E-mail direct.orders@marston.co.uk
EUROPE: Hogrefe Publishing, Merkelstr. 3, 37085 Göttingen, Germany
           Phone +49 551 99950-0, Fax +49 551 99950-111; E-mail publishing@hogrefe.com
OTHER OFFICES
CANADA: Hogrefe Publishing, 660 Eglinton Ave. East, Suite 119-514, Toronto, Ontario, M4G 2K2
SWITZERLAND: Hogrefe Publishing, Länggass-Strasse 76, CH-3000 Bern 9

Hogrefe Publishing
Incorporated and registered in the Commonwealth of Massachusetts, USA, and in Göttingen, Lower Saxony, Germany

No part of this book may be reproduced, stored in a retrieval system or transmitted, in any form or by any means, electronic, mechanical, photocopying, microfilming, recording or otherwise, without written permission from the publisher.

Cover design: MetaDesign AG
Printed and bound in Germany

ISBN 978-0-88937-437-9 (print) • ISBN 978-1-61676-437-1 (PDF) • ISBN 978-1-61334-437-8 (EPUB)
http://doi.org/10.1027/00437-000

Table of Contents

Part I: Introduction

Chapter 1   Assessment Beyond Self-Reports 3
           Tuulia M. Ortner and Fons J. R. van de Vijver

Part II: Modes and Theoretical Foundations

Chapter 2   Implicit Association Tests, Then and Now 15
           Marco Perugini, Giulio Costantini, Juliette Richetin, and Cristina Zogmaister

Chapter 3   A Model of Moderated Convergence Between Direct, Indirect, and
           Behavioral Measures of Personality Traits 29
           *Manfred Schmitt, Wilhelm Hofmann, Tobias Gschwendner,
           Friederike Gerstenberg, and Axel Zinkernagel*

Chapter 4   Narrative Content Coding 45
           Michael Bender

Chapter 5   Beyond Projection: Performance-Based Assessment 64
           Robert F. Bornstein

Part III: Measures

Chapter 6   Measuring Implicit Motives 81
           Athanasios Chasiotis

Chapter 7   Measures of Affect 97
           Martina Kaufmann and Nicola Baumann

Chapter 8   Implicit Measures of Attitudes 113
           Colin Tucker Smith and Kate A. Ratliff

Chapter 9   Objective Personality Tests 133
           Tuulia M. Ortner and René T. Proyer

Part IV: Domains of Application

Chapter 10 Indirect Measures in the Domain of Health Psychology 153
           Reinout W. Wiers, Katrijn Houben, Wilhelm Hofmann, and Alan W. Stacy

Chapter 11 Indirect Measures in Forensic Contexts 173
           Alexander F. Schmidt, Rainer Banse, and Roland Imhoff

Chapter 12 Implicit Measures in Consumer Psychology 195
           Malte Friese and Andrew Perkins

Chapter 13 Observation of Intra- and Interpersonal Processes 211
           Axel Schölmerich and Julia Jäkel

Contributors 221
Subject Index 224

Part I
Introduction

Chapter 1
Assessment Beyond Self-Reports

Tuulia M. Ortner[1] and Fons J. R. van de Vijver[2]

[1]Department of Psychology, University of Salzburg, Austria
[2]Department of Culture Studies, Tilburg University, The Netherlands

Self-reports have come under renewed scrutiny in the last few decades. Notably in social psychology, but spreading out to differential psychology, psychological assessment, and a number of applied fields of psychology, there is a tendency to refrain from using self-reports to collect data. This has led to a renewed interest in alternative modes of assessment. Objective measures or behavior-based measures are an example of such a method in which there is more interest than ever before, even though they have a long tradition, as shown here. This book provides an overview of the current state of the art in this field of assessment. In this introductory chapter we first give a short historical overview of the field, including a delineation of what we mean by *assessment beyond self-reports*. We then proceed by briefly describing the theme of each chapter. We conclude the chapter by drawing conclusions about the state of the field and its outlook.

A Short Look Back Into History

In the history of psychological assessment, behavior-based approaches for the measurement of personality characteristics and related constructs have played a major role from the very beginning. Early ancestors of personality psychology saw the relevance of behavioral indicators; examples are James McKeen Cattell, who in 1890 proposed behavioral tasks in his battery of mental tests, and Francis Galton, who in 1884 stated that the measurement of aspects of character deserves carefully recorded acts. Later, leading scholars of human personality also included behavioral data into their research. For example, Raymond Bernard Cattell and his team proposed three sources of information in their integral assessment of personality including so-called T-data (referring to reactions to standardized experimental situations, besides L-data and Q-data, which involve everyday behaviors and self-reported questionnaire data, respectively) represented in measurement by so-called cursive miniature situations (Cattell, 1941, 1944), later called objective tests. These tests aimed to stimulate the behavioral expression of personality while meeting common psychometric standards of psychological tests. Further earlier approaches of behavior-based assessment could be traced back to the early attempts of Herrmann Rorschach and his idea to interpret reactions to a set of ambiguous stimuli to refine clinical diagnoses by tapping into not explicitly verbalized aspects of personality (Rorschach, 1921).

Nowadays, the available behavior-based approaches for the measurement of personality, motivational variables, or constructs addressing aspects related to social behavior represent an impressive variety of methods. This variety precludes a clear definition. Therefore, we refer to these as measurement approaches beyond self-reports. Such approaches *beyond self-reports* include the *basic* form of behavior observation and coding methods (e.g., index systems, category systems) that were found to be especially useful in the assessment and investigation of interactions (e.g., Hill, Maskowitz, Danis, & Wakschlag, 2008; Reyna, Brown, Pickler, Myers, & Younger, 2012), personality in children and adolescents (Kilgus, Riley-Tillman, Chafouleas, Christ, & Welsh, 2014; Martin-Storey, Serbin, Stack, & Schwartzman, 2009), and in the context of work and aptitude testing (Hennessy, Maybe, & Warr, 1998; Schollaert & Lievens, 2012). Measures beyond self-reports may also include analyses of the consequences of persons' behavior, such as the investigation of the abrasion of the floor in a museum in order to analyze visitors' preferences (unobtrusive measures; Webb, Campbell, Schwartz, & Sechrest, 1966), or analyses of personal marks on the Internet, such as information given or activities conducted in social networks (Back et al., 2010). Also narratives, spoken or written statements or stories, represent written or recorded behavior and may serve as a source for personality assessment, using structured methods of content coding (Fiese & Spagnola, 2005; Kuefner, Back, Nestler, & Egloff, 2010). Furthermore, the use of psychophysiological measures as indicators of physiological arousal (e.g., Gannon, Beech, & Ward, 2008; Madsen, Parsons, & Grubin, 2004) or facial expressions as indicators of emotions (polygraph; Tracy, Robins, & Schriber, 2009; Vick, Waller, Parr, Pasqualini, & Bard, 2007) would fall into this category.

Measurement approaches beyond self-reports also include classic projective techniques (Lilienfeld, Wood, & Garb, 2000) that assess persons' responses to ambiguous stimuli. Their validity has been widely discussed in the last few decades (Bornstein, 1999; Viglione, 1999; Weiner, 1997) and newer developments, such as a semiprojective test, have been proposed with the aim of overcoming criticism leveled at projective tests, such as a shortage of objectivity in scoring and lack of interpretation of the scores based on normative samples (Sokolowski, Schmalt, Langens, & Puca, 2000). New computerized technologies further enabled a large number of testing procedures. The fledgling field is quickly growing, as demonstrated by a large number of new computerized objective personality tests building on Cattel's notion of the miniature situation (see Ortner & Schmitt, 2014) as well as by widely applied so-called indirect tests, mainly represented by reaction time measures (e.g., De Houwer, 2003; Greenwald, McGhee, & Schwartz, 1998; Payne, Cheng, Govorun, & Steward, 2005), but also including further indicators for indirect attitudes, such as evaluative decisions (Payne et al., 2005).

When addressing assessment instruments, procedures in the noncognitive domain (i.e., personality, affect, attitudes, and motivation), self-report questionnaires represent the dominant approach. All the behavior-based approaches mentioned are – compared with questionnaires assessing self-reports – much less frequently employed in most domains of psychological research (see Alonso-Arbiol & Van de Vijver, 2010; Ortner & Vormittag, 2011) and practice (Evers et al., 2012). Why are these approaches less visible, less used, and less within the focus of research compared with self-reports? As far as behavior observations, narratives, and most projective techniques are concerned, one of the main reasons may be the effort involved in collecting and processing behavioral observations to assess persons' characteristics. Most behavior-based approaches of assessment produce much more data than questionnaires – data that need to be sorted, integrated, or summarized. Thus, test economy and procedural efforts may often be the reason to refrain from using these methods. However, this disadvantage does not apply to newer computerized indirect or objective testing procedures. The new technology may have led to their increased visibility and impact in current research.

This volume is based on the premise that behavior-based assessment represents an essential element in the assessment process and should be included whenever possible. We propose the following reasons: First and foremost, objective measures suffer less or not at all from various well-documented problems of self-reports, such as response styles (e.g., Linden, Paulhus, & Dobson, 1986; Podsakoff & Organ, 1986) and the limitations of introspection (Howe, 1991; Nisbett & Wilson, 1977). For example, not all processes of interest in assessment can be accessed, remembered, and reported. Persons differ in their ability to identify real-life situations that are relevant to estimate certain constructs via self-reports and to integrate this information into a self-related judgment. Second, the nature and detail of assessed real behavior greatly exceed those of reported or estimated behavior. As the saying goes, actions speak louder than words. Third, researchers and practitioners do not have to pit one method against another by following the recommendation to use multiple methods in assessing a given construct in order to receive a more complete picture and to compensate the weaknesses that are inherent to specific measurement approaches (Fernandez-Ballesteros et al., 2001).

Chapters of the Book

In this volume we aim to address behavior-based assessment from researchers' and developers' perspective, up to its implementation in practice. The volume is divided into four parts. After this short introduction (Part I, Chapter 1), the second part (Part II) of the volume addresses particular modes of behavior-based assessment embedded in theoretical foundations. The first chapter of this part, Chapter 2, by Marco Perugini, Giulio Costantini, Juliette Richetin, and Cristina Zogmaister, presents an introduction to the Implicit Association Test (IAT) as the most prominent representative of indirect measures today. The authors provide a definition of indirect measures, discuss cognitive processes underlying the IAT effect, and address its psychometric aspects by discussing the scoring of the IAT and its reliability and validity. Chapter 3 by Manfred Schmitt, Wilhelm Hofmann, Tobias Gschwendner, Friederike Gerstenberg, and Axel Zinkernagel describes a new and innovative theoretical model. In line with the theory of planned behavior (Ajzen, 1987) and with the reflective impulsive model (RIM; Strack & Deutsch, 2004) they differentiate between manifest behavior, behavioral plans and intentions, and behavioral schemata or scripts. In their chapter, they postulate that the degree of convergence between direct, indirect, and behavioral measures is variable, not constant, and they propose a number of variables that moderate the convergence between the components of the model. Michael Bender gives an overview of thematic vs. structural analyses of texts and discusses these procedures and their usability in Chapter 4. He further addresses a number of practical areas of application, such as analyses of autobiographic narratives, eyewitness reports, and the assessment of depression. Robert Bornstein takes the reader to a journey into the theory and practice of the Rorschach Inkblot Method (RIM) as a representative of the huge family of projective techniques in Chapter 5. He addresses processes underlying Rorschach responses and discusses psychometric properties of this approach. His chapter closes with explicit guidelines for clinicians and clinical researchers for the use of RIM data.

Part III of this volume is dedicated to specific measures. The chapters in this part provide an introduction and overview on background information, psychometric properties, and recent developments of particular groups of measures. First, Athanasios Chasiotis presents different approaches to the measurement of implicit motives in Chapter 6. After an introduction into implicit and explicit motives, he presents the Picture Story Exercise (PSE) and the Operant

Motive Test (OMT) as content-coding methods for the assessment of implicit motives. He discusses theoretical foundations, practical aspects of presentation and scoring, as well as their psychometric properties. Behavior-based methods for the assessment of affect are summarized and presented by Martina Kaufmann and Nicola Baumann in Chapter 7. They systematically address particular measures assigned to three groups of methods: indirect, reaction time-based approaches; projective techniques; and behavioral observations to assess affect. They discuss the possibilities and limitations of the approaches. Colin Tucker Smith and Kate Ratliff present an overview of indirect measures for the assessment of attitudes and their psychometric properties in Chapter 8, such as different variations of the IAT, the Evaluative Priming Task, the Go/No-Go Association Task, the Extrinsic Affective Simon Task (EAST), the Sorting Paired Features Task, and the Affective Misattribution Procedure (AMP). In the next chapter (Chapter 9), Tuulia Ortner and René Proyer give an overview of tests that derive personality-related characteristics from observable behavior on performance tasks or other highly standardized miniature situations that lack face validity, so-called objective personality tests (OPTs). As an attempt to group this heterogeneous group of tests, they introduce three categories of different OPTs: (a) OPTs masked as achievement tasks, (b) OPTs that aim to represent real-life simulations, and (c) questionnaire-type OPTs that ask for evaluations or decisions, but lack face validity since different constructs than suggested are assessed. Psychometric properties are addressed by giving a number of examples of contemporary OPTs. The chapter closes with an analysis of the current state in research and practice.

Part IV provides insight into approaches, methods, and empirical findings with reference to specific areas of practical application. Reinout Wiers, Katrijn Houben, Wilhelm Hofmann, and Alan W. Stacy discuss indirect measures in the domain of health psychology in Chapter 10. They argue that initial, impulsive reactions, assessed by indirect measures, may be the most important predictor of health behaviors in some people in some situations. They introduce an impressing variety of measures and discuss their correlations in the health domain. In addition, they discuss the assessment of reflective processes. In Chapter 11, Alexander Schmidt, Rainer Banse, and Roland Imhoff give an overview of indirect measures in a forensic context with special attention to the assessment of deviant sexual interest. They present a large number of so-called *task-relevant* and *task-irrelevant* measures and carefully discuss empirical findings and psychometric properties of these measures. They complete their chapter with an outlook on the future with reference to methodological aims, theoretical demands, and aims with regard to clinical implementation of indirect assessment. Behavior-based approaches within consumer psychology are discussed by Malte Friese and Andrew Perkins in Chapter 12. They first present precursors of implicit measures and later provide an extensive review of empirical studies employing implicit measures in the consumer context. Finally, they provide an outlook and discuss some challenges for future research. In Chapter 13, Axel Schölmerich and Julia Jäkel present advantages and challenges of observational methods (OM) for the assessment of intra- and interpersonal processes. After an introduction into behavior observation systems, they discuss several specific behavior observation instruments and their psychometric properties. In their conclusion, they evaluate procedures for behavior observation and formulate demands for their future development.

What Can We Learn From the Chapters?

In our view, the current chapters provide the basis for the following conclusions about the current state of behavior-based assessment:

1. *The concrete relevance of behavior-based approaches depends on the context.* Various chapters clearly suggest that behavior-based approaches are most suitable in specific settings. For example, Robert Bornstein concludes in his chapter on current approaches for the use of projective techniques (Chapter 5) that the exclusive reliance on questionnaires assessing self-report is particularly critical in *clinical settings*, where self-reports of traits and symptoms reflect people's tendencies to view and (or) present themselves. A critical factor that should raise the interest in and relevance of behavior-based measures is lack of insight into characteristics of the construct being assessed (e.g., personality pathology). Another critical factor can be found in forensic psychology, where questionnaires and interviews are transparent and can easily be faked by respondents who are aware of the personal consequences of the assessment outcome; here, indirect approaches seem promising (Chapter 11). In health psychology, impulsive reactions captured by indirect approaches may be the most important predictor of health behaviors in some situations in some persons (Chapter 10). In other domains, such as consumer psychology, the attitudes of interest are not necessarily less accessible through self-reports, but researchers assume that indirect measures can nevertheless contribute in a meaningful way to the investigation of concepts and processes beyond self-reports (Chapter 12). We conclude that a number of different reasons may contribute to the inclusion of behavior-based approaches in different fields of application.

2. *Findings on the psychometric properties of one behavior-based measure cannot be generalized to another.* This means especially that reliability and validity need to be empirically examined and proven for each test or diagnostic procedure separately. This even means for most approaches in this volume that the same procedure, such as an IAT (or a behavior observation scheme, a narrative coding system, an OPT) that aims to assess one construct may be valid, whereas another IAT (or another behavior observation scheme, another narrative coding system, another OPT) that aims to assess another construct may not be (see, e.g., Chapter 2). We know from research on questionnaires that the usefulness of instruments critically depends on the stimuli used (or technical procedure implemented, data interpreted) and their suitability to evoke and therefore measure a certain construct.

3. *Not all behavior-based approaches are convenient to validly measure all constructs or all possible aspects of a construct.* Each of the presented approaches is more or less suitable to assess certain constructs or particular aspects of a construct – and not to assess all possible constructs or attitudes. For example, indirect approaches in general have proved to be more able to assess implicit aspects of attitudes (Chapters 2 and 8). As referred to by Ortner and Proyer (Chapter 9), interpersonal behavior and personality variables (e.g., extraversion) may not be validly assessed through computerized miniature situations as represented by OPTs, but they may be very validly assessed through behavior observation. It may be more difficult on the other hand to assess introspective processes or evaluations through behavior observations. This means that the valid assessment of a certain construct or attitude of interest is often inseparably bound to one or several methods of measurement.

4. *More research is needed.* The status of knowledge significantly differs between the approaches. The currently available body of scientific knowledge available is strong for some behavior-based approaches, and weaker for others. The Web of Knowledge indicated 25,288 journal entries including the keyword *behavior observation* in July 2014, 5,972 entries for *projective technique or projective test*, 3,551 journal entries for the keyword *implicit association test*, 219 results for *narrative content coding*, and 32 publications listed for the combined keywords of *objective personality tests* and *Cattell*. However, most research in the social and behavioral sciences is still based on self-reports; the corpus of knowledge regarding behavior-based approaches is widely behind the current research available on self-report questionnaires.

5. *Construct validity of behavior-based measures remains a challenge for future research.* As referred to by Schmitt et al. (Chapter 3), the construct validity of OPTs needs to be investigated by going beyond the traditional strategy of convergent and discriminant validation as employed in the multitrait-multimethod framework proposed by Campbell and Fiske (1959). The low convergence of certain behavior-based measures with questionnaires addressing self-reports with simultaneously demonstrated criterion validity deserves a new theoretical framework to explain and interpret the convergence or lack thereof. Cronbach and Meehl (1955) argued that a test's construct validity is given when empirical data confirm claims that were made based on a theory describing the given construct. The model proposed by Schmitt et al. in this volume (Chapter 3) postulates in line with dual-process theories (Strack & Deutsch, 2004) that explicit dispositions can be measured directly with self-report scales and that implicit dispositions can only be measured indirectly with procedures like the IAT. They further propose that explicit dispositions affect behavior via plans and intentions, and that implicit dispositions affect behavior via the automatic activation of behavioral scripts and schemata. This model goes beyond classic dual-process theories by assuming that these effects are moderated by personality and situation factors. In order to meet particular new challenges, inclusion of moderators of convergence in designs of validity studies may increase the convergence and indicate their validity more thoroughly compared with bare correlation coefficients. Nevertheless, the field is also open for further theoretical frameworks and developments.

6. *Reliability of (some) behavior-based measures needs further attention.* As referred to in several chapters, reliabilities for some behavior-based measures are low. For example, reliabilities differ widely across objective tests (see Chapter 9) and implicit measures (see Chapter 11). Besides, low reliabilities impact on correlations among measures and lead to difficulties in replicating findings (LeBel & Paunonen, 2011); low retest correlations may also, but not necessarily, indicate a higher amount of state variance assessed compared with trait variance (e.g., Koch, Ortner, Eid, & Schmitt, 2014; Schmukle & Egloff, 2004). Nevertheless, early studies revealed that behavior is more inconsistent than self-reported attitudes are (Hartshorne & May, 1928; Mischel, 1968; Ross & Nisbett, 1991). Therefore, even substantial efforts in test design and scoring may not raise the reliability of behavior-based measures to levels that are known from self-report questionnaires. We may therefore need to adjust our views on the reliability of behavior-based measures.

7. *There is ample room for further developments in behavior-based assessment.* Newer indirect methods, such as the IAT, have triggered an amazing interest in psychological research, as described in several chapters of this volume. The IAT in particular is a procedure that has been thoroughly investigated with reference to its functioning and, as Perugini and colleagues report, how to best develop and use it. Nevertheless, the IAT is not a task that could be implemented in order to assess individuals' characteristics or make reliable comparisons between individuals. Due to its psychometric properties, it is still a measure for the assessment of attitudes of groups instead of individuals. Perugini and colleagues point out that there is substantial room for improvements within the paradigm itself and make suggestions for future improvements of IATs. Future developments are also expected both in the currently underinvestigated field of OPTs and in all fields of application, where the use of behavior-based approaches is still underrepresented.

Coda

We hope that the publication of this book will enhance the understanding of behavior-based assessment and stimulate research on the topic. We would also like to encourage practitioners to use multimethod assessment by including various sources of information in the assessment process. We believe that we can only understand the complexity of human behavior by combining various theoretical and assessment perspectives. Behavior-based measures and their underlying models have an important role to play in this endeavor.

Acknowledgments

The editors gratefully acknowledge Karin C. Berkhout's skillful assistance in the editorial process.

References

Ajzen, I. (1987). Attitudes, traits, and actions: Dispositional prediction of behavior in personality and social psychology. In L. Berkowitz (Ed.), *Advances in experimental social psychology* (Vol. 20, pp. 1–63). New York, NY: Academic Press.

Alonso-Arbiol, I., & Van de Vijver, F. J. R. (2010). A historical analysis of the European Journal of Psychological Assessment: A comparison of the earliest (1992-1996) and the latest years (2005-2009). *European Journal of Psychological Assessment, 26*, 238–247. http://doi.org/10.1027/1015-5759/a000032

Back, M. D., Stopfer, J. M., Vazire, S., Gaddis, S., Schmukle, S. C., Egloff, B., & Gosling, S. D. (2010). Facebook profiles reflect actual personality, not self-idealization. *Psychological Science, 21*, 372–374. http://doi.org/10.1177/0956797609360756

Bornstein, R. F. (1999). Criterion validity of objective and projective dependency tests: A meta-analytic assessment of behavioral prediction. *Psychological Assessment, 11*, 48–57. http://doi.org/10.1037/1040-3590.11.1.48

Campbell, D. T., & Fiske, D. W. (1959). Convergent and discriminant validation by the multitrait-multimethod matrix. *Psychological Bulletin, 56*, 81–105. http://doi.org/10.1037/h0046016

Cattell, J. M. (1890). Mental tests and measurements. *Mind, 15*, 373–381. http://doi.org/10.1093/mind/os-XV.59.373

Cattell, R. B. (1941). An objective test of character-temperament I. *Journal of General Psychology, 25*, 59–73. http://doi.org/10.1080/00221309.1941.10544704

Cattell, R. B. (1944). An objective test of character-temperament II. *Journal of Social Psychology, 19*, 99–114. http://doi.org/10.1080/00224545.1944.9918805

Cronbach, L. J., & Meehl, P. E. (1955). Construct validity in psychological tests. *Psychological Bulletin, 52*, 281–302. http://doi.org/10.1037/h0040957

De Houwer, J. (2003). The Extrinsic Affective Simon Task. *Experimental Psychology and Health, 50*, 77–85. http://doi.org/10.1026//1618-3169.50.2.77

Evers, A., Muniz, J., Bartram, D., Boben, D., Egeland, J., Fernandez-Hermida, J. R., ... Urbanek, T. (2012). Testing practices in the 21st century developments and European psychologists' opinions. *European Psychologist, 17*, 300–319. http://doi.org/10.1027/1016-9040/a000102

Fernandez-Ballesteros, R., De Bruyn, E. E. J., Godoy, A., Hornke, L. F., Ter Laak, J., Vizcarro, C., ... Zaccagnini, J. L. (2001). Guidelines for the assessment process (GAP): A proposal for discussion. *European Journal of Psychological Assessment, 17*, 187–200. http://doi.org/10.1027//1015-5759.17.3.187

Fiese, B. H., & Spagnola, M. (2005). Narratives in and about families: An examination of coding schemes and a guide for family researchers. *Journal of Family Psychology, 19*, 51–61. http://doi.org/10.1037/0893-3200.19.1.51

Galton, F. (1884). Measurement of character. *Forthnightly Review, 36*, 179–185.

Gannon, T. A., Beech, A. R., & Ward, T. (2008). Does the polygraph lead to better risk prediction for sexual offenders? *Aggression and Violent Behavior, 13*, 29–44. http://doi.org/10.1016/j.avb.2007.08.001

Greenwald, A. G., McGhee, D. E., & Schwartz, J. K. L. (1998). Measuring individual differences in implicit cognition: The Implicit Association Test. *Journal of Personality and Social Psychology, 74*, 1464–1480. http://doi.org/10.1037/0022-3514.74.6.1464

Hartshorne, H., & May, M. A. (1928). *Studies in the nature of character. Studies in deceit (1)*. New York, NY: Macmillan.

Hennessy, J., Maybe, B., & Warr, P. (1998). Assessment Centre Observation Procedures: An experimental comparison of traditional, checklist and coding methods. *International Journal of Selection and Assessment, 6*, 222–231. http://doi.org/10.1111/1468-2389.00093

Hill, C., Maskowitz, K., Danis, B., & Wakschlag, L. (2008). Validation of a clinically sensitive, observational coding system for parenting behaviors: The Parenting Clinical Observation Schedule. *Parenting-Science and Practice, 8*, 153–185. http://doi.org/10.1080/15295190802045469

Howe, R. B. (1991). Introspection: A reassessment. *New Ideas in Psychology, 9*, 25–44. http://doi.org/10.1016/0732-118X(91)90038-N

Kilgus, S. P., Riley-Tillman, T. C., Chafouleas, S. M., Christ, T. J., & Welsh, M. E. (2014). Direct behavior rating as a school-based behavior universal screener: Replication across sites. *Journal of School Psychology, 52*, 63–82. http://doi.org/10.1016/j.jsp.2013.11.002

Koch, T., Ortner, T. M., Eid, M., & Schmitt, M. (2014). Evaluating the construct validity of Objective Personality Tests using a Multitrait-Multimethod-Multioccasion (MTMM-MO) approach. *European Journal of Psychological Assessment, 30*, 208–230. http://doi.org/10.1027/1015-5759/a000212

Kuefner, A. C. P., Back, M. D., Nestler, S., & Egloff, B. (2010). Tell me a story and I will tell you who you are! Lens model analyses of personality and creative writing. *Journal of Research in Personality, 44*, 427–435. http://doi.org/10.1016/j.jrp.2010.05.003

LeBel, E. P., & Paunonen, S. V. (2011). Sexy but often unreliable: The impact of unreliability on the replicability of experimental findings with implicit measures. *Personality and Social Psychology Bulletin, 37*, 570–583. http://doi.org/10.1177/0146167211400619

Lilienfeld, S. O., Wood, J. M., & Garb, H. N. (2000). The scientific status of projective techniques. *Psychological Science in the Public Interest, 1*(2), 27–66.

Linden, W., Paulhus, D. L., & Dobson, K. S. (1986). Effects of response styles on the report of psychological and somatic distress. *Journal of Consulting and Clinical Psychology, 54*, 309–313. http://doi.org/10.1037/0022-006X.54.3.309

Madsen, L., Parsons, S., & Grubin, D. (2004). A preliminary study of the contribution of periodic polygraph testing to the treatment and supervision of sex offenders. *Journal of Forensic Psychiatry & Psychology, 15*, 682–695. http://doi.org/10.1080/1478994042000270256

Martin-Storey, A., Serbin, L. A., Stack, D. M., & Schwartzman, A. E. (2009). The behaviour style observation system for young children predicts teacher-reported externalizing behaviour in middle childhood. *Infant and Child Development, 18*, 337–350. http://doi.org/10.1002/icd.601

Mischel, W. (1968). *Personality and assessment*. New York, NY: Wiley.

Nisbett, R. E., & Wilson, T. D. (1977). Telling more than we can know: Verbal reports on mental processes. *Psychological Review, 84*, 231–259. http://doi.org/10.1037/0033-295X.84.3.231

Ortner, T. M., & Schmitt, M. (2014). Advances and continuing challenges in objective personality testing. *European Journal of Psychological Assessment, 30*, 163–168. http://doi.org/10.1027/1015-5759/a000213

Ortner, T. M., & Vormittag, I. (2011). Articles published in EJPA 2009-2010: An analysis of the features of the articles and the characteristics of the authors. *European Journal of Psychological Assessment, 27*, 290–298. http://doi.org/10.1027/1015-5759/a000082

Payne, B. K., Cheng, C. M., Govorun, O., & Steward, B. D. (2005). An inkblot for attitudes: Affect misattribution as implicit measurement. *Journal of Personality and Social Psychology, 89*, 277–293. http://doi.org/10.1037/0022-3514.89.3.277

Podsakoff, P. M., & Organ, D. W. (1986). Self-reports in organizational research: Problems and prospects. *Journal of Management, 12*, 531–544. http://doi.org/10.1177/014920638601200408

Reyna, B. A., Brown, L. F., Pickler, R. H., Myers, B. J., & Younger, J. B. (2012). Mother-infant synchrony during infant feeding. *Infant Behavior & Development, 35*, 669–677. http://doi.org/10.1016/j.infbeh.2012.06.003

Rorschach, H. (1921). *Psychodiagnostik. Der Rorschach-Test* [Psychodiagnostics. The Rorschach Test]. Bern, Switzerland: Huber.

Ross, L., & Nisbett, R. E. (1991). *The person and the situation: Perspectives of social psychology*. New York, NY: McGraw-Hill.

Schmukle, S. C., & Egloff, B. (2004). Does the implicit association test for assessing anxiety measure trait and state variance? *European Journal of Personality, 18*, 483–494. http://doi.org/10.1002/per.525

Schollaert, E., & Lievens, F. (2012). Building situational stimuli in assessment center exercises: Do specific exercise instructions and role-player prompts increase the observability of behavior? *Human Performance, 25*, 255–271. http://doi.org/10.1080/08959285.2012.683907

Sokolowski, K., Schmalt, H. D., Langens, T. A., & Puca, R. M. (2000). Assessing achievement, affiliation, and power motives all at once: The Multi-Motive Grid (MMG). *Journal of Personality Assessment, 74*, 126–145. http://doi.org/10.1207/S15327752JPA740109

Strack, F., & Deutsch, R. (2004). Reflective and impulsive determinants of social behavior. *Personality and Social Psychology Review, 8*, 220–247. http://doi.org/10.1207/s15327957pspr0803_1

Tracy, J. L., Robins, R. W., & Schriber, R. A. (2009). Development of a FACS-verified set of basic and self-conscious emotion expressions. *Emotion, 9*, 554–559. http://doi.org/10.1037/a0015766

Vick, S.-J., Waller, B. M., Parr, L. A., Pasqualini, M. C. S., & Bard, K. A. (2007). A cross-species comparison of facial morphology and movement in humans and chimpanzees using the Facial Action Coding System (FACS). *Journal of Nonverbal Behavior, 31*, 1–20. http://doi.org/10.1007/s10919-006-0017-z

Viglione, D. J. (1999). A review of recent research addressing the utility of the Rorschach. *Psychological Assessment, 11*, 251–265. http://doi.org/10.1037/1040-3590.11.3.251

Webb, E. J., Campbell, D. T., Schwartz, R. D., & Sechrest, L. (1966). *Unobtrusive measures: Nonreactive research in the social sciences*. Chicago, IL: Rand McNally.

Weiner, I. B. (1997). Current status of the Rorschach Inkblot Method. *Journal of Personality Assessment, 68*, 5–19. http://doi.org/10.1207/s15327752jpa6801_2

Part II

Modes and Theoretical Foundations

Chapter 2
Implicit Association Tests, Then and Now

Marco Perugini, Giulio Costantini, Juliette Richetin, and Cristina Zogmaister

Department of Psychology, University of Milan-Bicocca, Italy

One of the ways to understand the importance of a scientific contribution is by looking at how many times it is cited in the scientific literature. The original paper by Greenwald, McGhee, and Schwartz (1998) that presented the Implicit Association Test (IAT), published in the *Journal of Personality and Social Psychology* (JPSP), has so far been cited 1,900 times (as retrieved from Web of Science, March 26, 2012) . Putting this figure into perspective, it is the most cited paper published in JPSP, the second most cited being a subsequent paper by Greenwald and colleagues on an improved scoring algorithm of the IAT (Greenwald, Nosek, & Banaji, 2003), and the fifth most cited paper in the whole field of psychology between 1998 and 2012. There is therefore little doubt that the IAT represents one of the most important developments in the field of psychology during the last 15 years. In this chapter we will first define direct and indirect measures, then present the IAT, discuss some cognitive processes behind its functioning, and briefly review some variants that have appeared in recent years. Adopting a psychometric perspective, the second part of this chapter will deal with issues such as the scoring of the IAT and its reliability and validity. The last part will focus on methodological issues relative to the development and the use of an IAT in a research context. Throughout the chapter our review will provide an overview of what has been done (*then*), what is the current state of knowledge (*now*), and what are the potential interesting developments (*future*).

Direct and Indirect Measures

In this chapter we use the terms *direct* and *indirect* to refer to the measures, and explicit and implicit to refer to the constructs. We should, however, clarify that we have modified the definitions provided by De Houwer and Moors (2010). According to the authors:

> …direct measures are characterized by two properties: (1) The measurement outcome is derived from a self-assessment by the participant. (2) The target of the self-assessment is the attribute that the measurement outcome is assumed to capture. If a measure does not have both of these properties, it can be called indirect. (p. 183)

This definition of a direct measure is problematic from a psychometric perspective because a direct self-assessment of a construct is never possible given that multiple items (questions) are by definition needed to measure a construct. Therefore, criterion 2 can never be respected apart from the trivial, and psychometrically deficient, case of using a single question to measure a construct[1]. Using this definition virtually no measure in psychology can be classified as direct from a psychometric perspective and the distinction put forward by De Houwer and Moors (2010) would be of little utility. We think that the taxonomic distinction by De Houwer and Moors (2010) is very important but, to increase its usefulness, we propose to modify the definition of a direct measure. We define a direct measure as *a measurement procedure that is characterized by* (a) *a personal evaluation* (e.g., questions such as "do you start conversations?" or "do you like chocolate?" requiring answers such as "very often" or "very much") *that is targeted to* (b) *an attribute* (c) *that could be included in the definition of the construct that the measurement outcome is assumed to capture* (e.g., extraversion, attitude toward chocolate).

The first property (*personal evaluation*) helps to differentiate a direct measure from a measure such as the IAT. The third property (*could be included in the definition of the construct*[2]) helps to differentiate standard questionnaires from measures such as the Name–Letter Task (NLT; Nuttin, 1985) that rely on a personal evaluation but that capture an attribute that would not be used to define the construct. In fact, starting conversations very often or affirming that one likes chocolate very much could be included in the definition of the constructs of extraversion and attitude toward chocolate, respectively. On the contrary, no one would include in the definition of self-esteem the preference for the letter of one's name. In other words, the critical question here is to ask oneself whether one would use the measured outcome as a potential defining element of the construct: If the answer is no, the measure is indirect. Of course, often this is a continuum that we are dichotomizing only as a means to clarify the property. The second property (*an attribute*) helps to accommodate the fact that psychological measurement is generally characterized by two levels of abstraction, items and construct (e.g., Edwards & Bagozzi, 2000). Therefore, the measurement outcome is an element (an attribute) related to the construct rather than the construct itself (*the* attribute).

Using this definition as a benchmark, all measures should ideally have the second property (i.e., they are multi-items or stimuli), direct measures have all properties, whereas indirect measures do not have at least one among the first and the third properties. Moreover, this definition could be useful to further distinguish between different types of indirect measures depending on which of the two differentiating properties are missing. For instance, one could argue that the IAT does not have the first and the third property whereas the NLT has the

---

[1] Concerning criterion 1, for the sake of simplicity, we will restrict our analysis to measurement procedures in which the self is the source of data and therefore this criterion is respected. We note, however, that there is another relevant dimension in a taxonomy of measurement procedures that is the source of the data (or method, using the psychometric jargon). There are in fact other sources of data such as peer reports, behavioral observations, and objective behavioral data, and each of them can be a valid source and, under some conditions and in some domains, can be as valid as or more valid than the self.

[2] An alternative formulation of the third property is *directly related to the construct*. In fact, the main point of this property is that some measures have a direct relation with the construct whereas others have an indirect relation. This concept can also be captured by the fact that the apparent target of measurement may be less or more concealed. For example, asking someone whether she thinks that the chocolate is good, tasty, and so on is a more direct (less concealed) way of measuring her attitude toward the chocolate than asking her to evaluate how much she likes a series of Chinese ideograms. In this sense, one type of measure can be more direct than another depending on whether the responses of the participants are closely or loosely connected to the to-be-measured construct (cf. De Houwer & Moors, 2010, p.183). However, on close inspection this alternative formulation may have the advantage of being straightforward but at the cost of having some elements of circularity because the term *direct* is contained both in what should be explained (*explanandum*) and in its explanation (*explanans*). For this reason we decided to formulate the third property as *could be included in the definition of the construct*, given that one key feature of having a direct/close vs. indirect/loose relation with the construct is that the measured outcome is more or less likely to be usable when defining the construct.

first but not the third property. In fact, as we will detail later, a typical IAT is a task that is not characterized by a personal evaluation (e.g., it does not require one to express a personal opinion), similar to indirect measures such as the Affective Evaluative Priming (AEP; Fazio, Sanbonmatsu, Powell, & Kardes, 1986). The Affective Misattribution Paradigm (AMP; Payne, Cheng, Govorun, & Stewart, 2005) and NLT instead rely on a personal evaluation (e.g., evaluate as positive or negative Chinese ideograms; evaluate alphabet letters) but the attributes they capture (e.g., preference for Chinese ideograms; preference for a letter) would not normally be used to define the construct (e.g., related to the primes in the AMP, self-esteem in the NLT).

What Is the Implicit Association Test?

The IAT is a paradigm that has been developed for the measurement of psychological constructs through the strength of associative links between concepts. It has been implemented to investigate a broad range of constructs (see the meta-analysis by Greenwald, Poehlman, Uhlmann, & Banaji, 2009). Unlike traditional interviews and questionnaires, in the IAT respondents are not requested to describe their own opinions or attitudes (e.g., by selecting their agreement to a question among several response options) but, rather, these are inferred based on their performance in a series of categorization tasks. Respondents see a series of stimuli appearing on a computer monitor (words or images) that represent two different (typically opposite) concepts and the two polarities of an attribute dimension. For each stimulus, they are required to press one of two different keys of the keyboard, depending on their category membership. For instance, in an IAT aimed to measure prejudice against Blacks, the two concepts could be the social categories Black and White, represented respectively by photographs of Black and White faces, and the attribute could be the positive–negative evaluation, represented by words (e.g., *rainbow, rotten*). The IAT is structured in different blocks. In the *simple categorization* blocks, the participants' task would be to press one key for White and the other for Black faces, or to press one key for positive and another key for negative words. Each stimulus belongs univocally to one category; the categorization task is therefore easy and the presence of an unambiguous relationship between each stimulus and its category is one of the prerequisites of a good implementation of IAT. The task is made more complex by the presence of two *double categorization critical* blocks, namely, blocks of trials in which exemplars representing the concept or the attributes are to be categorized. Continuing the previous example, in one of the critical blocks one key would be used for White faces and negative words, and the other for Black faces and positive words. The association between concepts and attributes is counterbalanced in the other critical block and therefore respondents would use one key for White faces and positive words and the other key for Black faces and negative words. The critical block in which the associations in response between a concept and an attribute is consistent with the cognitive associations of the respondent is called a compatible block, and the other is called an incompatible block. Based on speed and accuracy of performance in the critical blocks, the IAT score can be computed (Greenwald et al., 2003), which is typically interpreted as an indirect measure (Greenwald et al., 1998).

Which Cognitive Processes Underlie the IAT Effect?

Various theoretical explanations of the IAT effect have been proposed. According to De Houwer (2001), the IAT relies on a response compatibility effect. After repeated categorizations of exemplars of the attribute dimension by pressing two different keys of the keyboard, these acquire a specific meaning. If, for instance, the attribute dimension is evaluative, the key used for negative words acquires a temporary negative evaluation and the key for positive words a temporary positive evaluation. In critical blocks, when respondents have to categorize exemplars of the concept (e.g., based on racial membership), automatic affective reactions toward the concept trigger the consistent response. In the compatible task this facilitates the response on the concept dimension, while in the incompatible task the automatic reaction and the response tendency automatically triggered by the concept's valence interferes with the answer required by the semantic content, causing an increase in mistakes and/or latency.

Brendl, Markman, and Messner (2001; see also Klauer, Voss, Schmitz, & Teige-Mocigemba, 2007) propose a different explanation according to which categorization decisions in IAT are based on a random walk model. In a nutshell, during critical tasks respondents base their decision on how to categorize each stimulus on a progressive process of gathering evidence supporting the two options (i.e., press the right or left key), until evidence for one of the options reaches a threshold level. At this point the answer is given. While gathering this evidence, respondents process each stimulus both in terms of the concept (e.g., White or Black in a prejudice IAT) and of the attribute dimension (e.g., positive or negative). The consistency/inconsistency with which evidence coming from the two dimensions leads to action influences the time required for the decision. In the compatible block all evidence leads to the same direction and therefore the threshold is reached fast; in the incompatible block evidence from categorization of the stimulus in terms of concept guides the response to the opposite direction relative to evidence coming from the attribute dimension and therefore more processing is necessary to reach the threshold. Moreover, respondents perceive the greater difficulty of the task and therefore increase the threshold criterion; this second process causes a further slowdown. Results from work by Klauer and colleagues (2007) provide empirical evidence for this model and highlight that the increase in time required to reach the threshold causes variance that is related to the construct being investigated, but the increase in the criterion of threshold introduces error variance in the IAT score.

Another explanation of the IAT effect by Mierke and Klauer (2003) focuses on the cognitive control processes that are required in the critical blocks for the continuous switching from categorizations based on the concept to those based on the attribute and vice versa. These control processes cause a slowdown in response. The compatible block of IAT can be simplified to a unidimensional categorization, which reduces the cognitive costs. For instance, in the compatible block of an IAT measuring the preference for musical instruments as compared with weapons, a respondent who prefers musical instruments can simplify the task by pressing a key for all positive stimuli, including musical instruments, and the other key for all negative stimuli, including weapons. This simplification is not possible for the incompatible block. In short, the IAT effect is based on the costs of the cognitive control that is required in the incompatible block to a higher extent than in the compatible block. According to this model, empirically supported by Klauer, Schmitz, Teige-Mocigemba, and Voss (2010), individual differences in cognitive control abilities introduce systematic error variance in the IAT score.

The figure–ground model of Rothermund and Wentura (2001) is also based on the idea that respondents enact strategies to simplify the IAT tasks. According to this proposal, a categorization task can be simplified to a unipolar search by focusing on the most salient category. For instance, if a White individual is required to press one key for Black faces and the other for White faces, Black faces may be more salient; then, the respondent can simplify the task to "press one key for Black faces, and the other for anything else." Similarly, the categorization of words into positive and negative can be simplified by pressing one key for negative words, which are typically more salient, and the other key for anything else. In one of the critical blocks, the two most salient categories (Black faces and negative words) share the response key. The double categorization task can therefore be simplified to a unipolar search and the respondent can press one key for everything that is salient (*figure*), and the other key for anything else (*ground*). This simplification and facilitation is not possible in the other critical task, in which the two salient categories require different responses. Stimulus salience can be caused by reasons that are extraneous to the constructs of interest for the researcher, such as, for instance, familiarity, and in this case the mechanism described here would introduce error variance in the IAT score.

In sum, there is evidence supporting each of these explanations and suggesting therefore that different cognitive processes may cause the IAT effect. We are not aware of studies that have attempted to test the different explanations against each other and therefore little is known about the extent to which they are independent or redundant. It is important to note that these explanations help to understand the cognitive process underlying the IAT as a task but they do not necessarily challenge its validity. In fact, individual differences in these cognitive processes tend to introduce systematic error variance in the IAT score that is at least partly orthogonal to its valid variance. This is confirmed by various studies showing that in many different implementations of the IAT a substantial component of variance in the score is related to the construct of interest (e.g., Greenwald et al., 2009), hence it is reflecting valid variance, but it is useful nonetheless to stress that the IAT is a procedural format whose psychometric characteristics rely on the specific implementation. The role played by each of these processes is likely influenced by the specific stimuli chosen, by the construct being investigated, the circumstances, and the characteristics of the respondents.

Variants of the IAT

During the short life of the IAT several variants of the procedure have been proposed to improve the paradigm and overcome some of its limitations. For instance, a personalized IAT was proposed to remedy the critique that the IAT would be affected by *extrapersonal associations* (Olson & Fazio, 2004); a paper-and-pencil IAT was developed that does not require the use of a PC (e.g., Lowery, Hardin, & Sinclair, 2001), and a version based only on images was built to administer to very young children (Thomas, Burton-Smith, & Ball, 2007).

Probably, the most important variations that have been introduced so far are for overcoming the relative nature of the IAT. The IAT score indeed reflects the *preferential* association between a concept and a given polarity of the attribute dimension, as compared with the other concept. On the basis of an IAT score, we can, for instance, say that one's own social group is more associated to a positive evaluation than another group is, but we cannot determine how much this result can be described in terms of an ingroup bias toward one's own group or derogation of the outgroup. A variant of the IAT to measure associations concerning a single concept is the Single-Category IAT (Karpinski & Steinman, 2006), whereas an alternative paradigm is the Go/No-Go Association Task (Nosek & Banaji, 2001).

Another important limitation, for which no completely satisfying solution has so far been developed, is the *block* structure of the IAT. Indeed, some of the cognitive processes that can introduce error variance in the IAT are at work because of this block structure (e.g., De Houwer, 2003; Teige-Mocigemba, Klauer, & Sherman, 2010). An alternative of the IAT that was based on a single block of trials was the Extrinsic Affective Simon Task (EAST; De Houwer, 2003), which unfortunately seems to be characterized by lower levels of reliability compared with those typically observed for the IAT (De Houwer & De Bruycker, 2007). More recently, variants of the IAT such as the Single-Block IAT (Teige-Mocigemba, Klauer, & Rothermund,

2008) or the Recoding-Free IAT (Rothermund, Teige-Mocigemba, Gast, & Wentura, 2009) were elaborated but evidence concerning their psychometric properties is still insufficient.

Finally, concerning the figure–ground recoding strategy, it is worth mentioning the Brief IAT (Sriram & Greenwald, 2009). This variant has the typical block structure of the IAT, but it has the advantage of speed of administration with only a small loss of internal consistency. More important, it has been built with the aim of reducing spontaneous variability in the participants' strategy, because the roles of figure and ground are explicitly and systematically associated with the category dimensions. Unfortunately, to our knowledge, no study to date has investigated the impact of this explicit attribution of figure/ground roles on the systematic error variance of IAT scores.

Scoring of the IAT

The IAT performance is assessed using both latencies and errors. In the first publication on the IAT, Greenwald et al. (1998) computed IAT effects (i.e., difference between incompatible and compatible blocks) with three conventional scores using, respectively, untransformed latencies, log transformed latencies to correct for positive skewness, and errors. Later, Greenwald et al. (2003) elaborated on additional scoring procedures, tested them on thousands of data relative to different domains, and ended up recommending a new D score. The D score consists of taking the difference in reaction times between the two critical blocks and dividing it by the individual reaction time standard deviation (SD) of the two critical blocks (individual variability calibration). The D score was chosen because it reduces error variance due to individual differences in overall reaction times, order effects in the IAT (i.e., compatible vs. incompatible administered first), and practice effects in the case of multiple IATs. It also maximizes the correlation between the IAT and explicit measures (see Greenwald et al., 2003, for more details). Moreover, the D scores allow one to cope with possible speed–accuracy trade-offs by including a time penalty to error trials. Note that error rates in the IAT performance are on average very low (around 5–10%) and the data of participants showing more than 25% of errors are typically discarded. Three main types of D scores are usually calculated depending on whether the procedure (a) has a built-in penalty ($D2$) or, in case of no built-in penalty, the correction for errors is made (b) with 2 SDs based on correct latencies ($D3$ and $D5$) or (c) with a fixed 600 ms ($D4$ and $D6$). In addition to differences in terms of transformations and consideration of general speed, the scores differ in terms of how the outliers are treated. Indeed, for the conventional latency scores, trials greater than 3,000 ms and less than 300 ms are recoded into these upper and lower boundaries, whereas for the D scores cited above, trials greater than 10,000 ms and less than 400 ms are excluded (lower tail treatment only for $D5$ and $D6$). To our knowledge, since the development of the D scores, very little research has been devoted to develop and test a better alternative scoring algorithm. However, we believe that there is still room for improvement, especially when considering that some work showed different effects of the same factor depending on the scoring method used (e.g., Dambrun, Villate, & Richetin, 2008; Schmitz, Teige-Mocigemba, Klauer, & Voss, 2013). For example, Schmitz et al. (2013) demonstrated incongruities in the effect of cognitive load depending on the type of IAT scores and showed that these incongruities can be mainly explained by the type of transformation applied to the data (i.e., log-transformation or individual variability calibration). Furthermore, the authors demonstrated that depending on the outlier criterion, correlations between direct (self-report) and indirect measure (IAT) fluctuated.

Recent mathematical modeling work has been devoted to systematically identify and measure the different processes involved in the IAT performance in order to disentangle the construct-related components from other components. In these mathematical models the outcomes of an IAT (i.e., errors and reaction times) are modeled in terms of a set of variables or parameters that represent the components' processes (e.g., activation of association, detecting correct responses) and a set of equations that relate these parameters (see Sherman, Klauer, & Allen, 2010, for a review). Besides providing a test of the different processes of the IAT, this decompositional approach could offer an alternative to the D measure. In other words, one could isolate the estimate of the component process more directly related to the construct and test its relationship with other measures. Klauer et al. (2007) presented a diffusion-model analysis of the IAT and identified the IATv in accounting for construct-specific variance as demonstrated by its significant correlation with a direct measure of attitude. However, the diffusion-model analysis is complex and has some disadvantages such as the exclusion of data from participants who do not make errors (but see Krause, Back, Egloff, & Schmukle, 2011), lower reliability of the specific parameters, and difficulty of computation, although some software is now available that makes this type of analysis more accessible to nonspecialists. Incidentally, one should note that it is rare to reach this level of analysis in order to disentangle method variance from construct-related variance in the domain of direct measures.

A different approach for improving the D scoring could be to focus on diminishing the influence of error variance. In this perspective, modern robust statistical methods could provide some elements for an improved algorithm. In fact, robust statistics are immune to non-normal distribution and lack of homogeneity of variance (i.e., heteroscedasticity), which are the two main threats to classic parametric methods and are often observed in reaction times data. Logarithmic transformations of reaction times are intended to reduce skewness. However, this kind of transformation sometimes fails to produce normality (Erceg-Hurn & Mirosevich, 2008), compresses some information (see Schmitz et al., 2013) and, most important of all, does not deal with outliers in a systematic manner. As we outlined earlier, the way to deal with outliers is different depending on the scoring method and can affect psychometric properties such as convergent validity. In the D score, the individual variability calibration that consists of dividing the difference by the SD computed on trials of both compatible and incompatible trials is a way to deal with the heavy tails of the distributions. In fact, cognitive failures leading to long latencies affect both means and SD. By dividing the mean by the SD, one removes the extent to which the mean was inflated by long latencies (see Schmitz et al., 2013, for a more detailed explanation). We believe that applying robust statistical methods would allow one to deal more systematically with outliers, both at the individual level and the sample level (see Wilcox, 2012; Wilcox & Keselman, 2012), and it could result in an improved scoring of the IAT.

Psychometric Properties of the IAT

Many studies aimed at testing the psychometric properties of the IAT (see Teige-Mocigemba et al., 2010, for a review). We believe that this is a stage of initial development that will soon be crossed. In fact, strictly speaking, it is odd to determine whether the IAT is a psychometrically sound measure that could, for example, be employed in individual counseling or occupational assessment, much as it would be odd nowadays to establish the psychometric properties of a Likert-type scale. In fact, one can test the psychometric properties of a Self-Esteem IAT or of an Anxiety IAT but not of the IAT in general. Psychometric properties, consisting of aspects such as reliability and validity, are a contextualized issue concerning how well a specific measure works in assessing a particular concept. Nevertheless, at this stage a consideration of the psychometric qualities that the IAT showed in different fields may be useful because it provides an overview of its generic properties. However, whenever possible, one should investigate the psychometric properties of implementations of the IAT that are similar to one's own topic of research.

Reliability

Internal consistency is often estimated by dividing the IAT into two halves, computing the split-half reliability of the two sets of difference scores, and applying a Spearman–Brown correction. Reliability can also be estimated considering the differences between each compatible and incompatible trial as singletons to be integrated in the calculation of Cronbach's α. Both types of coefficients range from 0.70 to 0.90 (Nosek, Greenwald, & Banaji, 2007) and are usually higher than those observed for other indirect measures (e.g., De Houwer & De Bruycker, 2007). Reliability is also established by calculating test–retest correlations, thus estimating temporal stability. Usually test–retest stability is lower than internal consistency (from 0.25 to 0.70) although higher than for other indirect measures. The typical finding that test–retest stability is noticeably lower than internal consistency has been considered as an indication of the high malleability of the constructs or of the high dependency on the context of measurement. Therefore, in order to establish test–retest reliability, one might want to pay special attention to potential differences between the two measurement points. Note that there are different ways to increase reliability focusing on methodology (attention to special features or instructions of the task) or on statistics (use of more robust estimates; see Perugini, Richetin, & Zogmaister, 2010, for more details).

Validity

Convergent and Discriminant Validity

The convergent and discriminant validity of the IAT is estimated through correlations with both direct measures and other indirect measures. In terms of relations between the IAT and direct measures, the consistency between self-report measures and IAT is usually higher for attitude domains than for self-concept but in general is relatively modest: from 0.24 in the meta-analysis of Hofmann, Gawronski, Gschwendner, Le, and Schmitt (2005) to 0.37 in Nosek's analysis of Internet data (2005). Nosek (2005) demonstrated that the strength of the correlation is moderated by interpersonal (self-presentation, perceived distinctiveness from the norm) and intrapersonal (e.g., evaluative strength) features of attitudes. Self-esteem studies show that the correlation between direct and indirect measures depends on the conditions under which the measures are taken (LeBel, 2010). More specifically, when accessibility was high, direct and indirect measures of self-esteem were positively correlated, whereas they were not correlated under conditions of low accessibility. Moreover, research suggests that the relative lack of correlations is partly due to the structural fit or misfit between the IAT and direct measures (e.g., Payne, Burkley, & Stokes, 2008). Usually, convergent validity between the IAT and direct measures has been taken as evidence of a single construct measured in two different ways, whereas discriminant validity has been considered as evidence of the existence of implicit and explicit constructs of the same object (e.g., Greenwald & Farnham, 2000). However, the role of moderators such as structural fit or measurement conditions would suggest caution in the interpretation of the correlation between the IAT and direct measures as an indication of the cognitive structures underlying both types of score. In terms of correlations with other indirect measures, most research demonstrates a lack of correspondence (see Schnabel, Asendorpf, & Greenwald, 2008, for a review). This weak convergent validity of the IAT has mainly been explained in terms of unsatisfactory reliability of most of the other indirect measures, structural differences among indirect measures such as structural fit, relativity, and specific cognitive mechanisms involved (see Teige-Mocigemba et al., 2010, for a discussion). In sum, the lack of strong evidence of convergence between the IAT and other indirect or direct measures has not been interpreted as a lack of validity of the IAT but rather in terms of underlying processes or procedural details.

Predictive and Incremental Validity

The predictive validity of the IAT has attracted much attention in the literature (see Greenwald et al., 2009, and Perugini et al., 2010, for reviews on the predictive validity of numerous IATs). To properly establish the predictive and incremental validity of the IAT for a specific domain, one would probably want to examine it together with direct measures through the test of different patterns of prediction (Perugini, 2005; Perugini et al., 2010). Perugini et al. (2010) distinguished eight main validity patterns: simple association, moderation, additive, interactive/multiplicative, double dissociation, partial dissociation, and double additive. Examples of each pattern can be found in the literature (see Perugini et al., 2010, for a review). For instance, an interactive or multiplicative pattern has been demonstrated in the domain of self-esteem where indirect and direct measures of self-esteem significantly interact to predict the level of narcissism (e.g., Zeigler-Hill, 2006). Note that the additive and the double additive patterns, and to some extent also the partial dissociation pattern, allow for a test of incremental validity of the IAT in the sense that those patterns predict significant and simultaneous contributions of both the IAT and the direct measure for one (additive) or two (double additive) behaviors. The incremental validity for the IAT is a very important issue because the additional costs of including it should be overcome by the additional portion of variance it explains in behavior over and above direct measures. The moderation, the double dissociation, and the partial dissociation patterns all refer to an essential concept that is conditional predictive validity. In fact, the predictive validity of the IAT depends on many factors (for a review see Friese, Hofmann, & Schmitt, 2008; Perugini et al., 2010). Perugini et al. (2010) propose to organize these moderators in three main categories: types of behaviors (i.e., spontaneous vs. deliberate), situational moderators (e.g., self-activation), and personal moderators (e.g., working memory capacity). For example, it has been shown in different domains that an IAT uniquely predicts spontaneous behavior whereas a direct measure predicts more deliberate behavior (e.g., Perugini, 2005). In the domain of situational moderators, Perugini, O'Gorman, and Prestwich (2007) showed in four studies that the predictive validity of the IAT is increased when participants take part in a self-activation procedure before completing the IAT. In sum, the concept of conditional predictive validity means that some IATs predict some behaviors in some situations for some people.

Construct Validity

Since Greenwald et al. (1998) presented the IAT as providing an estimate of differential association between a set of two concepts and a set of two attributes, numerous publications have challenged this assumption both theoretically and empirically (e.g., Fiedler, Messner, & Bluemke, 2006). In fact, research has been devoted to identifying the possible confounding factors of the IAT effects such as recoding (e.g., Rothermund et al., 2009), cognitive abilities (e.g., Klauer et al., 2010), and salience asymmetry (e.g., Rothermund & Wentura, 2001). We have already focused on this issue when discussing the cognitive processes underlying the IAT. In general, this research underlines that numerous factors cause construct-unrelated variance in the IAT effect. Although there is no such thing as a psychological measure that reflects only a single specific process (process-pure), it appears important to identify the processes underlying the IAT effect in order to disentangle specific construct variance from construct-unrelated variance. Process models have tried to integrate some factors responsible for the IAT effects (see Teige-Mocigemba et al., 2010, for a detailed review of these models). With the same perspective of disentangling related from unrelated construct variance, mathematical modeling has been developed in order to identify and quantify the processes that account for performance on indirect measures such as the IAT (see Sherman et al., 2010, for a detailed review on the different mathematical models). Among the different models, the diffusion model (Klauer et al., 2007) seems to be more appropriate to the IAT because it takes into account both errors and reaction times, whereas most of the other models consider only error rates that are relatively low and uninformative in the IAT. In this model, the authors identified seven parameters that contribute to the IAT effect representing different decisional and nondecisional components and they were able to identify the differential drift rate (IATv) as the closest indicator of attitudinal (i.e., construct-related) responses. Finally, work that has demonstrated the ability of the IAT to be a significant moderator under theoretically relevant conditions could be considered as additional evidence of its construct validity. For example, the gatekeeper model predicts that whether priming has an effect on behavior depends on individual differences in the valence of the concept being automatically activated (Perugini & Prestwich, 2007). Given that these individual differences can be captured by a measure like the IAT, the implication is that the IAT should be a moderator of the effect of priming on behavior, such that a certain prime (e.g., helpful) will affect a relevant behavior (e.g., to volunteer) especially for those who have a high score in a relevant IAT (e.g., altruism; Perugini, Conner, & O'Gorman, 2011).

Methodological Considerations on the IAT

In this final section we focus our attention on a few methodological suggestions based on broader theoretical considerations and with an emphasis on making specific choices when developing or administering an IAT.

The Role of Structural Fit in the Development of the IAT

Structural fit is defined as "...the degree of methodological similarity between two different tests" (Payne et al., 2008, p. 17), and is especially important when comparing direct and indirect measures. Indirect and direct measures present many differences that are not necessarily connected to the distinction between implicit and explicit cognitions. For instance, while questionnaires require one to process verbal sentences and to answer on a numeric scale, indirect measures involve simpler stimuli, such as single words or images, and require simpler evaluations. A direct measure that consists of the ratings of the same stimuli presented in the indirect measures can provide a higher structural fit than germane self-report questionnaires. A series of studies (Payne et al., 2008) showed that correlations between the two types of measures increase substantially when structural fit is improved.

The concept of structural fit has some important implications for research involving the IAT. In particular, considerable attention and effort are required when selecting stimuli for an IAT.

Stimuli have a notable impact on the IAT, as they contextually define the corresponding categories (e.g., Bluemke & Friese, 2006): The definition of categories through stimuli should thus be as clear and as unambiguous as possible. Often stimuli for the target and contrast categories are selected simply on the basis of the intuition of the researcher and of the review of empirical and theoretical literature. Instead, we think that much more effort could be fruitfully devoted to this critical phase and we sketch a possible procedure that could be followed. The first step is to pre-select a large set of potential stimuli, according to the theoretical definition of the construct. Stimuli should be selected in bipolar pairs when possible to reduce irrelevant differences between the two opposite categories. The second step consists of a relatively large pilot study (we suggest a sample of at least 100 participants) where the stimuli are rated directly in terms of attitude toward or application to self. If desirable, the study might also include other established measures of the construct (e.g., self-report questionnaires). The analyses should then focus on establishing the factorial structure (e.g., with a principal component analysis), keeping an eye on the breadth of the construct, and optimal relations with the criteria (e.g., the questionnaire measures), if available. Besides the details that may vary, the main outcome of this study would be a set of stimuli that optimally reflect the target and contrast category as gauged by the explicit ratings. These stimuli would then be used for the main study both with the IAT and with an explicit rating measure. The main goal of this procedure is to maximize structural fit: This approach can not only improve the validity of the resulting indirect and direct measures but also facilitate cleaner theoretical interpretations of the results.

Context Effects and Contrast Category

Explicit measures are sensitive to contextual effects, both relative to the context of the items within the questionnaire and to the general measurement context (Podsakoff, MacKenzie, Lee, & Podsakoff, 2003; Schwarz & Oyserman, 2001). Contextual information can also affect indirect measures: Context is thought to influence the pattern activation of a concept defined as the subset of the associations in memory that is activated in a certain situation (Gawronski & Bodenhausen, 2006). The IAT has been proved to be sensitive to the context of administration and of the stimuli. For instance, studies that investigated racial prejudice showed that the IAT effect can be influenced by using names of liked/disliked Blacks and Whites as stimuli in the IAT (Mitchell, Nosek, & Banaji, 2003; Study 2). The IAT effect can be also affected by contextual motivational orientations: For instance, implicit attitude toward food is more positive for individuals who did not eat for a relatively long time compared with satiated individuals (Seibt, Häfner, & Deutsch, 2007). The context also influences indirect measures of self-concept, as has been shown for implicit aggressiveness that is higher when it is assessed after a session of violent video gaming (Bluemke, Friedrich, & Zumbach, 2010). The context can also be used to improve stability of the IAT over time, by keeping identical contextual information that activates similar concept-relevant associations across different administrations (Gschwendner, Hofmann, & Schmitt, 2008). In general the researcher should keep the context of administration, as well as contextual information included within stimuli, as stable and as neutral as possible to prevent potential confounds.

The contrast category can also be understood as a stable context that has the potential to foster a clear interpretation of the target category (Perugini et al., 2010). This happens seamlessly for complementary categories, such as for natural dichotomies or when liking one category implies disliking the contrast category. However, this is not always the case and there are categories without an obvious or unequivocal contrast. Under these circumstances, one solution is to use variants of the IAT that do not require a contrast category, such as the SC-IAT. It is also possible to use a traditional IAT but care must be taken that the contrast category, even if not opposite, provides a meaningful context within which the target category can be understood.

Concluding Remarks

In this chapter we have briefly reviewed a number of issues concerning the IAT. Research using this paradigm is currently extending to most fields in psychology and has started to find its way in other fields such as law, marketing, and political sciences. Much is known today about the functioning of the IAT and how to best develop it and use it. Although the IAT can be criticized in a number of ways, we still await a better alternative. We believe, however, that there is still substantial room for improvement within the paradigm itself and have suggested a few ways in which future IATs can be improved.

References

Bluemke, M., Friedrich, M., & Zumbach, J. (2010). The influence of violent and nonviolent computer games on implicit measures of aggressiveness. *Aggressive Behavior, 36*, 1–13. http://doi.org/10.1002/ab.20329

Bluemke, M., & Friese, M. (2006). Do features of stimuli influence IAT effects? *Journal of Experimental Social Psychology, 42*, 163–176. http://doi.org/10.1016/j.jesp.2005.03.004

Brendl, C. M., Markman, A. B., & Messner, C. (2001). How do indirect measures of evaluation work? Evaluating the inference of prejudice in the Implicit Association Test. *Journal of Personality and Social Psychology, 81*, 760–773. http://doi.org/10.1037/0022-3514.81.5.760

Dambrun, M., Villate, M., & Richetin, J. (2008). Implicit racial attitudes and their relationships with explicit personal and cultural beliefs: What personalized and traditional IATs measure. *Current Research in Social Psychology, 13*, 185–198.

De Houwer, J. (2001). A structural and process analysis of the Implicit Association Test. *Journal of Experimental Social Psychology, 37*, 443–451. http://doi.org/10.1006/jesp.2000.1464

De Houwer, J. (2003). The Extrinsic Affective Simon Task. *Experimental Psychology, 50*, 77–85. http://doi.org/10.1026//1618-3169.50.2.77

De Houwer, J., & De Bruycker, E. (2007). The Implicit Association Test outperforms the Extrinsic Affective Simon Task as a measure of interindividual differences in attitude. *British Journal of Social Psychology, 46*, 401–421. http://doi.org/10.1348/014466606X130346

De Houwer, J., & Moors, A. (2010). Implicit measures: Similarities and differences. In B. Gawronski & B. K. Payne (Eds.), *Handbook of implicit social cognition: Measurement, theory, and applications* (pp. 176–193). New York, NY: Guilford Press.

Edwards, J. R., & Bagozzi, R. P. (2000). On the nature and direction of the relationship between constructs and measures. *Psychological Methods, 5*, 155–174. http://doi.org/10.1037/1082-989X.5.2.155

Erceg-Hurn, D. M., & Mirosevich, V. M. (2008). Modern robust statistical methods: An easy way to improve the accuracy and power of your research. *American Psychologist, 63*, 591–601. http://doi.org/10.1037/0003-066X.63.7.591

Fazio, R. H., Sanbonmatsu, D. M., Powell, M. C., & Kardes, F. R. (1986). On the automatic activation of attitudes. *Journal of Personality and Social Psychology, 50*, 229–238. http://doi.org/10.1037/0022-3514.50.2.229

Fiedler, K., Messner, C., & Bluemke, M. (2006). Unresolved problems with the 'I', the 'A', and the 'T': A logical and psychometric critique of the Implicit Association Test (IAT). *European Review of Social Psychology, 17*, 74–147. http://doi.org/10.1080/10463280600681248

Friese, M., Hofmann, W., & Schmitt, M. (2008). When and why do implicit measures predict behavior? Empirical evidence for the moderating role of opportunity, motivation, and process reliance. *European Review of Social Psychology, 19*, 285–338. http://doi.org/10.1080/10463280802556958

Gawronski, B., & Bodenhausen, G. V. (2006). Associative and propositional processes in evaluation: An integrative review of implicit and explicit attitude change. *Psychological Bulletin, 132*, 692–731. http://doi.org/10.1037/0033-2909.132.5.692

Greenwald, A. G., & Farnham, S. D. (2000). Using the Implicit Association Test to measure self-esteem and self-concept. *Journal of Personality and Social Psychology, 79*, 1022–1038. http://doi.org/10.1037/0022-3514.79.6.1022

Greenwald, A. G., McGhee, D. E, & Schwartz, J. L. K. (1998). Measuring individual differences in implicit cognition: The Implicit Association Test. *Journal of Personality and Social Psychology, 74*, 1464–1480. http://doi.org/10.1037/0022-3514.74.6.1464

Greenwald, A. G., Nosek, B. A., & Banaji, M. R. (2003). Understanding and using the Implicit Association Test: I. An improved scoring algorithm. *Journal of Personality and Social Psychology, 85*, 481–481. http://doi.org/10.1037/h0087889

Greenwald, A. G., Poehlman, T. A., Uhlmann, E., & Banaji, M. R. (2009). Understanding and using the Implicit Association Test: III. Meta-analysis of predictive validity. *Journal of Personality and Social Psychology, 97*, 17–41. http://doi.org/10.1037/a0015575

Gschwendner, T., Hofmann, W., & Schmitt, M. (2008). Differential stability: The effects of acute and chronic construct accessibility on the temporal stability of the Implicit Association Test. *Journal of Individual Differences, 29*, 70–79. http://doi.org/10.1027/1614-0001.29.2.70

Hofmann, W., Gawronski, B., Gschwendner, T., Le, H., & Schmitt, M. (2005). A meta-analysis on the correlation between the Implicit Association Test and explicit self-report measures. *Personality and Social Psychology Bulletin, 31*, 1369–1385. http://doi.org/10.1177/0146167205275613

Karpinski, A., & Steinman, R. B. (2006). The single category Implicit Association Test as a measure of implicit social cognition. *Journal of Personality and Social Psychology, 91*, 16–32. http://doi.org/10.1037/0022-3514.91.1.16

Klauer, K. C., Schmitz, F., Teige-Mocigemba, S., & Voss, A. (2010). Understanding the role of executive control in the Implicit Association Test: Why flexible people have small IAT effects. *The Quarterly Journal of Experimental Psychology, 63*, 595–619. http://doi.org/10.1080/17470210903076826

Klauer, K. C., Voss, A., Schmitz, F., & Teige-Mocigemba, S. (2007). Process components of the Implicit Association Test: A diffusion-model analysis. *Journal of Personality and Social Psychology, 93*, 353–368. http://doi.org/10.1037/0022-3514.93.3.353

Krause, S., Back, M. D., Egloff, B., & Schmukle, S. C. (2011). Reliability of implicit self-esteem measures revisited. *European Journal of Personality, 25*, 239–251. http://doi.org/10.1002/per.792

LeBel, E. P. (2010). Attitude accessibility as a moderator of implicit and explicit self-esteem correspondance. *Self and Identity, 9*, 195–208. http://doi.org/10.1080/15298860902979166

Lowery, B. S., Hardin, C. D., & Sinclair, S. (2001). Social influence effects on automatic racial prejudice. *Journal of Personality and Social Psychology, 81*, 842–855. http://doi.org/10.1037/0022-3514.81.5.842

Mierke, J., & Klauer, K. C. (2003). Method-specific variance in the Implicit Association Test. *Journal of Personality and Social Psychology, 85*, 1180–1192. http://doi.org/10.1037/0022-3514.85.6.1180

Mitchell, J. P., Nosek, B. A., & Banaji, M. R. (2003). Contextual variations in implicit evaluation. *Journal of Experimental Psychology: General, 132*, 455–469. http://doi.org/10.1037/0096-3445.132.3.455

Nosek, B. A. (2005). Moderators of the relationship between implicit and explicit evaluation. *Journal of Experimental Psychology: General, 134*, 565–584. http://doi.org/10.1037/0096-3445.134.4.565

Nosek, B. A., & Banaji, M. R. (2001). The go/no-go association task. *Social Cognition, 19*, 625–666. http://doi.org/10.1521/soco.19.6.625.20886

Nosek, B. A., Greenwald, A. G., & Banaji, M. R. (2007). The Implicit Association Test at age 7: A methodological and conceptual review. In J. A. Bargh (Ed.), *Automatic processes in social thinking and behavior* (pp. 265–292). New York, NY: Psychology Press.

Nuttin, J. M. (1985). Narcissism beyond gestalt and awareness: The name letter effect. *European Journal of Social Psychology, 15*, 353–361. http://doi.org/10.1002/ejsp.2420150309

Olson, M. A., & Fazio, R. H. (2004). Reducing the influence of extrapersonal associations on the Implicit Association Test: Personalizing the IAT. *Journal of Personality and Social Psychology, 86*, 653–667. http://doi.org/10.1037/0022-3514.86.5.653

Payne, B. K., Burkley, M., & Stokes, M. B. (2008). Why do implicit and explicit attitude tests diverge? The role of structural fit. *Journal of Personality and Social Psychology, 94*, 16–31. http://doi.org/10.1037/0022-3514.94.1.16

Payne, B. K., Cheng, S. M., Govorun, O., & Stewart, B. D. (2005). An inkblot for attitudes: Affect misattribution as implicit measurement. *Journal of Personality and Social Psychology, 89*, 277–293. http://doi.org/10.1037/0022-3514.89.3.277

Perugini, M. (2005). Predictive models of implicit and explicit attitudes. *British Journal of Social Psychology, 44*, 29–45. http://doi.org/10.1348/014466604X23491

Perugini, M., Conner, M., & O'Gorman, R. (2011). Automatic activation of individual differences: A test of the gatekeeper model in the domain of spontaneous helping. *European Journal of Personality, 25*, 465–476. http://doi.org/10.1002/per.826

Perugini, M., O'Gorman, R., & Prestwich, A. (2007). An ontological test of the IAT: Self-activation can increase predictive validity. *Experimental Psychology, 54*, 134–147. http://doi.org/10.1027/1618-3169.54.2.134

Perugini, M., & Prestwich, A. (2007). The gatekeeper: Individual differences are key in the chain from perception to behavior. *European Journal of Personality, 21*, 303–317. http://doi.org/10.1002/per.633

Perugini, M., Richetin, J., & Zogmaister, C. (2010). Prediction of behavior. In B. Gawronski & K. Payne (Eds.), *Handbook of implicit social cognition: Measurement, theory, and applications* (pp. 255–277). New York, NY: Guilford Press.

Podsakoff, P. M., MacKenzie, S. B., Lee, J.-Y., & Podsakoff, N. P. (2003). Common method biases in behavioral research: A critical review of the literature and recommended remedies. *Journal of Applied Psychology, 88*, 879–903. http://doi.org/10.1037/0021-9010.88.5.879

Rothermund, K., Teige-Mocigemba, S., Gast, A., & Wentura, D. (2009). Eliminating the influence of recoding in the Implicit Association Test: The Recoding-Free Implicit Association Test (IAT-RF). *Quarterly Journal of Experimental Psychology, 62*, 84–98. http://doi.org/10.1080/17470210701822975

Rothermund, K., & Wentura, D. (2001). Figure-ground asymmetries in the Implicit Association Test (IAT). *Zeitschrift für Experimentelle Psychologie, 48*, 94–106.

Schmitz, F., Teige-Mocigemba, S., Klauer, K. C., & Voss, A. (2013). When scoring algorithms matter: Effects of working memory load on different IAT scores. *British Journal of Social Psychology, 52*, 103–121. http://doi.org/10.1111/j.2044-8309.2011.02057.x

Schnabel, K., Asendorpf, J. B., & Greenwald, A. G. (2008). Implicit Association Tests: A landmark for the assessment of implicit personality self-concept. In G. J. Boyle, G. Matthews, & D. H. Saklofske (Eds.), *Handbook of personality theory and testing* (pp. 508–528). London, UK: Sage.

Schwarz, N., & Oyserman, D. (2001). Asking questions about behavior: Cognition, communication, and questionnaire construction. *American Journal of Evaluation, 22*, 127–160. http://doi.org/10.1177/109821400102200202

Seibt, B., Häfner, M., & Deutsch, R. (2007). Prepared to eat: How immediate affective and motivational responses to food cues are influenced by food deprivation. *European Journal of Social Psychology, 37*, 359–379. http://doi.org/10.1002/ejsp.365

Sherman, J. W., Klauer, K. C., & Allen, T. J. (2010). Mathematical modeling of implicit social cognition: The machine in the ghost. In B. Gawronski & B. K. Payne (Eds.), *Handbook of implicit social cognition: Measurement, theory, and applications* (pp. 156–175). New York, NY: Guilford Press

Sriram, N., & Greenwald, A. G. (2009). The Brief Implicit Association Test. *Experimental Psychology, 56*, 283–294. http://doi.org/10.1027/1618-3169.56.4.283

Teige-Mocigemba, S., Klauer, K. C., & Rothermund, K. (2008). Minimizing method-specific variance in the IAT: A Single Block IAT. *European Journal of Psychological Assessment, 24*, 237–245. http://doi.org/10.1027/1015-5759.24.4.237

Teige-Mocigemba, S., Klauer, K. C., & Sherman, J. W. (2010). Practical guide to Implicit Association Task and related tasks. In B. Gawronski & B. K. Payne (Eds.), *Handbook of implicit social cognition: Measurement, theory, and applications* (pp. 117–139). New York, NY: Guilford Press.

Thomas, S., Burton-Smith, R., & Ball, P. (2007). Implicit attitudes in very young children: An adaptation of the IAT. *Current Research in Social Psychology, 13*, 75–85.

Wilcox, R. (2012). *Modern statistics for the social and behavioral sciences: A practical introduction.* New York, NY: CRC Press.

Wilcox, R., & Keselman, H. (2012). Modern regression methods that can substantially increase power and provide a more accurate understanding of associations. *European Journal of Personality, 26*, 165–174. http://doi.org/10.1002/per.860

Zeigler-Hill, V. (2006). Discrepancies between implicit and explicit self-esteem: Implications for narcissism and self-esteem instability. *Journal of Personality, 74*, 119–143. http://doi.org/10.1111/j.1467-6494.2005.00371.x

Chapter 3
A Model of Moderated Convergence Between Direct, Indirect, and Behavioral Measures of Personality Traits

Manfred Schmitt[1], Wilhelm Hofmann[2], Tobias Gschwendner[3], Friederike Gerstenberg[4], and Axel Zinkernagel[1]

[1]Department of Psychology, University of Koblenz-Landau, Germany
[2]Department of Psychology, University of Cologne, Germany
[3]Lebensberatung Trier, Counseling Center Trier, Germany
[4]Kreisdiakonieverband Esslingen, Psychological Counseling Center, Esslingen, Germany

The Variable Nature of Consistency and Convergence

Traits are useful as personality constructs to the extent that individual differences in behavior are consistent across similar situations and stable across time. Accordingly, measures of traits can be valid only to the extent that the indicators and methods that are used converge (Eid & Diener, 2006). Whether and how well these fundamental assumptions of the trait model are met has been a matter of repeated controversy in the history of psychology (Kenrick & Funder, 1988; Schmitt, 2006). The first controversy in the 1930s was initiated by research on the cross-situational consistency of moral behavior (Hartshorne & May, 1928); the second by Mischel's (1968) review of the predictive validity of personality and achievement tests.

Both controversies have followed a characteristic sequence of arguments and studies. First, the degree of consistency was debated, especially the degree of behavioral consistency across situations and the predictability of behavior from trait measures (the *how much* question). Second, boundary conditions of consistency were identified empirically (the *when* question). Finally, theoretical ideas were advanced for explaining person–situation interactions and submitted to empirical tests (the *why* question; Kenrick & Funder, 1988; Swann & Seyle, 2005).

Perhaps one of the most important results of both controversies was the recognition that consistency is not constant but variable (Baumeister & Tice, 1988; Chaplin, 1991; Schmitt, 2006;

Snyder & Ickes, 1985; Swann & Seyle, 2005). As a consequence of this insight, the theory-guided identification of moderators of consistency became an important goal for personality research. This research is important because not only does it aid our understanding of why behavior can be better predicted in some cases than in others, but it is also extremely relevant for psychological assessment since variable consistency, convergence, and behavioral predictability imply that the validity of trait measures depends on boundary conditions. Knowing these boundary conditions and understanding why they affect the validity of a measure is of utmost importance for the use of this measure in applied settings such as personnel selection or decision making in clinical psychology.

Recently, the consistency issue has been revived due to the low convergence that was found in many studies between direct self-report measures of attitudes and personality traits and indirect measures such as the Implicit Association Test (IAT; Greenwald, McGhee, & Schwartz, 1998). The results of these studies mirror the findings that were found between self-report personality measures (Q-data) and objective personality tests (T-data) as proposed by Cattell (1957; see also Chapter 9 in this volume). In both cases, the low correlations can mean either that the methods that were used lack convergent validity or that the methods measure different traits that are only moderately related (Wilson, Lindsey, & Schooler, 2000).

Our theoretical inquiry and empirical research over the last decade have been devoted to understanding these findings of low convergence between direct, indirect, and behavioral trait measures. Our thinking and our studies have been based on theoretical and methodological insights that were gained during earlier consistency debates. Most importantly, we assume that the degree of convergence between direct, indirect, and behavioral measures is variable. Therefore, identifying the moderator variables that shape convergence has been the primary goal of our work. The present chapter provides a summary of our views and findings.

We began our research program with a systematic analysis of the literature on implicit–explicit convergence and a meta-analysis of available findings (Hofmann, Gawronski, Gschwendner, Le, & Schmitt, 2005). This meta-analysis was limited to the IAT because at the beginning of our literature review in 2002, the IAT was by far the most often used indirect measure. On the basis of a sample of 126 studies, we obtained a mean correlation between direct and indirect (IAT) measures of the *same* construct of $r = .24$, with approximately half of the variability across correlations attributed to the moderator variables that we were able to consider. Correlations increased systematically as a function of (a) increasing spontaneity of self-reports and (b) increasing conceptual correspondence between measures. These findings are important for at least three reasons. First, they demonstrate that questionnaires measure different latent factors depending on the spontaneity with which they are answered. Second, it seems not only worthwhile but mandatory to search for moderators that affect the convergence of multiple methods that were designed to measure a construct. Third, the average convergence we found was so low that it seems unjustified to assume that direct and indirect methods that were designed for the same construct indeed measure the same trait. Rather, it seems plausible to assume that they measure different – albeit related – traits. The same conclusion probably applies to behavioral trait measures such as objective personality tests.

Building a Model of Moderated Convergence

Previous efforts aimed at identifying moderators of consistency and convergence taught us that only moderators that are thoroughly grounded in theory can be replicated. Moderators found in exploratory studies have hardly ever been replicable (Kenrick & Funder, 1988). For this reason, we decided to begin our systematic search for moderators by building a theoretical model. The model should account for the systematic variability in implicit–explicit consistency that was identified in our meta-analysis and in narrative reviews (Gschwendner, Hofmann, & Schmitt, 2006a; Hofmann, Gschwendner, Nosek, & Schmitt, 2005; Nosek, 2005, 2007). The model should also account for the variability in the predictability of behavior between direct and indirect trait measures (Friese, Hofmann, & Schmitt, 2009; Greenwald, Poehlmann, Uhlmann, & Banaji, 2009).

A second important reason for building a theoretical model first was that construct validity can be tested only on the basis of a theoretical model. A measure possesses construct validity only to the extent that it generates data that are in accordance with a theory that includes the construct being measured.

Based on the results of our meta-analysis and consistent with the predominant view in the current literature, our model assumes two types of mental representations of latent traits such as attitudes, personality factors, motives, self-concept dimensions, and self-esteem: Explicit traits are assumed to be represented in a propositional format (Gawronski & Bodenhausen, 2006), introspectively accessible, and measurable via direct self-report. They serve as a self-knowledge base for deliberate thinking and reasoned judgment. Implicit traits are assumed to be stored in an associative format as object-attribute links (me–anxious; cockroaches–disgusting). These associations are unconscious and introspectively opaque. Implicit dispositions provide the knowledge base for quick evaluations and intuitive judgments that occur outside a person's conscious awareness. This is why implicit dispositions can be measured only indirectly. In line with dual-process models (Smith & DeCoster, 2000; Strack & Deutsch, 2004), we assume that explicit dispositions feed into reasoned action based on the controlled processing of information such as the anticipation of consequences that a certain behavior might have. By contrast, implicit dispositions are assumed to affect behavior automatically via approach and avoidance impulses and the activation of behavioral schemata or scripts.

The most recent version of our model is depicted in Figure 3.1. It differs slightly from previous versions of the model (Hofmann, Gschwendner, Nosek et al., 2005; Gschwendner et al.,

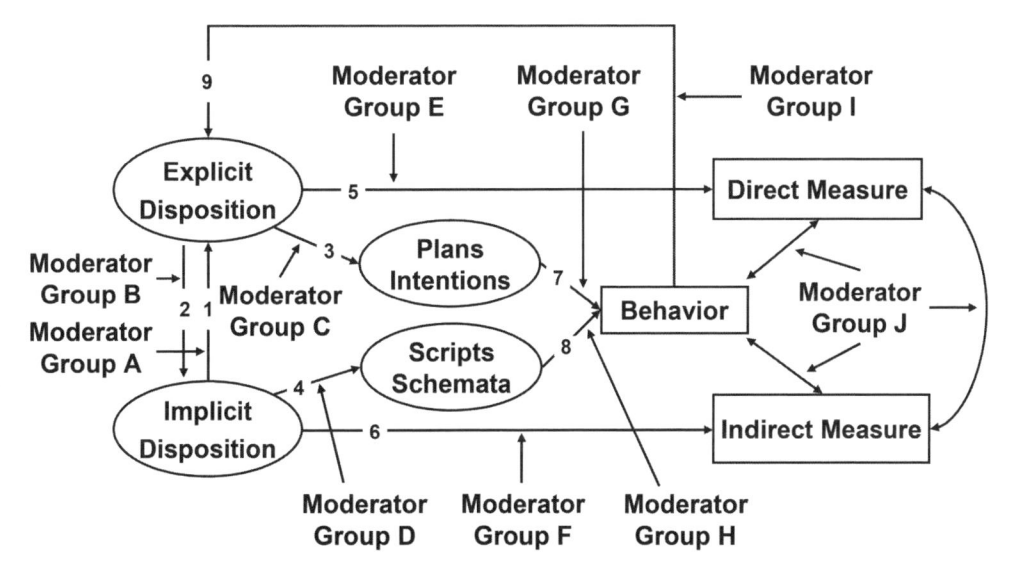

Figure 3.1. A model of moderated convergence between direct, indirect, and behavioral measures of latent traits and states.

2006a, 2006b). Unlike earlier versions, the current model includes behavior in addition to direct and indirect measures. Behavior was added to the model for two reasons. First, the consistency issue is not limited to direct and indirect measures of dispositions but encompasses all sorts of indicators including overt behavior. Moreover, overt behavior is often considered to be the ultimate criterion for the usefulness of a construct and the validity of a measure. Second, objective personality tests as proposed by Cattell (1957) consist of overt behavioral acts in highly standardized miniature situations (Cattell & Warburton, 1967). Therefore, the model we designed is not limited to being used for tracing moderators that affect the predictability of behavior from explicit and implicit dispositions. The model can also be used to search for moderators that explain the convergence of direct and indirect measures with objective personality tests (Gschwendner et al., 2006b).

The current model also differs from earlier versions in that it differentiates between manifest behavior, behavioral plans and intentions, and behavioral schemata or scripts. In line with action theories such as the theory of planned behavior (Ajzen, 1987), we assume that behavioral plans and intentions mediate the effect of explicit dispositions on manifest behavior. Further and in accordance with the reflective–impulsive model (RIM) proposed by Strack and Deutsch (2004), we assume that behavioral schemata and scripts mediate the effect of implicit dispositions on manifest behavior.

The model specifies nine effects (depicted as single-headed arrows in Figure 3.1) and three correlations (depicted as double-headed arrows). Most importantly with regard to our primary research interest, the model assumes that the sizes of all effects and correlations depend on moderator variables. Moreover, we deem it likely that the size of each effect and correlation depends on more than one moderator. For this reason, moderators were combined into groups. Each moderator group contains several factors including personality traits or characteristics of the situation in which measurement or behavior occurs. Moderator groups also include attributes of the construct at issue, such as the social desirability of a personality trait or an attitude, and attributes of their indicators, such as the degree of controllability (vs. automaticity) of a specific behavior or the reliability of a measure. These differentiations between types of moderators are not included in the model in order to keep it principled and parsimonious. In a similar vein, the model does not specify joint moderator effects. We assume, for instance, that functionally equivalent moderators such as the chronic and acute activation of associations will moderate the effect of implicit dispositions on indirect measures jointly in a synergistic fashion (Gschwendner et al., 2006c; Schmitt, 2009).

It is important to understand that implicit–explicit convergence cannot be observed directly on the level of constructs (circular frames in the model) but only on the level of manifest indicators (rectangular frames in the model). Note that most moderators are assumed to affect causal links between latent constructs (A, B, C, D) and the effects of these latent constructs on their manifest indicators (E, F, G, H). These assumptions cannot be tested directly. We can test only their implied effects on the correlations among the manifest indicators. This is not a specific limitation of our model but a limitation of any latent-variable model.

We should also note that although the model contains a substantial number of variables and paths, it is still a simplification. This is especially true for the moderators of the model. First, moderators are not specified as separate variables but only summarized as groups. Second, moderators are constructs that need to be either measured (personality factors) or varied experimentally (properties of the situation, the behavior, and the measures). Thus, a more complete version of the model would have to include latent and manifest moderator variables and, in addition, possible interactions between them. These details are not included in the model in order to keep it general and flexible. Thus, the model is not a detailed effect model for a specific trait but rather a theoretical framework that can be applied to a large variety of traits.

We first briefly describe the nine paths that are numbered accordingly in Figure 3.1.

Path 1: In line with other authors, we assume that object–attribute associations form the elementary basis of propositional thinking and explicit self-knowledge (Gawronski & Bodenhausen, 2006; Strack & Deutsch, 2004). This assumption is represented by the path from the implicit to the explicit disposition.

Path 2: Propositional thinking may in turn shape the structure of the underlying associative representations (Strack & Deutsch, 2004). Autosuggestion and self-instruction are examples. In the domain of attitudes, the intentional imagination of counter-attitudinal exemplars can weaken previous associations between attitude objects and values. The same process can lead to changes in implicit stereotypes, implicit self-esteem, and the implicit self-concept (Gawronski & Bodenhausen, 2006). This type of process is represented in the model by a path from the explicit disposition to the implicit disposition.

Path 3: Explicit dispositions shape behavior. A vast number of studies have shown that behavior can be predicted from personality factors, attitudes, self-concept dimensions, motive traits, self-esteem, and beliefs. In line with action theories such as the theory of planned behavior (Ajzen, 1987), and also in line with dual-process theories such as the RIM (Strack & Deutsch, 2004), we assume that explicit dispositions do not affect behavior directly but rather indirectly via action plans and behavioral intentions. People reason about the benefits and costs of the behavioral options they consider, and depending on these and other factors, they make choices. The preferred choice is turned into a behavioral intention. Moreover, many goals require sequences of behavioral steps. These need to be designed and represented mentally as action plans.

Path 4: Implicit dispositions also shape behavior. Although this assumption has been tested much less often than the previous one, recent reviews have provided clear evidence in support of Path 4 in our model (Friese et al., 2009; Greenwald et al., 2009). In line with dual-process models such as the RIM (Strack & Deutsch, 2004), we assume that implicit dispositions do not feed directly into behavior but rather impact behavior via behavioral schemata or scripts. More specifically, it is assumed that the activation of object–attribute links automatically co-activates behavioral schemata or scripts.

Path 5: This effect represents a notion that is common to all approaches to psychological assessment that are based on the latent-trait model. According to this view, self-reports are a specific form of behavior that reflect the self-knowledge people have about their traits. Moreover, it is assumed that the transformation of explicit dispositions into self-reports is a conscious and controlled process similar to the formation of intentions and behavioral plans that precede behavior (Path 3).

Path 6: Accordingly, Path 6 of our model represents the assumption that implicit dispositions cause the behaviors that are measured by indirect measurement procedures such as the IAT.

Path 7: This path represents a notion that is common to action theories. It reflects the idea that behavior is the controlled execution of previously formed plans and intentions (Ajzen, 1987).

Path 8: This effect reflects the core assumption of dual-process theories such as the RIM (Strack & Deutsch, 2004). It represents the idea that activated behavioral schemata feed automatically into behavior without conscious awareness.

Path 9: This final path of our model was derived from self-observation theory (Bem, 1972) and is included as one of several processes that may influence the size of the correlation between an implicit and an explicit disposition. Behavior is never entirely consistent with explicit dispositions because it is jointly determined by controlled and automatic processes. People are able to detect inconsistencies between their explicit dispositions and their behavior. Such inconsistencies generate cognitive dissonance that needs to be resolved. Changing explicit assumptions about the self is one way of dissolving such inconsistencies. Because this process is more likely to occur in cases in which behavior is driven automatically, it may be an important route by which implicit associations feed into explicit self-knowledge (Hofmann, Gschwendner, Nosek et al., 2005).

We now turn to moderators that affect the strengths of these paths and, in addition, the sizes of the correlations between direct, indirect, and behavioral measures of latent traits and states.

Moderator Group A: Explicit self-knowledge can draw upon implicit self-knowledge to the extent that implicit self-knowledge is accessible. The accessibility of associations depends on their strength. Several studies have shown, for instance, that strong attitudes are more accessible than weak attitudes (Petty & Krosnick, 1995). Compared with weak object–value associations, strong associations should feed more easily into explicit self-knowledge. The first support for this assumption comes from a study by Nosek (2005). The notion of associative strength can be generalized from attitudes to other dispositions such as stereotypes, personality traits, and self-concepts because these dispositions are also represented as associations between objects and attributes. A second important moderator is awareness. People differ in their motivation and ability to introspect (Fenigstein, Scheier, & Buss, 1975). The strength of Path 1 of our model should vary accordingly.

Moderator Group B: Auto-suggestion, self-instruction, and selective exposure to object–attribute combinations contribute to the translation of elaborate assumptions about the self into simpler representations of self-knowledge. Again, the effectiveness of this process should depend on motivational factors and on abilities. People who dislike their impulsive reactions to certain objects such as certain kinds of food sometimes consciously engage in counter-impulsive auto-suggestions. People who dislike their attitudes/stereotypes/self-concepts can engage in intentional imagination of counter-attitudinal exemplars of their attitudes/stereotypes/self-concepts (Blair, Ma, & Lenton, 2001). The effectiveness of this process will depend on knowledge about the underlying psychological principle, on motivational strength, and probably also on personality factors such as self-control and openness to experience.

Moderator Group C: Making plans requires both the motivation and the opportunity to deliberate about relevant information. Both can vary depending on stable individual differences between people and as a function of situational factors. If people have no time to deliberate, they cannot make plans. Further, making plans and carefully considering the pros and cons of various behavioral alternatives requires cognitive capacity and ability. More generally, all factors that contribute to the availability and usability of control resources will affect Path 3. In addition, some people rely more on intuition than on deliberation (Betsch, 2004; Epstein, Pacini, Denes-Raj, & Heier, 1996), and this will also contribute to how carefully action plans are made on the basis of relevant information. In the domain of attitudes, people may know that they hold negative attitudes that are politically incorrect. To the extent that they are motivated to control prejudiced reactions (Dunton & Fazio, 1997), they will refrain from translating their attitudes into consistent behavioral intentions. Additional moderators of this group are reviewed by Friese et al. (2009).

Moderator Group D: The strength with which behavioral schemata are activated in a specific situation depends on how closely they are linked to objects. This in turn will depend on how often both have been activated simultaneously during the person's learning history (Logan, 1988). Social learning and modeling may play important roles here. Consider a person who holds negative attitudes toward strangers and who repeatedly observes how peers with the same negative attitude treat strangers. Very likely, this person will not only develop a behavioral script vis-à-vis strangers but will also develop an associative link between the attitude object stranger and this script (Castelli, De Dea, & Nesdale, 2008).

Moderator Group E: People are not always willing to disclose their self-knowledge honestly. Rather, they tend to adjust self-reports to personal goals. Pervasive motivational sources of these goals are self-presentation, social desirability, and impression management. The strength of these motives varies across individuals, across dispositions, and across the measurement context. For instance, some individuals are more motivated than others to control prejudiced reactions (Dunton & Fazio, 1997), and several studies have confirmed that this moderator indeed affects the validity of self-reports (Hofmann, Gschwendner, Nosek et al., 2005). Furthermore, some situations will more likely trigger adjustment processes than others. Anonymous self-reports of socially undesirable attitudes, stereotypes, beliefs, motives, and personality traits are more valid than public self-reports on the same dispositions.

Moderator Group F: Indirect procedures such as the IAT are intended to measure behavior that is driven automatically by the activation of object–attribute associations. It follows directly from this assumption that the validity of such measures depends on the accessibility of the association at issue. This in turn depends on the strength of the relevant associations and thus on the person's learning history (Nosek, 2005). In addition, the validity of measures for object–attribute associations will vary depending on the strength with which these associations have been preactivated and the strength with which they are activated by the measurement procedure itself (Blair, 2002). Preactivation can be achieved via priming. Moreover, measurement procedures differ in the strength with which they activate associated concepts. For instance, embedding object-stimuli in a congruent context can promote activation and thus increase the validity of the indirect measure (Gschwendner et al., 2008a).

Moderator Group G: Action plans and behavioral intentions are not transformed automatically into behavior or chains of behavioral steps. Rather, they require self-regulation. Self-regulation consists of self-monitoring and self-management strategies such as the adjustment of one's behavior if goal discrepancy is beyond an acceptable limit. Self-monitoring (Snyder, 1974) and self-management abilities (Bandura, 1977) vary between individuals. In addition, self-regulation requires the availability (opportunity) and willingness to invest (motivation) control resources. In line with this reasoning, chronic and acute control resources have been shown to influence the relative weight of explicit and implicit dispositions on behavior (Hofmann, Gschwendner, Castelli, & Schmitt, 2008; Hofmann, Gschwendner, Wiers, Friese, & Schmitt, 2008).

Moderator Group H: Behavioral schemata and scripts feed automatically into behavior depending on the strength with which they are linked to the behavioral object, the strength with which they are activated, and the degree to which they are overridden by controlled processes. The first factor depends on the person's learning history (compare to Moderator Group D). The second moderator is a function of time. Activation fades away quickly, and therefore a schema will affect behavior automatically only if it follows within a short period. Whether and to what extent controlled processes override impulses depends on the moderators of Group G. The person's primary reliance on deliberation vs. intuition (compare to Moderator Group C) may also contribute to a moderator effect at this point.

Moderator Group I: Our model assumes that the self-observation of behavior will feed back into explicit self-knowledge, and this is even more likely if behavior is not consistent with previously held assumptions about the self. Inconsistencies are more likely to occur the more that behavior is driven by implicit associations and the behavioral schemata linked with these associations. This is more likely for behaviors that are difficult to control such as certain kinds of nonverbal behaviors (Asendorpf, Banse, & Mücke, 2002). We assume that the feedback effect will be stronger for people who are willing and able to self-observe and who are capable of adequately interpreting their behavior. The ability and willingness to self-observe vary with self-monitoring (Snyder, 1974) and private self-consciousness (Fenigstein et al., 1975). The ability to decode behavioral cues varies between individuals (Hefter, Manoach, & Barton, 2005). Next, people sometimes use display rules in order to disguise their feelings (Matsumoto, Yoo, Hirayama, & Petrova, 2005). Compared to individuals who express their emotions authentically, individuals who regularly use display rules will most likely not be able to make inferences about their emotional sensitivity when self-observing their facial expressions. Finally, people differ in their need for consistency and closure (Webster & Kruglanski, 1994). Those who are high in these needs behave more authentically in accordance with their self-concept. It seems less likely that they will self-observe behavior that is inconsistent with their self-view. Consequently, there is no reason for these individuals to modify their self-concept when they observe their own behavior.

Moderator Group J: The strengths of all direct and moderator effects we have mentioned thus far will, by implication, affect the correlations between direct measures, indirect measures, and behavior. In addition, the convergence of these indicators will depend on features of the measurement instruments that are known to affect the size of correlations. Important examples of these factors are the reliability and the symmetry of the measures in terms of content and specificity. For instance, the correlation between indirect and direct measures that capture different facets of a construct will be lower than the correlation between two such measures that capture the same facets (Schmitt & Borkenau, 1992). This moderator is very relevant because the kinds of behavior that have typically been used in studies of predictive validity often do not match in content and specificity with the measures that are employed for their prediction. This has been a recurring issue in research on attitude–behavior consistency (Ajzen & Fishbein, 1977). One of our recent studies has shown that the degree to which measures are similar with regard to both content and specificity systematically moderates the convergence between direct, indirect, and behavioral indicators of dispositions (Gschwendner et al., 2008b).

Empirical Evidence on the Validity of the Model

Our model has not been tested in its entire complexity. However, many of the assumed moderator effects have been investigated in our own research and in studies by others. The available evidence has been summarized in three narrative reviews (Friese et al., 2009; Gschwendner et al., 2006a; Hofmann, Gschwendner, Nosek et al., 2005). Because of limited space, we concentrate the present review on our own research and include recent data that were not yet reported in our previous reviews.

Joint Moderator Effects of Individual Differences in Awareness and Adjustment

Our first empirical study (Hofmann, Gschwendner, & Schmitt, 2005) addressed moderators of Group A (awareness) and Group E (adjustment). In two experiments on attitudes of West Germans toward East Germans and Turks, we tested a number of dispositional moderators pertaining to awareness and adjustment. Concerning moderators affecting awareness, no reliable first-order effects were found for private self-consciousness or attitudinal self-knowledge. However, replicating findings reported by Nosek (2005), attitude importance generated the expected effect. Concerning moderators influencing adjustment, consistent effects were obtained for motivation to control prejudiced reactions. Social desirability and self-monitoring did not moderate the implicit–explicit relation in the expected direction. Some evidence was found for a second-order moderator effect between awareness and adjustment, suggesting that adjustment effects may be more pronounced under conditions of high awareness.

Synergistic Moderator Effects of Person and Situation Factors of Awareness and Adjustment

In a next step, again using attitudes of Germans toward Turks as an application of our model, the previous study was extended by experimentally manipulating moderators of awareness (Group A) and adjustment (Group E) in addition to measuring individual differences in these moderators (Gschwendner et al., 2006c). Besides including experimentally manipulated moderators, this study differed from the previous one in that some moderator constructs of Groups A and E were replaced or measured with better measures. Results were as follows: Concerning moderators of adjustment, no effects on implicit–explicit consistency were obtained for situational variables. The expected synergistic interaction of personal and situational variables was also not significant. However, concerning moderators of awareness, a reliable first-order effect was found for private self-consciousness. Moreover, private self-consciousness and the experimentally manipulated motivation to introspect showed the assumed synergistic moderator effect.

The Effects of Acute and Chronic Construct Accessibility on the Temporal Stability of the IAT

Another study was devoted to Moderator Group F (Gschwendner et al., 2008a). We tested the assumption that the validity and thus the temporal stability of indirect measures increases with the accessibility of the associated concepts during the measurement process. Adopting a procedure employed by Wittenbrink, Judd, and Park (2001), accessibility was manipulated experimentally by including or not including background pictures in the IAT. In Study 1, the 2-week stability of an IAT assessing anxiety was higher when IAT stimuli were embedded in an anxiety-relevant background. In Study 2, this context effect was replicated in the domain of racial attitudes. Moreover, the context effect in Study 2 was especially pronounced for participants with high chronic access to the relevant concept.

The Moderating Role of Situationally Available Control Resources

Another study (Hofmann, Gschwendner, Castelli et al., 2008) tested the assumption that control resources have an effect on the strength with which explicit and implicit dispositions determine behavior (Moderator Groups C, D, G, H). More specifically, we investigated how implicit attitudes (IAT) and explicit attitudes (blatant/subtle prejudice) were related to interracial reactions of Italians toward an African interviewer (Study 1) and of Germans toward a Turkish interviewer (Study 2). For half of the interview questions, participants' control resources were reduced via a memory task. Across both studies, the Race IAT was more predictive of behavior when participants were taxed than when untaxed. Conversely, explicit attitudes were somewhat more predictive under full resources. Taken together, our findings suggest that available control resources moderate the predictive validity of implicit and explicit attitudes (for similar findings, see Hofmann, Rauch, & Gawronski, 2007).

The Moderating Role of Chronically Available Control Resources

Next, we tested whether chronically available control resources would have the same effect that we had predicted and found for acutely available control resources (Hofmann, Gschwendner, Wiers et al., 2008). The results were fully consistent with our expectations. In two studies – on sexual interest behavior (Study 1) and the consumption of tempting food (Study 2) – automatic attitudes toward the temptation of interest had a stronger influence on behavior for individuals who scored low rather than high in working memory capacity. Analogous results emerged in Study 3 on anger expression in a provoking situation when a measure of the automatic personality trait of angriness was employed. Conversely, controlled dispositions such as explicit attitudes (Study 1) and self-regulatory goals (Studies 2 and 3) guided behavior more effectively for participants who scored high rather than low in working memory capacity.

The Moderating Effect of Content Similarity and Specificity Similarity on the Consistency of Direct, Indirect, and Behavioral Construct Measures

Our next study looked at two moderators of Group J: content and specificity similarity (Gschwendner et al., 2008b). In the first session, different general and specific anxiety measures were administered, among them a general-anxiety IAT, a spider-anxiety IAT, and an IAT assessing speech anxiety. In the second session, participants had to deliver a speech. Behavioral indicators of speech anxiety were measured. In line with the moderator hypotheses, the results showed that (a) implicit and explicit anxiety measures were significantly correlated only if they were at the same level of specification and only if they measured the same content, and (b) specific speech anxiety measures best predicted concrete anxious behavior.

Self-Perception of Automatic Behavior as a Potential Source of Implicit–Explicit Consistency

Hofmann, Gschwendner, and Schmitt (2009) tested Path 9 of the model. Showing that the self-perception of automatic behavior feeds back into explicit self-knowledge and thus contributes to implicit–explicit consistency is a necessary prerequisite for exploring moderators of such a process. Across three studies, no reliable evidence was found for the assumed feedback process. In a follow-up study, Zinkernagel, Hofmann, Gerstenberg, and Schmitt (2013) used a refined methodology and a trait – disgust sensitivity – that seemed ideally suited for testing Path 9 because of the distinct facial reactions people show when exposed to disgusting stimuli (Ekman, 1992). As expected, Path 9 showed up reliably across two studies. More importantly in the present context, two moderator variables from Group I had reliable effects on Path 9: display rules and need for closure. The more subjects tended to use display rules, the less they re-adapted their explicit disgust sensitivity to self-observed disgust behavior. This means that people who use display rules do not learn from feedback regarding their facial expression because they know it is not authentic. Next, re-adaptation was smaller for individuals high in need for closure compared with participants low in need for closure. This means that subjects high in need for closure had no reason to re-adapt their explicit disgust sensitivity to their self-perceived behavior because they expressed their disgust sensitivity in a congruent manner. By contrast, subjects low in need for closure showed a less congruent facial expression, and this caused them to re-adapt their explicit self-concept after being confronted with their facial expression.

Moderated Convergence of Direct, Indirect, and Objective Risk Propensity Measures

So far, we have conducted and published one study (Dislich, Zinkernagel, Ortner, & Schmitt, 2010) that used objective personality tests as proposed by Cattell (1957). Specifically, we tested whether the convergence between direct, indirect, and objective risk propensity measures in the domain of gambling would depend on the impulsiveness vs. reflectiveness of the risk behavior (Moderator Groups C and G). Two objective personality tests (OPT) of risk taking were employed: the Balloon Analogue Risk Task (BART; Lejuez et al., 2002) and the Game of Dice Task (GDT; Brand et al., 2005). Whereas stopping to blow up the balloon in the BART before it explodes requires an intuitive decision, the risk in the GDT can be calculated rationally. We predicted that the intuitive behavior in the BART would depend more on implicit risk propensity, whereas the reflective behavior in the GDT would depend more on explicit risk propensity. In addition, we expected that self-control would amplify the effect of explicit risk propensity and attenuate the effect of implicit risk propensity. At Time 1, two direct questionnaire measures of explicit risk proneness, three indirect measures of implicit risk proneness, and a self-control measure were collected. At Time 2, the OPTs were administered. The assumed pattern of effects was obtained, however, only for one of the three indirect measures of implicit risk propensity.

Implicit–Explicit Consistency as an Independent Variable

The model depicted in Figure 3.1 and the studies we have reported explain when and why different indicators of a trait converge. Thus, convergence is the dependent variable to be explained by moderators. However, the degree of consistency may itself have descriptive and explanatory value. In fact, the idea that individuals differ systematically in the consistency of their behavior (including self-reports and other personality trait indicators) had been proposed quite early in the history of personality psychology (Newcomb, 1929) and has been mentioned repeatedly since then (Baumeister & Tice, 1988; Bem & Allen, 1974; Chaplin, 1991). Recently, this idea was applied to implicit–explicit consistency. Some studies on self-esteem have shown that certain combinations of explicit and implicit self-esteem are associated with relevant outcomes such as well-being. For example, implicit–explicit self-esteem discrepancies seem to make people vulnerable to threatening information about the self (Schröder-Abé, Rudolph, & Schütz, 2007; Schröder-Abé, Rudolph, Wiesner, & Schütz, 2007).

We have continued this line of research in the domains of the intelligence and scholastic aptitude self-concepts. More specifically, we have been exploring whether patterns of implicit–explicit consistency are systematically related to objective test performance and whether these patterns moderate the impact of situational factors on performance.

Implicit–Explicit Combinations of the Intelligence Self-Concepts and Performance on Intelligence Tests

In a first series of studies, we found that configurations of the implicit and explicit self-concepts of intelligence are systematically related to performance on intelligence tests (Dislich et al., 2012). For individuals who self-reported high intelligence (high explicit self-concept), a negative implicit self-concept (measured with the IAT) was associated with poor performance on intelligence tests. The same was true for participants with low explicit and high implicit self-concepts. These effects were replicated across three studies. In line with studies on self-esteem, our results suggest that discrepant self-concepts bear a psychological risk for the person. Our next studies demonstrated that the type of inconsistency matters. Under some conditions, self-inconsistency may even have advantageous consequences for the person.

Implicit–Explicit Combinations of the Mathematical Aptitude Self-Concept and Vulnerability to Stereotype Threat

In a second series of studies, we demonstrated that individuals with fragile self-concepts (high explicit and low implicit self-concepts) of mathematical aptitude are particularly vulnerable to stereotype threat (Gerstenberg, Imhoff, & Schmitt, 2012). Specifically, women who explicitly described themselves as rather mathematical but whose implicit self-concept contradicted these claims were vulnerable to stereotype threat effects on mathematical performance. This effect was robust across three studies and independent of the subtleness or content of the stereotype threat manipulation. Additionally, we showed that the effect was mediated by anxious worrying. In line with the previous studies, these results showed that self-consistency is descriptive of individuals, that types of inconsistency can be distinguished meaningfully, and that they have unique consequences for important outcomes.

Implicit–Explicit Combinations of the Intelligence Self-Concept and Reactions to Performance Feedback

A third series of studies addressed the question of how changes in intelligence test performance after a feedback intervention depend on combinations of the implicit (iSCI) and explicit self-concepts of intelligence (eSCI; Gerstenberg et al., 2013). In three studies, persons with a low eSCI and a high iSCI showed improved performance after negative feedback compared with persons with any other combination of implicit and explicit SCI. This effect was mediated by affective, cognitive, and motivational mechanisms. The mediating effects suggest that individuals with a low eSCI and a high iSCI are either modest or tend to strategically understate their intelligence. These individuals do not feel threatened by negative performance feedback. Deep inside, they seem to know that they can perform better if they want to. When told that their performance on an intelligence test is poor, they seem to feel challenged to reject such feedback as invalid. By contrast, individuals with a high eSCI and a low iSCI seem to have deep feelings of insecurity about their intelligence. As a consequence, they are especially vulnerable to negative feedback.

Implications

The theoretical model and the empirical findings we have presented in this chapter are relevant not only for advancing personality theory and assessment in basic research. They are also relevant for applied psychological assessment in occupational, clinical, and educational settings. The findings from the last series of studies we reported illustrate this claim. We found that students reacted quite differently to performance feedback depending on the specific pattern of their implicit–explicit intelligence self-concepts. For most students, negative feedback resulted in frustration and a decrease in achievement motivation. For one group of students, however, negative feedback had the opposite effect. These students were characterized by a low explicit intelligence self-concept but had strong implicit associations of the self with being intelligent. Students who either seem to be modest or who strategically underscore their aptitude feel challenged by negative feedback. Instead of reacting with anxiety, frustration, and a decrease in achievement motivation, they feel challenged to demonstrate that they can do better if they decide to do so. Knowing about these mechanisms is important for teachers because they can adapt their feedback in a way that is maximally helpful for students depending on their self-concepts.

We hope that the ideas we have presented here will also stimulate further basic research. The call for multimethod strategy assessment (Eid & Diener, 2006) is certainly appropriate. However, it might not be sufficient to aggregate data across methods in order to reduce method specificity. More information might be gained if moderators of convergence are included in assessment designs because these moderators, if appropriately chosen and included in the analysis, may increase the validity and predictive potential of the data that were collected for testing psychological theories.

References

Ajzen, I. (1987). Attitudes, traits, and actions: Dispositional prediction of behavior in personality and social psychology. In L. Berkowitz (Ed.), *Advances in experimental social psychology* (Vol. 20, pp. 1–63). New York, NY: Academic Press.

Ajzen, I., & Fishbein, M. (1977). Attitude-behavior relations: A theoretical analysis and review of empirical research. *Psychological Bulletin, 84*, 888–918. http://doi.org/10.1037/0033-2909.84.5.888

Asendorpf, J. B., Banse, R., & Mücke, D. (2002). Double dissociation between implicit and explicit personality self-concept: The case of shy behavior. *Journal of Personality and Social Psychology, 83*, 380–393. http://doi.org/10.1037/0022-3514.83.2.380

Bandura, A. (1977). Self-efficacy: Toward a unifying theory of behavioral change. *Psychological Review, 84*, 191–215. http://doi.org/10.1037/0033-295X.84.2.191

Baumeister, R. F., & Tice, D. M. (1988). Metatraits. *Journal of Personality, 56*, 571–598. http://doi.org/10.1111/j.1467-6494.1988.tb00903.x

Bem, D. J. (1972). Self-perception theory. In L. Berkowitz (Ed.), *Advances in experimental social psychology* (Vol. 6, pp. 1–62). New York, NY: Academic Press.

Bem, D. J., & Allen, A. (1974). On predicting some of the people some of the time: The search for cross-situational consistency in behavior. *Psychological Review, 81*, 506–520. http://doi.org/10.1037/h0037130

Betsch, C. (2004). Präferenz für Intuition und Deliberation (PID): Inventar zur Erfassung von affekt- und kognitionsbasiertem Entscheiden [Preference for intuition and deliberation (PID): An inventory for assessing affect- and cognition-based decision-making]. *Zeitschrift für Differentielle und Diagnostische Psychologie, 25*, 179–197.

Blair, I. V. (2002). The malleability of automatic stereotypes and prejudice. *Personality and Social Psychology Review, 6*, 242–261. http://doi.org/10.1207/S15327957PSPR0603_8

Blair, I. V., Ma, J. E., & Lenton, A. P. (2001). Imagining stereotypes away: The moderation of implicit stereotypes through mental imagery. *Journal of Personality and Social Psychology, 81*, 828–841. http://doi.org/10.1037/0022-3514.81.5.828

Brand, M., Fujiwara, E., Borsutzky, S., Kalbe, E., Kessler, J., & Markowitsch, H. J. (2005). Decision-making deficits of Korsakoff patients in a new gambling task with explicit rules: Associations with executive functions. *Neuropsychology, 19*, 267–277. http://doi.org/10.1037/0894-4105.19.3.267

Castelli, L., De Dea, C., & Nesdale, D. (2008). Learning social attitudes: Children's sensitivity to the nonverbal behavior of adult models during interracial interactions. *Personality and Social Psychology Bulletin, 34*, 1504–1513. http://doi.org/10.1177/0146167208322769

Cattell, R. B. (1957). *Personality and motivation structure and measurement*. New York, NY: World Book.

Cattell, R. B., & Warburton, F. W. (1967). *Objective personality and motivation tests: A theoretical introduction and practical compendium*. Champaign, IL: University of Illinois Press.

Chaplin, W. F. (1991). The next generation of moderator research in personality psychology. *Journal of Personality, 59*, 143–178. http://doi.org/10.1111/j.1467-6494.1991.tb00772.x

Dislich, F. X. R., Imhoff, R., Banse, R., Altstötter-Gleich, C., Zinkernagel, A., & Schmitt, M. (2012). Discrepancies between implicit and explicit self-concepts of intelligence predict performance on tests of intelligence. *European Journal of Personality, 26*, 212–220. http://doi.org/10.1002/per.827

Dislich, F. X. R., Zinkernagel, A., Ortner, T. M., & Schmitt, M. (2010). Convergence of direct, indirect, and objective risk-taking measures in gambling: The moderating role of impulsiveness and self-control. *Journal of Psychology, 218*, 20–27.

Dunton, B. C., & Fazio, R. H. (1997). An individual difference measure of motivation to control prejudiced reactions. *Personality and Social Psychology Bulletin, 23*, 316–326. http://doi.org/10.1177/0146167297233009

Eid, M., & Diener, E. (Eds.) (2006). *Handbook of multimethod measurement in psychology*. New York, NY: American Psychological Association. http://doi.org/10.1037/11383-000

Ekman, P. (1992). Are there basic emotions? *Psychological Review, 99*, 550–553. http://doi.org/10.1037/0033-295X.99.3.550

Epstein, S., Pacini, R., Denes-Raj, V., & Heier, H. (1996). Individual differences in intuitive-experiential and analytical-rational thinking styles. *Journal of Personality and Social Psychology, 71*, 390–405. http://doi.org/10.1037/0022-3514.71.2.390

Fenigstein, A., Scheier, M. F., & Buss, A. H. (1975). Public and private self-consciousness: Assessment and theory. *Journal of Consulting and Clinical Psychology, 42*, 522–527. http://doi.org/10.1037/h0076760

Friese, M., Hofmann, W., & Schmitt, M. (2009). When and why do implicit measures predict behavior? Empirical evidence for the moderating role of opportunity, motivation, and process reliance. *European Review of Social Psychology, 19*, 285–338. http://doi.org/10.1080/10463280802556958

Gawronski, B., & Bodenhausen, G. V. (2006). Associative and propositional processes in evaluation: An integrative review of implicit and explicit attitude change. *Psychological Bulletin, 132*, 692–731. http://doi.org/10.1037/0033-2909.132.5.692

Gerstenberg, F. X. R, Imhoff, R., Banse, R., Altstötter-Gleich, C., Zinkernagel, A., & Schmitt, M. (2013). How implicit-explicit consistency of the intelligence self-concept moderates reactions to performance feedback. *European Journal of Personality, 27*, 238–255. http://doi.org/10.1002/per.1900

Gerstenberg, F. X. R., Imhoff, R., & Schmitt, M. (2012). "Women are bad at math, but I'm not, am I?" Fragile mathematical self-concept predicts vulnerability to a stereotype threat effect on mathematical performance. *European Journal of Personality, 26*, 212–220.

Greenwald, A. G., McGhee, D. E., & Schwartz, J. L. K. (1998). Measuring individual differences in implicit cognition: The Implicit Association Test. *Journal of Personality and Social Psychology, 74*, 1464–1480. http://doi.org/10.1037/0022-3514.74.6.1464

Greenwald, A. G., Poehlman, T. A., Uhlmann, E. L., & Banaji, M. R. (2009). Understanding and using the Implicit Association Test: III. Meta-analysis of predictive validity. *Journal of Personality and Social Psychology, 97*, 17–41. http://doi.org/10.1037/a0015575

Gschwendner, T., Hofmann, W., & Schmitt, M. (2006a). Moderatoren der Konsistenz implizit und explizit erfasster Einstellungen und Persönlichkeitsmerkmale. [Moderators of the consistency of implicitly and explicitly assessed attitudes and personality traits]. *Psychologische Rundschau, 57*, 13–33. http://doi.org/10.1026/0033-3042.57.1.13

Gschwendner, T., Hofmann, W., & Schmitt, M. (2006b). Ein Modell des Zusammenhangs impliziter Reaktionszeitverfahren mit Fragebogenmaßen [A model of the association of implicit reaction time tests and inventory measures]. In R. T. Proyer, T. M. Ortner, & K. D. Kubinger (Eds.), *Theorie und Praxis objektiver Persönlichkeitstests* (pp. 69–86). Bern, Switzerland: Verlag Hans Huber.

Gschwendner, T., Hofmann, W., & Schmitt, M. (2006c). Synergistic moderator effects of situation and person factors of awareness and adjustment on the consistency of implicit and explicit attitudes. *Journal of Individual Differences, 27*, 47–56. http://doi.org/10.1027/1614-0001.27.1.47

Gschwendner, T., Hofmann, W., & Schmitt, M. (2008a). Differential stability: The effects of acute and chronic construct accessibility on the temporal stability of the Implicit Association Test. *Journal of Individual Differences, 29*, 70–79. http://doi.org/10.1027/1614-0001.29.2.70

Gschwendner, T., Hofmann, W., & Schmitt, M. (2008b). Convergent and predictive validity of implicit and explicit anxiety measures as a function of specificity similarity and content similarity. *European Journal of Psychological Assessment, 24*, 254–262. http://doi.org/10.1027/1015-5759.24.4.254

Hartshorne, H., & May, M. A. (Eds.). (1928). *Studies in the nature of character* (Vol. I: Studies in deceit). New York, NY: Macmillan.

Hefter, R., Manoach, D., & Barton, J. (2005). Perception of facial expression and facial identity in subjects with social developmental disorders. *Neurology, 65*, 1620–1625. http://doi.org/10.1212/01.wnl.0000184498.16959.c0

Hofmann, W., Gawronski, B., Gschwendner, T., Le, H., & Schmitt, M. (2005). A meta-analysis on the correlation between the Implicit Association Test and explicit self-report measures. *Personality and Social Psychology Bulletin, 31*, 1369–1385. http://doi.org/10.1177/0146167205275613

Hofmann, W., Gschwendner, T., Castelli, L., & Schmitt, M. (2008). Implicit and explicit attitudes and interracial interaction: The moderating role of situationally available control resources. *Group Processes and Intergroup Relations, 11*, 69–87. http://doi.org/10.1177/1368430207084847

Hofmann, W., Gschwendner, T., Nosek, B. A., & Schmitt, M. (2005). What moderates implicit-explicit consistency? *European Review of Social Psychology, 16*, 335–390. http://doi.org/10.1080/10463280500443228

Hofmann, W., Gschwendner, T., & Schmitt, M. (2005). On implicit-explicit consistency: The moderating role of individual differences in awareness and adjustment. *European Journal of Personality, 19*, 25–49. http://doi.org/10.1002/per.537

Hofmann, W., Gschwendner, T., & Schmitt, M. (2009). The road to the unconscious self not taken: Discrepancies between self- and observer-inferences about implicit dispositions from nonverbal behavioral cues. *European Journal of Personality, 23*, 243–366. http://doi.org/10.1002/per.722

Hofmann, W., Gschwendner, T., Wiers, R., Friese, M., & Schmitt, M. (2008). Working memory capacity and self-regulatory behavior: Toward an individual differences perspective on behavior determination by automatic versus controlled processes. *Journal of Personality and Social Psychology, 95*, 962–977. http://doi.org/10.1037/a0012705

Hofmann, W., Rauch, W., & Gawronski, B. (2007). And deplete us not into temptation: Automatic attitudes, dietary restraint, and self-regulatory resources as determinants of eating behavior. *Journal of Experimental Social Psychology, 43*, 497–504. http://doi.org/10.1016/j.jesp.2006.05.004

Kenrick, D. T., & Funder, D. C. (1988). Profiting from controversy: Lessons from the person-situation debate. *American Psychologist, 43*, 23–34. http://doi.org/10.1037/0003-066X.43.1.23

Lejuez, C. W., Read, J. P., Kahler, C. W., Richards, J. B., Ramsey, S. E., Stuart, G. L., Strong, D. R., & Brown, R. A. (2002). Evaluation of a behavioral measure of risk taking: The Balloon Analogue Risk Task (BART). *Journal of Experimental Psychology, 8*, 75–84.

Logan, G. D. (1988). Toward an instance theory of automatization. *Psychological Review, 95*, 492–527. http://doi.org/10.1037/0033-295X.95.4.492

Matsumoto, D., Yoo, S. H., Hirayama, S., & Petrova, G. (2005). Development and initial validation of a measure of display rules: The Display Rule Assessment Inventory (DRAI). *Emotion, 5*, 23–40. http://doi.org/10.1037/1528-3542.5.1.23

Mischel, W. (Ed.). (1968). *Personality and assessment.* New York, NY: Wiley.

Newcomb, T. M. (1929). *Consistency of certain extrovert-introvert behavior patterns in 51 problem boys.* New York, NY: Columbia University, Teachers College, Bureau of Publications.

Nosek, B. A. (2005). Moderators of the relationships between implicit and explicit evaluation. *Journal of Experimental Psychology: General, 134*, 565–584. http://doi.org/10.1037/0096-3445.134.4.565

Nosek, B. A. (2007). Implicit-explicit relations. *Current Directions in Psychological Science, 16*, 65–69. http://doi.org/10.1111/j.1467-8721.2007.00477.x

Petty, R., & Krosnick, J. A. (1995). *Attitude strength. Antecedents and consequences.* Mahwah, NJ: Erlbaum.

Schmitt, M. (2006). Conceptual, theoretical, and historical foundations of multimethod assessment. In M. Eid & E. Diener (Eds.), *Handbook of multimethod measurement in psychology* (pp. 9–25). New York, NY: American Psychological Association.

Schmitt, M. (2009). Person x situation – interactions as moderators. *Journal of Research in Personality, 43*, 267. http://doi.org/10.1016/j.jrp.2008.12.032

Schmitt, M., & Borkenau, P. (1992). The consistency of personality. In G.-V. Caprara & G. L. Van Heck (Eds.), *Modern personality psychology. Critical reviews and new directions* (pp. 29–55). New York, NY: Harvester-Wheatsheaf.

Schröder-Abé, M., Rudolph, A., & Schütz, A. (2007). High implicit self-esteem is not necessarily advantageous: Discrepancies between implicit and explicit self-esteem and their relationship with anger expression and psychological health. *European Journal of Personality, 21*, 319–339. http://doi.org/10.1002/per.626

Schröder-Abé, M., Rudolph, A., Wiesner, A., & Schütz, A. (2007). Self-esteem discrepancies and defensive reactions to social feedback. *International Journal of Psychology, 42*, 174–183. http://doi.org/10.1080/00207590601068134

Smith, E. C., & DeCoster, J. (2000). Dual-process models in social and cognitive psychology: Conceptual integration and links to underlying memory systems. *Personality and Social Psychology Review, 4*, 108–131. http://doi.org/10.1207/S15327957PSPR0402_01

Snyder, M. (1974). The self-monitoring of expressive behavior. *Journal of Personality and Social Psychology, 30*, 526–537. http://doi.org/10.1037/h0037039

Snyder, M., & Ickes, W. (1985). Personality and social behavior. In G. Lindzey & E. Aronson (Eds.), *Handbook of social psychology* (3rd ed., Vol. II, pp. 883–947). New York, NY: Random House.

Strack, F., & Deutsch, R. (2004). Reflective and impulsive determinants of social behavior. *Personality and Social Psychology Review, 8*, 220–247. http://doi.org/10.1207/s15327957pspr0803_1

Swann, W. B., & Seyle, C. (2005). Personality psychology's comeback and its emerging symbiosis with social psychology. *Personality and Social Psychology Bulletin, 31*, 155–165. http://doi.org/10.1177/0146167204271591

Webster, D. M., & Kruglanski, A. W. (1994). Individual differences in need for cognitive closure. *Journal of Personality and Social Psychology, 67*, 1049–1062. http://doi.org/10.1037/0022-3514.67.6.1049

Wilson, T., Lindsey, S., & Schooler, T. Y. (2000). A model of dual attitudes. *Psychological Review, 107*, 101–126. http://doi.org/10.1037/0033-295X.107.1.101

Wittenbrink, B., Judd, C. M., & Park, B. (2001). Spontaneous prejudice at the implicit level and its relationship between questionnaire measures. *Journal of Personality and Social Psychology, 72*, 262–274. http://doi.org/10.1037/0022-3514.72.2.262

Zinkernagel, A., Hofmann, W., Gerstenberg, F. X. R., & Schmitt, M. (2013). On the road to the unconscious self: Understanding when people gain self-knowledge of implicit disgust sensitivity from behavioral cues. *European Journal of Personality, 27*, 355–376. http://doi.org/10.1002/per.1910

Chapter 4
Narrative Content Coding

Michael Bender

Department of Social Psychology, Babylon, Center for the Study of the
Multicultural Society, Tilburg University, The Netherlands

> A man is always a teller of stories, he lives surrounded by his own stories and those of other people, he sees everything that happens to him in terms of these stories, and he tries to live his life as if he were recounting it. (Sartre, 1964, p. 39)

Narratives, sometimes referred to as stories, have been attracting scholars for a very long time with the promise of revealing the narrator's innermost intentions, attitudes, or motives – to name a few psychologically salient focal points of narrative research. Between 1933 and 2014, a total of 6,364 (PsycINFO) peer-reviewed articles were published that focused on narratives (as part of their title). The first listed article is an anthropological case study providing a thick description, an account not just of overt behavior, but of interpretative context (Geertz, 1973), of an elderly woman of the Arapaho tribe (Michelson, 1933). By contrast, recent publications exhibit a methodological focus on the functionality and frequency of specific words assessed by linguistic computer software (e.g., Linguistic Inquiry and Word Count, LIWC; Tausczik & Pennebaker, 2009). An underlying assumption of narrative content coding is that sharing such stories is behavior, or behavioral traces, that provide a unique window into psychological processing unfettered by problems surrounding scalar self-reports.

Scholars from various disciplines in psychology, using various qualitative and quantitative methodologies, have made narratives part of their research (for an overview see Holstein & Gubrium, 2012). Methodological choices are intertwined with the theoretical considerations in narrative content coding, producing a multitude of answers to the question "What is a narrative?" Finding a satisfying answer has become difficult with the increasing popularity of the term itself. The term *narrative* has never been more popular, prompting some researchers to describe its ubiquity as the "tyranny of narrative": The term is indiscriminately applied everywhere and has come to mean anything and everything (Kohler Riessman & Speedy, 2007, p. 428).

With the meaning having become diluted, and differing radically across disciplines, a basic working definition to capture the common aspects of narrative research is needed. To start with, narratives themselves exhibit a clear sequence (e.g., a beginning and an end), which sets them apart from mere open-ended text (see also Chapter 6 in this volume). Events or topics are selected, organized, interconnected, and then evaluated by one or more assessors as they are tailored to cater to a specific audience or recipient (Kohler Riessman, 2008). There is substantial variation in definitions of narratives. In anthropology, narratives often refer to an entire life story that is captured as a case study (see the first example in this chapter, Michelson, 1933). In sociolinguistics and related areas, narratives are oftentimes confined to relatively short and highly specific topics that are analyzed in depth. In psychology, narratives are investigated as (typically long) sections of text or talk, often culminating in extended accounts of lives in context that develop over the course of interviews (Holstein & Gubrium, 2012). In clinical practice, narratives occupy a special position as a tool of maintaining or re-establishing meaning during therapy (Habermas & De Silveira, 2008; for an introduction to narrative therapy, see Morgan, 2000).

What is also common to all approaches, irrespective of discipline, is that narratives are considered as raw, unprocessed materials, which do not speak for themselves and do not have merit in an unanalyzed form – narratives require coding and interpretation to be used. In this chapter I clarify that methodological choices regarding the coding can be situated along a continuum of two extremes: Researchers either focus on thematic or on structural content coding. In the former, attention is given to the interpreted, often overall meaning of a narrative, the latter instead focuses on syntactic elements or word counts in a narrative. In the following, I provide a bird's-eye perspective on these two prototypical (yet overlapping) approaches to the analysis of the content of narratives. Then, I showcase how topics and methodological techniques are related in the study of autobiographical narratives, the recollection of personally meaningful events across one's life (Rubin, 2006): Case studies include illustrations from studies focusing on cognitive structure, eyewitness accuracy, depression, mental health, the life story, and studies at the intersection of development and culture.

Overview: Two Approaches to Narrative Content Coding

A multitude of different typologies of narrative analyses exist depending on the subdiscipline within psychology and related fields (Cortazzi, 2001, for ethnographic approaches; for overviews, see Mishler, 1995; Kohler Riessman, 2008). An important aspect that complicates a systematic overview of narrative methods lies in the flexibility with which techniques are applied to narrative content, particularly when using qualitative methodologies. This heterogeneity is an impediment for comparisons and generalizability. A further impediment is the needless portrayal of methodological approaches as mutually exclusive, while in fact much can be gained from combination or even triangulation between quantitative and qualitative tools (see Van de Vijver & Chasiotis, 2010). Across all approaches there is an understanding – more or less tacit – that stories provide an access point to comprehend how individuals derive meaning from their experiences or, more generally, the psychological processes of how they organize information in a self-relevant manner.

Focus on the content and structure of narratives has surged since the so-called narrative (or linguistic) turn in psychology. Coined by Bruner, the narrative turn exemplifies the withdrawal from a strictly behavioral and positivist scientific stance, and the turning toward an appreciation of the narrative construction of reality, which fosters the focus on individual meaning making (Bruner, 1986). Bruner's seminal reasoning (1986, 1991) also provides us with an organizing principle that can help shed light on the continuum of narrative approaches by contrasting two primary modes of thinking exhibited by the narrator: the narrative mode and the paradigmatic mode. Narrative thinking is characterized by sequential, action-oriented, detail-driven thought. Paradigmatic thinking, by contrast, transcends particularities to achieve systematic, categorical cognition. In the former, stories and drama emerge, whereas in the latter, the focus is on the analysis of propositions linked by logical operators. Many variants of this basic distinction can be found, yet the common denominator remains the distinction between focusing on content or structure of a narrative (e.g., content analysis vs. narrative analysis, Smith, 2000; context of discovery vs. context of justification, McAdams, 2012). Bruner's basic distinction thus captures the spectrum in which narrative data can be processed: from a *thematic*, holistic or from a *structural*, linguistic perspective (Bruner, 1986).

Thematic Analysis – Focusing on the What

The inquiry for a theme of a narrative is the search for the focal point of the story. The *what* is emphasized and it is tacitly assumed that a narrative can provide the researcher with a direct and unambiguous route to understanding what the narrator perceives to be the meaning of a given event. Particularly from the perspective of grounded theory, researchers collect a multitude of narrative information, and inductively build a conceptual clustering of the emerging themes (for an overview, see Glaser & Strauss, 2009). Thematic analyses within psychology, however, are often based on theoretically deduced concepts (e.g., implicit motivation, Schultheiss & Brunstein, 2010; but see also thematic analyses for personality disorders, Jenkins, 2008).

Thematic analyses are often applied to content derived from projective tests, particularly Picture Story Exercises (PSEs), which are used to assess the implicit motivational disposition of a respondent (see also Chapter 6 in this volume). In such assessments, test takers are asked to write down narratives in response to ambiguous picture stimuli (see Smith, 1992). The resulting story is then content-coded for the presence or absence of motive imagery according to specific manuals (e.g., Winter, 1994; for a comprehensive overview, see also Schultheiss & Brunstein, 2010).

An illustration for a theoretically guided thematic analysis of narrative content is given by Imada (2010), who examined narratives sampled from American and Japanese school textbooks with regard to their cultural values: To identify theoretically relevant values, Schwartz's (1992) Value Survey and Kilby's (1993) Omnibus Values Questionnaire were consulted for individualistic values (individual goals, uniqueness, personal benefits, well-being as individualistic values) and collectivistic values (group goals, group unity, and interpersonal well-being). The values summarized in these tools were transformed into a coding system for textbooks (Han & Shavitt, 1996). Han and Shavitt classified advertisements according to their individualistic vs. collectivistic appeal. An appeal about individuality would be, "She's got a style all her own," while a focus on collective group well-being would be exemplified by, "We have a way of bringing people closer together" (Han & Shavitt, 1996; p. 346). Imada (2010) adapted this procedure for a rating system in which researchers judge the extent to which a specific value is present in a text. Coding for the mere presence or absence of a predefined topic or characteristic is usually a more economic procedure, but standardized rating instructions and reliabilities of multiple indicators ensure the prospect of replicability while allowing for a more differentiated picture (with interrater reliabilities higher than .89; see Imada, 2010, p. 582). US stories featured themes of individualism (e.g., self-direction, achievement), and Japanese textbook narratives focused more on themes of collectivism (conformity, group harmony). Note that the interpretative space is regulated by the theoretical choices (e.g., the choice of coding manual) – not the raw narrative data themselves.

A stronger focus on structure can be found in Imada's second set of analyses (2010, see previous section). Here the focus of coding is on cultural differences in the presence or absence (not intensity) of specific narrative characteristics: (a) the narrator of the story (main character, other character in the story, or third person); (b) topic of the story (success, failure, neither, or both); (c) attribution of story outcome (success and/or failure) and locus of control (internal, external, both, or neither); (d) number of people (none, one person, two people, or three or more people); (e) overall valence of the story (happy, sad, neutral/neither, or includes both happy and sad elements); and (f) the frequency of positive (e.g., happy, smiled), negative (e.g., sad, felt like crying), and neutral (e.g., surprised) emotional words/phrases. For instance, the narrator casting himself as the main person of the story would count toward an individualistic theme. This second illustration is an example of thematic coding that is highly structured, and reliability coefficients indicate a good prospect for replication (all > .85; Imada, 2010, p. 585).

Within thematic approaches in general, language is seen as a medium or resource that conveys a specific theme but is not the topic of investigation itself. One potential disadvantage can be the snapshot quality of the thematic analysis: Often, the context or perspective of the creator of the narratives is not, or not sufficiently, included in the consideration of the theme as an alternative prediction. Another issue could be that grouped narrative elements (see the second set of analyses in Imada, 2010) constituting a theme are often presented as interchangeable in strength or in association with the overarching theme, without referring to ambiguities and confounds in the narrative data. Highly structured thematic content-coding manuals (again, as those used for implicit motivation, see Chapter 6 in this volume) usually do not have these issues because the constituting elements can be investigated separately and have been assessed and replicated over multiple studies.

Structural Analysis – Focusing on the How

In an approach to a structural analysis of the narrative, the emphasis is shifted toward (or includes) the telling itself, which is *how* a story is narrated. Language and textual indicators are a focal point, and constitute the object of investigation. A discourse-analytic perspective investigates the function of a clause or narrative passage (or other forms of language use) and evaluates it in terms of the communicative value it achieves. Thus, a thematic overarching perspective is present to which the specific structural constituents contribute. In many cases, such thematic umbrellas are explicated from the vantage point of theoretical frameworks.

Labov's (1982) historical study on personal narratives about violence can serve as an illustrative blueprint for a structural approach that inspects how syntactic elements are functionally interrelated with outcomes (e.g., violent behavior). Labov investigated six theoretically derived discrete elements of a narrative structure: the abstract (summary of the narrative); orientation (time, place, characters, situation); complicating action (event sequence, often with turning points); evaluation (evaluative comment by the narrator); resolution (the outcome of the plot); and a coda (formally leaving the story). Not all stories may contain all elements. Associating the presence or absence of such elements with behavioral outcomes (here, violence) is seen as a method to abstract the psychological meaning-making that is represented in the narrative structure.

Data on validity and reliability of often very specific structural coding procedures are not very common, with the exception of word count procedures that come with the promise of easy administration and clear coding rules (e.g., the text analysis software package LIWC, Tausczik & Pennebaker, 2009). The LIWC manual provides not only information on the reliability of the software, but also includes data on how human judges have rated specific categories as a means of triangulating the word count procedures (for details see the manual, Pennebaker, Chung, Ireland, Gonzales, & Booth, 2007). In addition, multiple studies have provided support for the validity of constructs assessed with LIWC by comparing it with other, established measures (e.g., emotion expression, Bantum & Owen, 2009; Kahn, Tobin, Massey, & Anderson, 2007).

Structural approaches commonly require much in-depth analysis, often with regard to syntactic features of narratives, and highly specific rules for coding and interpreting linguistic elements from a semantic perspective. As a consequence, coding a single piece of text is labor-intensive, and necessitates a highly trained coder – which renders a structural analysis difficult to carry out for large numbers or long texts. This of course also applies to the preparation required for software like LIWC, which is only as good as the coding/counting rules it executes. From a linguistic or literary perspective, the microanalysis of cases, however, is useful to help build theoretical assumptions about the interrelation of language and meaning. The advantage over a thematic analysis can be that a structural analysis (particularly when it would be inductive) does not necessarily presuppose an emergent theme to be transparent for the narrator or writer.

Thematic and Structural Approaches: Different Labels but Overlapping Techniques

One of the striking features of a thematic analysis is given by its focus on the meaning and the abstracted topic or motive of a narrative. A structural analysis, on the other hand, hones in on the specific narrative elements, the form of the text (word count, syntax, order, etc.). Upon closer inspection, however, this distinction appears to be not a qualitative difference: both need to specify theme *and* structure, albeit to often radically different degrees. A thematic analysis is rooted in specific coding rules regarding themes that are present or absent in its structure. A structural investigation is typically concerned with the functionality of narrative elements in terms of an emerging topic. An example would be a personal narrative describing the career of an individual. The agentic theme in the story would be exhibited in form of achievement images in the individual's career trajectory (e.g., standards of excellence, feelings of accomplishment, etc.). The structure of the story may also be geared toward this direction (e.g., the relation between number of first person pronouns and others, as a sign of agentic self-focus). Both need to be related to the content of the story (or its constituting elements, like the pronouns).

Across diverse topics, there are attempts to automate the content coding by using software programs (Pennebaker & King, 1999; Schultheiss, 2013; Tauszik & Pennebaker, 2009). Automated software represents a structural narrative analysis that would be highly different from coder-based, thematic content-coding systems. The advantage of such techniques is their economic utility, but outcomes of such analyses are at a greater danger of decontextualizing the narrative than coder-based systems. There are indications that automated structural coding and coder-based thematic coding assess overlapping (but not congruent) portions of what is represented in the narrative data (Pennebaker & King, 1999; Schultheiss, 2013).

Leaning more toward the thematic or the structural approach has implications, and is associated with specific challenges. For instance, in discourse analytic studies there has been a tradition of separating intertextual (thematic) and linguistic (structural) analysis and arguing for a *systematic* application of both techniques (Fairclough, 1992). Fairclough (1992, 2013) argued that a focus on the content rather than the form of texts should be accompanied by a systematic application of rigorous content-coding techniques, while a textual analysis should be theoretically rooted (e.g., in a theory of language such as systematic-functional linguistics). Applied to the assessment situation, Fairclough suggests that thematic content coding is often at danger of being applied in an unsystematic fashion (too general coding rules, unspecific categories, etc.). Structural content coding, on the other hand, often comes in the shape of counting specific linguistic elements like pronouns or verbs, and usually does not exhibit this problem – but may instead be prone to focus less on theoretical considerations. Focusing both on systematic and replicable coding procedures as well as theoretical substantiation is recommended, as each approach can benefit from the strengths of the other, much like quantitative and qualitative research techniques can benefit from one another (Van de Vijver & Chasiotis, 2010; see also Chapter 6 in this volume).

Two further dangers are related to the context of a narrative. First, a structural focus on the linguistic characteristics may lead to a *decontextualized narrative*. In positive terms, enduring characteristics can be gleaned from the narratives – but the risk of over-interpreting their stability has to be considered. Researchers need to pay attention to the moderating role of context and situation (e.g., in personality psychology, Mischel & Shoda, 1995) and to historical, interactional, and institutional factors (from a sociological perspective, Kohler Riessman, 2008). Second, the specific *eliciting conditions* or context that prompted the narrative needs to be considered as an explanans or confound. From a discourse-oriented perspective, narratives are a social process combining both text and context and reveal ongoing social processes that affect and are affected by the narratives (Langellier, 1989, 1999; for symbolic interactionism, see Blumer, 1969; for an overview on discourse analysis, see Fairclough, 1992, and Gee, 2011). In short, narratives represent storied ways of representation and communication (Hinchman & Hinchman, 1997) and, particularly from an interactional perspective, are ecologically more valid forms of assessment than self-reports, which make them valuable in clinical assessment and psychotherapy (Jenkins, 2008).

Content-Coding Approaches to Autobiographical Narratives

In the wake of narrative psychology (Bruner, 1990; Sarbin, 1986), sociolinguistic studies have underscored the intimate link between narrative and autobiographical memory (Fivush, 2011). Autobiographical memories (AMs) foster self-continuity and psychodynamic integrity by providing a reference point to the self in the past (Pillemer, 1992), have a social and communicative function by facilitating bonding via sharing memories (Alea & Bluck, 2007), and a directive, problem-solving function by providing access to the wealth of previously applied problem-solving strategies and the personal knowledge of having mastered challenges (Pillemer, 2003). Researchers strongly agree that personal memories are functionally critical for sustaining an individual's current goals, self-theories, attitudes, and beliefs (Conway & Pleydell-Pearce, 2000; Pillemer, 2009; Ross, 1989; Singer & Salovey, 1993). It has been repeatedly demonstrated that how people represent, organize, disclose, and narrate personal information has effects on motivation and behavior (Gollwitzer, Wicklund, & Hilton, 1982; Powell & Fazio, 1984) and vice versa (Woike, 2008; Woike, Bender, & Besner, 2009).

In research on autobiographical narratives an enormous range of different techniques is applied, which renders it a useful arena to showcase some variations of thematic and structural approaches and their combinations. Several content areas like gender (Davis, 1999), life-span considerations (Bluck & Glück, 2004), or the investigation of intimate relationships (Alea & Bluck, 2007) are left out in favor of focusing on techniques that would likely see use across research topics.

Autobiographical Narrative Structure Indicates Function

The structure of autobiographical narratives can be thought of as a window into cognitive processing, how we structure personal life events when prompted to recall them. The construct of narrative cognitive complexity, one operationalization of structuring narratives, is generally understood to comprise two main processes: differentiation (perceiving differences between aspects) and integration (drawing connections between stimuli; Schroder, Driver, & Streufert, 1967; Suedfeld & Bluck, 1993; Suedfeld, Tetlock, & Streufert, 1992). In short, we can portray two elements to be different from one another ("Charlotte is *taller* than Maria"; differentiation), or we express them in a connected fashion ("*Both* Charlotte and Maria are going swimming"; integration). The assessment of these processes is based on specific narrative elements (see the italicized sample words in the previous sentence), not content-coded themes of a narrative.

These two structural categories have been suggested as indicators of a separated and connected way of processing information (Woike, 1994), akin to the distinction between communal and agentic needs (Bakan, 1966), or self and social functions of AM on a thematic level (Bluck, 2003). Structure also indicates function by defining "the parameters of potential functions" (Robinson & Swanson, 1990, p. 330): A hammer is a more appropriate tool for nailing, not sewing. Applied to narratives, integrated memories (full of connections) are likely better in social situations, while differentiated memories (full of analytic differences) might be more appropriate in setting yourself apart from others (Bender & Chasiotis, 2011; Chasiotis, Bender, Kiessling, & Hofer, 2010). Telling a friend a story about differences seeking to mend a relationship might not work as well as a narrative featuring much integration.

There are several manuals of coding the structure of autobiographical narratives, all of them with elaborate coder manuals and practice sets, facilitating replication and increasing reliability (Schroder et al., 1967; Suedfeld & Bluck, 1993; Suedfeld et al., 1992; Woike, 1994). For illustration, I focus on the manual for coding cognitive complexity by Woike (1994). Here, the two processes are operationalized at simple and elaborated levels. Typically, coding is restricted to elaborated levels of both (Woike, Gershkovich, Piorkowski, & Polo, 1999). Markers of elaborated differentiation reflect a narrative structure of separateness between attributes: Restriction of meaning refers to linguistic expressions that limit a perspective (e.g., "In my point of view"), relative comparisons refer to comparisons of two or more aspects on a single dimension (e.g., *more/most*), and contrasts comprise two objects that are presented as being opposite to each other (e.g., *happy/sad*). Elaborated integration comprises elements stressing a connected way of information processing: causal links (dynamic/causal relations; e.g., "His comment made me realize [...]"), statements of similarity (analogies, similarities; e.g., "Both my brothers congratulated me"), and resolutions (the central theme of the narrative; e.g., "The day I came to visit my sister will stick in my mind forever"; see Woike, 1997). Bender and Chasiotis (2011) have used indicators of cognitive complexity to study how autobiographical narratives are related to a person's ontogenetic childhood context across cultures (China, Cameroon, and Germany): Individuals growing up with more siblings structure their memories in a more integrated fashion, which renders narratives more appropriate for social purposes. They found that it is rather the number of siblings that is informative in determining autobiographical narrative structure, and not the cultural label (i.e., the country from which individuals come). This finding highlights that it is important to include contextual variables when explaining and attributing differences in narrative structure – which are not readily available from the narrative material itself (Bender & Chasiotis, 2011; see also Chasiotis, Bender, & Hofer, 2014).

Coding autobiographical memories for cognitive complexity represents a highly structured narrative content-coding procedure (with acceptable to high intercoder reliabilities (Bender & Chasiotis, 2011; Chasiotis et al., 2010; Woike & Matic, 2004), while still representing a mixture between a thematic and structural orientation. Cognitive complexity represents a theoretically well-defined psychological process that is coded when specific narrative indicators are observed. The threat of decontextualizing the narrative is relevant, given that the aggregate scores of differentiation and integration can be considered without interpreting the content of the story or the situation in which the narrative is produced. However, this danger is minimized in studies that are particularly interested in the interaction between autobiographical processing, personality, and situation, in the tradition of personality psychology (Mischel & Shoda, 1995). For instance, Woike and Matic (2004) not only investigated how memories of posttraumatic events are related to psychological distress, but also considered the personality disposition as a moderator of autobiographical recall.

Forensic Assessment: Accuracy of Eyewitness Narratives

The dangers of misinterpreting narratives are painstakingly obvious in the legal arena: In legal systems around the world, eyewitness statements are of substantial importance for judicial outcomes. A recurring problem is that self-professed certainty is not a good indicator of actual narrative accuracy (Sporer, Penrod, Read, & Cutler, 1995; for false or repressed memories, see Loftus, 1993, 1996). This is particularly problematic in child-abuse cases, when much time has passed since the event, and autobiographical memory becomes prone to errors and suggestibility (Ceci & Bruck, 1995; Haber & Haber, 1998). Usually, the assumption is that the descriptions (i.e., content and structure) of an event that actually happened would differ from those that did not, while this does not necessarily imply a conscious effort to alter a memory (Undeutsch, 1989).

Studies investigating what contributes to accuracy or inaccuracy in children's autobiographical narratives employ highly elaborate coding systems: Researchers either choose to focus on so-called Features-of-Events (FOE) checklists, which offer coding simplicity (basically as word-count procedures), but do not seem appropriate for complex narratives and events. By contrast, Units-of-Information (UOI) systems assess all information reported, regardless of event complexity, promise high ecological validity, but are difficult to execute (for an evaluation, see Dickinson & Poole, 2000). As an example of an FOE checklist, Gordon and colleagues (1993) investigated whether the inclusion of memory-relevant props (i.e., a doll) helps children recall details from an authentic pediatric check-up. The features to be recalled were compiled by physicians, nurses, and parents who were present during the check-up – which represents a nonexhaustive focus on features deemed salient. By contrast, Poole and White (1993) used a UOI coding system to assess the reports of participants recalling an event 2 years in the past. They counted syntactic (i.e., grammatical) units, including words describing an actor (she), an action (left), or a direct object (the apple). Thus, *she left the apple* contained three such units. In addition, quotes, descriptions (*her hair was black*), qualifiers (*she was very beautiful*), temporal information (*now*), and prepositional phrases (*on the bus*) were differentiated. Each unit was assessed as being accurate or inaccurate, and the proportion of accurate information in each child's responses was computed (Poole & White, 1993). A comparison between an FOE and a UOI system suggests that they differ in terms of thematic or structural focus, with an FOE system being more thematic, and a UOI system reflecting a more structurally exhaustive focus. Note, however, that both would be considered highly structural when compared with more inductive content-analytic techniques (e.g., grounded theory, Glaser & Strauss, 2009).

The study by Gordon and colleagues (1993) not only clarifies a specific approach to coding narratives, but also highlights that a personal recollection of the past depends on the recall conditions (here: with or without a doll as a mnemonic aid). Autobiographical memory is typically considered a product of both context (Barclay, 1996) and motivational factors, which shape the resulting reminiscence (Woike, 2008; Woike et al., 2009). It is therefore logical that eyewitness researchers, interested in the accuracy of autobiographical recall, seek to understand and minimize the effects of context. Context and moderating factors play an important role in the investigation of eye-witness testimonial narratives (for an overview, see Kassin, Tubb, Hosch, & Memon, 2001). This not only concerns the context at the time of encoding the information, but particularly the context at the time of recollection. For instance, a moderating factor for testimonial narratives is the amount of postevent information that distorts the actual eyewitness information (e.g., suggestive questions by police officers; see Searcy, Bartlett, & Memon, 2000). Suggestive effects of interviewers, peer pressure, and other social influences in the postevent condition are generally more pronounced for child witnesses (Kassin et al., 2001). For example, Poole and Lindsay (1995) investigated children's eyewitness testimony under conditions either designed to maximize or degrade the quality of their narrative reports – with substantial effects on how accurate children were in their recollection.

In eyewitness research, narrative analyses oscillate between more exhaustive approaches (e.g., UOIs) and those promising easy administration and high replicability. Particularly word count procedures, given their high interrater reliability, have often been considered useful alternatives to UOIs (for an overview, see Dickinson & Poole, 2000). But irrespective of how thematic or structural a narrative content-coding approach is, and its associated disadvantages, eyewitness research highlights how important it can be to include information *outside the narrative* itself (e.g., the inclusion of props or postevent information), that is, to contextualize the narrative. This is arguably of supreme importance when the accuracy of memories needs to be determined. But it is much less relevant when the function of a narrative is concerned: When a researcher is interested in the effects of recalling a memory (e.g., regulating mood by recalling a specific past success in the face of adversity, e.g., shortly before an exam), its actual veracity is often secondary to the experienced utility.

Clinical Assessment: Depression and Autobiographical Specificity

One area that has received increasing attention over the last two decades is the role that autobiographical narratives have for mental health. It has been shown consistently that overly categorical autobiographical memories are associated with depression. This phenomenon has been described as an *overgeneral memory* (OGM) retrieval style (Williams & Broadbent, 1986) or *reduced autobiographical memory specificity* (rAMS), with depressed individuals recalling less specific and more general memories than their nondepressed counterparts (for an overview, see King et al., 2010; Van Vreeswijk & De Wilde, 2004). The phenomenon is considered an enduring marker for depression (Williams et al., 2007), predicts its course (Sumner, Griffith, & Mineka, 2010), and it is accessible for treatment in nonclinical (Raes, Watkins, Williams, & Hermans, 2008) as well as dysphoric and depressed individuals (Watkins, 2004).

To assess whether there is an OGM/rAMS, researchers predominantly use variants of the Autobiographical Memory Test (AMT; Williams & Broadbent, 1986). The AMT is either administered by an interviewer or in written form (for methodological variants, see also Griffith et al., 2009). It prompts participants to recall a specific personal memory in response to word stimuli, usually five pleasant (e.g., *happy, safe*) and five unpleasant words (e.g., *angry, clumsy*), in a set time (~60 s). The narratives are then coded by trained assistants, either with a two-category system (i.e., general/specific; Williams & Broadbent, 1986) or with the recently more dominant four-category system (Mark, Williams, & Dritschel, 1992). The four categories are omissions (memory-unrelated content, e.g., "I am currently filling out a questionnaire"), categoric-general (description of a category of events, e.g., "… when a lot of people are around me"), extended (periods longer than a day, e.g., "Our honeymoon to Cornwall"), and specific (events lasting less than a day at a particular, identifiable point in time, e.g., "On January 13th, when my wife told me that she was pregnant"). The AMT features a very standardized procedure, increasingly refined coding rules, and is accessible to sophisticated statistical techniques to assess its appropriateness and validity (Griffith et al., 2009). It therefore represents an interesting example of a narrative content coding that requires categorical codes based on clear coding rules, although these are not (yet) necessarily rooted in distinct linguistic markers. Coding is differentiated mainly in terms of chronological classification (e.g., one point in time as specific, etc.). The AMT procedure is highly structured and abstracts a decontextualized categorization from a narrative, without necessarily considering its theme or linguistic elements (but see Bender, Carrera, & Alonso-Arbiol, 2015).

Health Interventions: The Healing Power of Personal Narratives

The creation of personal narratives – often autobiographical experiences of emotional upheaval like trauma and loss – can positively affect well-being and mental health. Studies have focused on assessing and understanding which elements of a narrative are particularly related to mental health, with a special emphasis on automated word count computer software (LIWC; Tausczik & Pennebaker, 2009). One researcher has been synonymous with the rapidly expanding literature on the power of expressing emotions in narratives (Pennebaker, 1997a, 1997b): Pennebaker and colleagues (Niederhoffer & Pennebaker, 2009) suggested that the sharing of an emotional event can help people gradually construct a social narrative, and facilitates coming to terms with its implications (very much in line with the psychodynamic self-function of AM; Bluck, 2003). The use of narratives has found its place in psychotherapy (Esterling, L'Abate, Murray, & Pennebaker, 1999; Pennebaker, 1997a, 1997b). Language in narratives has been widely investigated, including smoking interventions (Ames et al., 2005), how military couples handle deployment (Baddeley & Pennebaker, 2011), personality differences (Jones & Pennebaker, 2006; Pennebaker & Lay, 2002), job loss (Spera, Buhrfeind, & Pennebaker, 2014), the dynamics of illness support groups (Davison, Pennebaker, & Dickerson, 2000), the self (Pennebaker, Mehl, & Niederhoffer, 2003), and language use across the lifespan (Pennebaker & Stone, 2003).

What these studies have in common is their assessment focus: Narratives are analyzed by computer software, such as LIWC (Tausczik & Pennebaker, 2009). LIWC is a text analysis software program designed by Pennebaker, Booth, and Francis (2007; see also Tausczik & Pennebaker, 2009). LIWC compares words used in texts with dictionary categories, and provides a frequency for each of the employed categories. In total, there are more than 80 categories present in the LIWC dictionaries (varying by language version). Word categories encompass a wide variety of topics, ranging from agentic (work, achieve) or communal (social) issues, affect, cognitive mechanisms, but also linguistic elements of the narrative (words per sentence, number of words with more than six letters, articles, tense analysis, etc.). The software was developed by having judges evaluate the match of words or word stems with the categories. Pennebaker has used LIWC to investigate how the structure and content of narratives predict health outcomes (for an overview of some, see Pennebaker, 2000). Together with colleagues (Pennebaker, Mayne, & Francis, 1997), he found that the more people used positive-emotion words in their narratives, the more their health improved over time. Interestingly, both people using many negative words and those using very few were highly likely to have health problems – but not those with a moderate degree of negative words. Such findings are discussed with regard to emotion regulation (Pennebaker, 2000). He also conducted intervention studies, in which people were prompted to write for 15–30 min per day. Analyses with LIWC revealed that people's levels of insight and their use of causality changed over the course of writing – which is taken as support for the notion that construction of a personal narrative is a useful psychodynamic tool (Pennebaker, 2000; see also Alea & Bluck, 2003). LIWC, as a highly structured and automated content-coding instrument, may be at a particular risk of decontextualizing narratives. Validity remains therefore a prime issue when evaluating the appropriateness of the method, even when studies generally find good criterion validity and attest good psychometric properties to the LIWC (Bantum & Owen, 2009; Kahn et al., 2007).

Autobiographical Narratives and the Life Story

The crowning achievement of a personal narrative can be found in the notion of the life story (Barclay, 1996). McAdams's model (McAdams, 1985, 1993) describes the life story as "an individual's internalized, evolving, and integrated story of the self" (McAdams, 2008, p. 242). The inherently autobiographical stories people come up with are the medium by which personal meaning and a sense of coherence across life and diverse social contexts is derived. Life stories, and the associated life story schema, are seen as the most integrated autobiographical account (Bluck & Habermas, 2000). In their life stories, people strive for an integration of both positive and negative aspects of their lives to feel whole (Bluck, Alea, & Ali, 2014; McAdams, 2008). People who find redemption in challenge and adversity by means of life stories tend to enjoy higher levels of mental health, well-being, and maturity (McAdams & McLean, 2013).

Researchers have highlighted that the assessment of how coherent a life story narrative is informs coping, attachment, psychotherapeutic processes, and the organization of autobiographical memory (Habermas & Bluck, 2000; Habermas & De Silveira, 2008). Coherence can be differentiated into multiple constituting elements: Temporal and causal coherence helps put events into sequence, thematic coherence reveals the dominant strands in the life story, and a cultural concept of biography reflects culturally appropriate biographic milestones. Coherence has been approached with different methodological techniques. For local, temporal, causal, and thematic coherence, linguistic indicators were assessed at the level of propositions as well as by a global rating scale measuring the impressions of observers (Habermas & De Silveira, 2008), and the cultural appropriateness of biographic events was assessed with rating scales of discrete event descriptions (Habermas, 2007).

A global sense of coherence is often approximated by an overall observer rating (Habermas & De Silveira, 2008). Habermas and De Silveira coded all linguistic expressions that locate events in the sequence of the narrative, such as age, phase, date, or distance from the present, as indicative of temporal coherence (but not story-unrelated markers such as "and then" or "3 days earlier"). Causal coherence is expressed as causal relations, explanations of change in terms of enduring personal dispositions, and, vice versa, explanations referring to events related to changes in personality (e.g., lessons learned: "That's why I told myself, next time I fall in love, school work should not suffer from it", see Habermas & De Silveira, 2008). Thematic coherence is reflected in analogies or similarities, such as prototypical episodes and their variants (e.g., exemplifications: "I haven't learned to do things on my own [general statement], although I am able to use the subway on my own and stuff like that, but, for example, I do not have the faintest idea how to go about anything bureaucratic [exemplification]" p. 713, Habermas & De Silveira, 2008; see also McAdams, 1985).

As in other studies on autobiographical narratives (e.g., eyewitness research), the recollection of autobiographical events can be influenced by a multitude of factors (Woike et al., 2009). It can therefore be useful to avoid potentially suggestive interviewer prompts (for further details, see Habermas & De Silveira, 2008). The content coding for coherence indicators is an example of a theoretically deduced thematic analysis that seeks to find linguistically located representations of the conceptually formed categories, but restrains itself from decontextualizing specific linguistic indicators from the narrative. While much still has to be done, it is noteworthy that with care in the coding rules and the procedure and with an inclusion of confounds, replicability is likely to increase (as signified by high interrater agreements, κ >.87; Habermas & De Silveira, 2008, p. 712; see also McAdams, 2008).

Mother–Child Reminiscence as a Means of Socialization

While autobiographical memory is not exclusively language-based (it comprises all senses, see Conway & Pleydell-Pearce, 2000; Rubin, 2006), language-related elements are dominant when social interaction is concerned (Fivush, 2011). Communication about past experiences is a hallmark of establishing a notion of selfhood in infants (Reese, 2002). It is usually the adults with whom children interact that assist in linking and interpreting these often ephemeral personal accounts.

Research in the past 20 years has found that mothers (who were investigated more often than fathers) differ substantially in how they interact with their children when engaging in memory talk (Fivush, 2011). In particular, mothers differ in the extent to which they engage in an elaborative style of reminiscing with their children. An elaborative style, as opposed to a normative style, is characterized by long and detailed conversations about the past, rich in descriptive details, and evaluation. Specific intertextual elements of a highly elaborative style are asking open-ended questions ("What did we do in the morning?"), affirming and integrating the child's account ("Right, we went to the market! Who did we meet there?"), and providing prompts and assistance. By contrast, closed question formats or repeating the question until a desired answer is given is indicative of a less elaborative (normative) style (for an overview, see Fivush, 2011). The styles have been linked to many child outcomes such as self-regulation, literacy, and attachment among many others, with usually elaborative styles being related to more favorable constellations (for an overview, see Fivush, Haden, & Reese, 2006). It was also found that differences in the maternal reminiscing style predicts a substantial amount of variance in later adult memories, with a highly elaborative style leading to detailed and coherent memories in children, who even recall their first memory earlier than others (Fivush, 2011; Jack, MacDonald, Reese, & Hayne, 2009).

The different reminiscence styles parents employ have also been linked with cultural differences in the emergence of the self (for an overview, see Wang, 2011, 2013), particularly since family sharing practices are an important vehicle of acquiring literacy in culturally appropriate scripts and schemas (e.g., identifying appropriate biographical cornerstones; Bluck & Habermas, 2000). Findings from different cultural settings clarify that the assessment of what can be considered a "good" style of reminiscence hinges on whether it is appropriate in a specific cultural context (Wang & Brockmeier, 2002). In prototypical East Asian settings, self-expression and focusing on oneself in reminiscence might not be as prominent as in typical Western settings like the US. Research has consistently shown that Caucasian (Western) mother–child dyads are more likely to portray the child as the central character in a narrative, focus on feelings and thoughts, and to refer to personal attributes of the child (see also Schröder et al., 2013). By contrast, many Asian dyads emphasized behavioral expectations and social roles to a greater extent (Wang, 2001b; Wang, Leichtman, & Davies, 2000). Similar differences are found for 4- to 7-year-olds' memories (Wang, 2004; Wang & Leichtman, 2000) as well as adults (Wang, 2001a). In short, such memories often serve the purpose of fitting in rather than sticking out.

In these studies parent–child conversations, as well as children's and adult's memories, were assessed with a combination of both structural and thematic elements. For instance, Wang and Leichtman (2000) content-coded the occurrence of social engagement, moral code, concern with authority, autonomous orientation, aggression, emotional expressiveness, and narrative concreteness. All of these content categories include some references to specific linguistic markers, but require interpretation. Narrative concreteness, for instance, refers to background information that places the narrative in context (i.e., "Grandma's house was very clean and shiny"), which requires an intertextual, thematic perspective. On the other hand, direct expressions of positive and negative emotion states (counting toward emotional expressiveness) require less interpretation and are more firmly rooted in specific linguistic markers (for details, see Wang & Leichtman, 2000). Other markers are highly structural, such as memory volume (typically words or propositions) and other/self ratio (i.e., the proportion of self- and other references; Wang & Conway, 2004). There is a multitude of studies using the techniques described here, exhibiting high interrater reliabilities. Validation is usually sought by some form of triangulation, often in the form of using self-reports, other reports, and content-coding techniques within the same study (for an overview of studies, see Wang, 2011, 2013). Such triangulations, however, are rarely specified as such, but rather emerge from the studies, highlighting a clear need for formalization.

Conclusion

The purpose of the chapter was to provide an exemplary insight into the techniques used in narrative content coding. To that end, I have suggested Bruner's (1990) distinction between a thematic and structural narrative analysis as an organizing principle. Much of the narrative literature seems to be classifiable as leaning toward either a more structural or a thematic focus. In some areas, such as research on autobiographical memory, the often contrasted approaches coexist, however tacit, even within single studies: Techniques vary between linguistic frequency markers (such as LIWC categories) and thematic content coding of narratives (such as coding motive-relevant content; see Bender, Woike, Burke, & Dow, 2012).

The issues that are encountered mirror those currently discussed in mixed-method approaches (Van de Vijver & Chasiotis, 2010): Structural approaches are often convincing in their replicability and the range of statistical procedures that can be applied, while thematic approaches are often argued to be better equipped in capturing the psychological meaning (see McAdams, 2012). Some call that the differentiation between idiographic and nomothetic methods (Woike, 2001). The nature of narratives as one form of open-ended, free-response data gives individuals an opportunity to tell their story, less hindered by item formats and experimental procedures constraining their responses. This open-ended, free-response assessment comes with the promise of an increased ecological validity of the data, and the possibility to be surprised by the data and finding something unexpected – which is less likely in most self-report approaches. Of course, reaping such benefits ultimately depends on how the data are processed and analyzed. It is only pragmatic that researchers focus on specific aspects of a narrative, and even in thick ethnographic descriptions (Geertz, 1973) details are inevitably left out. In this relationship it becomes apparent that the difference between Bruner's (1990) approaches is artificial: A gradient toward generalizable and statistically accessible techniques begins, from idiographic, thematic, or intertextual analysis to nomothetic, structural, and linguistic analysis. An adaptive combination of the two, rather than presenting them as irreconcilable opponents, seems to offer the best of both worlds – which resonates with efforts in bridging the divide between qualitative and quantitative methods (Van de Vijver & Chasiotis, 2010). Such combinations can come in the form of explicitly triangulating different sources of data, or also transforming thematic data into quantitative data (often in research on implicit motivation, e.g., Bender et al., 2012).

It is clear that such a reconciliation comes with the burden of establishing reliability and validity of the measures in a standardized, replicable fashion, which is too often lacking in current studies. There is a clear need for future studies to focus on and compare the psychometrics of content-coding procedures. The scarcity of information on narrative content coding may be related to researchers increasingly turning toward automated assessments of narratives by way of computer software. However, this does not release the researcher from establishing the psychological meaning of what is investigated to consider the context in which the narrative occurs. A careful application of linguistic word count techniques(Bender et al., 2012; Schultheiss, 2013; Tauszcik & Pennebaker, 2009) could help retain narratives as a heuristic and hypothesis-testing method and safeguard against an overly confirmatory data perspective as an "excellent tool in the arsenal of the skeptical scientist" (Woike, 2001, p. 158) – but we need more data on that.

References

Alea, N., & Bluck, S. (2003). Why are you telling me that? A conceptual model of the social function of autobiographical memory. *Memory, 11*, 165–178. http://doi.org/10.1080/741938207

Alea, N., & Bluck, S. (2007). I'll keep you in mind: The intimacy function of autobiographical memory. *Applied Cognitive Psychology, 21*, 1091–1111. http://doi.org/10.1002/acp.1316

Ames, S. C., Patten, C. A., Offord, K. P., Pennebaker, J. W., Croghan, I. T., Tri, D. M., … Hurt, R. D. (2005). Expressive writing intervention for young adult cigarette smokers. *Journal of Clinical Psychology, 61*, 1555–1570. http://doi.org/10.1002/jclp.20208

Baddeley, J. L., & Pennebaker, J. W. (2011). A postdeployment expressive writing intervention for military couples: A randomized controlled trial. *Journal of Traumatic Stress, 24*, 581–585. http://doi.org/10.1002/jts.20679

Bakan, D. (1966). *The duality of human existence*. Chicago, IL: Rand McNally.

Bantum, E. O., & Owen, J. E. (2009). Evaluating the validity of computerized content analysis programs for identification of emotional expression in cancer narratives. *Psychological Assessment, 21*, 79–88. http://doi.org/10.1037/a0014643

Barclay, C. R. (1996). Autobiographical remembering: Narrative constraints on objectified selves. In D. C. Rubin (Ed.), *Remembering our past: Studies in autobiographical memory* (pp. 94–125). New York, NY: Cambridge University Press.

Bender, M., Carrera, M., & Alonso-Arbiol, I. (2015). *Autobiographical specificity, cognitive complexity, and depression: Narrative self-focus and specificity/overgenerality are differentially related among depressed and non-depressed*. Manuscript submitted for publication.

Bender, M., & Chasiotis, A. (2011). Number of siblings in childhood explains cultural variance in autobiographical memory in Cameroon, People's Republic of China, and Germany. *Journal of Cross-Cultural Psychology, 42*, 998–1017. http://doi.org/10.1177/0022022110381127

Bender, M., Woike, B. A., Burke, C. T., & Dow, E. A. A. (2012). The relationship between implicit and explicit motives, goal pursuit, and autobiographical memory content during a diary study. *Journal of Research in Personality, 46*, 374–383. http://doi.org/10.1016/j.jrp.2012.03.005

Bluck, S. (2003). Autobiographical memory: Exploring its functions in everyday life. *Memory, 11*, 113–123. http://doi.org/10.1080/741938206

Bluck, S., Alea, N., & Ali, S. (2014). Remembering the historical roots of remembering the personal past. *Applied Cognitive Psychology, 28*, 290–300. http://doi.org/10.1002/acp.2987

Bluck, S., & Glück, J. (2004). Making things better and learning a lesson: Experiencing wisdom across the lifespan. *Journal of Personality, 72*, 543–572. http://doi.org/10.1111/j.0022-3506.2004.00272.x

Bluck, S., & Habermas, T. (2000). The life story schema. *Motivation and Emotion, 24*, 121–147. http://doi.org/10.1023/A:1005615331901

Blumer, H. H. (1969). *Symbolic interactionism: Perspective and method.* Englewood Cliffs, NJ: Prentice Hall.

Bruner, J. (1986). *Actual minds, possible worlds.* Cambridge, MA: Harvard University Press.

Bruner, J. (1990). *Acts of meaning.* Cambridge, MA: Harvard University Press.

Bruner, J. (1991). The narrative construction of reality. *Critical Inquiry, 18*, 1–21. http://doi.org/10.1086/448619

Ceci, S. J., & Bruck, M. (1995). *Jeopardy in the courtroom: A scientific analysis of children's testimony.* Washington, DC: American Psychological Association. http://doi.org/10.1037/10180-000

Chasiotis, A., Bender, M., Kiessling, F., & Hofer, J. (2010). The emergence of the independent self: Autobiographical memory as a mediator of false belief understanding and sociocultural motive orientation in Cameroonian and German preschoolers. *Journal of Cross-Cultural Psychology, 41*, 368–390. http://doi.org/10.1177/0022022110361705

Chasiotis, A., Bender, M., & Hofer, J. (2014). Childhood context explains cultural differences in implicit prosocial motivation and explicit prosocial value orientation. *Evolutionary Psychology, 12*, 295–317.

Conway, M. A., & Pleydell-Pearce, C. W. (2000). The construction of autobiographical memories in the self-memory system. *Psychological Review, 107*, 261–288. http://doi.org/10.1037/0033-295X.107.2.261

Cortazzi, M. (2001). Narrative analysis in ethnography. In P. Atkinson, A. Coffey, S. Delamont, J. Lofland, & L. Lofland (Eds.), *Handbook of ethnography* (pp. 384–394). London, UK: Sage.

Davis, P. J. (1999). Gender differences in autobiographical memory for childhood emotional experiences. *Journal of Personality and Social Psychology, 76*, 498–510. http://doi.org/10.1037/0022-3514.76.3.498

Davison, K. P., Pennebaker, J. W., & Dickerson, S. S. (2000). Who talks? The social psychology of illness support groups. *American Psychologist, 55*, 205–217. http://doi.org/10.1037/0003-066X.55.2.205

Dickinson, J. J., & Poole, D. A. (2000). Efficient coding of eyewitness narratives: A comparison of syntactic unit and word count procedures. *Behavior Research Methods, Instruments, and Computers, 32*, 537–545. http://doi.org/10.3758/BF03200826

Esterling, B. A., L'Abate, L., Murray, E. J., & Pennebaker, J. W. (1999). Empirical foundations for writing in prevention and psychotherapy. *Clinical Psychology Review, 19*, 79–96. http://doi.org/10.1016/S0272-7358(98)00015-4

Fairclough, N. (1992). Discourse and text: Linguistic and intertextual analysis within discourse analysis. *Discourse & Society, 3*, 193–217. http://doi.org/10.1177/0957926592003002004

Fairclough, N. (2013). *Critical discourse analysis: The critical study of language.* Oxford, UK: Routledge.

Fivush, R. (2011). The development of autobiographical memory. In S. T. Fiske, D. L. Schacter, & S. E. Taylor (Eds.), *Annual Review of Psychology, 62*, 559–582.

Fivush, R., Haden, C. A., & Reese, E. (2006). Elaborating on elaborations: Role of maternal reminiscing style in cognitive and socioemotional development. *Child Development, 77*, 1568–1588. http://doi.org/10.1111/j.1467-8624.2006.00960.x

Gee, J. P. (2011). *An introduction to discourse analysis: Theory and method.* New York, NY: Routledge.

Geertz, C. (1973). *The interpretation of cultures.* London, UK: Fontana.

Glaser, B. G., & Strauss, A. L. (2009). *The discovery of grounded theory: Strategies for qualitative research.* New Brunswick, NJ: Aldine Transaction.

Gollwitzer, P. M., Wicklund, R. A., & Hilton, J. L. (1982). Admission of failure and symbolic self-completion: Extending Lewinian theory. *Journal of Personality and Social Psychology, 43*, 358–371. http://doi.org/10.1037/0022-3514.43.2.358

Gordon, B. N., Ornstein, P. A., Nida, R. E., Follmer, A., Crenshaw, M. C., & Albert, G. (1993). Does the use of dolls facilitate children's memory of visits to the doctor? *Applied Cognitive Psychology, 7*, 459–474. http://doi.org/10.1002/acp.2350070602

Griffith, J. W., Sumner, J. A., Debeer, E., Raes, F., Hermans, D., Mineka, S., ... Craske, M. G. (2009). An item response theory/confirmatory factor analysis of the Autobiographical Memory Test. *Memory, 17*, 609–623. http://doi.org/10.1080/09658210902939348

Haber, L., & Haber, R. N. (1998). Criteria for judging the admissibility of eyewitness testimony of long past events. *Psychology, Public Policy, and Law, 4*, 1135–1159. http://doi.org/10.1037/1076-8971.4.4.1135

Habermas, T. (2007). How to tell a life: The development of the cultural concept of biography. *Journal of Cognition and Development, 8*, 1–31. http://doi.org/10.1207/s15327647jcd0801_1

Habermas, T., & Bluck, S. (2000). Getting a life: The emergence of the life story in adolescence. *Psychological Bulletin, 126*, 748–769. http://doi.org/10.1037/0033-2909.126.5.748

Habermas, T., & De Silveira, C. (2008). The development of global coherence in life narratives across adolescence: Temporal, causal, and thematic aspects. *Developmental Psychology, 44*, 707–721. http://doi.org/10.1037/0012-1649.44.3.707

Han, S., & Shavitt, S. (1996). Persuasion and culture: Advertising appeals in individualistic and collectivistic societies. In S. Fein & S. Spencer (Eds.), *Readings in social psychology: The art and science of research* (pp. 110–124). Boston, MA: Houghton, Mifflin and Company.

Hinchman, L. P., & Hinchman, S. K. (Eds.). (1997). *Memory, identity, community: The idea of narrative in the human sciences*. Albany, NY: State University of New York Press.

Holstein, J. A., & Gubrium, J. F. (Eds.). (2012). *Varieties of narrative analysis*. Thousand Oaks, CA: Sage.

Imada, T. (2010). Cultural narratives of individualism and collectivism: A content analysis of textbook stories in the United States and Japan. *Journal of Cross-Cultural Psychology, 43*, 576–591. http://doi.org/10.1177/0022022110383312

Jack, F., MacDonald, S., Reese, E., & Hayne, H. (2009). Maternal reminiscing style during early childhood predicts the age of adolescents' earliest memories. *Child Development, 80*, 496–505. http://doi.org/10.1111/j.1467-8624.2009.01274.x

Jenkins, S. R. (2008). Introduction: Why "score" TATs, anyway? In S. R. Jenkins (Ed.), *A handbook of clinical scoring systems for thematic apperceptive techniques* (pp. 3–38). Mahwah, NJ: Erlbaum.

Jones, A. C., & Pennebaker, J. W. (2006). Expressive writing, psychological processes, and personality. In M. E. Vollrath (Ed.), *Handbook of personality and health* (pp. 277–298). New York, NY: Wiley.

Kahn, J. H., Tobin, R. M., Massey, A. E., & Anderson, J. A. (2007). Measuring emotional expression with the Linguistic Inquiry and Word Count. *The American Journal of Psychology, 120*, 263–286.

Kassin, S. M., Tubb, V. A., Hosch, H. M., & Memon, A. (2001). On the "general acceptance" of eyewitness testimony research: A new survey of the experts. *American Psychologist, 56*, 405–416. http://doi.org/10.1037/0003-066X.56.5.405

Kilby, R. W. (1993). *The study of human values. The study of human values*. Lanham, MD: University Press of America.

King, M. J., MacDougall, A. G., Ferris, S. M., Levine, B., MacQueen, G. M., & McKinnon, M. C. (2010). A review of factors that moderate autobiographical memory performance in patients with major depressive disorder. *Journal of Clinical and Experimental Neuropsychology, 32*, 1122–1144. http://doi.org/10.1080/13803391003781874

Kohler Riessman, C. (2008). *Narrative methods for the human sciences*. Thousand Oaks, CA: Sage.

Kohler Riessman, C., & Speedy, J. (2007). Narrative inquiry in the psychotherapy professions: A critical review. In D. J. Clandinin (Ed.), *Handbook of narrative inquiry: Mapping a methodology* (pp. 426–456). Thousand Oaks, CA: Sage.

Labov, W. (1982). Speech actions and reactions in personal narrative. In D. Tannen (Ed.) *Analyzing discourse: Text and talk*. Washington, DC: Georgetown University Press.

Langellier, K. M. (1989). Personal narratives: Perspectives on theory and research. *Text and Performance Quarterly, 9*, 243–276. http://doi.org/10.1080/10462938909365938

Langellier, K. M. (1999). Personal narrative, performance, performativity: Two or three things I know for sure. *Text and Performance Quarterly, 19*, 125–144. http://doi.org/10.1080/10462939909366255

Loftus, E. F. (1993). The reality of repressed memories. *American Psychologist, 48*, 518–537. http://doi.org/10.1037/0003-066X.48.5.518

Loftus, E. F. (1996). *Eyewitness testimony*. Cambridge, MA: Harvard University Press.

Mark, J., Williams, G., & Dritschel, B. (1992). Categoric and extended autobiographical memories. In M. Conway, D. Rubin, H. Spinnler, & W. Wagenaar (Eds.), *Theoretical perspectives on autobiographical memory SE - 23* (Vol. 65, pp. 391–410). Dordrecht, The Netherlands: Kluwer Academic Publishers.

McAdams, D. P. (1985). *Power, intimacy, and the life story: Personological inquiries into identity*. New York, NY: Guilford Press.

McAdams, D. P. (1993). *The stories we live by: Personal myths and the making of the self*. New York, NY: William Morrow.

McAdams, D. P. (2008). Personal narratives and the life story. In O. P. John, R. W. Robins, & L. A. Pervin (Eds.), *Handbook of personality: Theory and research* (3rd ed., pp. 242–262). New York, NY: Guilford Press.

McAdams, D. P. (2012). Exploring psychological themes through life-narrative accounts. In J. A. Holstein & F. J. Dudrium (Eds.), *Varieties of narrative analysis* (pp. 15–32). Thousand Oaks, CA: Sage.

McAdams, D. P., & McLean, K. C. (2013). Narrative identity. *Current Directions in Psychological Science, 22*, 233–238. http://doi.org/10.1177/0963721413475622

Michelson, T. (1933). Narrative of an Arapaho woman. *American Anthropologist, 35*, 595–610. http://doi.org/10.1525/aa.1933.35.4.02a00030

Mischel, W., & Shoda, Y. (1995). A cognitive-affective system theory of personality: Reconceptualizing situations, dispositions, dynamics, and invariance in personality structure. *Psychological Review, 102*, 246–268. http://doi.org/10.1037/0033-295X.102.2.246

Mishler, E. G. (1995). Models of narrative analysis: A typology. *Journal of Narrative & Life History, 5*, 87–123.

Morgan, A. (2000). *What is narrative therapy? An easy-to-read introduction.* Adelaide, Australia: Dulwich Centre Press.

Niederhoffer, K. G., & Pennebaker, J. W. (2009). Sharing one's story: On the benefits of writing or talking about emotional experience. In S. J. Lopez & C. R. Snyder (Eds.), *Oxford handbook of positive psychology* (2nd ed., pp. 621–632). New York, NY: Oxford University Press.

Pennebaker, J. W. (1997a). *Opening up: The healing power of expressing emotions.* New York, NY: Guilford.

Pennebaker, J. W. (1997b). Writing about emotional experiences as a therapeutic process. *Psychological Science, 8*, 162–166. http://doi.org/10.1111/j.1467-9280.1997.tb00403.x

Pennebaker, J. W. (2000). Telling stories: The health benefits of narrative. *Literature and Medicine, 19*, 3–18. http://doi.org/10.1353/lm.2000.0011

Pennebaker, J. W., Booth, R. J., & Francis, M. E. (2007). Linguistic inquiry and word count: LIWC [Computer software]. Austin, TX: LIWC.net.

Pennebaker, J. W., Chung, C. K., Ireland, M., Gonzales, A., & Booth, R. J. (2007). *The development and psychometric properties of LIWC2007.* Austin, TX: LIWC.net.

Pennebaker, J. W., & King, L. A. (1999). Linguistic styles: Language use as an individual difference. *Journal of Personality and Social Psychology, 77*, 1296–1312. http://doi.org/10.1037/0022-3514.77.6.1296

Pennebaker, J. W., & Lay, T. C. (2002). Language use and personality during crises: Analyses of Mayor Rudolph Giuliani's press conferences. *Journal of Research in Personality, 36*, 271–282. http://doi.org/10.1006/jrpe.2002.2349

Pennebaker, J. W., Mayne, T. J., & Francis, M. E. (1997). Linguistic predictors of adaptive bereavement. *Journal of Personality and Social Psychology, 72*, 863–871. http://doi.org/10.1037/0022-3514.72.4.863

Pennebaker, J. W., Mehl, M. R., & Niederhoffer, K. G. (2003). Psychological aspects of natural language. use: our words, our selves. *Annual Review of Psychology, 54*, 547–577. http://doi.org/10.1146/annurev.psych.54.101601.145041

Pennebaker, J. W., & Stone, L. D. (2003). Words of wisdom: Language use over the life span. *Journal of Personality and Social Psychology, 85*, 291–301. http://doi.org/10.1037/0022-3514.85.2.291

Pillemer, D. B. (1992). Remembering personal circumstances: A functional analysis. In E. Winograd & U. Neisser (Eds.), *Affect and accuracy in recall: Studies of "flashbulb" memories* (pp. 236–264). New York, NY: Cambridge University Press.

Pillemer, D. B. (2003). Directive functions of autobiographical memory: The guiding power of the specific episode. *Memory, 11*, 193–203. http://doi.org/10.1080/741938208

Pillemer, D. B. (2009). Twenty years after Baddeley (1988): Is the study of autobiographical memory fully functional? *Applied Cognitive Psychology, 23*, 1193–1208. http://doi.org/10.1002/acp.1619

Poole, D. A., & Lindsay, D. S. (1995). Interviewing preschoolers: Effects of nonsuggestive techniques, parental coaching, and leading questions on reports of nonexperienced events. *Journal of Experimental Child Psychology, 60*, 129–154. http://doi.org/10.1006/jecp.1995.1035

Poole, D. A., & White, L. T. (1993). Two years later: Effect of question repetition and retention interval on the eyewitness testimony of children and adults. *Developmental Psychology, 29*, 844–853. http://doi.org/10.1037/0012-1649.29.5.844

Powell, M. C., & Fazio, R. H. (1984). Attitude accessibility as a function of repeated attitudinal expression. *Personality and Social Psychology Bulletin, 10*, 139–148. http://doi.org/10.1177/0146167284101016

Raes, F., Watkins, E. R., Williams, J. M. G., & Hermans, D. (2008). Non-ruminative processing reduces overgeneral autobiographical memory retrieval in students. *Behaviour Research and Therapy, 46*, 748–756. http://doi.org/10.1016/j.brat.2008.03.003

Reese, E. (2002). Social factors in the development of autobiographical memory: The state of the art. *Social Development, 11*, 124–142. http://doi.org/10.1111/1467-9507.00190

Robinson, J. A., & Swanson, K. L. (1990). Autobiographical memory: The next phase. *Applied Cognitive Psychology, 4*, 321–335. http://doi.org/10.1002/acp.2350040407

Ross, M. (1989). Relation of implicit theories to the construction of personal histories. *Psychological Review, 96*, 341–357. http://doi.org/10.1037/0033-295X.96.2.341

Rubin, D. (2006). Autobiographical memory. In *Encyclopedia of Cognitive Science*. New York, NY: Wiley.

Sarbin, T. R. (1986). The narrative as a root metaphor for psychology. In T. R. Sarbin (Ed.), *Narrative psychology: The storied nature of human conduct* (pp. 3–21). Westport, CT: Praeger Publishers/Greenwood Publishing Group.

Sartre, J.-P. (1964). *The words*. New York, NY: Braziller.

Schroder, H. M., Driver, M. J., & Streufert, S. (1967). *Human information processing*. New York, NY: Holt, Rinehart & Winston.

Schröder, L., Keller, H., Kärtner, J., Kleis, A., Abels, M., Yovsi, R. D., ... Papaligoura, Z. (2013). Early reminiscing in cultural contexts: Cultural models, maternal reminiscing styles, and children's memories. *Journal of Cognition and Development, 14*, 10–34. http://doi.org/10.1080/15248372.2011.638690

Schultheiss, O. C. (2013). Are implicit motives revealed in mere words? Testing the marker-word hypothesis with computer-based text analysis. *Frontiers in Psychology, 4*, 748. http://doi.org/10.3389/fpsyg.2013.00748

Schultheiss, O. C., & Brunstein, J. C. (Eds.). (2010). *Implicit motives*. New York, NY: Oxford University Press. http://doi.org/10.1093/acprof:oso/9780195335156.001.0001

Schwartz, S. H. (1992). Universals in the content and structure of values: Theoretical advances and empirical tests in 20 countries. In M. P. Zanna (Ed.), *Advances in experimental social psychology, Vol. 25* (pp. 1–65). San Diego, CA: Academic Press.

Searcy, J., Bartlett, J. C., & Memon, A. (2000). Influence of post-event narratives, line-up conditions and individual differences on false identification of young and older eyewitnesses. *Legal and Criminological Psychology, 5*(Part 2), 219–235. http://doi.org/10.1348/135532500168100

Singer, J. A., & Salovey, P. (1993). *The remembered self: Emotion and memory in personality*. New York, NY: Free Press.

Smith, C. P. (1992). *Motivation and personality: Handbook of thematic content analysis*. Cambridge, UK: Cambridge University Press. http://doi.org/10.1017/CBO9780511527937

Smith, C. P. (2000). Content analysis and narrative analysis. In H. T. Reis & C. M. Judd (Eds.), *Handbook of research methods in social and personality psychology* (pp. 313–335). New York, NY: Cambridge University Press.

Spera, S. P., Buhrfeind, E. D., & Pennebaker, J. W. (2014). Expressive writing and coping with job loss. *Academy of Management, 37*, 722–733. http://doi.org/10.2307/256708

Sporer, S. L., Penrod, S., Read, D., & Cutler, B. (1995). Choosing, confidence, and accuracy: A meta-analysis of the confidence-accuracy relation in eyewitness identification studies. *Psychological Bulletin, 118*, 315–327. http://doi.org/10.1037/0033-2909.118.3.315

Suedfeld, P., & Bluck, S. (1993). Changes in integrative complexity accompanying significant life events: Historical evidence. *Journal of Personality and Social Psychology, 64*, 124–130. http://doi.org/10.1037/0022-3514.64.1.124

Suedfeld, P., Tetlock, P. E., & Streufert, S. (1992). Conceptual/integrative complexity. In C. P. Smith, J. W. Atkinson, D. C. McClelland, & J. Veroff (Eds.), *Motivation and personality: Handbook of thematic content analysis* (pp. 393–400). New York, NY: Cambridge University Press.

Sumner, J. A., Griffith, J. W., & Mineka, S. (2010). Overgeneral autobiographical memory as a predictor of the course of depression: A meta-analysis. *Behaviour Research and Therapy, 48*, 614–625. http://doi.org/10.1016/j.brat.2010.03.013

Tausczik, Y. R., & Pennebaker, J. W. (2009). The psychological meaning of words: LIWC and computerized text analysis methods. *Journal of Language and Social Psychology, 29*, 24–54. http://doi.org/10.1177/0261927X09351676

Undeutsch, U. (1989). The development of statement reality analysis. In J. C. Yuille (Ed.), *Credibility assessment* (pp. 101–119). New York, NY: Kluwer Academic/Plenum Publishers.

Van de Vijver, F. J. R., & Chasiotis, A. (2010). Making methods meet: Mixed design in cross-cultural research. In J. A. Harkness, M. Braun, B. Edwards, T. P. Johnson, L. Lyberg, P. P. Mohler, ... T. W. Smith (Eds.), *Survey methods in multinational, multiregional, and multicultural contexts* (pp. 455–473). Hoboken, NJ: Wiley.

Van Vreeswijk, M. F., & De Wilde, E. J. (2004). Autobiographical memory specificity, psychopathology, depressed mood and the use of the Autobiographical Memory Test: A meta-analysis. *Behaviour Research and Therapy, 42*, 731–743. http://doi.org/10.1016/S0005-7967(03)00194-3

Wang, Q. (2001a). Culture effects on adults' earliest childhood recollection and self-description: Implications for the relation between memory and the self. *Journal of Personality and Social Psychology, 81*, 220–233. http://doi.org/10.1037/0022-3514.81.2.220

Wang, Q. (2001b). "Did you have fun?" American and Chinese mother-child conversations about shared emotional experiences. *Cognitive Development, 16*, 693–715.

Wang, Q. (2004). The emergence of cultural self-constructs: Autobiographical memory and self-description in European American and Chinese children. *Developmental Psychology, 40*, 3–15. http://doi.org/10.1037/0012-1649.40.1.3

Wang, Q. (2011). Autobiographical memory and culture. *Online Readings in Psychology and Culture, 5*.

Wang, Q. (2013). The cultured self and remembering. In *The Wiley Handbook on the Development of Children's Memory* (pp. 605–625). New York, NY: Wiley.

Wang, Q., & Brockmeier, J. (2002). Autobiographical remembering as cultural practice: Understanding the interplay between memory, self and culture. *Culture & Psychology, 8*, 45–64. http://doi.org/10.1177/1354067X02008001618

Wang, Q., & Conway, M. A. (2004). The stories we keep: Autobiographical memory in American and Chinese middle-aged adults. *Journal of Personality, 72*, 911–938. http://doi.org/10.1111/j.0022-3506.2004.00285.x

Wang, Q., & Leichtman, M. D. (2000). Same beginnings, different stories: A comparison of American and Chinese children's narratives. *Child Development, 71*, 1329–1346. http://doi.org/10.1111/1467-8624.00231

Wang, Q., Leichtman, M. D., & Davies, K. I. (2000). Sharing memories and telling stories: American and Chinese mothers and their 3-year-olds. *Memory, 8*, 159–177. http://doi.org/10.1080/096582100387588

Watkins, E. (2004). Adaptive and maladaptive ruminative self-focus during emotional processing. *Behaviour Research and Therapy, 42*, 1037–1052. http://doi.org/10.1016/j.brat.2004.01.009

Williams, J. M., & Broadbent, K. (1986). Autobiographical memory in suicide attempters. *Journal of Abnormal Psychology, 95*, 144–149. http://doi.org/10.1037/0021-843X.95.2.144

Williams, J. M. G., Barnhofer, T., Crane, C., Herman, D., Raes, F., Watkins, E., & Dalgleish, T. (2007). Autobiographical memory specificity and emotional disorder. *Psychological Bulletin, 133*, 122–148. http://doi.org/10.1037/0033-2909.133.1.122

Winter, D. G. (1994). *Manual for scoring motive imagery in running text* (4th ed.). Unpublished manuscript, Department of Psychology, University of Michigan, Ann Arbor, MI.

Woike, B. A. (1994). The use of differentiation and integration processes: Empirical studies of "separate" and "connected" ways of thinking. *Journal of Personality and Social Psychology, 67*, 142–150. http://doi.org/10.1037/0022-3514.67.1.142

Woike, B. A. (1997). *Categories of cognitive complexity: A scoring manual*. Unpublished manuscript, Barnard College, Department of Psychology, New York, NY, USA.

Woike, B. A. (2001). Working with free response data: Let's not give up hope. *Psychological Inquiry, 12*, 157–159.

Woike, B. A. (2008). A functional framework for the influence of implicit and explicit motives on autobiographical memory. *Personality and Social Psychology Review, 12*, 99–117. http://doi.org/10.1177/1088868308315701

Woike, B. A., Bender, M., & Besner, N. (2009). Implicit motivational states influence memory: Evidence for motive by state-dependent learning in personality. *Journal of Research in Personality, 43*, 39–48. http://doi.org/10.1016/j.jrp.2008.10.009

Woike, B. A., Gershkovich, I., Piorkowski, R., & Polo, M. (1999). The role of motives in the content and structure of autobiographical memory. *Journal of Personality and Social Psychology, 76*, 600–612. http://doi.org/10.1037/0022-3514.76.4.600

Woike, B. A., & Matic, D. (2004). Cognitive complexity in response to traumatic experiences. *Journal of Personality, 72*, 633–657. http://doi.org/10.1111/j.0022-3506.2004.00275.x

Chapter 5

Beyond Projection

Performance-Based Assessment

Robert F. Bornstein

Derner Institute of Advanced Psychological Studies, Adelphi University, Garden City, NY, USA

> If a professional psychologist is evaluating you and asks for responses to inkblots…walk out of that psychologist's office. Going through with such an examination creates the danger of having a serious decision made about you on totally invalid grounds. (Dawes, 1994, p. 152–153)

It has been more than 90 years since Rorschach (1921/1942) developed his now-famous inkblots. Although Rorschach initially intended that his inkblot stimuli be used to assess perceptual-cognitive style and refine diagnoses, his views regarding the core processes that underlie inkblot responses began to shift shortly after publication of *Psychodiagnostik*, as he became increasingly interested in content analysis and the possibility that his inkblots might tap latent, unverbalized aspects of personality. Following Rorschach's death in 1922 his work was continued by students and colleagues, and over time two dominant perspectives emerged, with Beck (1937) adhering closely to Rorschach's initial focus on perceptual-cognitive processes, and Klopfer (1937) emphasizing the idiographic, psychodynamic aspects of inkblot responses. It was primarily within the context of this psychodynamic tradition that Frank (1939) formulated the projective hypothesis, and coined the term *projective method* to describe tests and tasks – like the Rorschach – that are to varying degrees unstructured and provide great latitude for the testee to respond. Frank (1939) noted:

> When we scrutinize the actual procedures that may be called projective methods we find a wide variety of techniques and materials being employed for the same general purpose, to obtain from the subject "what he cannot or will not say", frequently because he does not know himself and is not aware of what he is revealing about himself through his projections. (p. 404)

The Rorschach Inkblot Method (RIM) has generated considerable controversy in recent years, as critics (e.g., Dawes, 1994; Lilienfeld, Wood, & Garb, 2000) and proponents (e.g., Viglione, 1996; Weiner, 2001) argued their respective positions with considerable vigor. Although debate regarding the validity and utility of the Rorschach has rarely been characterized by its current level of intensity, the measure has historically elicited strong opinions pro and con. Those who favor the RIM have described it as a "psychological x-ray" (Piotrowski, 1980, p. 86) and "perhaps the most powerful psychometric instrument ever envisioned" (Board of Professional Affairs, 1998, p. 392). Those who question the usefulness of the measure have argued that it is not merely invalid, but outright destructive, a position exemplified by Jensen's

(1965, p. 509) assertion that "the rate of scientific progress in clinical psychology might well be measured by the speed and thoroughness with which it gets over the Rorschach." Dawes's (1994) quote that opens this chapter expresses similar sentiments. Hunsley and Bailey (1999, p. 266) summarized the situation well when they noted that "the Rorschach has the dubious distinction of being, simultaneously, the most cherished and most reviled of all psychological assessment tools."

As will be outlined in the following, evidence confirms that when properly administered, carefully scored, and interpreted actuarially using adequate norms, the RIM can in fact generate useful data regarding aspects of the respondent's personality, cognitive style, coping and defense style, self-concept, perceptions of others, and underlying needs and motives. However, the psychological processes that help shape RIM responses are more complex than early Rorschach scholars realized (e.g., Beck, 1937; Klopfer, 1937), and findings suggest that projection may play a role in certain RIM responses, but not in all – or even most – that emerge during a typical Rorschach assessment (see Bornstein, 2007; Exner, 1989). As a result, the term projective test has fallen out of favor in recent years, replaced by more descriptively accurate terms like *free-response test, performance-based test,* and *stimulus attribution test* (see Bornstein, 2010, 2011).

Although other measures (e.g., the Holtzman [1961] Inkblot Technique; Wagner's [1962] Hand Test) may also be described as performance-based, they have been much less widely used than the RIM, and studied far less frequently by researchers. For better or worse, clinicians' attitudes regarding performance-based testing stand or fall based on their perceptions (and misperceptions) of evidence bearing on the Rorschach. Thus, this chapter focuses on the RIM as an exemplar of performance-based testing, recognizing that many of the principles and guidelines discussed here generalize to other performance-based tests in this sense as well.

Contemporary Scoring Systems

By most accounts the modern era of Rorschach practice and research began with the publication of Exner's (1974) Comprehensive System (CS), as the first empirically grounded framework for RIM scoring and interpretation that combined features of five well-established systems available at that time. The CS was revised in 1986, and refined again in 1991 (see also Exner, 2001; Exner & Erdberg, 2005). Although Exner's (1974, 1986, 1991) system has elicited its fair share of criticism (e.g., Wood, Nezworski, Lilienfeld, & Garb, 2003), it provided a single overarching framework that incorporated both structural and content scoring, and was eventually adopted by the majority of RIM users. The empirical foundation of the RIM was strengthened as a result of Exner's work (1974, 1986, 1991) and the test achieved a degree of respectability that it had not enjoyed for many years (see Meyer, 1999; Weiner, 2000a, 2000b). The utility of the CS was further enhanced by the delineation of detailed international norms (Shaffer, Erdberg, & Meyer, 2007), and the development of rigorous empirical frameworks for the derivation and validation of RIM scores (McGrath, 2008; Meyer, 1996; Weiner, 2001).

Although Exner's CS has remained the dominant RIM scoring and interpretation system during the past several decades (see Meyer & Archer, 2001; Weiner, 2004), a number of well-validated RIM scoring systems designed to assess narrower, more focused constructs (e.g., thought disorder, interpersonal dependency, potential to benefit from psychotherapy) also garnered attention from Rorschach researchers, and have to varying degrees been utilized in the laboratory, clinic, and field. Table 5.1 summarizes the core features of eight of these narrower systems, all of which generate RIM scores that meet accepted criteria for test score reliability

Table 5.1. Domain-specific Rorschach scoring and interpretation systems

System	Construct assessed	Key sources
Rorschach Prognostic Rating Scale (RPRS)	Potential to benefit from psychotherapy	Meyer & Handler (1997); Meyer (2000)
Thought Disorder Index (TDI)	Perceptual inaccuracy, distorted logic, autistic thinking, and unusual verbalization	Johnston & Holtzman (1979); Holtzman, Levy, & Johnston (2005)
Concept of the Object on the Rorschach Scale (COR)	Qualities of internalized mental images/introjects (both structural and content-related)	Blatt et al. (1976); Levy, Meehan, Auerbach, & Blatt (2005)
Rorschach Oral (ROD) Scale	Intensity of underlying dependency needs	Masling (1986); Bornstein (1996)
Mutuality of Autonomy (MOA) Scale	Degree to which interactions with others are seen as beneficial/constructive vs. malevolent	Holaday & Sparks (2001); Bombel, Mihura, & Meyer (2009)
Barrier and Penetration (BPS) Scoring System	Preoccupation with vulnerability of body; bodily resilience/integrity	Fisher & Cleveland (1968); O'Neill (2005)
Primary Process (PriPro) Scoring	Degree to which primary process/impulse-dominated thinking is evident in verbalizations	Holt (1960, 2005)
The Lerner Defense Scale (LDS)	Reliance on denial, devaluation, splitting, idealization, and projective identification	Lerner & Lerner (1988); Lerner (1996)

Note. Detailed discussions of these Rorschach Inkblot Method systems, along with construct validity evidence and outcome data, are summarized in Bornstein and Masling (2005).

and validity (see also Bornstein & Masling, 2005; Hunsley & Bailey, 2001; Meyer & Handler, 1997; and Viglione & Hilsenroth, 2001, for reviews).

To further enhance the empirical foundation and clinical utility of the RIM, Meyer, Viglione, Mihura, Erard, and Erdberg (2011) developed the Rorschach Performance Assessment System (R-PAS). Building upon the strengths of Exner's (1974, 1986, 1991) CS, and incorporating aspects of narrower scoring systems with strong empirical foundations (e.g., Masling, Rabie, & Blondheim's, 1967, Rorschach Oral Dependency [ROD] scale), the R-PAS was developed to optimize RIM administration, refine RIM scoring, and enhance RIM interpretation. As Meyer et al. (2011) noted, among the key goals of R-PAS are to: (a) distinguish variables with strong empirical support from those with weaker support; (b) provide a simplified system of terminology, symbols, and calculations to increase parsimony; (c) describe in detail the empirical evidence and theoretical rationale for each RIM variable; (d) optimize the number of responses given, and provide statistical procedures to adjust for overall complexity of a record, to ensure that each record is interpretable; and (e) provide a more intuitive, graphic procedure for comparing respondents' scores with those of a large international reference sample, facilitating RIM interpretation.

Psychometric Properties of RIM Scores

Although criticisms of the RIM are often couched in broad and general terms (e.g., Herbert's [2009, p. 27] assertion that "The real problem with the Rorschach test is ... It doesn't work"), much of the controversy surrounding the RIM in recent years has actually centered on norms and psychometric properties. Several critics have questioned the adequacy and representativeness of clinical and nonclinical CS norms (e.g., Lilienfeld et al., 2000). In addition, researchers who question the clinical utility of the measure have argued that RIM scores do not meet acceptable criteria for reliability and validity. Those who argue in support of the test contend that – while not perfect – the RIM fares well in this regard when compared with other widely used assessment tools (see Bornstein, 2002, 2012, and Weiner, 2000a, 2000b, for reviews of evidence in this area).

Examining the construct validity of RIM scores is complicated by the fact that reliability and validity data vary from system to system, and from variable to variable within complex systems (like the CS) that generate multiple scores (Hunsley & Bailey, 1999; Meyer & Archer, 2001). As Bornstein (2012) and Viglione and Taylor (2003) noted, examining the reliability and validity of RIM ratios, percentages, and derivations is particularly challenging, because it is not always obvious which components of multiscore variables are to blame when reliability or validity data are poor. With these caveats in mind, it is possible to make some general statements regarding the psychometrics of RIM scores, and provide the reader with sources for more detailed analyses.

Reliability

Grønnerød (2003, 2006) used meta-analytic procedures to estimate retest correlations for a broad array of CS and non-CS RIM scores, finding that both short- and long-term retest reliabilities were generally good, with reliability coefficients (r) for the majority of RIM scores in the range of .70–.80. Retest reliability evidence for narrower RIM scoring systems is summarized in Bornstein and Masling (2005). As Meyer (2004) and Weiner (2004) noted, in evaluating RIM retest reliability researchers should distinguish those scores that are expected to be relatively stable over time (e.g., defense style, ego impairment) from those that are more state-like (e.g., suicidality, experienced stress), so reliability coefficients can be properly contextualized.

As Acklin, McDowell, and Verschell (2000) and Viglione and Taylor (2003) pointed out, intraclass correlation coefficient (ICC) statistics tend to yield the most conservative and rigorous estimates of interrater reliability, especially for those RIM variables that have low base rates. Janson and Olsson's (2001) iota coefficient, a multivariate generalization of the kappa coefficient that corrects for expected agreement among diverse raters, is also useful in this context. Extensive reviews of interrater reliability for a broad array of RIM variables are provided by Meyer (2004) and Meyer et al. (2002). As these reviews show, interrater reliability for most RIM variables is adequate, and comparable to that associated with interrater reliability estimates for other variables in psychology and medicine.

Validity

RIM scores differ in the degree to which they show adequate concurrent and predictive validity. Reviews of evidence bearing on the validity of CS and non-CS variables are provided by Bornstein and Masling (2005), Hunsley and Bailey (1999), Lilienfeld et al. (2000), Meyer and Handler (1997), and Viglione and Hilsenroth (2001); evidence in this area has come from a variety of participant samples (e.g., psychiatric patients, medical patients, community adults), involving a broad array of outcome measures (e.g., depression, aggressiveness, impulsivity, narcissism, dependency; see Bornstein, 2012, for a review). Many CS variables have demonstrated excellent validity in these domains; those that fared poorly in this regard have been dropped from the R-PAS system, or modified to enhance their predictive validity (see Meyer et al., 2011). As Hunsley and Meyer (2003) noted, because the RIM is a labor-intensive instrument that requires extensive training to administer and score properly, it is not enough for RIM scores to show adequate validity in laboratory investigations to justify their inclusion in a psychological test battery; they must also provide incremental validity – unique, clinically relevant information that other measures in the battery do not provide.

Several other findings from studies of the convergent and discriminant validity of RIM scores are worth noting, as these findings have implications for use of the RIM in various applied settings:

1. *RIM scores predict spontaneous behavior better than goal-directed responding.* As McClelland, Koestner, and Weinberger (1989) noted, this pattern holds for other performance-based tests as well (see also Bornstein, 1999). As Bornstein (1998b) demonstrated, the concurrent validity of RIM scores (specifically ROD scores) actually increases when participants' attention is directed away from task-relevant behavior (in this case dependency-related help-seeking), and decreases when participants' attention is focused on the relevance of the task so their behavior becomes more goal-directed. These patterns hold for children as well as adults, and clinical as well as nonclinical samples.
2. *RIM scores correlate as expected with scores from other performance-based tests.* As would be expected given shared method variance, RIM scores tend to correlate strongly with scores on other performance-based tests that assess parallel constructs (e.g., the Thematic Apperception Test, the Holtzman Inkblot Test), with intertest correlations (r) typically .50 or greater. RIM scores also correlate strongly with behavioral indices of parallel constructs (e.g., dependency-related help-seeking), regardless of whether these behaviors are examined in the laboratory or in vivo. For example, Bornstein (1998b) found that RIM indices of interpersonal dependency predicted help-seeking behavior exhibited in a controlled laboratory setting, as well as in a college campus setting when students' help-seeking behaviors were assessed periodically over several weeks using a diary sampling method (see also Bornstein, 1999, for a meta-analytic review of evidence bearing on the behaviorally referenced validity of RIM scores).
3. *RIM scores show modest correlations with self-reports.* In general, RIM scores tend to correlate with questionnaire and interview-based self-reports of similar constructs in the range of .20–.30. Although these modest correlations have been incorrectly cited as evidence of problems with the validity of RIM scores (Wood et al., 2003), in fact they represent compelling evidence for the discriminant validity of RIM scores, which would be expected to correlate modestly with self-reports (see Bornstein, 2002, 2009, 2012, for discussions of this issue).

Processes Underlying Rorschach Responses

Two issues are germane in this regard: (a) the processes (response strategies) in which respondents engage as they interpret inkblots, and (b) the underlying cognitive and affective dynamics that shape RIM responses.

Response Strategies

As Bornstein (2009) noted, two well-established findings regarding RIM scores – their ability to predict spontaneous real-world behavior, and their modest correlation with self-report data – both stem from the psychological processes that underlie Rorschach responses and the manner in which these processes differ from those that occur when self-report measures are used. At least three psychological processes occur when respondents complete self-report (i.e., questionnaire) test items. First, testees engage in *introspection*, turning their attention inward to determine if the statement captures some aspect of their feelings, thoughts, motives, or behaviors. Second, *a retrospective memory search* occurs, as testees attempt to retrieve instances wherein they experienced or exhibited the responses described in the test item. Finally, testees may engage in *deliberate self-presentation*, deciding whether, given the context and setting in which they are being evaluated, it is better to answer honestly or modify their response to depict themselves in a particular way.

A very different set of psychological processes occur as people engage in the RIM. Here the fundamental challenge is to create meaning in a stimulus that can be interpreted in multiple ways. To do this, testees must direct their attention outward rather than inward, and focus on the stimulus (not the self). Put another way, if the testee engages in the task as instructed, deliberate, goal-directed introspection plays no role in shaping RIM responses. As several Rorschach researchers have noted, the respondent's main challenge during testing is to attribute meaning to each of the 10 stimuli; these attributions are based on properties of the inkblot (what Weiner, 1997, 2004, described as "card pull"), the associations primed by these stimulus properties (Bornstein, 2009), and the respondent's particular way of encoding and organizing information.

RIM scores have sometimes been conceptualized as tapping only implicit processes (e.g., Piotrowski, 1980), but most Rorschach responses (and therefore most Rorschach scores) are best conceptualized as reflecting some combination of implicit processes (e.g., underlying motives, needs states, perceptual tendencies, and organizing principles) that are moderated by conscious strategies used by participants to select among possible percepts, censor responses that seem ill-advised, and take into account situational factors (e.g., the context in which testing takes place) that alter respondents' self-presentation goals (see Exner, 1989; Exner & Erdberg, 2005; Weiner, 2001, 2004). Many psychologists not familiar with the RIM assume that test results reflecting thought disorder or other significant psychopathology only occur when respondents generate particularly idiosyncratic responses, but in fact this can also result from injudicious and incomplete censorship of the most idiosyncratic of these percepts. In other words, if the sequence of processes that occur during Rorschach responding is broken down into five phases – perception/encoding, categorization/labeling, generation of responses, selection among responses, and verbalization (see Bornstein, 2001a, 2001b; Weiner, 2004) – a high proportion of RIM responses with inappropriate content or flawed structure can potentially reflect difficulties that occur early in the process (during encoding and categorization) or difficulties that come later (during selection or verbalization).

Cognitive and Affective Dynamics

Although RIM variables have sometimes been grouped into two broad categories: thematic (content) variables and structural (perceptual) variables, the distinctions between these two categories are less sharp than once thought (Ritzler, 1995; Viglione, 2001), and clinical and forensic predictions typically draw upon both types of scores (Exner & Erdberg, 2005; Hilsenroth & Stricker, 2004). Elevated scores on many content variables are in part a product of chronic or momentary activation of particular nodes in the respondent's associative network (Bornstein, 2007). Scores on structural variables reflect underlying cognitive and perceptual processes, including the respondent's habitual strategies for encoding and organizing information (Smith, Bistis, Zahka, & Blais, 2007), moderated by the individual's information processing style (e.g., attentional focus, integrative tendencies; see Weiner, 1977, 2000a, 2000b). Complex RIM variables that reflect both content and structure (e.g., certain quotients and ratios) may involve aspects of both strategies.

Beyond the implicit–explicit distinction, it is also useful to distinguish intrapersonal/dispositional influences on RIM responses from interpersonal/situational ones. Although some intrapersonal processes are shaped by interpersonal concerns (e.g., a desire to present oneself to the examiner in a positive or negative way), others are largely driven by the context in which testing takes place (Masling, 2002). Situational influences on RIM responding include the physical setting in which the test is administered, the manner in which the tester introduces the procedure and interacts with the respondent, and the respondent's past experiences in similar types of situations (e.g., a patient who had an unpleasant experience in a previous psychological testing is likely to respond differently than one whose past testing experiences were more positive).

Combining Self-Report and Performance-Based Test Data

A more complete picture of a patient's affective patterns, defenses, motives, and need states requires that performance-based test data be combined with self-report test data. Research on interpersonal dependency illustrates this approach, and evidence confirms that in this domain integrating self-report and performance-based dependency scores provides better predictive power than reliance on one type of score alone. For example, Bornstein (1998a) found that college students who scored high on both RIM and self-report measures of interpersonal dependency showed high levels of dependent personality disorder symptoms, whereas college students who scored high on RIM indices of dependency – but not self-report measures of dependency – showed high levels of histrionic personality disorder symptoms (see also Craig, Koestner, & Zuroff, 1994, and Koestner, Weinberger, & McClelland, 1991, for parallel findings regarding other clinically relevant constructs).

Using interpersonal dependency as an example, Bornstein (2002, 2009) showed that there are four possible outcomes when self-report and performance-based test data are collected from the same patient. In most of these investigations, Masling et al.'s (1967) ROD scale was used to assess underlying dependency, and Hirschfeld et al.'s (1977) Interpersonal Dependency Inventory (IDI) was used to assess self-attributed dependency. As Bornstein noted, it is possible that in this situation a particular patient will score high or low on both types of measures; either of these outcomes would indicate a convergence between that patient's implicit and self-attributed dependency needs, and suggest that self-reports are a reasonably accurate reflection of the person's underlying dependency strivings. There are also two possible patterns of divergence. In one the person appears to have high levels of underlying dependency but either is unaware of this or is unwilling to acknowledge it when asked (unacknowledged dependency). In the other the person appears to have low levels of implicit dependency needs but nonetheless chooses to present him- or herself as being highly dependent (a dependent self-presentation).

These patterns have proved useful in refining Axis II diagnoses. For example, Bornstein (1998a) used the Personality Diagnostic Questionnaire-Revised (PDQ-R) to select college students with clinically elevated symptoms of dependent personality disorder (PD), histrionic PD, another DSM-IV PD, or no PD; he then administered the ROD scale and the IDI to obtain information regarding implicit and self-attributed dependency strivings in the four groups. Students in the dependent PD and histrionic PD groups obtained significantly higher scores on the ROD scale than did students in the other two groups, suggesting that dependent PD and histrionic PD are both associated with high levels of implicit dependency strivings. Only those students in the dependent PD group obtained elevated IDI scores, however; the IDI scores of histrionic PD students did not differ from those with other PDs, or no PD. Thus, both dependent PD and histrionic PD are associated with elevated implicit dependency strivings, but those with dependent PD acknowledge those strivings when asked whereas those with histrionic PD do not (see also Cogswell, Alloy, Karpinsky, & Grant, 2010, for related findings).

Other studies show that implicit and self-attributed dependency test data, used in combination, can predict spontaneous dependency-related behavior in vivo. Bornstein (1998b) used experience-sampling procedures to assess help-seeking behaviors in college students who had been prescreened using the IDI and ROD scale, and divided into high dependent (HD), low dependent (LD), unacknowledged dependency (UAD), and dependent self-presentation (DSP) groups. Data were collected over a 4-week period, with participants asked to provide behavioral descriptions several times each day, at predetermined reporting times randomly assigned to each participant. Analyses of participants' behavioral descriptions revealed that HD and DSP participants made a significantly greater number of direct requests for help than did LD and UAD participants (e.g., asking parents for money, asking a professor for advice, and asking a friend to help move belongings). A different pattern was obtained when indirect requests for help were assessed, however (e.g., hinting to a lab partner that assistance was needed on an assignment, implying that a ride to the mall was needed without asking directly). When indirect help-seeking was assessed UAD, HD, and DSP students all showed elevated help-seeking. Apparently unacknowledged dependency is associated with subtle, indirect help-seeking, but not overt, direct help-seeking.

Effective Use of RIM Data: Guidelines for Clinicians and Clinical Researchers

Findings such as these (see also McGrath, 2008; Meyer, 1996, 1997; Viglione, 1996, 2001) allow us to draw reasonably firm conclusions regarding what RIM scores can and cannot do. On the positive side, abundant evidence confirms that across an array of trait domains, and in a variety of contexts and settings (e.g., clinical, forensic, laboratory), Rorschach scores are a valid indicator of underlying needs and motives that are not always fully accessible to consciousness (see Bornstein & Masling, 2005). Evidence also confirms that RIM scores reflect a respondent's perceptual-cognitive style and way of processing and organizing information (Weiner, 2000a, 2004). On the negative side, Rorschach data are not a useful index of respondents' self-perceptions and self-reports. They are also not useful in rendering diagnoses, although as Bornstein's (1998a) data illustrate, they may be helpful in differential diagnosis, especially for personality disorders. It may be that RIM data ultimately prove more useful in refining PDM than DSM or ICD diagnoses, because PDM symptom descriptions are more dynamic and process-focused than the symptom descriptions of the DSM or ICD (see Bornstein, 2011). These patterns notwithstanding, critics of the Rorschach who cite modest associations between RIM

Table 5.2. Effective use of Rorschach data in clinical, forensic, and research settings

Setting	Uses
Clinical	Assess cognitive style, personality, psychopathology, coping and defense, risk of self-harm, dangerousness, and other constructs that may not always be assessed reliably via self-report; use in conjunction with self-report test data to examine divergences between implicit and self-attributed traits, attitudes, emotional patterns, and other constructs
Forensic	Assess dissimulation (both faking good and faking bad), reality testing, impulsivity, affect modulation, and other constructs relevant to culpability (in criminal cases), and ability to manage complex responsibilities and stressful situations (in custody cases); use in conjunction with self-report test data to contextualize veracity of self-reports
Research	Assess a broad array of constructs that are reflected in open-ended responses to ambiguous stimuli (e.g., interpersonal dependency, experienced stress) but that may not be fully accessible to consciousness; use in conjunction with self-report test data to explore domain-specific convergences and divergences across assessment modalities

Note. Useful sources include Huprich & Ganellen (2006) and Weiner (2000b) – clinical; Hildebrand & De Ruiter (2008) and Hilsenroth & Stricker (2004) – forensic; Bornstein (2009) and Meyer & Archer (2001) – research.

variables and diagnostic criteria as evidence of a flaw or limitation in the Rorschach are simply incorrect: The RIM is not an appropriate index of self-attributions or psychological symptoms and diagnoses, and would not be expected to predict them.

Table 5.2 summarizes in broad terms how RIM data may be used effectively in clinical, forensic, and research settings. Continued effort aimed at enhancing the utility of RIM scores in these settings is important for at least three reasons. First, as McGrath (2001), Bornstein (2010) and others have noted, contemporary personality assessment is characterized by a number of features that undermine the appropriate use of assessment data in clinical contexts and reduce the quality of empirical research in this area as well. Several decades ago psychological assessment almost invariably included a battery consisting of measures designed to tap different levels of functioning and experience (e.g., questionnaires and performance-based tests; see Allison, Blatt, & Zimet, 1968), but due in part to the demands of managed care (Sperling, Sack, & Field, 2000), and to the ascendance of trait-based perspectives on personality that rely primarily on patient self-reports (e.g., Costa & McCrae, 1992), psychological assessment now consists primarily of the administration, scoring, and interpretation of questionnaires.

Exclusive reliance on self-reports, in and of itself, limits the inferences that may be drawn from personality test data; this situation is exacerbated by the fact that in both research and clinical settings, self-reports of traits and symptoms are often conceptualized as veridical indices of these traits and symptoms rather than as self-attributions that reflect people's tendencies to view themselves (and present themselves) in particular ways (see McClelland et al., 1989; Shedler, Mayman, & Manis, 1993). The equating of self-report with actual behavior occurs even for those domains wherein lack of insight is regarded as a hallmark of the construct being assessed (e.g., personality pathology; see Huprich & Ganellen, 2006). When Bornstein (2003) conducted a systematic survey of personality disorder research published in five major psychology and psychiatry journals between 1991 and 2000, he found that over 80% of studies relied exclusively on self-report data (only 4% assessed observable behavior).

Second, the RIM can play a critical role in personality and psychopathology research, complementing self-report data to provide a more complete picture of patient functioning. Following the tradition established by Campbell and Fiske (1959), for the past 50 years construct validity research has tended to focus primarily on documenting the convergence of scores on different measures of the same construct, even when the measures use very different methods to quantify these constructs. As Meyer (1996, 1997) noted, however, scales that employ markedly different formats should in fact show only modest test score intercorrelations in most instances. Moreover, test score divergence for measures that use different methods to measure similar constructs can be as informative and meaningful as test score convergence, sometimes more so (Bornstein, 2002, 2009).

Given these patterns, it is not surprising that certain RIM scores (e.g., those derived from the Rorschach Prognostic Rating Scale or the Ego Impairment Index) have been shown to have incremental validity (i.e., unique predictive value) in diagnostic and therapeutic settings (Meyer, 2000; Perry, Minassian, Cadenhead, & Braff, 2003). The RIM has not been used as frequently in basic personality research in recent years, but has considerable potential to add incremental validity in this domain as well (Bornstein, 1998b; Cogswell, 2008; Mihura, Nathan-Montano, & Alperin, 2003). Paralleling the patterns found in research on personality pathology (Bornstein, 2003), Bornstein (2001b) found that a sizeable proportion of studies examining personality dynamics in nonclinical samples also relied exclusively on participant self-report. A survey of the literature from 1991 to 2000 indicated that the majority of articles appearing in the American Psychological Association's seven most widely subscribed journals during this period – about 65% of published studies overall – relied exclusively on questionnaire outcome measures (Bornstein, 2001b). By introducing into these investigations well-validated measures that tap the implicit components of constructs heretofore assessed primarily via self-report methods (e.g., dependency, narcissism, impulsivity, and self-regulation), personality and clinical researchers may obtain a more complete and nuanced picture of patients and nonclinical participants (see Morf, 2006; Oltmanns & Turkheimer, 2009).

References

Acklin, M. W., McDowell, C. J., & Verschell, M. S. (2000). Interobserver agreement, intraobserver reliability, and the Rorschach Comprehensive System. *Journal of Personality Assessment, 74*, 15–47. http://doi.org/10.1207/S15327752JPA740103

Allison, J., Blatt, S. J., & Zimet, C. N. (1968). *The interpretation of psychological tests*. New York, NY: Harper & Row.

Beck, S. J. (1937). *Introduction to the Rorschach method: A manual of personality study*. New York, NY: American Orthopsychiatric Association. http://doi.org/10.1037/12226-000

Blatt, S. J., Brennies, B., Schimak, J., & Glick, M. (1976). Normal development and psychopathological impairment of the concept of the object on the Rorschach. *Journal of Abnormal Psychology, 85*, 364–373. http://doi.org/10.1037/0021-843X.85.4.364

Board of Professional Affairs, American Psychological Association. (1998). Award for distinguished professional contributions: John Exner. *American Psychologist, 53*, 391–392. http://doi.org/10.1037/0003-066X.53.4.391

Bombel, G., Mihura, J. L., & Meyer, G. J. (2009). An examination of the construct validity of the Rorschach Mutuality of Autonomy Scale. *Journal of Personality Assessment, 91*, 227–238. http://doi.org/10.1080/00223890902794267

Bornstein, R. F. (1996). Construct validity of the Rorschach Oral Dependency Scale: 1967-1995. *Psychological Assessment, 8*, 200–205. http://doi.org/10.1037/1040-3590.8.2.200

Bornstein, R. F. (1998a). Implicit and self-attributed dependency needs in dependent and histrionic personality disorders. *Journal of Personality Assessment, 71*, 1–14. http://doi.org/10.1207/s15327752jpa7101_1

Bornstein, R. F. (1998b). Implicit and self-attributed dependency strivings: Differential relationships to laboratory and field measures of help-seeking. *Journal of Personality and Social Psychology, 75*, 778–787. http://doi.org/10.1037/0022-3514.75.3.778

Bornstein, R. F. (1999). Criterion validity of objective and projective dependency tests: A meta-analytic assessment of behavioral prediction. *Psychological Assessment, 11*, 48–57. http://doi.org/10.1037/1040-3590.11.1.48

Bornstein, R. F. (2001a). Clinical utility of the Rorschach Inkblot Method: Reframing the debate. *Journal of Personality Assessment, 77*, 39–47. http://doi.org/10.1207/S15327752JPA7701_03

Bornstein, R. F. (2001b). Has psychology become the science of questionnaires? A survey of research outcome measures at the close of the 20th century. *The General Psychologist, 36*, 36–40.

Bornstein, R. F. (2002). A process dissociation approach to objective-projective test score interrelationships. *Journal of Personality Assessment, 78*, 47–68. http://doi.org/10.1207/S15327752JPA7801_04

Bornstein, R. F. (2003). Behaviorally referenced experimentation and symptom validation: A paradigm for 21st century personality disorder research. *Journal of Personality Disorders, 17*, 1–18. http://doi.org/10.1521/pedi.17.1.1.24056

Bornstein, R. F. (2007). Might the Rorschach be a projective test after all? Social projection of an undesired trait alters Rorschach Oral Dependency scores. *Journal of Personality Assessment, 88*, 354–367. http://doi.org/10.1080/00223890701333514

Bornstein, R. F. (2009). Heisenberg, Kandinsky, and the heteromethod convergence problem: Lessons from within and beyond psychology. *Journal of Personality Assessment, 91*, 1–8. http://doi.org/10.1080/00223890802483235

Bornstein, R. F. (2010). Psychoanalytic theory as a unifying framework for 21st century personality assessment. *Psychoanalytic Psychology, 27*, 133–152. http://doi.org/10.1037/a0015486

Bornstein, R. F. (2011). From symptom to process: How the PDM alters goals and strategies in psychological assessment. *Journal of Personality Assessment, 93*, 142–150. http://doi.org/10.1080/00223891.2011.542714

Bornstein, R. F. (2012). Rorschach score validation as a model for 21st century personality assessment. *Journal of Personality Assessment, 94*, 26–38. http://doi.org/10.1080/00223891.2011.627961

Bornstein, R. F., & Masling, J. M. (2005). Oral dependency and latency of volunteering to serve as experimental subjects: A replication. *Journal of Personality Assessment, 49*, 306–310. http://doi.org/10.1207/s15327752jpa4903_17

Bornstein, R. F., & Masling, J. M. (Eds.). (2005). *Scoring the Rorschach: Seven validated systems.* Mahwah, NJ: Erlbaum.

Campbell, D. T., & Fiske, D. (1959). Convergent and discriminant validation by means of the multitrait-multimethod matrix. *Psychological Bulletin, 56*, 85–105. http://doi.org/10.1037/h0046016

Cogswell, A. (2008). Explicit rejection of an implicit dichotomy: Integrating two approaches to assessing dependency. *Journal of Personality Assessment, 90*, 26–35. http://doi.org/10.1080/00223890701468584

Cogswell, A., Alloy, L. B., Karpinsky, A., & Grant, D. A. (2010). Assessing dependency using self-report and indirect measures: Examining the significance of discrepancies. *Journal of Personality Assessment, 92*, 306–316. http://doi.org/10.1080/00223891.2010.481986

Costa, P. T., & McCrae, R. R. (1992). Normal personality assessment in clinical practice: The NEO Personality Inventory. *Psychological Assessment, 4*, 5–13. http://doi.org/10.1037/1040-3590.4.1.5

Craig, J. A., Koestner, R., & Zuroff, D. C. (1994). Implicit and self-attributed intimacy motivation. *Journal of Social and Personal Relationships, 11*, 491–507. http://doi.org/10.1177/0265407594114001

Dawes, R. M. (1994). *House of cards: Psychology and psychotherapy built on myth.* New York, NY: Free Press.

Exner, J. E. (1974). *The Rorschach: A comprehensive system.* New York, NY: Wiley.

Exner, J. E. (1986). *The Rorschach: A comprehensive system, Volume 1: Basic foundations* (2nd ed.). New York, NY: Wiley.

Exner, J. E. (1989). Searching for projection in the Rorschach. *Journal of Personality Assessment, 53*, 520–536. http://doi.org/10.1207/s15327752jpa5303_9

Exner, J. E. (1991). *The Rorschach: A comprehensive system, Volume 2* (2nd ed.). New York, NY: Wiley.

Exner, J. E. (2001). *A Rorschach workbook for the comprehensive system* (5th ed.). Asheville, NC: Rorschach Workshops.

Exner, J. E., & Erdberg, P. (2005). *The Rorschach: A comprehensive system, Volume 2: Advanced interpretation* (3rd ed.). Hoboken, NJ: Wiley.

Fisher, S., & Cleveland, S. (1968). *Body image and personality* (2nd ed.). New York, NY: Dover.

Frank, L. K. (1939). Projective methods for the study of personality. *Journal of Psychology, 8*, 389–413. http://doi.org/10.1080/00223980.1939.9917671

Grønnerød, C. (2003). Temporal stability in the Rorschach method: A meta-analytic review. *Journal of Personality Assessment, 80*, 272–293. http://doi.org/10.1207/S15327752JPA8003_06

Grønnerød, C. (2006). Reanalysis of the Grønnerød (2003) Rorschach temporal stability meta-analysis data set. *Journal of Personality Assessment, 86*, 222–225. http://doi.org/10.1207/s15327752jpa8602_12

Herbert, W. (2009, July 30). *The real problem with the Rorschach test: It doesn't work*. Newsweek. Retrieved from http://www.newsweek.com/id/209502

Hildebrand, M., & De Ruiter, C. (2008). Psychological assessment with the Rorschach and the MMPI-2 in a forensic psychiatric hospital. *Rorschachiana, 29*, 151–182. http://doi.org/10.1027/1192-5604.29.2.151

Hilsenroth, M. J., & Stricker, G. (2004). A consideration of challenges to psychological assessment instruments used in forensic settings: Rorschach as exemplar. *Journal of Personality Assessment, 83*, 141–152. http://doi.org/10.1207/s15327752jpa8302_08

Hirschfeld, R. M. A., Klerman, G. L., Gough, H. G., Barrett, J., Korchin, S. J., & Chodoff, P. (1977). A measure of interpersonal dependency. *Journal of Personality Assessment, 41*, 610–618. http://doi.org/10.1207/s15327752jpa4106_6

Holaday, M., & Sparks, C. L. (2001). Revised guidelines for Urist's Mutuality of Autonomy Scale. *Assessment, 8*, 145–154. http://doi.org/10.1177/107319110100800203

Holt, R. R. (1960). Cognitive controls and primary process. *Journal of Psychological Researches, 4*, 105–112.

Holt, R. R. (2005). The PriPro scoring system. In R. F. Bornstein & J. M. Masling (Eds.), *Scoring the Rorschach: Seven validated systems* (pp. 191–235). Mahwah, NJ: Erlbaum.

Holtzman, P. S., Levy, D. L., & Johnston, M. H. (2005). The use of the Rorschach technique for assessing formal thought disorder. In R. F. Bornstein & J. M. Masling (Eds.), *Scoring the Rorschach: Seven validated systems* (pp. 55–95). Mahwah, NJ: Erlbaum.

Holtzman, W. H. (1961). *Guide to administration and scoring: Holtzman Inkblot Technique*. New York, NY: Psychological Corporation.

Hunsley, J., & Bailey, J. M. (1999). The clinical utility of the Rorschach: Unfulfilled promises and an uncertain future. *Psychological Assessment, 11*, 266–277. http://doi.org/10.1037/1040-3590.11.3.266

Hunsley, J., & Bailey, J. M. (2001). Whither the Rorschach? An analysis of the evidence. *Psychological Assessment, 13*, 472–485. http://doi.org/10.1037/1040-3590.13.4.472

Hunsley, J., & Meyer, G. J. (2003). The incremental validity of psychological testing and assessment: Conceptual, methodological, and statistical issues. *Psychological Assessment, 15*, 446–455. http://doi.org/10.1037/1040-3590.15.4.446

Huprich, S. K., & Ganellen, R. J. (2006). The advantages of assessing personality disorders with the Rorschach. In S. K. Huprich (Ed.), *Rorschach assessment of the personality disorders* (pp. 27–53). Mahwah, NJ: Erlbaum.

Janson, H., & Olsson, U. (2001). A measure of agreement for interval or nominal multivariate observations. *Educational and Psychological Measurement, 61*, 277–289. http://doi.org/10.1177/00131640121971239

Jensen, A. R. (1965). Review of the Rorschach. In O. K. Buros (Ed.), *The sixth mental measurements yearbook* (pp. 501–509). Highland Park, NJ: Gryphon Press.

Johnston, M. H., & Holtzman, P. S. (1979). *Assessing schizophrenic thinking*. San Francisco, CA: Jossey-Bass.

Klopfer, B. (1937). The present status of the theoretical developments of the Rorschach method. *Rorschach Research Exchange, 1*, 142–147. http://doi.org/10.1080/08934037.1937.10381209

Koestner, R., Weinberger, J., & McClelland, D. C. (1991). Task-intrinsic and social-extrinsic sources of arousal for motives assessed in fantasy and self-report. *Journal of Personality, 59*, 57–82. http://doi.org/10.1111/j.1467-6494.1991.tb00768.x

Lerner, H. (1996). Rorschach assessment of cognitive impairment from an object relations perspective. *Bulletin of the Menninger Clinic, 60*, 351–365.

Lerner, H., & Lerner, P. (Eds.) (1988). *Primitive mental states and the Rorschach*. Madison, CT: International Universities Press.

Levy, K. N., Meehan, K. B., Auerbach, J. S., & Blatt, S. J. (2005). Concept of the object on the Rorschach Scale. In R. F. Bornstein & J. M. Masling (Eds.), *Scoring the Rorschach: Seven validated systems* (pp. 97–133). Mahwah, NJ: Erlbaum.

Lilienfeld, S. O., Wood, J. M., & Garb, H. N. (2000). The scientific status of projective techniques. *Psychological Science in the Public Interest, 1*, 27–66.

Masling, J. M. (1986). Orality, pathology, and interpersonal behavior. In J. M. Masling (Ed.), *Empirical studies of psychoanalytic theories* (Vol. 2, pp. 73–106). Hillsdale, NJ: Erlbaum.

Masling, J. M. (2002). Speak, memory, or goodbye Columbus. *Journal of Personality Assessment, 78*, 4–30. http://doi.org/10.1207/S15327752JPA7801_02

Masling, J. M., Rabie, L., & Blondheim, S. H. (1967). Obesity, level of aspiration, and Rorschach and TAT measures of oral dependence. *Journal of Consulting Psychology, 31*, 233–239. http://doi.org/10.1037/h0020999

McClelland, D. C., Koestner, R., & Weinberger, J. (1989). How do self-attributed and implicit motives differ? *Psychological Review, 96*, 690–702. http://doi.org/10.1037/0033-295X.96.4.690

McGrath, R. E. (2001). Toward more clinically relevant assessment research. *Journal of Personality Assessment, 77*, 307–332. http://doi.org/10.1207/S15327752JPA7702_12

McGrath, R. E. (2008). The Rorschach in the context of performance based personality assessment. *Journal of Personality Assessment, 90*, 465–475. http://doi.org/10.1080/00223890802248760

Meyer, G. J. (1996). Construct validation of scales derived from the Rorschach method: A review of issues and introduction to the Rorschach Rating Scale. *Journal of Personality Assessment, 67*, 598–628. http://doi.org/10.1207/s15327752jpa6703_14

Meyer, G. J. (1997). On the integration of personality assessment methods: The Rorschach and MMPI. *Journal of Personality Assessment, 68*, 297–330. http://doi.org/10.1207/s15327752jpa6802_5

Meyer, G. J. (1999). The convergent validity of MMPI and Rorschach scales: An extension using profile scores to define response and character styles on both methods and a re-examination of simple Rorschach response frequency. *Journal of Personality Assessment, 72*, 1–35. http://doi.org/10.1207/s15327752jpa7201_1

Meyer, G. J. (2000). The incremental validity of the Rorschach Prognostic Rating Scale over the MMPI Ego Strength Scale and IQ. *Journal of Personality Assessment, 74*, 356–370. http://doi.org/10.1207/S15327752JPA7403_2

Meyer, G. J. (2004). The reliability and validity of the Rorschach and Thematic Apperception Test (TAT) compared to other psychological and medical procedures: An analysis of systematically gathered evidence. In M. Hersen, D. L. Segal, & M. J. Hilsenroth (Eds.), *Comprehensive handbook of psychological assessment, Volume 2: Personality assessment* (pp. 315–342). Hoboken, NJ: Wiley.

Meyer, G. J., & Archer, R. P. (2001). The hard science of Rorschach research: What do we know and where do we go? *Psychological Assessment, 13*, 486–502. http://doi.org/10.1037/1040-3590.13.4.486

Meyer, G. J., & Handler, L. (1997). The ability of the Rorschach to predict subsequent outcome: A meta-analysis of the Rorschach Prognostic Rating Scale. *Journal of Personality Assessment, 69*, 1–38. http://doi.org/10.1207/s15327752jpa6901_1

Meyer, G. J., Hilsenroth, M. J., Baxter, D., Exner, J. E., Fowler, J. C., Piers, C. C., & Resnick, J. (2002). An examination of interrater reliability for scoring the Rorschach Comprehensive System in eight data sets. *Journal of Personality Assessment, 78*, 219–274. http://doi.org/10.1207/S15327752JPA7802_03

Meyer, G. J., Viglione, D. J., Mihura, J. L., Erard, R. E., & Erdberg, P. (2011). *Rorschach Performance Assessment System: Administration, coding, interpretation, and technical manual*. Toledo, OH: Rorschach Performance Assessment System.

Mihura, J. L., Nathan-Montano, E., & Alperin, R. J. (2003). Rorschach measures of aggressive drive derivatives: A college student sample. *Journal of Personality Assessment, 80*, 41–49. http://doi.org/10.1207/S15327752JPA8001_12

Morf, C. C. (2006). Personality reflected in a coherent idiosyncratic interplay of intra- and interpersonal self-regulatory processes. *Journal of Personality, 74*, 1527–1556. http://doi.org/10.1111/j.1467-6494.2006.00419.x

Oltmanns, T. F., & Turkheimer, E. (2009). Person perception and personality pathology. *Current Directions in Psychological Science, 18*, 32–36. http://doi.org/10.1111/j.1467-8721.2009.01601.x

O'Neill, R. M. (2005). Body image, body boundary, and the Barrier and Penetration Rorschach Scoring System. In R. F. Bornstein & J. M. Masling (Eds.), *Scoring the Rorschach: Seven validated systems* (pp. 159–189). Mahwah, NJ: Erlbaum.

Perry, W., Minassian, A., Cadenhead, K., & Braff, D. (2003). Use of the Ego Impairment Index across the schizophrenia spectrum. *Journal of Personality Disorders, 80,* 50–57.

Piotrowski, Z. A. (1980). CPR: The psychological x-ray in mental disorders. In I. B. Sidowski, J. H. Johnson, & T. A. Williams (Eds.), *Technology in mental health care delivery systems* (pp. 85–108). Norwood, NJ: Ablex.

Ritzler, B. (1995). Putting your eggs in the content analysis basket: A response to Aronow, Reznikoff, and Moreland. *Journal of Personality Assessment, 64,* 229–234. http://doi.org/10.1207/s15327752jpa6402_2

Rorschach, H. (1942). *Psychodiagnostik.* Bern, Switzerland: Bircher. (Original work published 1921.)

Shaffer, T. W., Erdberg, P., & Meyer, G. J. (2007). Introduction to the JPA Special Supplement on international reference samples for the Rorschach Comprehensive System. *Journal of Personality Assessment, 89,* S2–S6. http://doi.org/10.1080/00223890701629268

Shedler, J., Mayman, M., & Manis, M. (1993). The illusion of mental health. *American Psychologist, 48,* 1117–1131. http://doi.org/10.1037/0003-066X.48.11.1117

Smith, S. R., Bistis, K., Zahka, N. E., & Blais, M. A. (2007). Perceptual-organizational characteristics of the Rorschach task. *The Clinical Neuropsychologist, 21,* 789–799. http://doi.org/10.1080/13854040600800995

Sperling, M. B., Sack, A., & Field, C. L. (2000). *Psychodynamic practice in a managed care environment.* New York, NY: Guilford Press.

Viglione, D. J. (1996). Data and issues to consider in reconciling self-report and the Rorschach. *Journal of Personality Assessment, 67,* 579–587. http://doi.org/10.1207/s15327752jpa6703_12

Viglione, D. J. (2001). A review of recent research addressing the utility of the Rorschach. *Psychological Assessment, 11,* 251–265. http://doi.org/10.1037/1040-3590.11.3.251

Viglione, D. J., & Hilsenroth, M. J. (2001). The Rorschach: Facts, fictions, and future. *Psychological Assessment, 13,* 452–471. http://doi.org/10.1037/1040-3590.13.4.452

Viglione, D. J., & Taylor, N. (2003). Empirical support for interrater reliability of Rorschach Comprehensive System coding. *Journal of Clinical Psychology, 59,* 111–121. http://doi.org/10.1002/jclp.10121

Wagner, E. E. (1962). *The Hand Test: Manual for administration, scoring, and interpretation.* Los Angeles, CA: Western Psychological Services.

Weiner, I. B. (1977). Approaches to Rorschach validation. In M. A. Rickers-Ovsiankina (Ed.), *Rorschach psychology* (2nd ed., pp. 575–608). Huntington, NY: Robert E. Krieger.

Weiner, I. B. (1997). Current status of the Rorschach Inkblot Method. *Journal of Personality Assessment, 68,* 5–19. http://doi.org/10.1207/s15327752jpa6801_2

Weiner, I. B. (2000a). Making Rorschach interpretation as good as it can be. *Journal of Personality Assessment, 74,* 164–174. http://doi.org/10.1207/S15327752JPA7402_2

Weiner, I. B. (2000b). Using the Rorschach properly in practice and research. *Journal of Clinical Psychology, 56,* 435–438. http://doi.org/10.1002/(SICI)1097-4679(200003)56:3<435::AID-JCLP17>3.0.CO;2-L

Weiner, I. B. (2001). Advancing the science of psychological assessment: The Rorschach Inkblot Method as exemplar. *Psychological Assessment, 13,* 423–432. http://doi.org/10.1037/1040-3590.13.4.423

Weiner, I. B. (2004). Rorschach Inkblot Method. In M. E. Maruish (Ed.), *The use of psychological testing for treatment planning and outcomes assessment* (3rd ed., pp. 553–588). Mahwah, NJ: Erlbaum.

Wood, J. M., Nezworski, M. T., Lilienfeld, S. O., & Garb, H. N. (2003). *What's wrong with the Rorschach?* San Francisco, CA: Jossey-Bass.

Part III
Measures

Chapter 6

Measuring Implicit Motives

Athanasios Chasiotis

School of Social and Behavioral Sciences, Department of Social Psychology,
Tilburg University, The Netherlands

The key to progress in science lies not only in theoretical clarification, but also in adequate measurement. (McClelland, 1987, p. 588)

Implicit and Explicit Motives

There is a long tradition in psychology to distinguish between experiences of which we are aware and others of which we are not aware (Kihlstrom, 2002). The claim that both of these conscious and unconscious psychological forces cause goal-directed behavior is reflected in many prominent psychological theories (e.g., Erikson, 1950; Maslow, 1954; McClelland, 1987). In the course of the so-called cognitive revolution (e.g., Neisser, 1967), cognitive models of motivation became popular to explain individuals' behavioral acts. At the same time, research interest on motivational processes that are difficult to access by introspection has clearly abated for decades. Fortunately, recent years have witnessed a renewed interest in nonconscious aspects of cognition, emotion, and behavior. It has become increasingly evident that experiences, thoughts, and actions can be influenced by mental contents or some event in the current stimulus environment of which we are unaware (Kihlstrom, 2002). Consequently, empirical research also is rediscovering the fact that unconscious psychological forces like implicit motives can have effects on human behavior (for overviews see Hofer, 2010; Hofer & Chasiotis, 2011; Van de Vijver, Hofer, & Chasiotis, 2010).

Implicit motives are defined as the unconsciously represented propensity to engage in situations that afford certain incentives (Schultheiss, 2008). They are general dispositions to act in specific ways and determine spontaneous choice of behavior. In their seminal theoretical approach, McClelland, Koestner, and Weinberger (1989) contrast implicit with explicit motives. McClelland and colleagues argue that goal-directed behavior is caused by two types of qualitatively different motives, namely, implicit motives (e.g., need for affiliation-intimacy) and explicit (self-attributed) motives (e.g., motivational orientation toward interpersonal relatedness) that direct and energize human goal-directed striving. According to McClelland and colleagues (1989), both types of motives are acquired and shaped at different times during ontogeny and are associated with different classes of behaviors. It is assumed that implicit motives are built on early prelinguistic affective experiences and remain affectively aroused by them rather than by salient social experiences (McClelland & Pilon, 1983; for indirect evidence, see Chasiotis, Bender, Kiessling, & Hofer, 2010; Chasiotis, Bender, & Hofer, 2014). This seems to be the reason for their substantial predictive validity concerning long-term behavior compared with self-reported explicit goals and values. Data showing that implicit motives are also strongly related to endocrinological processes, whereas explicit self-reports are not, support these findings (e.g., Mazur & Booth, 1998; Schultheiss, Dargel, & Rohde, 2003).

The second motivational system involving individuals' values, goals, beliefs, and attitudes evolves later in ontogeny when further cognitive structures have developed. Particularly, the mastery of language is supposed to be crucial for children to acquire advanced access to and control over their mental processes. There is evidence that explicit teaching by parents and others with respect to what is important for the child (e.g., to follow certain rules) shapes components of the explicit motivational system. Obviously, learning by instructions can take place only after children have acquired an advanced mastery of language, which enables them to grasp the significance of the linguistic information, and to organize its meaning into such constructs as self, others, and sociocultural norms (McClelland et al., 1989). Available evidence suggests that explicit motives, which are more apt to be stimulated by extrinsic social demands and expectations (Weinberger & McClelland, 1990), influence actions and choice behavior in constrained situations in which individuals cognitively decide on a course of action (Ajzen & Fishbein, 1970; for recent empirical evidence, see also Aydinli, Bender, Chasiotis, Cemalcilar, & Van de Vijver, 2014).

Due to being shaped primarily in the prelinguistic period, implicit motives lack symbolic representation and, thus, operate outside of conscious awareness and control, and are difficult to verbalize. However, implicit motives express themselves in individuals' fantasies and can therefore be measured by fantasy-based methods. Research focuses, above all, on the so-called Big Three of implicit motivation, that is, the needs for affiliation-intimacy, achievement, and power. The affiliation-intimacy motive represents a concern for warm, close relationships and for establishing, maintaining, or restoring a positive affective relationship with a person or group. The achievement motive is defined as a need to enhance one's performance or to surpass certain standards of excellence. Finally, the power motive is defined as one's desire to influence the behavior or emotions of other people (for details, see Smith, 1992). To assess implicit motives, content analyses methods like the Picture Story Exercise (PSE), based on the classic Thematic Apperception Test (TAT; Murray, 1943), have been routinely used (for an overview, see Schultheiss & Brunstein, 2010).

In the following, two prominent PSE methods with satisfying psychometric properties for coding implicit motives will be presented, one classic and one a modification of the former. First, the PSE based on the TAT will be portrayed and a short overview on psychometric issues and coding characteristics will be given, followed by a short review on methodological issues in measuring implicit motives across cultures and the description of a more recent and promising PSE version, the Operant Motive Test (OMT). We will refrain from including the Implicit Association Test in this chapter (IAT, see Greenwald et al., 1998, 2002), because of its controversial validity (Mierke & Klauer, 2003; Rothermund & Wentura, 2004) and the fact that there are still very few empirical studies in which the IAT was used to measure implicit motives (Brunstein & Schmitt, 2004; Sheldon, King, Houser-Marko, Osbaldiston, & Gunz, 2007; for an overview, see Brunstein & Schmitt, 2010; for other methods like the grid technique, see Schmalt, 1999; Sokolowski, Schmalt, Langens, & Puca, 2000). The concluding part elaborates on further perspectives on implicit motives measurement.

Content Coding Methods for Implicit Motives

The Picture Story Exercise Based on the Thematic Apperception Test

Atkinson and McClelland (1948) were the first who came up with the idea to use Murray's (1943) TAT to measure implicit motives (Schultheiss & Brunstein, 2010). The abbreviations still used for the three basic motives or needs adhere to Murray's (1938) original terminology (n Achievement, n Affiliation, and n Power). Since McClelland and coworkers' (1989) seminal paper "How do self-attributed and implicit motives differ?" in which they distinguished implicit and explicit motivation and discussed methodological consequences of this distinction, there has been a switch in terminology from TAT to PSE as the official name for the picture story methods commonly used to assess implicit motives. This switch reflects the fact that motive researchers rarely used original TAT stimuli or the administration procedures associated with it (Schultheiss & Brunstein, 2010), making the PSE the most widely used method for assessing implicit motives today. The PSE is based on the assumption that needs can be inferred from imaginative material in response to pictorial, verbal, or textual cues like political speeches, diaries, and literary sources. Most nonclinical research in implicit motives uses the PSE by requiring participants to write imaginative stories in response to ambiguous picture stimuli that depict people in everyday situations; the story protocols are then analyzed for motive imagery using coding systems (e.g., Kuhl & Scheffer, 2001; Smith, 1992; Winter, 1994).

There are about 18 commonly studied PSE picture stimuli (see Table 5.2 in Pang, 2010, pp. 127–128). Participants are presented with a subset of these ambiguous pictures and asked to write a story in response to each of the pictures within 5 min. As an example, the following is an excerpt of instructions according to Schultheiss and Pang (2007):

> In the Picture Story Exercise, your task is to write a complete story about each of a series of x pictures (…). Try to portray who the people in each picture are, what are they feeling, thinking, and wishing for. Try to tell what led to that situation (…) and how everything will turn out in the end. (…) Don't worry about grammar, spelling, or punctuation (…) they are of no concern here. (p. 135)

Some guiding questions, usually printed at the top left-hand corner of every writing page, are provided to help participants in writing each story (e.g., "Who are the people on the picture?"; "What do they want?"; "What is happening now and how will the story end?").

PSE Coding Systems

PSE coding systems of implicit motives share the feature that they identify differences in strength of a given motive. The most commonly used coding system for *n* Achievement, *n* Power, and *n* Affiliation is compiled in Smith (1992). Sometimes, the Affiliation motive is subcategorized into *n* Intimacy, too (McAdams, 1980). Winter's (1994) Manual for Scoring Motive Imagery in Running Text is an abbreviated version and less time consuming to learn and therefore the most popular coding system. They all categorize behavior as being instrumental for fulfilling a certain need, accompanied by subcategories like positive or negative affect and positive or negative goal anticipation. First, a scoring decision is made for the absence or presence of a certain motive before moving to a subcategory. For example, stories are scored for achievement-related imagery if there is a mention of competition with a standard of excellence, before going on to score for the subcategories like instrumental activity, positive and negative anticipatory goal states, and blocks to goal progress. Affiliation-related imagery is scored whenever there is a concern for establishing, maintaining, or restoring a positive relationship, followed by similar subcategories to those for *n* Achievement. *n* Intimacy-related imagery is scored when a dialogue or any verbal or nonverbal communicative exchange occurs, followed by subcategories like psychological growth and time- and space-transcending quality of a relationship (McAdams, 1980). Finally, power-related imagery is scored whenever a character in a story is concerned about having impact on others, with possible subcategories like prestige of actor and stated need for power (see Winter, 1973).

PSE tests were criticized because they do not satisfy classical psychometric criteria, especially internal consistency and test-retest reliability (e.g., Entwistle, 1972). Traditional notions of internal consistency are based on the idea that picture cues in the PSE test are comparable to items on a test that measure related aspects of the same construct. Therefore, the larger the correlation coefficients between items, the more reliable the measure (Nunnally, 1978). Internal consistency measures are usually suitable for evaluating self-report measures of self-attributed or explicit motives while questions about the typically lower consistency of PSE measures have been raised from early on (Entwistle, 1972). There are several possible explanations for these findings derived from the literature: According to the dynamics of action theory (DOA; Atkinson & Birch, 1970), the sheer act of expressing a motive reduces its strength or intensity, thereby causing a less strong reaction to the next picture cue. Technically speaking, according to DOA, the axiom of local stochastic statistical independence of the items would not hold for PSE picture cues. Hence, internal consistency may not be a suitable tool for assessing PSE measures, rather the combined motive scores of all PSE cues. However, Tuerlinckx, De Boeck, and Lens (2002) using models of item response theory could not find evidence for this DOA effect (see Pang, 2010, for further discussion).

Another important characteristic of a motive is its behavioral variability or motive extensity (McClelland, 1987): Knowing that someone is affiliation motivated does not help in predicting which action the individual will express to satisfy this need (e.g., partying or writing a letter). This has two implications for the internal consistency: Firstly, a PSE measure with dissimilar picture cues may reveal data indicating lower internal consistency, but may reveal a higher validity. That is a problem of bandwidth fidelity, that is, the trade-off between highly specified, multidimensional and variable assessment on the one hand and more simplistic but reliable measures on the other (Schultheiss & Pang, 2007). Secondly, the validity of the PSE can be increased by choosing PSE picture sets with a sufficient variety of motive-arousing situations. Although a PSE may not necessarily have high interpicture correlations, it can still be a valid measure for motives if pictures with similarly motivationally relevant contents are being correlated (Schultheiss, Liening, & Schad, 2008).

Coder Training and Coding Procedure

Practice materials consisting of sample picture descriptions and expert coding answers are usually provided in manuals. Generally, coders are recommended to undergo at least 12 hr of practice scoring to reach a minimum of 85% agreement with provided coding materials before starting to code PSE protocols (Pang, 2010). The coder should be able to justify each coding decision; if an image does not fall into any of the available categories, it should not be scored ("when in doubt, leave it out"). In the next step, coders should check for outliers, and examine score distributions. Since motive scores usually also correlate with protocol length, corrections for word count should be implemented. A simple method is to multiply the total motive score by 1,000 and then the result by the total word count of each participant. However,

Table 6.1. Selected studies on psychometric characteristics of the Picture Story Exercise (PSE)

Factors	Measurement standard				Stage of measurement					Selected studies
	TRR	IR	IC	V	PRE	T	RT	SCORE	POST	
Administration										
Mode of administration (verbal, written, typed)	X			X	X	X				3; 17
Group size (individual, group)				X	X	X				15; 17
Instructions	X			X	X	X	X			10; 12; 17; 22
Situational factors	X			X	X	X				19; 21
Experimenter characteristics (gender, authority, formality)	X			X	X	X				1; 7; 19; 21
Participant characteristics										
Social context (culture, race, gender)				X	X	X				2; 5; 6; 20
Degree of sample heterogeneity				X	X	X				4
Recent life changes				X		X	X			8
Data processing and analysis										
Data entry format		X							X	17
Word count correction			X						X	17
Selection of scoring scheme			X					X		17; 18
Coder training		X						X		17
Calculating interrater reliability		X						X		11; 23
Picture cues										
Ambiguity	X		X	X	X	X				19
Universality	X		X	X	X	X				6; 19
Cue strength	X		X	X	X	X				5; 6; 19
Content themes	X		X	X	X	X				9; 13; 16
Number of pictures (fatigue, variability in scores, motives measured)	X	X			X	X				6; 14; 17
Picture position			X		X	X				17
Number of motives being measured	X		X	X	X	X				17
Gender depicted			X	X	X	X				24

Note. This is a modified and extended version of Table 5.1 in Pang (2010). TRR = test–retest reliability; IR = interrater reliability; IC = internal consistency; V = validity; PRE= pretesting; T = testing; RT = retest; POST = posttest; SCORE = scoring.

List of selected studies:
1. Atkinson, 1958
2. Bellak, 1975
3. Blankenship & Zoota, 1998
4. Cramer, 1996
5. Hofer & Chasiotis, 2004
6. Hofer et al., 2005
7. Klinger, 1967
8. Koestner, Franz, & Hellman, 1991
9. Langan-Fox & Grant, 2006
10. Lundy, 1988
11. Meyer et al., 2002
12. Murstein, 1965
13. Pang & Schultheiss, 2005
14. Reitman & Atkinson, 1958
15. Schultheiss & Brunstein, 2001
16. Schultheiss & Brunstein, 2005
17. Schultheiss & Pang, 2007
18. Smith, 1992
19. Smith, Feld, & Franz, 1992
20. Stewart & Chester, 1982
21. Veroff, 1992
22. Winter & Stewart, 1977
23. Winter, 1994
24. Worchel, Aaron, & Yates, 1990

this correction sometimes creates artifacts because the corrected motive scores are not always uncorrelated with word count. Another method is to use the regression residuals of the motive score in subsequent analyses after having partialled out the effect of word count on motive scores (Schultheiss & Pang, 2007).

Most participants typically produce stories with about 100 words per picture. Experienced coders need 2–5 min to score a PSE story; thus, a typical study with six picture protocols from 100 participants will take about 20–50 hr (Pang, 2010). If there is more than one coder, an adequate degree of agreement of at least 85% must be obtained. There are a number of methods to determine an interrater reliability score like Spearman's rank, index of concordance, or the intraclass correlation coefficient (see http://psychmserver.uzh.ch/forum/ for a very useful user forum for PSE coding problems based on the coding manual of Winter, 1994; and Pang, 2010, pp. 124–125, for a detailed documentation of psychometric properties and validation studies on the PSE).

Conducting a Pretest for a PSE

Depending on the hypotheses and goals of the research, one has to decide if the PSE is the most expedient method of data collection. Sometimes, archival and natural occurring materials, even broadcasts and email exchanges, may be more informative and ecologically more valid than motive scores from an experimentally administered set of picture cues like the PSE. A widely used set of pictures includes the pictures depicting a couple by the river, a man at a desk, a ship captain, a man with children, trapeze artists, and a man with a cigarette (Smith, 1992, 2000; for a more comprehensive set, see Pang, 2010, pp. 127–128; for their psychometric propensities in cross-cultural research see Chasiotis & Hofer, 2003, and Hofer, Chasiotis, Friedlmeier, Busch, & Campos, 2005). Pretesting new pictures is labor intensive and time consuming; however, especially in cross-cultural research, this is sometimes the best way to ensure using culture-informed stimuli (see Hofer & Chasiotis, 2011). These pictures can come from various sources like advertisements, newspapers, magazines, or even movie screenshots. In general, pictures should depict one or more persons engaging or preparing to engage in a certain behavior. It is also advisable to select relatively ambiguous pictures with a less detailed background to avoid recognizably extreme/unknown samples or contexts. Though one can find suggestions to use more contemporary and familiar rather than dated pictures and uncommon contexts, the demonstrated cross-cultural applicability of most of the classic TAT picture cues qualifies this concern (Hofer & Chasiotis, 2011, see "On the Validity of Measuring Implicit Motives Across Cultures," this chapter).

Number of Pictures

According to the TAT coding, to avoid motive score distributions being skewed to the left, no less than four (Schultheiss & Pang, 2007) but no more than eight pictures should be used to avoid decreasing validity because of fatigue. Motive scores start to resemble a normal distribution with a five-picture battery. Thus, the mostly used set is about six pictures (Pang, 2010).

Characteristics of Picture Cues

Selection of picture cues is mainly based on the characteristics of cue strength, cue ambiguity, and universality (for a more detailed discussion, see Pang, 2010). *Cue strength or stimulus pull* is the average number of imagery for a particular motive elicited by a picture cue. A picture cue eliciting one codable image from at least 50% of the individuals tested is considered as having a high pull (Schultheiss & Brunstein, 2001; see Pang, 2010, for an overview on stimulus pulls of the most common picture cues based on the TAT; for cross-cultural motive cue strengths, see Hofer & Chasiotis, 2004; Hofer et al., 2005; for cue strengths of the OMT, see Chasiotis & Hofer, 2003, and Baumann, Kazén, & Kuhl, 2010). *Cue ambiguity* refers to the ability of a picture to evoke multiple motives and usually has an inverse relation to cue strength. Some authors suggest selecting pictures with low ambiguity since pictures with low ambiguity evoke a particular motive more often and therefore show high test–retest reliability (Haber & Alpert, 1958). Cue ambiguity, however, might also enhance variance and lower distorting effects of defense mechanisms and reactance: For example, in the classic study by Clark and Sansibar (1955), the less ambiguous picture cue set of nude pinup girls elicited significantly lower amounts of sexual arousal in male undergraduates than a set of landscaping and architecture. Thus, picture cues should elicit a sufficient amount of ambiguity to provide enough variance while also having moderately to high cue strength to evoke motives. Finally, *universality* refers to the tendency of picture cues to evoke similar motives across all members of a population and across cultures (for an overview, see Hofer & Chasiotis, 2011, and the next section). As a related characteristic, pictures should also be representative of common situations in which motives typically can be aroused (also called *extensivity* of a picture, see Schultheiss & Pang, 2007).

On the Validity of Measuring Implicit Motives Across Cultures

Most research efforts in mainstream psychology are still limited to Euro-American cultural contexts. By contrast, culture was a significant concept in early studies on implicit motives that were probably set off by the pioneering work of McClelland and colleagues on the need for achievement at the collective (national) level (McClelland, 1961; McClelland, Atkinson, Clark, & Lowell, 1953).

Early research on implicit motives across cultures at the individual level (e.g., Rosen, 1962) is difficult to interpret because methodological details are not easily accessed (e.g., possible nonequivalence of stimulus materials; language differences, etc.). The crucial concept in evaluating the adequacy of cross-cultural assessment procedures and test scores is bias, which generally refers to the occurrence of systematic error in a measure. Only if test scores are unbiased are they equivalent and can be meaningfully compared across cultural groups (Van de Vijver & Leung, 1997). The problem of bias is often studied for self-report measures but has been widely neglected for PSE measurements (Van de Vijver, 2000). However, like any other test instruments, PSEs have to be scrutinized for validity-threatening factors. In principle, three types of bias are distinguished that affect equivalence of measurements at different levels. Construct bias is present when the definition of a construct only partially overlaps across cultures. Depending on its main source, three types of method bias are differentiated: administration bias (e.g., communication problems between test administrator and participants), instrument bias (e.g., differential familiarity with test settings and methods of assessment), and sample bias (e.g., sampling differences in participants' test-relevant background characteristics). Finally, item bias is based on characteristics of single items (e.g., items' content or wording is not equivalent). An item shows bias when participants with the same underlying psychological construct (e.g., need for achievement) from different cultural samples react diversely to a given item (e.g., PSE stimulus card). In a study conducted by Hofer et al. (2005), an integrated examination of construct, method, and item bias in their cross-cultural research on implicit needs for power and affiliation-intimacy was implemented. In the study, construct equivalence of needs for power and affiliation-intimacy was established by inspecting meaningfulness of established motive indicators in samples from Cameroon, Costa Rica, and Germany. These cultures were chosen due to well-known differences in self-construal (Markus & Kitayama, 1991) and prototypical family interaction models (Kagitcibasi, 2005). A number of precautions were already set in the design of the study to circumvent the occurrence of method bias when collecting the data. For example, cultural samples were balanced with respect to relevant background characteristics (e.g., level of education), local test administrators were extensively trained, fixed rules were applied in data scoring, and interrater agreements were examined. Referring to instrument bias, the most significant problems that thwart equivalence of test scores are group differences in familiarity with test material (e.g., items and response procedures) and response styles (e.g., extremity ratings, and social desirability). To reduce differences in familiarity with stimulus material and testing between cultural groups, Hofer and colleagues (Hofer et al., 2005; see also Hofer & Chasiotis, 2004) adapted PSE test instructions as participants from non-Western cultures were more likely to produce mere descriptions of picture cards rather than to create fantasy stories. Thus, group differences were minimized by giving participants from all cultural groups a detailed and vivid introduction to the PSE.

Item bias (differential item functioning) was also statistically examined in the study. Due to theoretical considerations on culture-bound situational incentives for motive pull, namely, item/picture bias, Hofer et al. (2005) aimed to identify contexts (picture cards depicting various scenes) that elicit motive imagery to an equal extent among participants, regardless of their culture of origin. In an earlier study, Hofer and Chasiotis (2004) could demonstrate noticeable cross-cultural differences in cue strength of picture cards between samples from Germany and Zambia. Also in the study conducted in 2005, half of the picture cards had to be removed in pretests because they aroused motives differently across cultures. Thus, even if individuals have universally a desire for affiliation and power, contexts for motive realization, as depicted in the picture cards, differ to some extent across cultures (for an overview, see Hofer & Chasiotis, 2011).

Other PSE Variants: The Operant Motive Test

The Operant Motive Test (OMT) represents a PSE that is based on the TAT (Murray, 1943). Within the TAT, ambiguous pictures are presented and persons are instructed to imagine a story in response to each of the pictures. The OMT cuts both administration and coding time considerably while allowing for presentation of more pictures (12 to 15 instead of four to eight in the TAT). As opposed to the classic PSE procedure, test takers in the OMT are not instructed to write down the complete story (as in other PSEs) but have to choose one main character from those depicted in the picture and answer three to four short questions: (a) "What is important for the person in this situation and what is he/she doing?"; (b) "How does the person feel?"; (c) "Why does the person feel this way?"; and (d) "How does the story end?" (the last question is not included in some more recent studies, e.g., Chasiotis, Bender, & Hofer, 2014). The reduction of the explicit response format to verbal associations rather than full stories is chosen here to reduce distortions by logical reasoning. These responses are then content-coded for the presence of the three basic implicit motives (achievement, power, and affiliation) as in most PSE coding procedures (Winter, 1994). In addition to identifying the presence of one motive per picture (only one code is given), the particular modes of motive realization, that is, the cognitive and affective mechanisms guiding the motive pursuit are identified as well. The OMT therefore allows for the differentiation of four approach components and one avoidance component for each motive. This is achieved by crossing two affective sources of motivation (positive vs. negative) with different degrees of self-determined vs. incentive-focused forms of motivation. In other words, a motive realization can either be positively or negatively affectively toned and either be grounded in the self or in external incentives (Kuhl, 2001; see also Deci & Ryan, 2000). This results in five combinations for each basic implicit motive: (a) is a positively toned motivation characterized by self-activation (i.e., being rooted in the self); (b) is a striving for a motive associated with positive affect based on external rewards; (c) is a motive characterized by negative affect and activation of the self; (d) is coded if the story is lacking in self-activation; and, finally, (e) if a negative affect is combined with the absence of self-activation, the passive, avoidant component of the motive is scored (see Table 6.2; a fourth motive [autonomy, see Alsleben, 2010], which is included in more recent versions of the OMT coding manual, will not be presented here because of its pending validation).

Findings on OMT Psychometric Properties

The OMT shows sufficient reliability even according to classic test theory indices such as, for example, internal consistencies of .70 to .78 across the four approach levels of affiliation, achievement, and power, and retest stabilities across the four approach components of $r = .60$ to $r = .72$ (Scheffer, Kuhl, & Eichstädt, 2003). As regards the OMT construct validity, in the last couple of years, extensive research has been carried out on the convergence of the OMT with the traditional TAT, also with regard to behavioral correlates (Baumann, Kaschel, & Kuhl, 2005; for an overview, see Baumann et al., 2010). For example, Chasiotis and Hofer (2003) did not find the expected convergent correlations between a TAT-based PSE and the OMT in their cross-cultural samples. However, both PSE measures showed predictive validity, with some OMT categories even showing incremental validity in more outcome criteria like school achievement than the common PSE (see also Busch, Hofer, Chasiotis, & Campos, 2013; and Baumann & Scheffer, 2011, for a similar result with flow experience as outcome criterion). Recent work on the OMT suggests that the reliability and validity of the OMT are improved by separating the assessment of motives and their implementation components (Baumann et al., 2005; Chasiotis, Hofer, & Campos, 2006; Scheffer, Eichstädt, Chasiotis, & Kuhl, 2007). These incremental aspects do not discount the merits of TAT measures of the PSE since they might tap different levels of motive measurement that describe the degree to which the self participates in motive-guided fantasy and behavior (Baumann et al., 2010). Classic PSE methods focus on the preconceptual level of motive imagery, while the OMT focuses more on the self-integration level of motive measurement.

The OMTs cross-cultural appropriateness has been repeatedly demonstrated by Chasiotis and colleagues and a 12-picture set has proved to be applicable for the measurement of implicit motivation and its specific modes of realization in countries like Cameroon, Costa Rica, China, Germany, The Netherlands, Turkey, and the US (e.g., Aydinli et al., 2014; Busch et al., 2013; Chasiotis et al., 2006; Chasiotis et al., 2014; Hofer, Busch, Chasiotis, Kärtner & Campos, 2008; for overviews, see Hofer & Chasiotis, 2011, and Chasiotis & Hofer, in press).

Table 6.2. Five-level model and content categories of the Operant Motive Test (OMT)

Dominant macro-systems	Motive		
	Affiliation	Achievement	Power
1. PA (self-regulated) Task involvement; context-sensitive switching among microsystems	1.1. Intimacy *Affective sharing* – Interaction (mutual, joyful–intuitive exchange) – Process-like relation; love – Empathy	2.1. Flow – Curiosity and interest; feedback – Learning something – Being absorbed; concentrated – Fun with a task; variety	3.1. Guidance – Helping and protecting others – Pass on knowledge; educate – Convey values – Convince; calmness
2. PA (incentive-based) Incentive-orientation; intuitive behavior control	1.2. Sociability – Extroverted contact (superficial) – Interest; entertainment – Good mood – Erotic; flirt	2.2. Inner standards – Pride; focused on results – Doing something well – Solving tasks – Persistence in thinking	3.2. Status – Being the focus of attention – Receiving recognition – Having prestige and authority – Observing others
3. NA (self-regulated) Self-regulated coping; extension memory (acknowledging problem or NA and constructive coping)	1.3. Coping with rejection – Positive reevaluation of a rejection – Attempts to restore an relationship (positive outcome)	2.3. Coping with failure – Positive reevaluation of a failure – Perception of threat associated with active coping – Identification of problems – Task rejection ("disengagement")	3.3. Coping with power-related threats – Having influence – Expressing feelings and wishes – Relaxing – Making decisions
4. NA (incentive-based) Goal-oriented behavior; intention memory and intuitive behavior control (denial of anxiety by action)	1.4. Avoiding insecurity *Familiarity* – Acting with hope for – Safety – Security – Closeness – Being loved	2.4. Pressure to achieve – Social standards; trying to be the best – Effort (with success); hope – Relief (after success) – Avoiding failure; passing exams – Persistence; solving difficult tasks	3.4. Inhibited power, dominance – Fear of using power – Denial of power; sense of duty (*must*) – Many actions – Dominance
5. Low PA and high NA Passive fear (rumination); object recognition and intention memory (conscious focus on fear)	1.5. Dependence – Being lonely – Feeling left alone; abandoned – Desperate, hopeless, sad – Rejected – Not being understood	2.5. Failure – Stressed – Helpless – Disappointed – Anxiety – Looking for help	3.5. Powerlessness – Obedient, guilty, sick – Being a petitioner

Note. This is a modified version of Table 13.1 in Baumann et al. (2010). PA = positive affect; NA = negative affect.

Further Perspectives on Implicit Measurement

Computerized Coding of PSE Stories

PSE stories can be captured on computers or through the Internet using survey programs. For example, Hogenraad (2005) used the *Motive Dictionary* and content analysis software PROTAN to demonstrate that the increasing gap between implicit power words and affiliation words in the political speeches of George W. Bush in the 19 months prior to the invasion of Iraq in 2003 can be regarded as predictive for the subsequent war in Iraq. The development of a computer-based coding system for implicit motives would greatly facilitate psychological practice and research in the field alike. Laborious human training and coding of stories can be minimized, focusing only on flagged stories that appear to have troubling content that may violate the assumptions of established coding systems (e.g., a story with the phrase *wants to win* might not be achievement motivated if it also contains the word *lottery*, see Blankenship, 2010). It remains to be seen how accurate and valid a fully computerized coding system of PSE stories will be able to become.

Assessment of Implicit Motivation in Children

According to McClelland (1987), implicit motives represent highly generalized preferences derived from individuals' experiences during early, preverbal childhood. However, our knowledge on motive development in various cultural contexts is still very limited (e.g., McClelland & Pilon, 1983) due to a lack of psychometrically sound instruments to measure implicit motivation in children. As a first attempt to fill this gap, in a cross-cultural study in which a preschooler version of an instrument measuring implicit motives was applied to 5-year-olds from Cameroon and Germany, Chasiotis et al. (2010) were able to demonstrate that culture-specific combinations of the three implicit motives in preschoolers are related to significant sociocognitive abilities like autobiographical memory and mentalistic understanding (theory of mind).

Conclusion

Content analysis of PSE stories is labor intensive and time consuming, but these disadvantages are outweighed by the gained richness of information: Rescoring of the same set of texts for a number of different psychological constructs is possible as well as scoring motives at a distance, or by coding data from deceased subjects, remote geographical areas, or historical times (Pang, 2010). The biggest advantage, however, might be the nonreactive nature of the narratives that are not subject to response bias and other methodological distortions of self-report data (Daly & Wilson, 1999; Nisbett & Wilson, 1977; see also Chasiotis, 2011). The fields of application for PSEs beyond mainly research-oriented approaches are also manifold. There are successful applications in the political sciences (Winter, 2010) as well as in organizational (Lang, Zettler, Ewen, & Hülsheger, 2012; McClelland, 1987), counseling (e.g., Kaschel & Kuhl, 2004), educational (e.g., Schultheiss & Köllner, 2014), and clinical contexts (e.g., Baumann et al., 2005; McClelland, 1989; McClelland, Alexander, & Marks, 1982; Schüler & Kuster, 2011; for overviews, see Weinberger, Cotler, & Fishman, 2010; and Schultheiss & Brunstein, 2010).

If we are to do a better job at predicting behavior both within and across cultural groups, we need to supplement our typical reliance on explicit measures of personality with implicit measures of motivation. It remains to be seen if the implicit motives measured by different PSE versions (like TAT and OMT) are operationalizations of one single, some complementary (Baumann et al., 2010), or even different motivational dimensions (Schultheiss & Brunstein, 2010; for discussion, see also Chasiotis & Hofer, in press). Despite these shortcomings, available empirical findings suggest that motive-guided fantasy and behavior can be reliably and validly assessed from content analysis based-PSEs.

References

Ajzen, I., & Fishbein, M. (1970). The prediction of behavior from attitudinal and normative variables. *Journal of Experimental Social Psychology, 6*, 466–487. http://doi.org/10.1016/0022-1031(70)90057-0
Alsleben, P. (2010). *Das Bedürfnis nach Freiheit: Selbst-Integration als viertes Basismotiv*. [The need for freedom: Self-integration as a fourth basic motive]. Munich, Germany: VDM.
Atkinson, J. W. (Ed.). (1958). *Motives in fantasy, action, and society*. Princeton, NJ: VanNostrand.
Atkinson, J. W., & Birch, D. (1970). *The dynamics of action*. New York, NY: Wiley.
Atkinson, J. W., & McClelland, D. C. (1948). The projective expression of needs. II. The effects of different intensities of the hunger drive on thematic apperception. *Journal of Experimental Psychology, 28*, 643–658. http://doi.org/10.1037/h0061442
Aydinli, A., Bender, M., Chasiotis, A., Cemalcilar, Z., & Van de Vijver, F. J. R. (2014). When does self-reported prosocial motivation lead to helping? – the moderating role of implicit prosocial motivation. *Motivation and Emotion, 38*, 645–658. http://doi.org/10.1007/s11031-014-9411-8
Baumann, N., Kaschel, M., & Kuhl, J. (2005). Striving for unwanted goals: Stress-dependent discrepancies between explicit and implicit achievement motives reduce subjective well-being and increase psychosomatic symptoms. *Journal of Personality and Social Psychology, 89*, 781–799. http://doi.org/10.1037/0022-3514.89.5.781
Baumann, N., Kazén, M., & Kuhl, J. (2010). Implicit motives: A look from Personality Systems Interaction Theory. In O. C. Schultheiss & J. C. Brunstein (Eds.), *Implicit motives* (pp. 375–403). New York, NY: Oxford University Press.
Baumann, N., & Scheffer, D. (2011). Seeking flow in the achievement domain: The achievement flow motive behind flow experience. *Motivation and Emotion, 35*, 267–284. http://doi.org/10.1007/s11031-010-9195-4
Bellak, L. (1975). *The Thematic Apperception Test, the Children's Apperception Test and the Senior Apperception Technique in clinical use*. New York, NY: Grune & Stratton.
Blankenship, V. (2010). Computer-based modeling, assessment, and coding of implicit motives. In O. C. Schultheiss & J. C. Brunstein (Eds.), *Implicit motives* (pp. 186–208). New York, NY: Oxford University Press.
Blankenship, V., & Zoota, A. L. (1998). Comparing power imagery in TATs written by hand or on the computer. *Behavior Research Methods, Instruments & Computers, 30*, 441–448. http://doi.org/10.3758/BF03200677
Brunstein, J. C., & Schmitt, C. H. (2010). Assessing individual differences in achievement motivation with the Implicit Association Test: Predictive validity of a chronometric measure of the self-concept "me = successful". In O. C. Schultheiss & J. C. Brunstein (Eds.), *Implicit motives* (pp. 151–185). New York, NY: Oxford University Press.
Brunstein, J. C., & Schmitt, C. H. (2004). Assessing individual differences in achievement motivation with the Implicit Association Test. *Journal for Research in Personality, 38*, 536–555. http://doi.org/10.1016/j.jrp.2004.01.003
Busch, H., Hofer, J., Chasiotis, A., & Campos, D. (2013). The achievement flow motive as an element of the autotelic personality: Predicting educational attainment in three cultures. *European Journal of Psychology of Education, 28*, 239–254. http://doi.org/10.1007/s10212-012-0112-y
Chasiotis, A. (2011). An epigenetic view on culture: What evolutionary developmental psychology has to offer for cross-cultural psychology. In F. J. R. van de Vijver, A. Chasiotis, & S. M. Breugelmans (Eds.), *Fundamental questions in cross-cultural psychology* (pp. 376–404). Cambridge, UK: Cambridge University Press.

Chasiotis, A., Bender, M., & Hofer, J. (2014). Childhood context explains cultural variance in implicit parenting motivation: Results from two studies with six samples from Cameroon, Costa Rica, Germany, and PR China. *Evolutionary Psychology, 12*, 295–317.

Chasiotis, A., Bender, M., Kiessling, F., & Hofer, J. (2010). The emergence of the independent self: Autobiographical memory as a mediator of false belief understanding and motive orientation in Cameroonian and German preschoolers. *Journal of Cross-Cultural Psychology, 41*, 368–390. http://doi.org/10.1177/0022022110361705

Chasiotis, A., & Hofer, J. (in press). Implicit prosocial power motivation: Views from evolutionary and developmental cross-cultural psychology. In N. Baumann, T. Goschke, M. Kazén, S. Koole, & M. Quirin (Eds.), *Julius Kuhl Festschrift in honour of his 65th birthday*. Berlin, Germany: Springer.

Chasiotis, A., & Hofer, J. (2003). *Die Messung impliziter Motive in Deutschland, Costa Rica und Kamerun* [Measurement of implicit motives in Germany, Costa Rica, and Cameroon.] (Research report to the German Research Foundation [DFG]). Bonn, Germany: DFG.

Chasiotis, A., Hofer, J., & Campos, D. (2006). When does liking children lead to parenthood? Younger siblings, implicit prosocial power motivation, and explicit love for children predict parenthood across cultures. *Journal of Cultural and Evolutionary Psychology, 4*, 95–123. http://doi.org/10.1556/JCEP.4.2006.2.2

Clark, R. A., & Sansibar, M. R. (1955). The relationship between symbolic and manifest projections of sexuality with some incidental correlates. *The Journal of Abnormal and Social Psychology, 50*, 327–334. http://doi.org/10.1037/h0047775

Cramer, P. (1996). *Storytelling, narrative, and the Thematic Apperception Test*. New York, NY: Guilford.

Daly, M., & Wilson, M. (1999). Human evolutionary psychology and animal behavior. *Animal Behaviour, 57*, 509–519. http://doi.org/10.1006/anbe.1998.1027

Deci, E. L., & Ryan, R. M. (2000). The "what" and "why" of goal pursuits: Human needs and the self-determination of behavior. *Psychological Inquiry, 11*, 227–268. http://doi.org/10.1207/S15327965PLI1104_01

Entwistle, D. R. (1972). To dispel fantasies about fantasy-based measures of achievement motivation. *Psychological Bulletin, 77*, 377–391. http://doi.org/10.1037/h0020021

Erikson, E. H. (1950). *Childhood and society*. New York, NY: Norton.

Greenwald, A. G., Banaji, M. R., Rudman, L. A., Farnham, S. D., Nosek, B. A., & Mellott, D. S. (2002). A unified theory of implicit attitudes, stereotypes, self-esteem, and self-concept. *Psychological Review, 109*, 3–25. http://doi.org/10.1037/0033-295X.109.1.3

Greenwald, A. G., McGhee, D. E., & Schwartz, J. L. K. (1998). Measuring individual differences in implicit cognition: The implicit association test. *Journal of Personality and Social Psychology, 74*, 1464–1480. http://doi.org/10.1037/0022-3514.74.6.1464

Haber, R. N., & Alpert, R. (1958). The role of situation and picture cues in projective measurement of the achievement motive. In J. W. Atkinson (Ed.), *Motives in fantasy, action, and society* (pp. 644–663). New York, NY: Van Nostrand.

Hofer, J. (2010). Research on implicit motives across cultures. In O. C. Schultheiss & J. C. Brunstein (Eds.), *Implicit motives* (pp. 433–467). New York, NY: Oxford University Press.

Hofer, J., Busch, H., Chasiotis, A., Kärtner, J., & Campos, D. (2008). Concern for generativity and its relation to implicit power motivation, generative goals, and satisfaction with life: A cross-cultural investigation. *Journal of Personality, 76*, 1–30. http://doi.org/10.1111/j.1467-6494.2007.00478.x

Hofer, J., & Chasiotis, A. (2011). *Implicit motives across cultures (Online readings in psychology and culture, Unit 4)*. Grand Valley State University, Allendale, MI: International Association for Cross-Cultural Psychology. Retrieved from http://scholarworks.gvsu.edu/orpc/vol4/iss1/5

Hofer, J., & Chasiotis, A. (2004). Methodological considerations of applying a TAT-type picture-story test in cross-cultural research: A comparison of German and Zambian adolescents. *Journal of Cross-Cultural Psychology, 35*, 224–241. http://doi.org/10.1177/0022022103262246

Hofer, J., Chasiotis, A., Friedlmeier, W., Busch, H., & Campos, D. (2005). The measurement of implicit motives in three cultures: Power and Affiliation in Cameroon, Costa Rica, and Germany. *Journal of Cross-Cultural Psychology, 36*, 689–716. http://doi.org/10.1177/0022022105280510

Hogenraad, R. (2005). What the words of war can tell us about the risk of war. *Journal of Peace Psychology, 11*, 137–151. http://doi.org/10.1207/s15327949pac1102_2

Kagitcibasi, C. (2005). Autonomy and relatedness in cultural context: Implications for self and family. *Journal of Cross-Cultural Psychology, 36*, 403–422. http://doi.org/10.1177/0022022105275959

Kaschel, R., & Kuhl, J. (2004). Motivational counseling in an extended functional context: Personality systems theory and assessment. In W. M. Cox & E. Klinger (Eds.), *Handbook of motivational counseling: Concepts, approaches, and assessment* (pp. 99–119). New York, NY: Wiley.

Kihlstrom, J. F. (2002). The unconscious. In V. S. Ramachandran (Ed.), *Encyclopedia of the human brain* (Vol. 4, pp. 635–646). San Diego, CA: Academic.

Klinger, E. (1967). Modeling effects on achievement imagery. *Journal of Personality and Social Psychology, 7*, 49–62. http://doi.org/10.1037/h0024936

Koestner, R., Franz, C. E., & Hellman, C. (1991). *Life changes and the reliability of TAT motive assessment*. Unpublished manuscript.

Kuhl, J. (2001). *Motivation und Persönlichkeit* [Motiviation and personality]. Göttingen, Germany: Hogrefe.

Kuhl, J., & Scheffer, D. (2001). *The Operant Motive Test: Scoring manual*. Osnabrück, Germany: University of Osnabrück.

Lang, J. W., Zettler, I., Ewen, C., & Hülsheger, U. R. (2012). Implicit motives, explicit traits, and task and contextual performance at work. *Journal of Applied Psychology, 97*, 1201–1217. http://doi.org/10.1037/a0029556

Langan-Fox, J., & Grant, S. (2006). The Thematic Apperception Test: Toward a standard measure of the Big Three motives. *Journal of Personality Assessment, 87*, 277–291. http://doi.org/10.1207/s15327752jpa8703_09

Lundy, A. (1988). Instructional set and Thematic Apperception Test validity. *Journal of Personality Assessment, 52*, 309–320. http://doi.org/10.1207/s15327752jpa5202_12

McAdams, D. P. (1980). A thematic coding system for the intimacy motive. *Journal of Research in Personality, 14*, 413–443. http://doi.org/10.1016/0092-6566(80)90001-X

Markus, H. R., & Kitayama, S. (1991). Culture and the self: Implications for cognition, emotion, and motivation. *Psychological Review, 98*, 224–253. http://doi.org/10.1037/0033-295X.98.2.224

Maslow, A. (1954). *Motivation and personality*. New York, NY: Harper & Row.

Mazur, A., & Booth, A. (1998). Testosterone and dominance in men. *Behavioral and Brain Sciences, 21*, 353–397. http://doi.org/10.1017/S0140525X98001228

McClelland, D. C. (1961). *The achieving society*. Princeton, NJ: Van Nostrand. http://doi.org/10.1037/14359-000

McClelland, D. C. (1987). *Human motivation*. New York, NY: Cambridge University Press.

McClelland, D. C. (1989). Motivational factors in health and disease. *American Psychologist, 44*, 675–683. http://doi.org/10.1037/0003-066X.44.4.675

McClelland, D. C., Alexander, C., & Marks, E. (1982). The need for power, stress, immune function, and illness among male prisoners. *Journal of Abnormal Psychology, 91*, 61–70. http://doi.org/10.1037/0021-843X.91.1.61

McClelland, D. C., Atkinson, J. W., Clark, R. A., & Lowell, E. L. (1953). *The achievement motive*. New York, NY: Appleton-Century-Crofts. http://doi.org/10.1037/11144-000

McClelland, D. C., Koestner, R., & Weinberger, J. (1989). How do self-attributed and implicit motives differ? *Psychological Review, 96*, 690–702. http://doi.org/10.1037/0033-295X.96.4.690

McClelland, D. C., & Pilon, D. A. (1983). Sources of adult motives in patterns of parent behavior in early childhood. *Journal of Personality and Social Psychology, 44*, 564–574. http://doi.org/10.1037/0022-3514.44.3.564

Meyer, G. J., Hilsenroth, M. J., Baxter, D., Exner, J. E., Fowler, J. C., Piers, C. C., & Resnick, J. (2002). An examination of interrater reliability for scoring the Rorschach comprehensive system in eight data sets. *Journal of Personality Assessment, 78*, 219–274. http://doi.org/10.1207/S15327752JPA7802_03

Mierke, J., & Klauer, K. C. (2003). Method-specific variance in the Implicit Association Test. *Journal of Personality and Social Psychology, 85*, 1180–1192. http://doi.org/10.1037/0022-3514.85.6.1180

Murray, H. A. (1938). *Explorations in personality*. New York, NY: Oxford University Press.

Murray, H. A. (1943). *Thematic Apperception Test manual*. Cambridge, MA: Harvard University Press.

Murstein, B. I. (1965). Projection of hostility on the TAT as a function of stimulus background, and personality variables. *Journal of Consulting Psychology, 29*, 43–48. http://doi.org/10.1037/h0021666

Neisser, U. (1967). *Cognitive psychology.* New York, NY: Appleton-Century-Crofts.
Nisbett, R. E., & Wilson, T. D. (1977). Telling more than we can know: Verbal reports on mental processes. *Psychological Review, 84,* 231–259. http://doi.org/10.1037/0033-295X.84.3.231
Nunnally, J. C. (1978). *Psychometric theory.* New York, NY: McGraw-Hill.
Pang, J. S. (2010). Content coding methods in implicit motive assessment: Standards of measurement and best practices for the Picture Story Exercise. In O. C. Schultheiss & J. C. Brunstein (Eds.), *Implicit motives* (pp. 119–150). New York, NY: Oxford University Press.
Pang, J. C., & Schultheiss, O. C. (2005). Assessing implicit motives in U.S. college students: Effects of picture type and position, gender and ethnicity, and cross-cultural comparisons. *Journal of Personality Assessment, 85,* 280–294.
Rosen, B. C. (1962). Socialization and achievement motivation in Brazil. *American Sociological Review, 27,* 612–624. http://doi.org/10.2307/2089619
Reitman, W. R., & Atkinson, J. W. (1958). Some methodological problems in the use of thematic apperceptive measures of human motives. In J. W. Atkinson (Ed.), *Motives in fantasy, action, and society* (pp. 664–683). Princeton, NJ: Van Nostrand.
Rothermund, K., & Wentura, D. (2004). Underlying processes in the Implicit Association Test: Dissociating salience from associations. *Journal of Experimental Psychology: General, 133,* 139–165. http://doi.org/10.1037/0096-3445.133.2.139
Scheffer, D., Eichstädt, J., Chasiotis, A., & Kuhl, J. (2007). Towards an integrated measure of need affiliation and agreeableness derived from the Operant Motive Test. *Psychology Science, 49,* 308–324.
Scheffer, D., Kuhl, J., & Eichstädt, J. (2003). Der Operante Motiv-Test (OMT): Inhaltsklassen, Auswertung, psychometrische Kennwerte und Validierung [The operant motive test (OMT): Contents, scoring, psychometric properties, and validation]. In J. Stiensmeier-Pelster & F. Rheinberg (Eds.), *Diagnostik von Motivation und Selbstkonzept* [Diagnostics of motivation and self-concept] (pp. 151–167). Goettingen, Germany: Hogrefe.
Schmalt, H.-D. (1999). Assessing the achievement motive using the grid technique. *Journal of Research in Personality, 33,* 109–130. http://doi.org/10.1006/jrpe.1999.2245
Schüler, J., & Kuster, M. (2011). Binge eating as a consequence of unfulfilled basic needs: The moderating role of implicit achievement motivation. *Motivation and Emotion, 35,* 89–97. http://doi.org/10.1007/s11031-010-9200-y
Schultheiss, O. C. (2008). Implicit motives. In O. P. John, R. W. Robins, & L. A. Pervin (Eds.), *Handbook of personality: Theory and research* (3rd ed., pp. 603–633). New York, NY: Guilford.
Schultheiss, O. C., & Brunstein, J. C. (2001). Assessment of implicit motives with a research version of the TAT: Picture profiles, gender differences, and relations to other personality measures. *Journal of Personality Assessment, 77,* 71–86. http://doi.org/10.1207/S15327752JPA7701_05
Schultheiss, O. C., & Brunstein, J. C. (2005). An implicit motive perspective on competence. In A. J. Elliot & C. S. Dweck (Eds.), *Handbook of competence and motivation* (pp. 31–51). New York, NY: Guilford Publications.
Schultheiss, O. C., & Brunstein, J. C. (Eds.). (2010). *Implicit motives.* New York, NY: Oxford University Press. http://doi.org/10.1093/acprof:oso/9780195335156.001.0001
Schultheiss, O. C., Dargel, A., & Rohde, W. (2003). Implicit motives and gonadal steroid hormones: Effects of menstrual cycle phase, oral contraceptive use, and relationship status. *Hormones and Behavior, 43,* 293–301. http://doi.org/10.1016/S0018-506X(03)00003-5
Schultheiss, O. C., & Köllner, M. G. (2014). Implicit motives, affect, and the development of competencies. In R. Pekrun & L. Linnenbrink-Garcia (Eds.), *International handbook of emotions in education* (pp. 73–95). New York, NY: Taylor & Francis.
Schultheiss, O. C., Liening, S., & Schad, D. (2008). The reliability of a Picture Story Excercise measure of implicit motives: Estimates of internal consistency, retest reliability and ipsative stability. *Journal of Research in Personality, 42,* 1560–1571. http://doi.org/10.1016/j.jrp.2008.07.008
Schultheiss, O. C., & Pang, J. S. (2007). Measuring implicit motives. In R. W. Robins, R. C. Fraley, & R. F. Krueger (Eds.), *Handbook of research methods in personality psychology* (pp. 322–344). New York, NY: Guilford.
Sheldon, K. M., King, L. A., Houser-Marko, L., Osbaldiston, R., & Gunz, A. (2007). Comparing IAT and TAT measures of power versus intimacy motivation. *European Journal of Personality, 21,* 263–280. http://doi.org/10.1002/per.630

Smith, C. P. (Ed.). (1992). *Motivation and personality: Handbook of thematic content analysis*. New York, NY: Cambridge University Press. http://doi.org/10.1017/CBO9780511527937

Smith, C. P. (2000). Content analysis and narrative analysis. In H. T. Reis & C. M. Judd (Eds.), *Handbook of research methods in social and personality psychology* (pp. 313–335). New York, NY: Cambridge University Press.

Smith, C. P., Feld, S. C., & Franz, C. E. (1992). Methodological considerations: steps in research employing content analysis systems. In C. P. Smith (Ed.), *Motivation and personality: Handbook of thematic content analysis* (pp. 515–536). New York, NY: Cambridge University Press.

Sokolowski, K., Schmalt, H.-D., Langens, T. A., & Puca, R. M. (2000). Assessing achievement, affiliation, and power motives all at once: The Multi-Motive Grid (MMG). *Journal of Personality Assessment, 74*, 126–145. http://doi.org/10.1207/S15327752JPA740109

Stewart, A. J., & Chester, N. L. (1982). Sex differences in human social motives: Achievement, affiliation, and power. In A. J. Stewart (Ed.), *Motivation and society* (pp. 172–218). San Francisco, CA: Jossey-Bass.

Tuerlinckx, F., De Boeck, P., & Lens, W. (2002). Measuring needs with Thematic Apperception Test: A psychometric study. *Journal of Personality and Social Psychology, 82*, 448–461. http://doi.org/10.1037/0022-3514.82.3.448

Van de Vijver, F. J. R. (2000). The nature of bias. In R. H. Dana (Ed.), *Handbook of cross-cultural and multi-cultural personality assessment* (pp. 87–106). Mahwah, NJ: Erlbaum.

Van de Vijver, F. J. R., Hofer, J., & Chasiotis, A. (2010). Methodological aspects of cross-cultural developmental studies. In M. Bornstein (Ed.), *Handbook of cross-cultural developmental science* (pp. 21–37). Mahwah, NJ: Erlbaum.

Van de Vijver, F. J. R., & Leung, K. (1997). *Methods and data analysis for cross-cultural research*. Newbury Park, CA: Sage.

Veroff, J. (1992). Thematic apperceptive methods in survey research. In C. P. Smith (Ed.), *Motivation and personality: Handbook of thematic content analysis* (pp. 100–109). New York, NY: Cambridge University Press.

Weinberger, J., Cotler, T., & Fishman, D. (2010). Clinical implications of implicit motives. In O. C. Schultheiss & J. C. Brunstein (Eds.), *Implicit motives* (pp. 468–509). New York, NY: Oxford University Press.

Weinberger, J., & McClelland, D. C. (1990). Cognitive versus traditionalmotivationalmodels. Irreconcilable or complementary? In E. T. Higgins & R. M. Sorrentino (Eds.), *Handbook of motivation and cognition: Vol. 2. Foundations of social behavior* (pp. 562–597). New York, NY: Guilford Press.

Winter, D. G. (1973). *The power motive*. New York, NY: Free Press.

Winter, D. G. (1994). *Manual for scoring motive imagery in running text*. Ann Arbor, MI: University of Michigan.

Winter, D. G. (2010). Political and historical consequences of implicit motives. In O. C. Schultheiss & J. C. Brunstein (Eds.), *Implicit motives* (pp. 407–432). New York, NY: Oxford University Press.

Winter, D. G., & Stewart, A. J. (1977). Power motive reliability as a function of retest instructions. *Journal of Consulting and Clinical Psychology, 45*, 436–440. http://doi.org/10.1037/0022-006X.45.3.436

Worchel, F. T., Aaron, L. L., & Yates, D. F. (1990). Gender bias on the Thematic Apperception Test. *Journal of Personality Assessment, 55*, 593–602. http://doi.org/10.1080/00223891.1990.9674093

Chapter 7
Measures of Affect

Martina Kaufmann and Nicola Baumann

Department of Psychology, University of Trier, Germany

The very first reactions toward stimuli are almost always accompanied by some kind of affect. There is no single definition of *affect*. It is rather a label for the superordinate category of moods, feelings, and emotions. Basically the term affect refers to a positive and negative evaluative response tendency, which can vary from time to time (i.e., mood state), from stimulus to stimulus (i.e., emotion), as well as from person to person (i.e., sensitivity to positive/negative affects), and, therefore, can be measured both as a state and as a trait (e.g., Watson & Clark, 1992; Watson, Clark, & Tellegen, 1988). Seeing the world through blue- or rose-colored glasses is a popular saying; however, research shows that this is more than just a metaphor. Affect can have an enormous influence on cognition and behavior (for a review, see Schwarz & Clore, 2007). How affect can be measured is, therefore, of vital interest in many fields of psychological investigation and intervention.

Sometimes, people are not willing or not able to communicate their true affect. For this case alternatives to self-report measures are needed. Over the last few years there was a boom in the development of new, indirect measurement techniques. In this chapter, we illustrate some of these procedures that may be used for the measurement of affect. Because of their large number, this review is, however, necessarily selective. It is assumed that affect that cannot or will not be verbalized is very different from affect that is verbalized. In this chapter we describe three categories of measures that attempt to capture the former type of affect, on the basis of the following theoretical statements (e.g., Kuhl, 2000, 2001; Smith & DeCoster, 2000; Strack & Deutsch, 2004; for an overview see Evans, 2008):

1. Affect is stored in memory in different formats: In contrast to explicit affect, which can be verbalized and which is stored in memory as conceptual propositions, implicit affect to which people do not necessarily have conscious access and that cannot be verbalized is thought to be cognitively represented in the form of preconceptual associations.
2. Affect influences judgment making: Where explicit affect primarily influences judgment making concerning the source of affect, implicit affect influences a larger range of judgments, including those which are completely unrelated to the source of affect.
3. Affect manifests itself in behavior: Where explicit affect expresses in reasoned actions and planned behaviors, implicit affect rather should be inferred from people's noncontrolled reactions.

On the basis of these assumptions, we describe *measures of associations, projective measures*, and *behavioral observations of affect* in the remainder of this chapter.

Association-Based Measures of Affect

Implicit affect is thought to be mentally represented in the form of preconceptual associations. Instruments that attempt to measure the strength of the association between a target category and the concepts of *good* and *bad* are, for instance, the Implicit Association Test (IAT), Affective Priming, and the Affective Misattribution Procedure.

The Implicit Association Test as Measure for Implicit Affect

The most frequently used indirect measure of affect in research is arguably the IAT. Greenwald's IAT (Greenwald, McGhee, & Schwartz, 1998; Greenwald, Nosek, & Banaji, 2003; Greenwald, Poehlman, Uhlmann, & Banaji, 2009) measures reaction times when people categorize both positive and negative items and items of the stimulus category (and a contrast category) in cases where the stimulus category (e.g., in some cases, Black faces) shares the same response key with positive items (e.g., positive trait words) and in cases where the stimulus and negative items (e.g., negative trait words) share the same response key (see also Chapter 2 in this volume).

Research from different fields suggest that the IAT score is a good indicator of affect (i.e., with high internal consistency; $\alpha > 0.80$; Perugini, 2005; see also Greenwald et al., 2009). Perhaps because of its frequent use in research, special effort has been devoted to address shortcomings of the procedure. In its original version, the IAT consists of five phases (for a detailed description of the IAT, see Chapter 2 in this volume). Most critique refers to its complexity (e.g., requires task-switching) and its relative nature (e.g., requires a contrast stimulus). Therefore, in recent years, several new variants have been proposed, ranging from a Single-Category IAT (Karpinski & Steinman, 2006) over a Single-Attribute IAT (Penke, Eichstaedt, & Asendorpf, 2006) to a Single-Block IAT (Teige-Mocigemba, Klauer, & Rothermund, 2008) and even a Personalized IAT (Olson & Fazio, 2004).

In order to address several shortcomings of the original IAT, Zinkernagel, Hofmann, Dislich, Gschwendner, and Schmitt (2011) recently proposed a Single-Block–Single-Target (SB-ST) IAT. In this SB-ST-IAT, test takers are simply required to press one of two response keys whenever a picture of the stimulus or another negative picture flashes in the upper part of the screen and the other key whenever the stimulus or a positive item appears in the lower part of the screen (see Figure 7.1). Depending on their valence and the location of their appearance on the screen (either in the upper or lower part of the screen), the stimuli automatically create compatible and incompatible trials. As support for the appropriateness of this measure, it has been found that people with evident disgust to worms (i.e., show withdrawal of the upper body when exposed to a box of worms) responded faster when pictures of worms were presented in the same location as negative pictures than when pictures of worms appeared in the same location as positive pictures (Zinkernagel et al., 2011). However, since data on the psychometric properties of those new variants of the classic IAT such as the SB-ST-IAT are still limited, further research is needed in order to decide to what extent these are appropriate instruments for indirectly measuring affect.

Using Affective Priming for the Assessment of Implicit Affect

Another very popular method is Affective Priming as proposed by Fazio and colleagues (Fazio, Jackson, Dunton, & Williams, 1995; Fazio, Sanbonmatsu, Powell, & Kardes, 1986). The speed

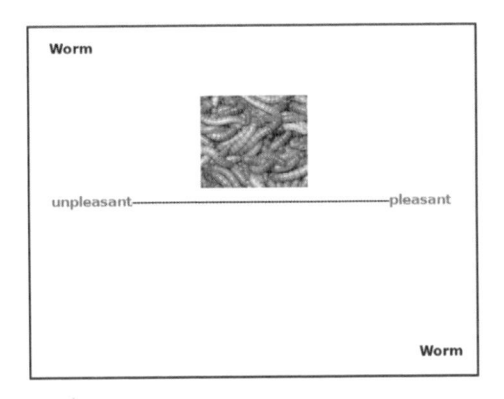

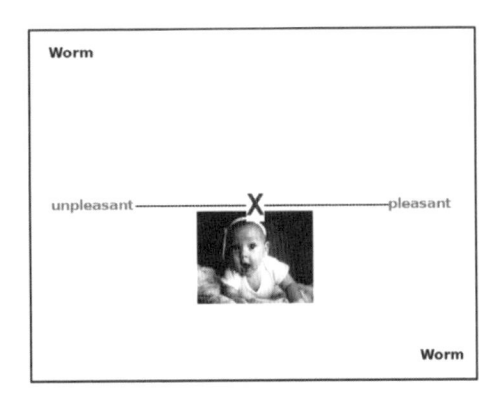

Figure 7.1. A schematic description of the Single-Block–Single-Target IAT (SB-ST-IAT). Reprinted with permisson from Zinkernagel, Hofmann, Dislich, Gschwender, & Schmitt (2011).

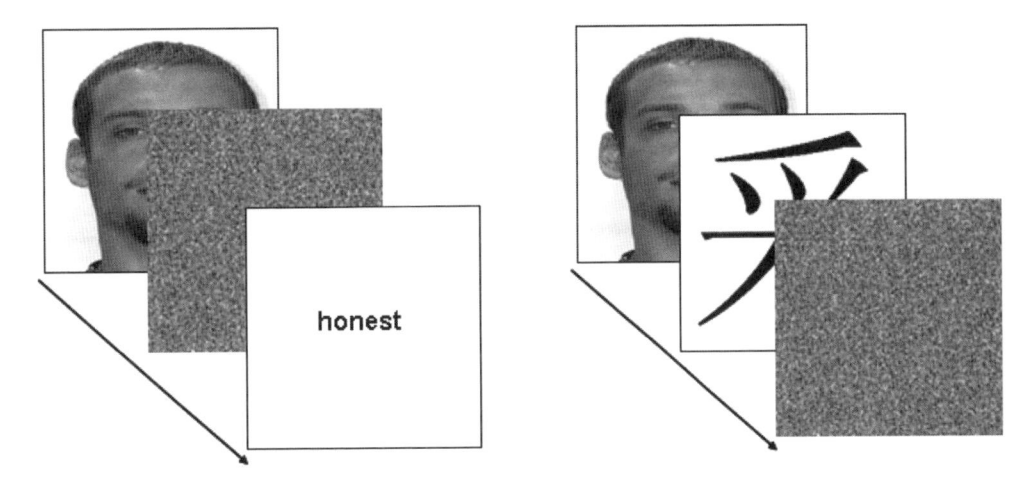

Figure 7.2. Left side: Affective Priming (Fazio et al., 1995; Fazio et al., 1986). Right side: Affect Misattribution Procedure (AMP; Greenwald et al., 1998).

at which test takers categorize items of positive and negative valence shortly after viewing items of the category of interest (as opposed to another, contrast category) is recorded. The idea is that if the priming with items of the category of interest speeds up responses toward positive stimuli, this category is associated with the concept *positive*, whereas if it facilitates responses toward negative stimuli, it is more strongly associated with the concept *negative* instead. Similar to the IAT, the assessed score is the response time in presumably compatible trials (i.e., prime and target are of the same valence) relative to the response time in presumably incompatible trials (i.e., prime and target are of different valence). In Fazio et al. (1995), for example, White test takers with racial prejudice responded faster to negative trait words when these were preceded by Black faces, than when these were preceded by White faces; and when primed with White faces, they responded faster to positive trait words (see left side of Figure 7.2).

Affective Priming is also a standard measure of affect (sometimes deemed to have low reliability; e.g., $\alpha \leq 0.26$, Banse, 2001; but see Fazio & Olson, 2003, for a review of results). In recent years, several successful variants of this procedure have been proposed. This method is viewed as a good candidate for the measurement of implicit affect; with *subliminal affective priming* (e.g., Niedenthal, 1990) or *masked affective priming* (e.g., Frings & Wentura, 2003) the described effect can be found even when test takers lack any knowledge about the presentation of the primes (i.e., they perceive it as just a short flicker). In this way, Neumann and Lozo (2012), for example, recently presented test takers with verbal emotion labels as primes (i.e., German words for disgust and fear) and measured the speed with which these individuals responded to subsequently presented emotional pictures. They found that test takers reacted faster to disgust-evoking pictures when these were preceded by the word disgust, and they recognized fear-arousing pictures faster when primed with the word fear, suggesting that even emotion-specific associations can be traced using this method, beyond positive and negative affect.

The Affect Misattribution Procedure for Measuring Affect

In the Affect Misattribution Procedure (AMP; Payne, Cheng, Govorun, & Stewart, 2005; see right side of Figure 7.2), the priming with the stimulus is typically above the threshold of awareness. The rationale behind this procedure is that test takers cannot immunize themselves against the influence of the affect activated by the prime (e.g., a Black face), and will automatically misattribute their affect to stimuli immediately presented thereafter. Therefore, after being primed with the category of interest, test takers have to categorize novel, ambiguous stimuli into the categories of positive and negative. And the AMP score then reflects the proportion of positive and negative categorizations following the primes (as compared with other, control primes). In a study by Payne et al. (2005), for example, test takers with resentments toward Black people, categorized Chinese pictographs more frequently as negative, when these were preceded by Black faces than when these were preceded by neutral control primes (Payne et al., 2005; Payne, Govorun, & Arbuckle, 2008; Payne, McClernon, & Dobbins, 2007).

The AMP has good psychometric properties (i.e., good internal consistency; $0.69 < \alpha < 0.90$; Payne et al., 2005; Payne, Burkley, & Stokes, 2008). It is important to note that there is some debate over whether the AMP truly addresses hot, emotional processes. It has been found, for example, that emotional face primes influence reactions to subsequently presented pictographs irrespective of test takers' emotions and the personal significance of the primes (Blaison, Imhoff, Hühnel, Hess, & Banse, 2012). It is important, however, to consider that, as opposed to the aforementioned *associative measures* (IAT; Affective Priming) the AMP induces affect and then assesses the extent to which this is misattributed to subsequently presented novel stimuli. It could be that the extent to which affect is misattributed strongly depends on the sort of affect induced by the primes (i.e., object-specific or not object-related) and the sort of stimuli presented immediately thereafter. People may not misattribute their unspoken affect to all other stimuli.

Affect Assessed by Projective Measures

It is assumed that affect influences the interpretation of novel and ambiguous stimuli and situations. Measures that attempt to assess affect that is read into by novel, ambiguous stimuli are summarized as projective measures. Since the introduction of the original Rorschach Inkblot Test, significant developments have occurred in this field (see Chapter 5 in this volume). To illustrate, we next describe the Implicit Positive and Negative Affect Test (IPANAT), the Operant Motive Test, and figure placement techniques.

The Implicit Positive and Negative Affect Test

The IPANAT (Quirin, Kazén, & Kuhl, 2009) assumes that test takers' momentary affective responses show up in judgments of nonsense words. The words were pretested for pleasantness, familiarity, semantic meaning, and associative value. Test takers are, however, told that the words (i.e., SAFME, VIKES, TUNBA) express various affects and that they should guess to which extent these words fit diverse positive affect states (i.e., happy, cheerful, energetic) and negative affect states (i.e., helpless, tense, inhibited), using 4-point scales. From high scores on the positive items, positive affect is deduced, and from high scores on the negative items, negative affect is deduced. The intriguing results obtained support this assumption and demonstrate discriminant validity of the scales. For example, the positive affect score (but not the negative affect score) correlated with circadian cortisol release, and the negative affect score (but not the positive affect score) correlated with a cortisol response to an acute stressor (Quirin, Kazén, Rohrmann, & Kuhl, 2009).

The Operant Motive Test

In the Operant Motive Test (Kuhl & Scheffer, 1999; Scheffer, 2005; Scheffer, Eichstaedt, Chasiotis, & Kuhl, 2007) test takers are required to interpret pictures. They are shown 15 pictures depicting situations that are representative of the three major motive themes: affiliation, achievement, and power. They are asked to mark one of the displayed characters as the main character and answer the following questions: (a) "What is important for the person in this situation and what is the person doing?"; (b) "How does the person feel?"; (c) "Why does the person feel this way?"; (d) "How does the story end?" (see Figure 7.3). The first question addresses the presence of a motive (i.e., affiliation, achievement, and power). If a motive is present, one of the 15 categories described in Table 7.1 is coded (3 motives × 5 implementation strategies; for the complete coding scheme, see Kuhl & Scheffer, 1999). On the basis of crossing the two sources of motivation – positive and negative affect – with self-determined and incentive-focused forms of motivation, the coding scheme differentiates for each motive theme four forms of approach behaviors from avoidance behavior.

Test takers' affect is inferred from their preferred type of behavior across the motive themes (therefore the implementation strategies are identified by the OMT; see Table 7.1). For example, negative affect is inferred when in achievement-related narrations the protagonist experiences feelings of relief after success (instead of pride), and relationship-related narrations are

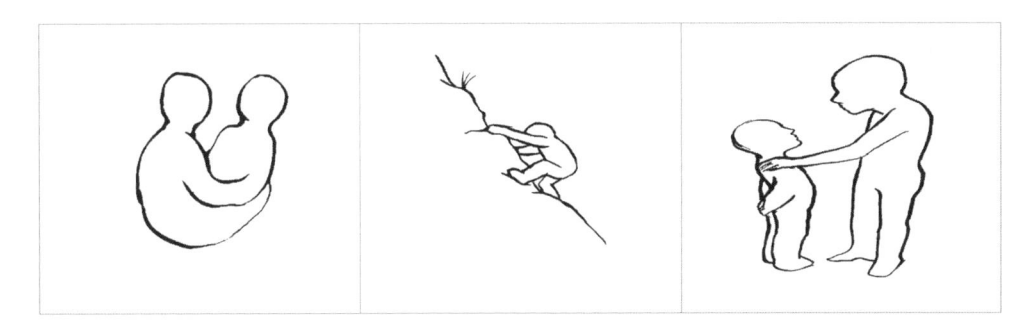

Figure 7.3. Three sample pictures of the Operant Motive Test (OMT). Reprinted with permission from Kuhl &Scheffer (1999).

Table 7.1. Five implementation strategies for three motives in the Operant Motive Test (OMT)

		Affiliation	Achievement	Power
Approach behavior driven by				
Positive affect				
1	Self-regulated	Intimacy – Mutual, joyful exchange – Love, empathy	Flow – Curiosity and interest – Absorption, fun with a task	Guidance – Helping and protecting others – Conveying values, feeling calm
2	Incentive-focused	Sociability – Extraverted contact, interest – Entertainment, good mood	Inner standards – Doing something well – Feeling proud after success	Status – Being the focus of attention – Having prestige and authority
Negative affect				
3	Self-regulated	Coping with rejection – Positive reevaluation of rejection – Restoring an attachment – Delimitation, dislike, disgust	Coping with failure – Positive reevaluation of failure – Seeing demands as challenges – Task rejection (disengagement)	Coping with power-related threats – Asserting wishes – Expressing feelings – Relaxation despite opposition
4	Incentive-focused	Avoiding insecurity – Safety, security, familiarity – Closeness – Being loved	Pressure to achieve – Social standards, trying to be best – Effort (with success), hope – Feeling relieved after success	Inhibited power or dominance – Fear of using power – Many actions, having survived – Overt dominance
Avoidance behavior				
5	Conscious fear (explicit negative affect)	Dependence – Being lonely, rejected – Desperate, hopeless, sad	Failure – Feeling stressed, helpless – Disappointed, anxious	Powerlessness – Being a petitioner – Feeling obedient, guilty, sick

about security and *being loved* (instead of intimacy and *mutually loving*). Although relief and security may be subjectively experienced as positive, with the OMT it can be revealed that they primarily indicate successful removal of negative affect, such as fear of insecurity, to which people have no conscious access (Kuhl, 2001; MacDonald, 1992; Scheffer, 2005).

The evaluation of the validity of each of the 15 OMT categories is a monumental task that is far from finished. There are, however, some promising results to support the use of this method for the measurement of affect. For example, according to terror management theory mortality salience is a primer of implicit negative affect (rather than explicit negative affect; Solomon, Greenberg, & Pyszczynski, 2004). Consistent with this assumption, under high (vs. low) mortality salience, OMT stories show significantly more approach behaviors driven by negative affect across motives (rows 3 and 4 in Table 7.1), but not more avoidance behaviors (row 5; Lüdecke & Baumann, 2015). Positive affect, in turn, is assumed to result, for example, in conditions where information is easy to process (e.g., Winkielman & Cacioppo, 2001). Consistent with this assumption, OMT indicators of positive affect (e.g., row 1 in Table 7.1) have been associated with

Figure 7.4. An example of a figure placement (Family System Test [FAST]). Reprinted with permission from Gehring (1998).

diverse forms of processing facilitation, for example, flow is associated with reduced Stroop interference (Baumann & Scheffer, 2010) and intimacy and guidance with better self-access (i.e., shorter self-classification latencies; Baumann, Kazén, & Kuhl, 2010).

Figure Placement Techniques

Figure placement techniques require test takers to place figures representing themselves and others on a board (see Figure 7.4). This instrument is frequently used to assess family structures and early child–parent relationships. From retrospective placements of family structures (i.e., the distance and hierarchy between figures) conclusions can be made concerning the degree of social warmth and threat in early childhood (e.g., Family System Test, FAST; Gehring, 1998; Gehring, Debry, & Smith, 2001). Since warmth and threat in early parent–child interactions are the developmental basis for the experience of positive and negative affect in later life (MacDonald, 1992), the placements on the board may also be used as indirect measures of test takers' affect.

Supporting this assumption, research suggests that the distance between mother and child figures in retrospective placements can be taken as an indicator of sensitivity to positive affect later in life (Baumann & Scheffer, 2008). Moreover, Field and Storksen-Coulson (2007) recently traced momentary affect using this method. Using a special variant of the figure placement technique, they measured experimentally induced fear in children. Specifically, in their studies children given fear-arousing information about a fictitious animal (as opposed to those who were not) placed a Lego figure representing themselves at a Nature Reserve Board farther away from a picture of that animal (see also Field & Field, 2013).

Behavior Observations of Affect

Because affect is thought to be expressed in behaviors, we finally illustrate how in research affect is inferred from these channels. Following Darwin's (1872/1965) pioneering work on expressions of emotion, we concentrate on the three major channels: *bodily expressions, vocal characteristics*, and *facial expressions*.

Bodily Expressions

Positive affect is assumed to facilitate approach-oriented behaviors and negative affect is assumed to facilitate avoidance-oriented behaviors (e.g., Gray & McNaughton, 2000). These tendencies can be measured very subtly, as well. For example, the speed at which people pull and push a lever in response to stimuli can be measured. Typically, when viewing positive stimuli respondents are faster in pulling a lever toward them, and, when viewing negative stimuli, they are faster in pushing it away from them (e.g., Solarz, 1960). This effect can be observed even when test takers are required to respond to nonvalent features of the stimuli (e.g., Chen & Bargh, 1999), suggesting that this method assesses affect indirectly. In addition, it has been found that in order to avoid a stimulus, individuals scoring high in the trait fear, tend to use the lever more forcefully than those scoring low in this trait (Puca, Rinkenauer, & Breidenstein, 2006). Taken together these results suggest that this method can be used for the measurement of both trait affect and state affect.

Vocal Characteristics

Another channel from which affect can be inferred are vocal characteristics (Juslin & Scherer, 2005). The most robust finding is a positive relationship between affective arousal and vocal pitch (fundamental frequency; Kappas, Hess, & Scherer, 1991). The vocal pitch measure, however, does not allow differentiating between positive or negative affect (Bachorowski, 1999). An increased vocal pitch can be a sign of both positive and negative affect (i.e., joy and anger, Johnstone & Scherer, 2000). Current research, therefore, aims at identifying sets of voice markers for emotions (e.g., Patel, Scherer, Björkner, & Sundberg, 2011).

Facial Expressions

A very popular instrument for the analysis of facial expressions of affect is the Facial Action Coding System proposed by Ekman (FACS; Ekman, Friesen, & Hager, 2002). An even more fine-grained instrument is facial electromyography (EMG). In contrast to the FACS, facial EMG is posited to identify affect markers in the activity of facial muscles before the affect can be seen on the face. Typically, when viewing positive stimuli, observers pull the lip corners up and back (smiling), and therefore show greater activity in the zygomatic muscle. When viewing negative stimuli they in turn, for example, knit the eyebrows (frowning) and therefore demonstrate greater activity in the corrugator muscle (for a complete coding scheme see Fridlund & Cacioppo, 1986; Larsen, Norris, & Cacioppo, 2003). With facial EMG, activity in the muscle can be measured even in a condition where test takers lack any knowledge about the presentation of the stimuli (e.g., Dimberg, Thunberg, & Elmehed, 2000). An increasing set of studies attempts to assess specific emotions using this method. Results show that individuals react to emotion labels and emotional faces with discrete patterns of facial muscle activity even when they lack any knowledge about their presentation (for an overview, see Hess 2009).

Final Questions

As illustrated, affect can be traced in a variety of ways. The measures of affect described here infer the presence of affect from response latencies, judgments of novel stimuli, placements of objects, and other overt behaviors. The fact that the results achieved with these measures often show low correlations with self-reports suggests that they capture implicit affect. However, to what extent do these measures really overcome limitations of self-reports? And, do they indeed purely assess affect? These questions are addressed in the remainder of this chapter.

To What Extent Do These Measures Overcome Limitations of Self-Reports of Affect?

Self-reports of affect alone may provide limited information about an individual's affect. Moreover, an individual may report positive affect when actually experiencing negative affect. In the following passage we discuss to what extent the described measures can circumvent limitations of self-reports.

Cognitive Limitations

Self-reports can be biased, for example, due to *introspective limits* (Evans, 2008; Kuhl, 2000, 2001), *intrusive beliefs* about the most probable or appropriate affective response in the given situation (Parkinson & Manstead, 1992; Robinson & Clore, 2002), or just through *thinking* about personal affect (Wilson & Schooler, 1991). By not directly asking for a judgment of personal affect, the illustrated indirect measures seem to circumvent these problems. However, how results can still be confounded with cognitive processes is illustrated in the next passage.

Motivational Influences

Self-reports can be further distorted by motives of *self-presentation, self-deception*, and *faking* (e.g., Cronbach, 1990; Paulhus, 1984; Tetlock & Manstead, 1985). Since indirectly measuring affect captures processes outside the individual's conscious control and monitoring, initially many researchers believed that indirect measures are immune to such motivational influences. There is, however, reason to doubt this belief. In the IAT, test takers can depict themselves more positively, for example, when they slow down their reactions in trials that are presumed to be compatible (see also Chapter 2 in this volume, for further discussion). In particular, behavioral demonstrations of affect have a social communicative function, above and beyond their expressive function. Therefore, they are not completely immune to motivational influences. Another result that illustrates this fact quite well is, for instance, the observation that people smile more often in public as compared with private contexts, and smile publically, even after a failure feedback (Schneider & Josephs, 1991).

Emotion Regulation

When confronted with an emotional cue, perceivers may spontaneously engage in emotion regulation (e.g., Erber, Wegner, & Therriault, 1996; Gross, 1999). Research suggests that such regulatory processes can occur automatically. It has been found, for example, that regulation of negative affect can involve enhanced fluency of positive memories (e.g., DeWall et al., 2011). Against this backdrop, positive associations are not always unambiguous signals of positive affect, but can also indicate (the regulation of) negative affect instead (e.g., Boden & Baumeister, 1997; DeWall et al., 2011; Sheppes & Meiran, 2007).

That is, even by using an indirect measure it could happen that we may mistakenly assign positive affect to an individual where (the regulation of) a negative affect is true instead (for an exception see the OMT). Therefore, caution is warranted when interpreting the results achieved with described measures.

Do These Measures Tap Implicit Affect?

In the following section, we outline three findings that might be important to consider before interpreting scores on indirect measures as (implicit) affect.

Processes Mediating the Scores on the Measures

First and foremost, if all indirect measures could truly and exclusively assess affect, we would expect at least medium-sized convergent correlations between data gained using the different measures. There is, however, evidence for surprisingly low correspondence among different indirect measures (e.g., Schnabel, Asendorpf, & Greenwald, 2008, for a review). Moreover, several findings show that virtually the same experimental manipulation can even produce opposite effects on the measures (i.e., Affective Priming vs. AMP; e.g., Deutsch & Gawronski, 2009; Gawronski & Bodenhausen, 2005). Accordingly, these instruments may not actually be measuring the same phenomenon. Indeed, very little is yet known about the processes mediating the results achieved with the measures (see Chapter 2 in this volume, for results in the IAT). And indeed, it could be that some measures do not assess pure affect (see Blaison et al., 2012, for a further discussion).

Results in the IAT and the Affective Priming Response, for example, may be explained in part by response conflicts. The resultant scores are assumed to represent the strength of the association of a target category with the concepts of *positive* and *negative*. In fact, however, during the procedures test takers learn to associate the concepts of positive and negative with certain response behaviors (e.g., press key A for positive words; press B for negative ones). Accordingly, at the time of the presentation of the target category, both the concept of positive or negative and the corresponding reaction (e.g., press A) are activated. Therefore, responding faster in certain trials as opposed to others may not be due merely to a stronger association between the target category and the concept of negative or positive, but can be due to the activation of a specific response alternative, which in turn either fits or does not fit with the required one. That is, test takers respond faster, because the preactivated reaction is the required one (e.g., the test requires that A be pressed), and will need relatively more time to react, because the preactivated reaction is not compatible with the required one (e.g., the test requires that B be pressed; for an overview of response conflicts in the measures, see De Houwer, 2003; see also Chapter 2 in this volume). As this example illustrates, in order to understand low correlations among the different measures, more insight into the processes producing the scores on the measures is needed.

Relative Nature of Test Scores

Second, to date most measures provide only an aggregated score, containing information about the negative evaluation of a target category relative to its positive evaluation, and vice versa (with the exception of the IPANAT). This type of measurement implies that positive and negative affect are opposite ends of a single bipolar continuum. There is, however, evidence that positive and negative should be regarded as separable phenomena (Larsen, McGraw, Mellers, & Cacioppo, 2004; MacDonald, 1992; Watson, Wiese, Vaidya, & Tellegen, 1999). The existence of mixed feelings, ambivalence, and conflict is a clear sign that positive and negative affect can exist in parallel. Furthermore, conflicts may also reveal whether or not regulatory processes attempt to cover affect. From this viewpoint, positive and negative affect should be regarded as separate phenomena and their measurement should be able to identify ambivalence or conflict. Until now this information is not captured by most of the described measures. However, since it is conjectured that positive and negative affect do not act in opposition, unless an individual is required for an action toward a stimulus (Cacioppo, Gardner, & Berntson, 1999), it is indeed not easy to capture this information with the described measures (for an exception, see IPANAT or OMT).

Strength of the Relations Between Affect and Behavior

Third, notwithstanding the fact that almost all of the described measures turned out to be good predictors of affect-related behaviors, there is reason to doubt that the same type of affect always manifests itself in the same type of behavior. Consider the finding that people are faster in pulling a lever toward them when viewing positive stimuli and faster in pushing it away from them when viewing negative stimuli. This robust finding has long been considered as evidence for a strong affect–behavior link. There is, however, growing evidence against such a hard-wired perspective. New research shows that the observed effect suddenly disappears and reverses to the opposite one when test takers are told that pulling the lever means *downward* and pushing it means *upward*. In this case, when viewing negative items they are faster in pulling the lever and when viewing positive items are faster in pushing it (Eder & Rothermund, 2008). This reversed effect possibly occurred because test takers may have tended to associate the label downward with the concept of negative, and upwards with the concept of positive.

As this example illustrates, virtually the same type of affect can show up in very different behavioral tendencies. Also, the same behavior may not always be indicative of the same type of affect (see smiling after failure feedback). Whether a certain behavior indicates a certain type of affect (or the regulation of another instead) seems to depend on how strongly this behavior itself is associated with the type of affect. That is, whether pulling or pushing the lever indicates positive affect seems to depend on the meaning associated with the reaction and whether it is strongly associated with the concept of positive, as well. This assumption is at least well in harmony with the notion that (implicit) affect is stored in memory in an associative format.

Concluding Remarks

When people are not willing or not able to indicate their true affect, the illustrated indirect measures can provide valuable information that cannot be obtained with self-reports. Moreover, even when an individual tends to report a positive affect these instruments can reveal an underlying negative affect. However, indirect measures do not generally possess a higher validity (for further discussion of indirect measures, see Gawronski, 2009). Because to date little is known about the processes mediating the results achieved with the measures, and because these results are often of a relative nature, caution is warranted before one interprets a score on indirect measures as pure affect.

Since there are strong indications that affect that cannot or will not be verbalized does not act in similar ways to affect that is verbalized, and since the former can be covered by automatic regulatory processes, it is still not easy to capture affect by using the available alternatives to self-reports. Because we found no measure of affect with superior validity, we would recommend the use of multiple methods to validate observations. Moreover, the problem of confounds with regulatory processes may require that affect and emotions are measured as processes rather than as states.

References

Bachorowski, J.-A. (1999). Vocal expression and perception of emotion. *Current Directions in Psychological Science, 8,* 53–57. http://doi.org/10.1111/1467-8721.00013

Banse, R. (2001). Affective priming with liked and disliked persons: Prime visibility determines congruency and incongruency effects. *Cognition and Emotion, 15,* 501–520. http://doi.org/10.1080/02699930126251

Baumann, N., Kazén, M., & Kuhl, J. (2010). Implicit motives: A look from Personality Systems Interaction theory. In O. C. Schultheiss & J. C. Brunstein (Eds.), *Implicit motives* (pp. 375–403). New York, NY: Oxford University Press.

Baumann, N., & Scheffer, D. (2008). Operanter Motivtest und Leistungs-Flow [Operant motive test and flow in the achievement domain]. In W. Sarges & D. Scheffer (Eds.), *Innovative Ansätze für die Eignungsdiagnostik. Psychologie für das Personalmanagement* (pp. 65–76). Göttingen, Germany: Hogrefe.

Baumann, N., & Scheffer, D. (2010). Seeing and mastering difficulty: The role of affective change in achievement flow. *Cognition and Emotion, 24,* 1304–1328. http://doi.org/10.1080/02699930903319911

Blaison, C., Imhoff, R., Hühnel, I., Hess, U., & Banse, R. (2012). The affect misattribution procedure: Hot or not? *Emotion, 12,* 403–412. http://doi.org/10.1037/a0026907

Boden, J. M., & Baumeister, R. F. (1997). Repressive coping: Distraction using pleasant thoughts and memories. *Journal of Personality & Social Psychology, 73,* 45–62. http://doi.org/10.1037/0022-3514.73.1.45

Cacioppo, J. T., Gardner, W. L., & Berntson, G. G. (1999). The affect system has parallel and integrative processing components: Form follows function. *Journal of Personality and Social Psychology, 76,* 839–855. http://doi.org/10.1037/0022-3514.76.5.839

Chen, M., & Bargh, J. A. (1999). Consequences of automatic evaluation: Immediate behavioral predispositions to approach or avoid the stimulus. *Personality and Social Psychology Bulletin, 25,* 215–224. http://doi.org/10.1177/0146167299025002007

Cronbach, L. J. (1990). *Essentials of psychological testing* (5th ed.). New York, NY: Harper & Row.

Darwin, C. (1965). *The expression of the emotions in man and animals.* Chicago, IL: University of Chicago Press. (Original work published 1872)

De Houwer, J. (2003). A structural analysis of indirect measures of attitudes. In J. Musch & K. C. Klauer (Eds.), *The psychology of evaluation: Affective processes in cognition and emotion* (pp. 219–244). Mahwah, NJ: Erlbaum.

Deutsch, R., & Gawronski, B. (2009).When the method makes a difference: Antagonistic effects on "automatic evaluations" as a function of task characteristics of the measure. *Journal of Experimental Social Psychology, 45*, 101–114. http://doi.org/10.1016/j.jesp.2008.09.001

DeWall, C. N., Twenge, J. M., Koole, S. L., Baumeister, R. F., Marquez, A., & Reid, M. W. (2011). Automatic emotion regulation after social exclusion: Tuning to positivity. *Emotion, 11*, 623–636. http://doi.org/10.1037/a0023534

Dimberg, U., Thunberg, M., & Elmehed, K. (2000). Unconscious facial reactions to emotional facial expressions. *Psychological Science, 11*, 86–89. http://doi.org/10.1111/1467-9280.00221

Eder, A., & Rothermund, K. (2008). When do motor behaviors (mis)match affective stimuli? An evaluative coding view of approach and avoidance reactions. *Journal of Experimental Psychology: General, 137*, 262–281. http://doi.org/10.1037/0096-3445.137.2.262

Ekman, P., Friesen, W. V., & Hager, J. C. (2002). *The facial action coding system*. Salt Lake City, UT: Research Nexus eBook.

Erber, R., Wegner, D. M., & Therriault, N. (1996). On being cool and collected: Mood regulation in anticipation of social interaction. *Journal of Personality and Social Psychology, 70*, 757–766. http://doi.org/10.1037/0022-3514.70.4.757

Evans, J. S. B. T. (2008). Dual-processing accounts of reasoning, judgment, and social cognition. *Annual Review of Psychology, 59*, 255–278. http://doi.org/10.1146/annurev.psych.59.103006.093629

Fazio, R. H., Jackson, J. R., Dunton, B. C., & Williams, C. J. (1995). Variability in automatic activation as an unobtrusive measure of racial attitudes: A bona fide pipeline? *Journal of Personality and Social Psychology, 69*, 1013–1027. http://doi.org/10.1037/0022-3514.69.6.1013

Fazio, R. H., & Olson, M. A. (2003). Implicit measures in social cognition: Their meaning and use. *Annual Review of Psychology, 54*, 297–327. http://doi.org/10.1146/annurev.psych.54.101601.145225

Fazio, R. H., Sanbonmatsu, D. M., Powell, M. C., & Kardes, F. R. (1986). On the automatic activation of attitudes. *Journal of Personality and Social Psychology, 50*, 229–238. http://doi.org/10.1037/0022-3514.50.2.229

Field, Z. C., & Field, A. P. (2013). How trait anxiety, interpretation bias and memory affect acquired fear in children learning about new animals. *Emotion, 13*, 409–423. http://doi.org/10.1037/a0031147

Field, A. P., & Storksen-Coulson, H. (2007). The interaction of pathways to fear in childhood anxiety: A preliminary study. *Behaviour Research and Therapy, 45*, 3051–3059. http://doi.org/10.1016/j.brat.2007.09.001

Fridlund, A. J., & Cacioppo, J. T. (1986). Guidelines for human electromyographic research. *Psychophysiology, 23*, 567–589. http://doi.org/10.1111/j.1469-8986.1986.tb00676.x

Frings, C. G., & Wentura, D. (2003). Who is watching Big Brother? TV consumption predicted by masked affective priming. *European Journal of Social Psychology, 33*, 779–791. http://doi.org/10.1002/ejsp.167

Gawronski, B. (2009). Ten frequently asked questions about implicit measures and their frequently supposed, but not entirely correct answers. *Canadian Psychology, 50*, 141–150. http://doi.org/10.1037/a0013848

Gawronski, B., & Bodenhausen, G. V. (2005). Accessibility effects on implicit social cognition: The role of knowledge activation versus retrieval experiences. *Journal of Personality and Social Psychology, 89*, 672–685. http://doi.org/10.1037/0022-3514.89.5.672

Gehring, T. M. (1998). *Family System Test (FAST)*. Seattle, WA: Hogrefe & Huber Publishers.

Gehring, T. M., Debry, M., & Smith, P. K. (2001). *The Family System Test (FAST): Theory and application*. London, UK: Routledge.

Gray, J. A., & McNaughton, N. (2000). *The neuropsychology of anxiety: An enquiry into the functions of the septo-hippocampal system* (2nd ed.). Oxford, UK: Oxford University Press.

Greenwald, A. G., McGhee, D. E., & Schwartz, J. K. L. (1998). Measuring individual differences in implicit cognition: The Implicit Association Test. *Journal of Personality and Social Psychology, 74*, 1464–1480. http://doi.org/10.1037/0022-3514.74.6.1464

Greenwald, A. G., Nosek, B. A., & Banaji, M. R. (2003). Understanding and using the Implicit Association Test: I. An improved scoring algorithm. *Journal of Personality and Social Psychology, 85*, 197–216. http://doi.org/10.1037/h0087889

Greenwald, A. G., Poehlman, T. A., Uhlmann, E., & Banaji, M. R. (2009). Understanding and using the Implicit Association Test: III. Meta-analysis of predictive validity. *Journal of Personality and Social Psychology, 97*, 17–41. http://doi.org/10.1037/a0015575

Gross, J. J. (1999). Emotion regulation: Past, present, future. *Cognition and Emotion, 13*, 551–573. http://doi.org/10.1080/026999399379186

Hess, U. (2009). Facial EMG. In E. Harmon-Jones & J. S. Beer (Eds.), *Methods in the neurobiology of social and personality psychology* (pp. 70–91). New York, NY: Guilford Press.

Johnstone, T., & Scherer, K. R. (2000).Vocal communication of emotion. In M. Lewis & J. M. Haviland-Jones (Eds.), *Handbook of emotions* (pp. 220–235). New York, NY: Guilford Press.

Juslin, P. N., & Scherer, K. R. (2005). Vocal expression of affect. In J. Harrigan, R. Rosenthal, & K. Scherer (Eds.), *The new handbook of methods in nonverbal behavior research* (pp. 65–135). Oxford, UK: Oxford University Press.

Kappas, A., Hess, U., & Scherer, K. R. (1991). Voice and emotion. In R. S. Feldman & B. Rimé (Eds.), *Fundamentals of nonverbal behavior* (pp. 200–238). Cambridge, UK: Cambridge University Press.

Karpinski, A., & Steinman, R. B. (2006). The single category implicit association test as a measure of implicit social cognition. *Journal of Personality and Social Psychology, 91*, 16–32. http://doi.org/10.1037/0022-3514.91.1.16

Kuhl, J. (2000). A functional-design approach to motivation and volition: The dynamics of personality systems interactions. In M. Boekaerts, P. R. Pintrich, & M. Zeidner (Eds.), *Self-regulation: Directions and challenges for future research* (pp. 111–169). New York, NY: Academic Press.

Kuhl, J. (2001). *Motivation und Persönlichkeit: InteraktionpsychischerSysteme* [Motivation and personality: Interaction of psychological systems]. Göttingen, Germany: Hogrefe.

Kuhl, J., & Scheffer, D. (1999). *Manual for scoring the Operant Motive Test (OMT)*. Osnabück, Germany: University of Osnabrück.

Larsen, J. T., McGraw, A. P., Mellers, B. A., & Cacioppo, J. T. (2004).The agony of victory and the thrill of defeat: Mixed emotional reactions to disappointing wins and relieving losses. *Psychological Science, 13*, 325–330. http://doi.org/10.1111/j.0956-7976.2004.00677.x

Larsen, J. T., Norris, C. J., & Cacioppo, J. T. (2003). Effects of positive affect and negative affect on electromyographic activity over zygomaticus major and corrugator supercilii. *Psychophysiology, 40*, 776–785. http://doi.org/10.1111/1469-8986.00078

Lüdecke, C., & Baumann, N. (2015). *Experiencing terror but not knowing it: Evidence for implicit negative affect under mortality salience*. Manuscript submitted for publication.

MacDonald, K. (1992). Warmth as a developmental construct: An evolutionary analysis. *Child Development, 63*, 753–773. http://doi.org/10.2307/1131231

Neumann, R., & Lozo, L. (2012). Priming the activation of fear and disgust: Evidence for semantic processing. *Emotion, 12*, 223–228. http://doi.org/10.1037/a0026500

Niedenthal, P. M. (1990). Implicit perception of affective information. *Journal of Experimental Social Psychology, 26*, 505–527. http://doi.org/10.1016/0022-1031(90)90053-O

Olson, M. A., & Fazio, R. H. (2004). Reducing the influence of extra-personal associations on the implicit association test: Personalizing the IAT. *Journal of Personality and Social Psychology, 86*, 653–667. http://doi.org/10.1037/0022-3514.86.5.653

Parkinson, B., & Manstead, A. S. R. (1992). Appraisal as a cause of emotion. In M. S. Clark (Ed.), *Review of personality and social psychology* (Vol. 13, pp. 122–149). Newbury Park, CA: Sage.

Patel, S., Scherer, K. R., Björkner, E., & Sundberg, J. (2011). Mapping emotions into acoustic space: The role of voice production. *Biological Psychology, 87*, 93–98. http://doi.org/10.1016/j.biopsycho.2011.02.010

Paulhus, D. L. (1984). Two-component models of socially desirable responding. *Journal of Personality and Social Psychology, 46*, 598–609. http://doi.org/10.1037/0022-3514.46.3.598

Payne, B. K., Burkley, M. A., & Stokes, M. B. (2008). Why do implicit and explicit attitude tests diverge? The role of structural fit. *Journal of Personality and Social Psychology, 94*, 16–31. http://doi.org/10.1037/0022-3514.94.1.16

Payne, B. K., Cheng, S. M., Govorun, O., & Stewart, B. D. (2005). An inkblot for attitudes: Affect misattribution as implicit measurement. *Journal of Personality and Social Psychology, 89*, 277–293. http://doi.org/10.1037/0022-3514.89.3.277

Payne, B. K., Govorun, O., & Arbuckle, N. L. (2008). Automatic attitudes and alcohol: Does implicit liking predict drinking? *Cognition and Emotion, 22*, 238–271. http://doi.org/10.1080/02699930701357394

Payne, B. K., McClernon, J. F., & Dobbins, I. G. (2007). Automatic affective responses to smoking cues. *Experimental and Clinical Psychopharmacology, 15*, 400–409. http://doi.org/10.1037/1064-1297.15.4.400

Penke, L., Eichstaedt, J., & Asendorpf, J. B. (2006). Single attribute Implicit Association Tests (SA-IAT) for the assessment of unipolar constructs: The case of sociosexuality. *Experimental Psychology, 53*, 283–291. http://doi.org/10.1027/1618-3169.53.4.283

Perugini, M. (2005). Predictive models of implicit and explicit attitudes. *British Journal of Social Psychology, 44*, 29–45. http://doi.org/10.1348/014466604X23491

Puca, R.M., Rinkenauer, G., & Breidenstein, C. (2006). Individual differences in approach and avoidance movements: How the avoidance motive influences response force. *Journal of Personality, 74*, 979–1014. http://doi.org/10.1111/j.1467-6494.2006.00400.x

Quirin, M., Kazén, M., & Kuhl, J. (2009). When nonsense sounds happy or helpless: The Implicit Positive and Negative Affect Test (IPANAT). *Journal of Personality and Social Psychology, 97*, 500–516. http://doi.org/10.1037/a0016063

Quirin, M., Kazén, M., Rohrmann, S., & Kuhl, J. (2009). Implicit but not explicit affectivity predicts circadian and reactive cortisol: Using the implicit positive and negative affect test. *Journal of Personality, 77*, 401–425. http://doi.org/10.1111/j.1467-6494.2008.00552.x

Robinson, M. D., & Clore, G. L. (2002). Episodic and semantic knowledge in emotional self-report: Evidence for two judgment processes. *Journal of Personality and Social Psychology, 83*, 663–677. http://doi.org/10.1037/0022-3514.83.1.198

Scheffer, D. (2005). *Implizite motive* [Implicit motives]. Göttingen, Germany: Hogrefe.

Scheffer, D., Eichstaedt, J., Chasiotis, A., & Kuhl, J. (2007). Towards an integrated measure of need affiliation and agreeableness derived from the Operant Motive Test. *Psychological Science, 49*, 308–324.

Schnabel, K., Asendorpf, J. B., & Greenwald, A. G. (2008). Assessment of individual differences in implicit cognition: A review of IAT measures. *European Journal of Psychological Assessment, 25*, 210–217. http://doi.org/10.1027/1015-5759.24.4.210

Schneider, K., & Josephs, I. (1991). The expressive and communicative functions of preschool children's smiles in an achievement-situation. *Journal of Nonverbal Behaviour, 15*, 185–198. http://doi.org/10.1007/BF01672220

Schwarz, N., & Clore, G. L. (2007). Feelings and phenomenal experiences. In E. T. Higgins & A. W. Kruglanski (Eds.), *Social psychology: Handbook of basic principles* (2nd ed., pp. 385–407). New York, NY: Guilford.

Sheppes, G., & Meiran, N. (2007). Better late than never? On the dynamics of on-line regulation of sadness using distraction and cognitive reappraisal. *Personality and Social Psychology Bulletin, 33*, 1518–1532. http://doi.org/10.1177/0146167207305537

Smith, E. R., & DeCoster, J. (2000). Dual-process models in social and cognitive psychology: Conceptual integration and links to underlying memory systems. *Personality and Social Psychology Review, 4*, 108–131. http://doi.org/10.1207/S15327957PSPR0402_01

Solarz, A. K. (1960). Latency of instrumental responses as a function of compatibility with the meaning of eliciting verbal signs. *Journal of Experimental Psychology, 59*, 239–245. http://doi.org/10.1037/h0047274

Solomon, S., Greenberg, J., & Pyszczynski, T. (2004). The cultural animal: Twenty years of terror management theory and research. In J. Greenberg, S. L. Koole, & T. Pyszczynski (Eds.), *Handbook of experimental existential psychology* (pp. 13–34). New York, NY: Guilford.

Strack, F., & Deutsch, R. (2004). Reflective and impulsive determinants of social behavior. *Personality and Social Psychology Review, 8*, 220–247. http://doi.org/10.1207/s15327957pspr0803_1

Teige-Mocigemba, S., Klauer, K. C., & Rothermund, K. (2008). Minimizing method-specific variance in the IAT: The Single Block IAT. *European Journal of Psychological Assessment, 25*, 237–245. http://doi.org/10.1027/1015-5759.24.4.237

Tetlock, P. E., & Manstead, A. S. R. (1985). Impression management versus intrapsychic explanations in social psychology: A useful dichotomy? *Psychological Review, 92*, 67–82. http://doi.org/10.1037/0033-295X.92.1.59

Watson, D., & Clark, L. A. (1992). On traits and temperament: General and specific factors of emotional experience and their relation to the five-factor model. *Journal of Personality, 60*, 441–476. http://doi.org/10.1111/j.1467-6494.1992.tb00980.x

Watson, D., Clark, L.A., & Tellegen, A. (1988). Development and validation of brief measures of positive and negative affect: The PANAS scales. *Journal of Personality and Social Psychology, 54*, 1063–1070. http://doi.org/10.1037/0022-3514.54.6.1063

Watson, D., Wiese, D., Vaidya, J., & Tellegen, A. (1999). The two general activation systems of affect: Structural findings, evolutionary considerations, and psychobiological evidence. *Journal of Personality and Social Psychology, 76*, 820–838. http://doi.org/10.1037/0022-3514.76.5.820

Wilson, T. D., & Schooler, J. W. (1991). Thinking too much: Introspection can reduce the quality of preferences and decisions. *Journal of Personality and Social Psychology, 60*, 181–192. http://doi.org/10.1037/0022-3514.60.2.181

Winkielman, P., & Cacioppo, J. T. (2001). Mind at ease puts a smile on the face: Psychophysiological evidence that processing facilitation elicits positive affect. *Journal of Personality and Social Psychology, 81*, 989–1000. http://doi.org/10.1037/0022-3514.81.6.989

Zinkernagel, A., Hofmann, W., Dislich, F. X. R., Gschwendner, T., & Schmitt, M. (2011). Indirect assessment of implicit disgust sensitivity. *European Journal of Psychological Assessment, 27*, 237–243. http://doi.org/10.1027/1015-5759/a000078

Chapter 8

Implicit Measures of Attitudes

Colin Tucker Smith and Kate A. Ratliff

Department of Psychology, University of Florida, Gainesville, FL, USA

Asking people to self-report their thoughts and feelings is a simple and straightforward method for measuring attitudes. For example, if you tell me that you think highly of a new colleague, Susan, I now have useful and important information regarding your attitude toward Susan. However, researchers have long known that such self-report measures are imperfect indicators of attitudes for at least three reasons. First, self-report measures are subject to social desirability and self-presentational concerns (Paulhus, 1991). Knowing that I am friendly with Susan is likely to influence what you are willing to say about her. Second, self-report measures are notoriously sensitive to contextual factors that are unrelated to the attitude itself (Schwarz, 1999). For example, asking you to report your attitude toward Susan immediately after she declined your request to serve on a committee is likely to lead to a different attitude than you would report if she had agreed. Finally, reliance on self-report measures erroneously assumes that one has introspective access to one's attitudes (Nisbett & Wilson, 1977). For example, you might be unaware that your attitude toward Susan is influenced by her gender or other group memberships.

To minimize the problems with self-report, researchers have developed a wide variety of measures that assess thoughts, feelings, and behaviors in a way that does not require introspection. Such *implicit measures* of attitudes typically do not alert the respondent to what is being measured, or do not allow the respondent control over their response even if they do know what is being measured. In addition to providing a richer assessment of evaluations, the inclusion of implicit measures in attitude research can be important for predicting behaviors (e.g., Greenwald, Poehlman, Uhlmann, & Banaji, 2009).

Chapter Overview

The purpose of the current chapter is to describe a variety of implicit measures of attitudes. In the next section we provide summary information regarding the general method and important methodological features of eight such measures (and their variations). A common source of misunderstanding is that some researchers use the terms implicit and explicit to refer to features of the attitude that is being measured (i.e., a measure of implicit attitudes; e.g., Greenwald & Banaji, 1995) and others use the terms implicit and explicit to refer to features of the measurement (i.e., an implicit measure of attitudes; e.g., Petty, Fazio, & Briñol, 2009). In the current chapter, we take the latter approach (see also Chapter 1 in this volume). We consider a measure to be implicit if the measurement outcome is thought to rely on processes that are some combination of uncontrolled, unintentional, autonomous, unconscious, efficient, or fast (De Houwer & Moors, 2015). Further, many of the measures that we describe can be used to assess other constructs (e.g., identity, stereotypes, self-esteem); however, in this chapter we focus singularly on the measurement of attitude – a psychological tendency that is expressed by evaluating a particular entity with some degree of favor or disfavor (Eagly & Chaiken, 1998).

The descriptions that follow provide a basic introduction to each implicit measure of attitudes. As such, the interested reader is directed to previous reviews of implicit attitude measures that have approached this issue in complementary ways (De Houwer, 2003a; De Houwer, 2009; Fazio & Olson, 2003; Gawronski & Payne, 2010; Nosek, Hawkins, & Frazier, 2011; Uhlmann et al., 2012). For each measure, we describe: (a) a general overview of the procedure, (b) the benefits and drawbacks of its use, and (c) its relation to other measures and to behavior.

Implicit Association Test and Its Variants

Overview and Procedure

The Implicit Association Test (IAT; Greenwald, McGhee, & Schwartz, 1998) is by far the most widely used implicit measure of attitudes, accounting for more than 40% of total citations through the year 2010 (Nosek et al., 2011; see also Chapter 2 in this volume). The IAT has generated (and, arguably, withstood) a level of criticism virtually unheard of in research psychology and – partially as a function of that criticism – has seen periodic improvements (see Lane, Banaji, Nosek, & Greenwald, 2007, for a review). The IAT is a response-competition task based on the assumption that closely associated concepts facilitate response to one another. The IAT measures the strength of associations between two concept categories (e.g., Black people and White people) and two evaluative attributes (e.g., good and bad). The stimuli used to represent the concept categories and evaluative attributes can be words (e.g., Black, African American, good, bad) or pictures (e.g., pictures of positive or negative objects). A typical IAT consists of seven blocks of trials (Nosek, Greenwald, & Banaji, 2005). The first two blocks of the IAT are practice blocks in which the participant categorizes words that appear in the center of the screen using two different keys on the keyboard (e.g., *E* and *I*) that correspond to category labels that appear on the left and right side of the screen, respectively. In the first block, the participant sorts words into the categories *good* and *bad*; in the second block the participant sorts words into the categories *Black people* and *White people*. The third and fourth blocks are critical blocks in which one response key is used to categorize good words or Black people and another is used to categorize bad words or White people. In the fifth block the participant practices categorizing pictures of Black and White people using the opposite keys than they used previously (i.e., if the category Black people was on the left and White people on the right, the category labels and corresponding response keys switch). The number of trials in this block is typically twice what was used in the first practice blocks in order to reduce potential learning effects. The sixth and seventh blocks are critical blocks with the opposite pairing of the third and fourth blocks; in this case, one response key would now be used to categorize bad words or Black people and another to categorize good words or White people. The underlying idea of the IAT is that one should be faster to categorize words when closely related items share the same response key. A more negative association with Black people than White people is inferred if people are able to complete the task more quickly when Black people + bad and White people + good share response keys relative to when Black people + good and White people + bad share the same response key. Greenwald, Nosek, and Banaji (2003) provide more specific information about scoring the IAT.

Relation to Behavior and Other Measures

IAT scores have been shown to predict a wide variety of important, real-world outcomes such as Whites' behavior in interracial interactions (Dovidio, Kawakami, & Gaertner, 2002), race-based disparities in physicians' treatment of patients (Green et al., 2007), the longevity of romantic relationships (LeBel & Campbell, 2009), suicidal behavior (Nock et al., 2010), voting behavior (Friese, Smith, Plischke, Bluemke, & Nosek, 2012), consumer behavior (Maison, Greenwald, & Bruin, 2004), and consumption behavior (Friese, Hofmann, & Wänke, 2008). Greenwald, Poehlman, et al. (2009) provide a meta-analysis of 184 studies using the IAT to predict behavior, concluding that the average correlation is $r = .27$, and that the IAT is particularly valuable in predicting behavior in socially sensitive domains (compare to Oswald, Mitchell, Blanton, Jaccard, & Tetlock, 2013). The relationship between the IAT and explicit measures has proved to be highly variable. A review of 57 attitude objects indicated that the average correlation was .36, but this ranged from no significant relationship to a high of $r = .70$ based on the attitude object, with the strongest relationships found for political attitudes (Nosek, 2005). A number of other moderators of the relationship between the IAT and explicit attitudes have been discovered (for additional reviews, see Hofmann, Gawronski, Gschwendner, Le, & Schmitt, 2005; and Hofmann, Gschwendner, Nosek, & Schmitt, 2005). In short, explicit attitudes are more related to the IAT when self-presentational concerns are low (Hofmann, Gschwendner et al., 2005; Nosek, 2005), when the attitude is of high importance (Karpinski, Steinman, & Hilton, 2005) or strongly held (Nosek, 2005), and when mood is positive (Huntsinger & Smith, 2009) or marked by anger (Huntsinger, 2013). Additionally, the relationship is stronger to the extent that explicit measures are related to spontaneous, gut-level, affective responses (Gawronski & LeBel, 2008; Hofmann, Gawronski, et al., 2005; Hofmann, Gschwendner, et al., 2005; Ranganath, Smith, & Nosek, 2008; Smith & Nosek, 2011). See also Chapter 11 in this volume on the convergence of different measures.

Benefits and Drawbacks

The IAT has excellent psychometric properties including high reliability (ranging from .70 to .90; Gawronski & De Houwer, 2014), good convergent and discriminant validity (Gawronski, 2002), and high predictive validity (Greenwald, Poehlman, et al., 2009)[1].

A number of criticisms have been leveled against the IAT, each sparking response from IAT proponents. These concerns (see Fiedler, Messner, & Bluemke, 2006, for an overview) include that participants can be instructed to fake their scores on the IAT (e.g., De Houwer, Beckers, & Moors, 2007; Fiedler & Bluemke, 2005; Steffans, 2004) and that the metric on which the IAT is scored may be problematic (Blanton & Jaccard, 2006). In addition, some researchers made changes to the measure in an attempt to tackle concerns they had; we describe those measures next.

Personalized Implicit Association Test

The Personalized IAT (PIAT; Olson & Fazio, 2004) was designed to address concerns that the standard version of the IAT may be "contaminated" by cultural knowledge (i.e., associations

---

[1] Although we refer to *the IAT*, individual IATs should be evaluated separately based on the specific procedures used (e.g., amount of time between trial, format and font options, stimuli choices, and whether the IAT assesses attitudes, stereotypes, beliefs, self-esteem, or something else). Numbers provided here are based on meta-analysis.

in mind that are "extrapersonal") rather than assessing associations that are truly evaluative in nature. For example, Olson and Fazio (2004) argue that, in a traditional race IAT, participants in the US may respond more quickly to the White people + good/Black people + bad pairing than to the reverse pairing because they are aware of their culture's long history of discrimination, and not necessarily because of their personal associations. While other researchers have argued that dividing mental associations in this way may not be theoretically meaningful (Gawronski, Peters, & LeBel, 2008; Nosek & Hansen, 2008; Uhlmann, Poehlman, & Nosek, 2012), the PIAT was developed to eliminate this perceived confound.

The PIAT procedure is identical to that of the standard IAT, with two key differences. First, the evaluative category labels (*good* and *bad*) are changed to *I like* and *I dislike*. Also, no error feedback is given (although some recent instantiations of the PIAT have reintroduced error feedback such as Han, Olson, & Fazio, 2006, and Olson, Crawford, & Devlin, 2009). This measure has gained a fairly strong foothold in the literature; the original paper has been cited more than 200 times at the time of writing. The PIAT has been used to measure attitudes toward alcohol (Houben & Wiers, 2007), consumer goods (Han, Czellar, Olson, & Fazio, 2010; Smith, De Houwer, & Nosek, 2013), stigmatized groups (Goff, Eberhardt, Williams, & Jackson, 2008; Olson et al., 2009), and smoking (De Houwer, Custers, & De Clercq, 2006). Although a formal review has yet to be published, in general the PIAT shows psychometric properties comparable to those of the classic IAT (e.g., Smith et al., 2013).

Single-Block Implicit Association Test and Recoding-Free Implicit Association Test

Two related measures have been designed to address concerns that the blocked structure of the IAT can lead participants to adopt recoding strategies to simplifying the task (e.g., De Houwer, Geldof, & De Bruycker, 2005; Rothermund, Wentura, & De Houwer, 2005; Wentura & Rothermund, 2007). For example, a participant might adopt the strategy of combining the White people and good categories into a single mental category of *Things I like* and the Black people and bad categories into *Things I don't like*. An artificial inflation of IAT scores results when participants find it more difficult to simplify the reverse pairings in a similar way. In response to these concerns, researchers developed the Recoding-Free IAT (IAT-RF; Rothermund, Teige-Mocigemba, Gast, & Wentura, 2009) and the Single-Block IAT (SB-IAT; Teige-Mocigemba, Klauer, & Rothermund, 2008). In the IAT-RF, the category labels (White people, Black people) switch sides randomly between trials, preventing an idiosyncratic method of recoding the task. On each trial of the IAT-RF, the new category pairings are presented for 1,000 ms and then a fixation cross is presented for 500 ms where the stimuli will appear to reorient the participant's attention. In the IAT-RF, as with the IAT, participants first practice good and bad words, and then practice sorting pictures of Black people and White people before combining these two types of trials into a *critical block*. A preference for White people compared with Black people is inferred if people are able to complete the task more quickly on the trials in which Black people + bad and White people + good share response keys relative to the trials in which Black people + good and White people + bad share the same response key. The IAT-RF typically has reliability ranging from .40 to .70 (Gawronski & De Houwer, 2014). To date, there is only one use of the IAT-RF that includes a self-report measure and behavior. That study showed that an alcohol IAT-RF was not related to heavy drinkers' explicit attitudes or to problematic alcohol behavior, but that the IAT-RF did predict self-reported alcohol use (Houben, Rothermund, & Wiers, 2009).

A similar measure that was also designed to mitigate potential problems with participant recoding strategies is the S-BIAT. A participant faced with an S-BIAT would see the congruent (White people + good/Black people + bad) and incongruent (White people + bad, Black people + good) pairings on the same screen, one on the top, the other on the bottom. The pairings are separated by a dotted line and participants are instructed to sort target words using the pairings at the top of the screen when a stimulus is presented above the dotted line, and to use the pairings at the bottom of the screen when a stimulus is presented below the dotted line. A greater preference for Black people compared with White people is inferred if people are able to complete the task more quickly on the trials in which Black people + good and White people + bad share response keys relative to the trials in which Black people + bad and White people + good share the same response key, regardless of whether the pairing was at the top or bottom of the screen. The S-BIAT typically has reliability ranging from .60 to .90 (Gawronski & De Houwer, 2014). In the one investigation of the relationship between the S-BIAT and outcome measures, S-BIAT scores showed a moderate correlation (r = .43) with explicit political attitudes and predicted voting intentions; predictive ability of the S-BIAT disappeared when entered into a simultaneous regression that included explicit attitudes (Teige-Mocigemba et al., 2008).

The Single-Category Implicit Association Test and Single-Target Implicit Association Test

The Single-Category IAT (SC-IAT; Karpinski & Steinman, 2006) and Single-Target IAT (ST-IAT; Bluemke & Friese, 2008) are nearly identical measures and, in practice, the names are used interchangeably. The sole difference between the SC-IAT and the ST-IAT is that the original version of the SC-IAT required a response deadline of 1,500 or 2,000 ms in an attempt to induce a sense of speed to the task, whereas the ST-IAT does not. To avoid unnecessary confusion, we will refer to the measure as the ST-IAT.

The ST-IAT improves upon the IAT by allowing for the measurement of associations between evaluations and one single category (e.g., Black people + good and Black people + bad) rather than requiring two categories. The ST-IAT procedure is identical to that of the IAT after dropping one of the four categories (White people, in the current example). Participants sort Black people + good with one key, while using the other key to sort words into the category bad. They then complete a block during which Black people are paired with bad, and the other key is used for the category good. A more negative association with Black people is inferred if people are able to complete the task more quickly on the trials in which Black people + bad share a response key relative to the trials in which Black people + good share a response key. (For more information about scoring, see Karpinski & Steinman, 2006.)

The ST-IAT is easy to modify, measures a single attitude object with good reliability (r = .70–.90; Bar-Anan & Nosek, 2014; Gawronski & De Houwer, 2014), making it a highly recommendable implicit measure. On the down side, the ST-IAT is easier to fake than the traditional IAT (Stieger, Göritz, Hergovich, & Voracek, 2011), this is possibly caused by its simpler structure that is easier for participants to figure out and employ successful faking strategies. The ST-IAT has successfully predicted behavior in several different contexts. For example, more positive attitudes on a nuclear power ST-IAT predicted test takers' support for increasing governmental reliance on nuclear power and less reluctance to have a nuclear plant placed near their home (Truelove, Greenberg, & Powers, 2013) and a political party

ST-IAT predicted voting in the 2002 German parliamentary elections (Friese, Bluemke, & Wänke, 2007).

Brief Implicit Association Test

General Procedure

Although its name implies that it is a shorter version of the IAT, the Brief Implicit Association Test (BIAT; Sriram & Greenwald, 2009) differs structurally from the original IAT in important ways, and therefore we chose not to include it in the section on IAT variations. It is also important to know that the BIAT does not necessarily take less time for a participant to complete. Like other versions of the IAT, the BIAT is a response-competition measure. A participant faced with a BIAT is asked to press one key for any stimulus that fits into either of two focal categories (e.g., Black people and good) and a second key for any other stimuli (e.g., White people and bad). In the other block, the participant would press one key for any stimulus that fits into the category of White people and good, and a second key for any other stimuli (e.g., Black people and bad). The original authors recommend preceding these blocks with a training phase in which the participant practices how the task works, but using different categories than during the test itself; for example, participants can use one key to sort the focal categories of birds and curved objects and another key to sort the nonfocal categories of mammals and angled objects (see Sriram & Greenwald, 2009). An implicit preference for Black people is inferred if participants are able to complete the task more quickly on trials in which Black people + good share a response key relative to the trials in which White people + good share a response key. For more information about scoring, see Sriram and Greenwald (2009). Note also that the BIAT has shown to have better psychometric properties when the focal evaluative attribute is good than when it is bad (Sriram & Greenwald, 2009), although the reason for this is not yet well understood.

Relation to Behavior and Other Measures

In a comparison of seven different implicit measures, the BIAT showed the strongest relationship with explicit measures and with other implicit measures (Bar-Anan & Nosek, 2014). To date, the BIAT has only been used to predict voting behavior; a political party BIAT predicted voting intention in the 2008 Serbian parliamentary elections (Pavlović & Žeželj, 2013) and implicit race bias on the BIAT predicted voting behavior in the 2008 US presidential race between John McCain and Barack Obama (Greenwald, Smith, Sriram, Bar-Anan, & Nosek, 2009).

Benefits and Drawbacks

One of the strongest benefits of the BIAT is its high reliability (ranging from .55 to .95; Bar-Anan & Nosek, 2014; Gawronski & De Houwer, 2014). Additionally, the BIAT can be used to assess comparative associations with good between a (theoretically) infinite number of attitude objects. In order to add a third category (e.g., Asian people), a block would be added in which participants pressed the *K* key for the focal categories of Asian people and good, and the *D* key for the nonfocal categories of Black people, White people, and bad. In addition,

Asian people would be added to the nonfocal group when Black people and White people were focal. The number of categories measured is only limited by the time and energy (and patience) of the participant. This is a particular advantage of the BIAT that has been underutilized to date.

One drawback of the BIAT is the impact of order effects. At the level of the experiment, it is important to counterbalance the order of these blocks to ameliorate the effects of block order. Order effects can be reduced for individual scores by cutting each of the two critical blocks in half and randomizing the resulting four blocks (for an example, see Bar-Anan & Nosek, 2014). In addition, the BIAT is similar enough to the IAT that it suffers from similar task-specific influences such as potential recoding processes, salience asymmetries, and effects of particular stimuli (Rothermund & Wentura, 2010).

Evaluative Priming Task

Overview and Procedure

The Evaluative Priming task (EP task; Fazio, Sanbonmatsu, Powell, & Kardes, 1986) was instrumental in opening new frontiers in attitude theory and measurement. It is the second most commonly used measure in psychological research, accounting for nearly 20% of all citations using an implicit measure through 2010 (Nosek et al., 2011). The EP task is based on the assumption that the activation of one concept automatically activates (or primes) related concepts. For example, the activation of the concept *doctor* might automatically activate the concept *nurse*. The assumption of the EP task is that, to the extent that an attitude is strong, the activation of one concept automatically activates an evaluation. Responding to a *target* stimulus should be faster to the extent that the prime and evaluative target are associated. A participant faced with a typical EP task would be presented with a series of trials in which they would briefly see a picture of a Black or White individual (the prime; e.g., 200 ms) followed by a blank screen (e.g., 50 ms), and then a positive or negative word (the target). The participant's objective is to press one key (e.g., *E*) if the target is a positive word, and another key (e.g., *I*) if the target is a negative word. A stronger association between Black people and bad relative to White people and bad would be inferred if pictures of Black people facilitate (i.e., speed up) responding to negative words to a greater extent than pictures of White people facilitate responding to negative words. Although a number of variants exist, it is recommended to instantiate the measure by presenting three blocks of 60 trials each (Fazio, Jackson, Dunton, & Williams, 1995). See Wittenbrink (2007) for more specific information about scoring the EP task.

Relation to Behavior and Other Measures

The literature on the EP task is too vast to review here, and therefore we point the interested reader to the most recent review paper (Herring et al., 2013). The EP task has been shown to predict behavior in important domains; less positive attitudes toward African Americans on the part of White participants led to a more negative interracial interaction as rated by their African American experimenter (Fazio et al., 1995). Similarly, for adolescents, more negative attitudes toward Turks were related to more discriminatory behavior during a ball-tossing task (Degner, Wentura, Gniewosz, & Noack, 2007). In addition, an EP task measuring attitudes toward the television show "Big Brother" predicted minutes spent watching that show, although the predictive ability of this measure declined to nonsignificance when controlling for explicit attitudes (Frings & Wentura, 2003). A recent review of uses of an EP task to measure attitudes found that the measure related to explicit self-reports at $r = .13$ and to behavior at $r = .25$ (Cameron, Brown-Iannuzzi, & Payne, 2012).

Benefits and Drawbacks

The mechanisms and outcomes of the EP task have been studied more than almost any other measure, providing researchers with a great deal of guidance in its use (e.g., De Houwer, Teige-Mocigemba, Spruyt, & Moors, 2009; Herring et al., 2013; Klauer & Musch, 2003). Another major benefit of the EP task as an implicit measure of attitudes is that one can separately calculate associations between different primes and target categories. For example, the inclusion of a neutral baseline condition in a race EP task allows one to separately estimate the association between Black people and good, Black people and bad, White people and good, and White people and bad. However, like the IAT and SC-IAT, it may be possible for a motivated participant to deliberately control the outcome of the EP task (Teige-Mocigemba & Klauer, 2008). The primary drawback of the EP task is a big one – its reliability is notoriously low, rarely exceeding .50 and typically even lower than that (Gawronski & De Houwer, 2014).

Go/No-Go Association Task

General Procedure

The Go/No-Go Association Task (GNAT; Nosek & Banaji, 2001) assesses automatic associations between a single concept (e.g., Black people) and two evaluative categories (e.g., good, bad). A participant faced with the GNAT is instructed to hit a key (e.g., the space bar) when an item belongs to one of two labeled categories presented at the top of the computer screen (i.e., *Go*) and to do nothing when an item belongs to any other category (i.e., *No-go*). For example, in a first block, a participant might be asked to go for images of Black people and good words (and do nothing for images of White people and bad words), and then in a second block they would be required to go for images of Black people and bad words (and do nothing for images of White people and good words). The GNAT is scored using either signal detection (*d*-prime) or response latencies. If a signal detection approach is utilized (see Nosek & Banaji, 2001, for details on this scoring procedure), then a response window of 500–850 ms is advised in order to induce an appropriate level of errors necessary for scoring. If latencies are used for scoring, a response window is not necessary, although the authors do recommend using a latency deadline of 2,000 ms for target stimuli (and 1,000 ms for distractor stimuli) to encourage automatic responding. A red X is presented if participants respond incorrectly, either by mistakenly hitting the space bar during a distractor trial or by not hitting the space bar quickly enough during a target trial. When using latencies, the task is scored by calculating the average of the responses to each of the four types of trials. These averages can be compared with one another directly, or can be turned into a single indicator of evaluation toward Black people by subtracting the average latency during trials when the category of Black people is paired with the category good from trials when Black people are paired with bad words.

The GNAT has not enjoyed widespread use, but has shown good flexibility in that it has been modified to measure attitudes toward genetically modified food (Spence & Townsend, 2007), gender (Mitchell, Nosek, & Banaji, 2003), race (Sherman, Stroessner, Conrey, & Azam, 2005), and sexuality (Ranganath et al., 2008). Williams and Kaufmann (2012) provide an in-depth investigation of issues regarding GNAT design and resulting implications for reliability estimates and Vianello and Robusto (2010) of the benefits of applying a many-facet Rasch model to GNAT scoring.

Relation to Behavior and Other Measures

The GNAT relates to explicit attitudes and to other implicit measures at approximately the same level as the IAT (both r values around .40; Bar-Anan & Nosek, 2014). In terms of predicting behavior, a GNAT measuring implicit attitudes toward genetically modified food predicted spontaneous valuation of a box of chocolates described as being genetically modified (Spence & Townsend, 2007). In addition, increasingly negative attitudes toward Black people predicted less willingness to vote for Barack Obama in the 2009 presidential election and less support for his health-care plan, even when controlling for explicit prejudice (Knowles, Lowery, & Schaumberg, 2010).

Benefits and Drawbacks

The GNAT has good psychometric properties (Williams & Kaufman, 2012) including acceptable reliability (ranging from .45 to .75; Bar-Anan & Nosek, 2014; Gawronski & De Houwer, 2014). As noted above, the GNAT can be scored using a signal detection approach that is unique among implicit measures and that may be considered a benefit. The GNAT has been used very little and, as such, relatively little is known about its operation.

The Extrinsic Affective Simon Task

General Procedure

The Extrinsic Affective Simon Task (EAST; De Houwer, 2003b) assesses automatic associations between a single concept (e.g., Black people) and two evaluations categories (e.g., good, bad). In the EAST, participants see good and bad adjectives in white font and attitude-relevant stimuli in colored font (e.g., green and blue). When words are in white font, participants are instructed to sort the words on the basis of their evaluative meaning (e.g., sort good words to the left using the Q key and bad words to the right using the P key). In this way, the two keys gain a consistent valence. When the words are in color, they are instructed to sort the words based on their color (e.g., sort blue words to the left using the Q key and green words to the right using the P key). Importantly, however, all of the words for one attitude object are presented in one color (e.g., gay people in blue) while all of the words for another attitude object are presented in another color (e.g., straight people in green). Thus, the shared key structure of the IAT is duplicated, but with a less obvious evaluative flavor, which may help to reduce demand characteristics in the participant. The EAST can be scored either using the percentage of errors committed or response latencies during each of the types of responses. Assessing errors is based on the assumption that an error response indicates difficulty with the task analogous to slowing down (i.e., fewer errors is related to a stronger mental association). In the case of errors, the percentage of trials is calculated on which a participant made an error, and this number is compared with percentages in the other trials. For example, if a person makes more errors when the *Q* key is used to sort good words and words in blue (which all relate to gay people) than they do when using the *P* key to sort bad words and words in blue, it indicates a negative implicit evaluation of gay people. One can do the same thing using latencies by calculating the average latency of a participant in sorting each of the types of stimuli. Because the original EAST did not perform well as a measure of interindividual differences, the Identification-EAST (De Houwer & De Bruycker, 2007) was developed, which used lower case and upper case words in the place of colors and which showed better psychometric properties. The EAST has been modified for use as a measure of attitudes toward alcohol (De Houwer, Crombez, Koster, & De Beul, 2004; De Jong, Wiers, van de Braak, & Huijding, 2007), back pain (Houben, Gijsen, Peterson, De Jong, & Vlaeyen, 2005), spiders (Huijding & De Jong, 2006), and stigmatized groups (Degner & Wentura, 2008). The EAST has also been modified to include the use of pictures rather than words (Huijding & De Jong, 2005).

Relation to Behavior and Other Measures

Positive attitudes on an alcohol EAST predict increased alcohol use and problems with alcohol (De Jong et al., 2007).

Benefits and Drawbacks

A drawback of the EAST is its relatively low reliability (De Houwer & De Bruycker, 2007; *r* = .60–.70; Gawronski & De Houwer, 2014). The EAST has been used very little and, as such, relatively little is known about its strengths and weaknesses.

The Sorting Paired Features Task

General Procedure

The Sorting Paired Features Task (SPF; Bar-Anan, Nosek & Vianello, 2009), which shares structural similarity with the S-BIAT, is an especially interesting variant of the IAT. Like the IAT, the SPF was designed based on the assumption that it is easier to respond quickly to paired concepts that are more strongly associated in the mind. However, in the SPF this pairing occurs both at the category level and the stimulus level. In other words, rather than sorting individual stimuli into two categories in the upper left and upper right corners of the screen – as in the IAT – in the SPF, the four category combinations appear simultaneously in the four corners of the screen. In this way both *congruent* and *incongruent* blocks are presented simultaneously. Specifically, pairs of stimuli are presented in the center of the screen, one from one of the two evaluative categories, and one from one of the two attitude objects (e.g., *tall people* and *good*). The task is to sort these paired stimuli into one of the four corners of the computer screen (e.g., *tall people + good, tall people + bad, short people + good, short people + bad*) as quickly as possible, using four keys (e.g., *Q, P, C,* and *M*). If a mistake is made, a red *X* appears, and the participant must correct the mistake to continue. Latencies are recorded from the appearance of a stimulus pair until a correct response is made. Successful instantiations of the SPF have ranged from a low of 120 trials to a high of 216 trials (both in Bar-Anan et al., 2009), organized into between two and four blocks, with the positions of the paired categories either held constant or randomized across those blocks. Scores are calculated by first calculating the average latency of categorizing each of the four types of trials (e.g., tall people + good). Those scores are then used to calculate an implicit attitude toward tall people by subtracting trials in which the category tall people was paired with bad from when tall people was paired with good. Similarly, an implicit attitude toward short people is indexed by subtracting short people and bad from short people and good. From these two scores, one can calculate a relative preference by subtracting evaluations of short people from evaluations of tall people.

Relation to Behavior and Other Measures

The SPF has not yet been used to predict behavior. It is only modestly related to other implicit measures and to explicit attitudes (Bar-Anan & Nosek, 2014).

Benefits and Drawbacks

A benefit of this measurement procedure is that it allows for both the calculation of an attitude toward a single attitude object and a relative preference. Additionally, it may ameliorate order effects and effects of task recoding. The SPF has been used rarely and, as such, relatively little is known about its operation.

The Affect Misattribution Procedure

General Procedure

The Affect Misattribution Procedure (AMP; Payne, Cheng, Govorun, & Stewart, 2005) is based on the idea that the valence of a viewed stimuli will automatically transfer to a subsequently presented neutral stimuli. In particular, the AMP is composed of trials that consist of a prime (e.g., an image of a Black person presented for 75 ms), followed by a blank screen (e.g., 125 ms), then a Chinese pictograph (e.g., for 100 ms), and then a mask. The participant is instructed to ignore the prime and evaluate the pictogram; they press one key (e.g., *E*) if they find the pictograph "more pleasant than average" and another key (e.g., *I*) if they find the pictograph "less pleasant than average." In one third of the trials in the original AMP procedure, the pictograph is preceded by a neutral prime (i.e., a gray square); some subsequent instantiations have not included the neutral prime trials (Payne, Burkley, & Stokes, 2008). Unlike most implicit measures, the AMP is not scored by comparing response latencies. Instead, one calculates a proportion of the times a participant responds that a pictograph is more pleasant than average and less pleasant than average following each of the primes. For example, in an AMP with 36 trials, with 12 trials each of Black people, White people, and gray squares, it is possible to calculate the implicit positivity toward Black people (i.e., number of *pleasant* responses following pictures of Black people, divided by 12) and White people (i.e., number of pleasant responses following pictures of white people, divided by 12). Responses toward the gray squares can be used as an individual's baseline of positive responding. The AMP has been used to measure attitudes toward political candidates (Payne et al., 2005), racial groups (Payne et al., 2005), alcohol (Payne, Govorun, & Arbuckle, 2008), consumer goods (Smith et al., 2013), moral behavior (Hofmann & Baumert, 2010), and smoking (Payne, McClernon, & Dobbins, 2007). Recently, De Houwer and Smith (2013) showed that instructing participants to focus on their gut-level affective responses while completing an AMP increased effect sizes on the measure, suggesting an improvement to the commonly used task instructions.

Relation to Behavior and Other Measures

The AMP relates to self-report measures fairly well (average $r = .30$; Cameron et al., 2012). Its relationship to other implicit measures is slightly lower, perhaps owing to its uniqueness regarding procedural and scoring elements (Bar-Anan & Nosek, in press). The AMP predicts several different kinds of behaviors. For example, positivity toward alcohol is related to alcohol use (Payne, Govorun, et al., 2008); scores on an AMP measuring morality predicted emotional responses to a moral dilemma and a fairness violation (Hofmann & Baumert, 2010); and race bias on the AMP predicted voting behavior in the 2008 US presidential race between John McCain and Barack Obama (Greenwald et al., 2009; Pasek et al., 2009; Payne et al., 2010).

Benefits and Drawbacks

Use of the AMP has increased quickly in a short time period. This is likely because: (a) its internal reliability is one of the highest among implicit measures (approximately .70–.90; Gawronski & De Houwer, 2014), (b) its number of trials in the task is one of the lowest of implicit measures, making it easy to use in a short experimental session, and (c) it is possible to calculate a relative preference or an attitude toward a single category. Note that AMP effects are more pronounced for participants who admit to directly rating the primes rather than the Chinese pictographs (Bar-Anan & Nosek, 2012; compare to Payne et al., 2013). Additionally, Blaison, Imhoff, Hühnel, Hess, and Banse (2012) argue that the processes underlying the AMP might be more cold and rational than the name suggests. However, it remains an open question what this might mean for interpreting the AMP (as in Imhoff, Schmidt, Bernhardt, Dierksmeier, & Banse, 2011; Sava et al., 2012). Finally, it is important to note that the AMP cannot be used with participants who are familiar with Chinese pictographs.

The Implicit Relational Assessment Procedure

General Procedure

The Implicit Relational Assessment Procedure (IRAP; Barnes-Holmes, Hayden, Barnes-Holmes, & Stewart, 2008) is based on the idea that we can understand attitudes by understanding verbal relations between relevant stimuli. On each trial of the IRAP, participants see two stimuli, one from one of two attitude categories (e.g., *old people* and *young people*) and, underneath that, one from one of two evaluative categories (e.g., *good* or *bad*). Participants are asked to respond using two keys, where one key (e.g., *D*) indicates that the two words are *similar* and the other key (e.g., *K*) indicates that the two words are *opposite*. This occurs in two sets of blocks, the rules for which only become clear to participants as they receive feedback during the task. During the *consistent* block, a red *X* informs participants that they have made an error when they choose similar for the pairing old people and good; during the *inconsistent* block they receive error feedback when they choose similar for the pairing old people and bad.

The participant must then make the correct classification in order to continue, thereby reinforcing the rules of the particular block. The IRAP is scored by calculating the average latency to complete the block under the two rules, so that a faster score when old people and bad (and young people and good) necessitate a similar response than when they require an opposite response indicates an implicit preference for young people relative to old people.

The IRAP has not been used extensively, but appears to have promise as an implicit measure. It has been successfully modified to measure attitudes toward age groups (Cullen, Barnes-Holmes, Barnes-Holmes, & Stewart, 2009), food (Barnes-Holmes, Murtagh, Barnes-Holmes, & Stewart, 2010), the self (Vahey, Barnes-Holmes, Barnes-Holmes, & Stewart, 2009), nationalities (Power, Barnes-Holmes, Barnes-Holmes, & Stewart, 2009), and overweight people (Roddy, Stewart, & Barnes-Holmes, 2010) in addition to proving able to index newly formed attitudes (Hughes & Barnes-Holmes, 2011).

Relation to Behavior and Other Measures

Although it has been used infrequently, the original authors of the IRAP argue that it shows predictive validity comparable to the IAT (e.g., Barnes-Holmes et al., 2010; Roddy et al., 2010). A spider-evaluation IRAP distinguished between participants high and low in spider fear and predicted approach behavior toward a tarantula (Nicholson & Barnes-Holmes, 2012).

Benefits and Drawbacks

One benefit of the IRAP is that it seems to be relatively immune to faking strategies (McKenna, Barnes-Holmes, Barnes-Holmes, & Stewart, 2007). The IRAP has been used rarely beside by the original authors and, as such, relatively little is known about its strengths and weaknesses.

Conclusion

The measures described in this chapter can be considered *implicit* to the extent that the measurement outcome relies on processes that are some combination of uncontrolled, unintentional, autonomous, unconscious, efficient, or fast (De Houwer & Moors, 2015). Each is designed to promote a more complete understanding of attitudes by providing an assessment of evaluations regardless of whether an individual is willing or able to introspect and self-report their attitude. Implicit measures were once thought to capture long-lasting and trait-like attitudes that would be less malleable than people's self-reported attitudes. Indeed, some researchers even floated the premise that such measures had the potential to index a person's "true" attitude (e.g., Fazio et al., 1995). Since that time it has become clear that there is no perfect measure of an individual person's attitudes. Rather, implicit measures solve some problems with measurement (e.g., it is *relatively* difficult to fake results on them) while introducing new ones (e.g., effects of task recoding). This should not come as a surprise. After all, evaluation is exceedingly complex even before attempting to measure attitude constructs that occur automatically or outside of conscious awareness.

It is important to note in closing that a great deal of methodological and statistical rigor has been brought to bear in the development of implicit measures of attitudes, both on the side of advocates of such measures and on the side of intellectual opponents. Indeed, the sophistication and range of these measures and conversation surrounding them has been quite remarkable. However, it remains the case that implicit measures should be used with appropriate caution. For example, while millions of people have insight into their implicit attitudes on websites where you can try an implicit measure and receive feedback, such as https://implicit.harvard.edu, even researchers with the utmost confidence in the utility of implicit measures for such purposes would be extremely hesitant to use the results of a single test for diagnostic purposes. Implicit measures are currently inappropriate to use for labelling an individual person – especially based on an individual experience with an individual measure. That said, implicit measures are powerful indicators of group-level biases, and they have quickly contributed to our knowledge base in dramatic ways across a wide variety of fields. Clearly, the last two decades have been a golden age in attitude measurement as hundreds of researchers have tinkered with implicit measures – modifying them to measure countless attitude objects, while simultaneously fixing perceived flaws and continually creating new measures to diversify the ability to capture the essence of evaluations. We believe that the ongoing, vigorous debate over the use of implicit measures is a sign of a young and healthy field and look forward with great interest to the refinement of current measures and development of new measures that are sure to come.

References

Bar-Anan, Y., & Nosek, B. A. (2012). Reporting intentional rating of the primes predicts priming effects in the Affective Misattribution Procedure. *Personality and Psychology Bulletin, 38*, 1194–1208. http://doi.org/10.1177/0146167212446835

Bar-Anan, Y., & Nosek, B. A. (2014). A comparative investigation of seven implicit measures of social cognition. *Behavior Research Methods, 46*, 668–688. http://doi.org/10.3758/s13428-013-0410-6

Bar-Anan, Y., Nosek, B. A., & Vianello, M. (2009). The sorting paired features task: A measure of association strengths. *Experimental Psychology, 56*, 329–343. http://doi.org/10.1027/1618-3169.56.5.329

Barnes-Holmes, D., Hayden, E., Barnes-Holmes, Y., & Stewart, I. (2008). The Implicit Relational Assessment Procedure (IRAP) as a response-time and event-related-potentials methodology for testing natural verbal relations: A preliminary study. *The Psychological Record, 58*, 497–516.

Barnes-Holmes, D., Murtagh, L., Barnes-Holmes, Y., & Stewart, I. (2010). Using the Implicit Association Test and the Implicit Relational Assessment Procedure to measure attitudes toward meat and vegetables in vegetarians and meat-eaters. *The Psychological Record, 60*, 287–306.

Blaison, C., Imhoff, R., Hühnel, I., Hess, U., & Banse, R. (2012). The affect misattribution procedure: Hot or not? *Emotion, 12*, 403–412. http://doi.org/10.1037/a0026907

Blanton, H., & Jaccard, J. (2006). Arbitrary metrics in psychology. *American Psychologist, 61*, 27–41. http://doi.org/10.1037/0003-066X.61.1.62

Bluemke, M., & Friese, M. (2008). Reliability and validity of the Single-Target IAT (ST-IAT): Assessing automatic affect towards multiple attitude objects. *European Journal of Social Psychology, 38*, 977–997. http://doi.org/10.1002/ejsp.487

Cameron, C. D., Brown-Iannuzzi, J. L., & Payne, B. K. (2012). Sequential priming measures of implicit social cognition. A meta-analysis of associations with behavior and explicit attitudes. *Personality and Social Psychology Review, 16*, 330–350. http://doi.org/10.1177/1088868312440047

Cullen, C., Barnes-Holmes, D., Barnes-Holmes, Y., & Stewart, I. (2009). The Implicit Relational Assessment Procedure (IRAP) and the malleability of ageist attitudes. *The Psychological Record, 59*, 591–620.

Degner, J., & Wentura, D. (2008). The extrinsic affective Simon task as an instrument for indirect assessment of prejudice. *European Journal of Social Psychology, 38*, 1033–1043. http://doi.org/10.1002/ejsp.536

Degner, J., Wentura, D., Gniewosz, B., & Noack, P. (2007). Hostility-related prejudice against Turks in adolescents: Masked affective priming allows for a differentiation of automatic prejudice. *Basic and Applied Social Psychology, 29*, 245–256. http://doi.org/10.1080/01973530701503150

De Houwer, J. (2003a). The extrinsic affective Simon task. *Experimental Psychology, 50*, 77–85. http://doi.org/10.1026//1618-3169.50.2.77

De Houwer, J. (2003b). A structural analysis of indirect measures of attitudes. In J. Musch & K. C. Klauer (Eds.), *The psychology of evaluation: Affective processes in cognition and emotion* (pp. 219–244). Mahwah, NJ: Erlbaum.

De Houwer, J. (2009). Comparing measures of attitudes at the procedural and functional level. In R. E. Petty, R. H. Fazio, & P. Briñol (Eds.), *Attitudes: Insights from the new implicit measures* (pp. 361–390). New York, NY: Psychology Press.

De Houwer, J., Beckers, T., & Moors, A. (2007). Novel attitudes can be faked on the Implicit Association Test. *Journal of Experimental Social Psychology, 43*, 972–978. http://doi.org/10.1016/j.jesp.2006.10.007

De Houwer, J., Crombez, G., Koster, E. H., & De Beul, N. (2004). Implicit alcohol-related cognitions in a clinical sample of heavy drinkers. *Journal of Behavior Therapy and Experimental Psychiatry, 35*, 275–286. http://doi.org/10.1016/j.jbtep.2004.05.001

De Houwer, J., Custers, R., & De Clercq, A. (2006). Do smokers have a negative implicit attitude towards smoking? *Cognition and Emotion, 20*, 1274–1284. http://doi.org/10.1080/02699930500484506

De Houwer, J., & De Bruycker, E. (2007). The identification-EAST as a valid measure of implicit attitudes toward alcohol-related stimuli. *Journal of Behavior Therapy and Experimental Psychiatry, 38*, 133–143. http://doi.org/10.1016/j.jbtep.2006.10.004

De Houwer, J., Geldof, T., & De Bruycker, E. (2005). The Implicit Association Test as a general measure of similarity. *Canadian Journal of Experimental Psychology, 59*, 228–239. http://doi.org/10.1037/h0087478

De Houwer, J., & Moors, A. (2015). Levels of explanation in social psychology. In B. Gawronski & G. Bodenhausen (Eds.), *Theory and explanation in social psychology* (pp. 24–40). New York, NY: Guilford press.

De Houwer, J., & Smith, C. T. (2013). Go with your gut! Effects in the Affect Misattribution Procedure become stronger when participants are encouraged to rely on their gut feelings. *Social Psychology, 44*, 299–302. http://doi.org/10.1027/1864-9335/a000115

De Houwer, J., Teige-Mocigemba, S., Spruyt, A., & Moors, A. (2009). Implicit measures: A normative analysis and review. *Psychological Bulletin, 135*, 347–368. http://doi.org/10.1037/a0014211

De Jong, P. J., Wiers, R. W., Van de Braak, M., & Huijding, J. (2007). Using the Extrinsic Affective Simon Test as a measure of implicit attitudes towards alcohol: Relationship with drinking behavior and alcohol problems. *Addictive Behaviors, 32*, 881–887. http://doi.org/10.1016/j.addbeh.2006.06.017

Dovidio, J. F., Kawakami, K., & Gaertner, S. L. (2002). Implicit and explicit prejudice and interracial interaction. *Journal of Personality and Social Psychology, 82*, 62–68. http://doi.org/10.1037/0022-3514.82.1.62

Eagly, A. H., & Chaiken, S. (1998). Attitude structure and function. In D. T. Gilbert, S. T. Fiske, & G. Lindzey (Eds.), *The handbook of social psychology* (4th ed., Vols. 1 & 2, pp. 269–322). New York, NY: McGraw-Hill.

Fazio, R. H., Jackson, J. R., Dunton, B. C., & Williams, C. J. (1995). Variability in automatic activation as an unobtrusive measure of racial attitudes: A bona fide pipeline? *Journal of Personality and Social Psychology, 69*, 1013. http://doi.org/10.1037/0022-3514.69.6.1013

Fazio, R. H., & Olson, M. A. (2003). Implicit measures in social cognition research: Their meaning and use. *Annual Review of Psychology, 54*, 297–327. http://doi.org/10.1146/annurev.psych.54.101601.145225

Fazio, R. H., Sanbonmatsu, D. M., Powell, M. C., & Kardes, F. R. (1986). On the automatic activation of attitudes. *Journal of Personality and Social Psychology, 50*, 229–238. http://doi.org/10.1037/0022-3514.50.2.229

Fiedler, K., & Bluemke, M. (2005). Faking the IAT: Aided and unaided response control on the Implicit Association Tests. *Basic and Applied Social Psychology, 27*, 307–316. http://doi.org/10.1207/s15324834basp2704_3

Fiedler, K., Messner, C., & Bluemke, M. (2006). Unresolved problems with the "I", the "A", and the "T": A logical and psychometric critique of the Implicit Association Test (IAT). *European Review of Social Psychology, 17*, 74–147. http://doi.org/10.1080/10463280600681248

Friese, M., Bluemke, M., & Wänke, M. (2007). Predicting voting behavior with implicit attitude measures. *Experimental Psychology, 54,* 247–255. http://doi.org/10.1027/1618-3169.54.4.247

Friese, M., Hofmann, W., & Wänke, M. (2008). When impulses take over: Moderated predictive validity of implicit and explicit attitude measures in predicting food choice and consumption behavior. *British Journal of Social Psychology, 47,* 397–419. http://doi.org/10.1348/014466607X241540

Friese, M., Smith, C. T., Plischke, T., Bluemke, M., & Nosek, B. A. (2012). Do implicit attitudes predict actual voting behavior particularly for undecided voters? *PLoS ONE, 7,* e44130. http://doi.org/10.1371/journal.pone.0044130

Frings, C., & Wentura, D. (2003). Who is watching Big Brother? TV consumption predicted by masked affective priming. *European Journal of Social Psychology, 33,* 779–791. http://doi.org/10.1002/ejsp.167

Gawronski, B. (2002). What does the Implicit Association Test measure? A test of the convergent and discriminant validity of prejudice-related IATs. *Experimental Psychology, 49,* 171–180. http://doi.org/10.1027//1618-3169.49.3.171

Gawronski, B., & De Houwer, J. (2014). Implicit measures in social and personality psychology. In H. T. Reis & C. M. Judd (Eds.), *Handbook of research methods in social and personality psychology* (2nd ed., pp. 283–310). New York, NY: Cambridge University Press.

Gawronski, B., & LeBel, E. P. (2008). Understanding patterns of attitude change: When implicit measures show change, but explicit measures do not. *Journal of Experimental Social Psychology, 44,* 1355–1361. http://doi.org/10.1016/j.jesp.2008.04.005

Gawronski, B., & Payne, B. K. (Eds.) (2010). *Handbook of implicit social cognition: Measurement, theory, and applications.* New York: NY: Guilford Press.

Gawronski, B., Peters, K. R., & LeBel, E. P. (2008). What makes mental associations personal or extrapersonal? Conceptual issues in the methodological debate about implicit attitude measures. *Social and Personality Psychology Compass, 2,* 1002–1023. http://doi.org/10.1111/j.1751-9004.2008.00085.x

Goff, P. A., Eberhardt, J. L., Williams, M. J., & Jackson, M. (2008). Not yet human: Implicit knowledge, historical dehumanization, and contemporary consequences. *Journal of Personality and Social Psychology, 94,* 292–306. http://doi.org/10.1037/0022-3514.94.2.292

Green, A. R., Carnet, D. R., Pallin, D. J., Ngo, L. H., Raymond, K. L., Iezzoni, L. I., & Banaji, M. R. (2007). Implicit bias among physicians and its prediction of thrombolysis decisions for black and white patients. *Journal of General Internal Medicine, 22,* 1231–1238. http://doi.org/10.1007/s11606-007-0258-5

Greenwald, A. G., & Banaji, M. R. (1995). Implicit social cognition: Attitudes, self-esteem, and stereotypes. *Psychological Review, 102,* 4–27. http://doi.org/10.1037/0033-295X.102.1.4

Greenwald, A. G., McGhee, D. E., & Schwartz, J. L. K. (1998). Measuring individual differences in implicit cognition: The Implicit Association Test. *Journal of Personality and Social Psychology, 74,* 1464–1480. http://doi.org/10.1037/0022-3514.74.6.1464

Greenwald, A. G., Nosek, B. A., & Banaji, M. R. (2003). Understanding and using the Implicit Association Test: I. An improved scoring algorithm. *Journal of Personality and Social Psychology, 85,* 197–216. http://doi.org/10.1037/h0087889

Greenwald, A. G., Poehlman, T. A., Uhlmann, E., & Banaji, M. R. (2009). Understanding and using the Implicit Association Test: III. Meta-analysis of predictive validity. *Journal of Personality and Social Psychology, 97,* 17–41. http://doi.org/10.1037/a0015575

Greenwald, A. G., Smith, C. T., Sriram, N., Bar-Anan, Y., & Nosek, B. A. (2009). Race attitude measures predicted vote in the 2008 U. S. presidential election. *Analysis of Social Issues and Public Policy, 9,* 241–253. http://doi.org/10.1111/j.1530-2415.2009.01195.x

Han, H. A., Czellar, S., Olson, M. A., & Fazio, R. H. (2010). Malleability of attitudes or malleability of the IAT? *Journal of Experimental Social Psychology, 46,* 286–298. http://doi.org/10.1016/j.jesp.2009.11.011

Han, H. A., Olson, M. A., & Fazio, R. H. (2006). The influence of experimentally-created extrapersonal associations on the Implicit Association Test. *Journal of Experimental Social Psychology, 42,* 259–272. http://doi.org/10.1016/j.jesp.2005.04.006

Herring, D. R., White, K. R., Jabeen, L. N., Hinojos, M., Terrazas, G., Reyes, S. M., … Crites, S. L. (2013). On the automatic activation of attitudes: A quarter century of evaluative priming research. *Psychological Bulletin, 139,* 1062–1089. http://doi.org/10.1037/a0031309

Hofmann, W., & Baumert, A. (2010). Immediate affect as a basis for intuitive moral judgement: An adaptation of the affect misattribution procedure. *Cognition and Emotion, 24*, 522–535. http://doi.org/10.1080/02699930902847193

Hofmann, W., Gawronski, B., Gschwendner, T., Le, H., & Schmitt, M. (2005). A meta-analysis on the correlation between the Implicit Association Test and explicit self-report measures. *Personality and Social Psychology Bulletin, 31*, 1369–1385. http://doi.org/10.1177/0146167205275613

Hofmann, W., Gschwendner, T., Nosek, B. A., & Schmitt, M. (2005). What moderates implicit-explicit consistency? *European Review of Social Psychology, 16*, 335–390. http://doi.org/10.1080/10463280500443228

Houben, R. M. A., Gijsen, A., Peterson, J., De Jong, P. J., & Vlaeyen, J. W. S. (2005). Do health care providers' attitudes towards back pain predict their treatment recommendations? Differential predictive validity of implicit and explicit attitude measures. *Pain, 114*, 491–498. http://doi.org/10.1016/j.pain.2005.01.017

Houben, K., Rothermund, K., & Wiers, R. W. (2009). Predicting alcohol use with a recoding-free variant of the Implicit Association Test. *Addictive Behaviors, 34*, 487–489. http://doi.org/10.1016/j.addbeh.2008.12.012

Houben, K., & Wiers, R. W. (2007). Are drinkers implicitly positive about drinking alcohol? Personalizing the alcohol-IAT to reduce negative extrapersonal contamination. *Alcohol and Alcoholism, 42*, 301–307. http://doi.org/10.1093/alcalc/agm015

Hughes, S., & Barnes-Holmes, D. (2011). On the formation and persistence of implicit attitudes: New evidence from the Implicit Relational Assessment Procedure (IRAP). *The Psychological Record, 61*, 391–410.

Huijding, J., & De Jong, P. J. (2005). A pictorial version of the Extrinsic Affective Simon Task: Sensitivity to generally affective and phobia-relevant stimuli in high and low spider fearful individuals. *Experimental Psychology, 52*, 289–295. http://doi.org/10.1027/1618-3169.52.4.289

Huijding, J., & De Jong, P. J. (2006). Specific predictive power of automatic spider-related affective associations for controllable and uncontrollable fear responses toward spiders. *Behaviour Research and Therapy, 44*, 161–176. http://doi.org/10.1016/j.brat.2005.01.007

Huntsinger, J. R. (2013). Anger enhances correspondence between implicit and explicit attitudes. *Emotion, 13*, 350–357. http://doi.org/10.1037/a0029974

Huntsinger, J. R., & Smith, C. T. (2009). First thought, best thought: Positive mood maintains and negative mood disrupts implicit-explicit attitude correspondence. *Personality and Social Psychology Bulletin, 35*, 187–197. http://doi.org/10.1177/0146167208327000

Imhoff, R., Schmidt, A. F., Bernhardt, J., Dierksmeier, A., & Banse, R. (2011). An inkblot for sexual preference: A semantic variant of the Affect Misattribution Procedure. *Cognition and Emotion, 25*, 676–690. http://doi.org/10.1080/02699931.2010.508260

Karpinksi, A., & Steinman, R. B. (2006). The Single Category Implicit Association Test as a measure of implicit social cognition. *Journal of Personality and Social Psychology, 91*, 16–32. http://doi.org/10.1037/0022-3514.91.1.16

Karpinski, A., Steinman, R. B., & Hilton, J. L. (2005). Attitude importance as a moderator of the relationship between implicit and explicit attitude measures. *Personality and Social Psychology Bulletin, 31*, 949–962. http://doi.org/10.1177/0146167204273007

Klauer, K., & Musch, C. (2003). Affective priming: Findings and theories. In J. Musch & K. C. Klauer (Eds.), *The psychology of evaluation: Affective processes in cognition and emotion* (pp. 7–49). Mahwah, NJ: Erlbaum.

Knowles, E. D., Lowery, B. & Schaumberg, R. L. (2010). Racial prejudice predicts opposition to Obama and his health care reform plan. *Journal of Experimental Social Psychology, 46*, 420–423. http://doi.org/10.1016/j.jesp.2009.10.011

Lane, K. A., Banaji, M. R., Nosek, B. A., & Greenwald, A. G. (2007). Understanding and using the Implicit Association Test: IV. What we know (so far). In B. Wittenbrink & N. S. Schwarz (Eds.), *Implicit measures of attitudes: Procedures and controversies* (pp. 59–102). New York, NY: Guilford Press.

LeBel, E. P., & Campbell, L. (2009). Implicit partner affect, relationship satisfaction, and the prediction of romantic breakup. *Journal of Experimental Social Psychology, 45*, 1291–1294. http://doi.org/10.1016/j.jesp.2009.07.003

Maison, D., Greenwald, A. G., & Bruin, R. H. (2004). Predictive validity of the Implicit Association Test in studies of brands, consumer attitudes, and behavior. *Journal of Consumer Psychology, 14*, 405–415. http://doi.org/10.1207/s15327663jcp1404_9

McKenna, I. M., Barnes-Holmes, D., Barnes-Holmes, Y., & Stewart, I. (2007). Testing the fake-ability of the Implicit Relational Assessment Procedure (IRAP): The first study. *International Journal of Psychology and Psychological Therapy, 7*, 253–268.

Mitchell, J. P., Nosek, B. A., & Banaji, M. R. (2003). Contextual variations in implicit evaluation. *Journal of Experimental Psychology: General, 132*, 455–469. http://doi.org/10.1037/0096-3445.132.3.455

Nicholson, E., & Barnes-Holmes, D. (2012). The Implicit Relational Assessment Procedure (IRAP) as a measure of spider fear. *Psychological Record, 62*, 263–278.

Nisbett, R. E., & Wilson, T. D. (1977). Telling more than we can know: Verbal reports on mental processes. *Psychological Review, 84*, 231–259. http://doi.org/10.1037/0033-295X.84.3.231

Nock, M. K., Park, J. M., Finn, C. T., Deliberto, T. L., Dour, H., J., & Banaji, M. R. (2010). Measuring the "suicidal mind": Implicit cognition predicts suicidal behavior. *Psychological Science, 21*, 511–517. http://doi.org/10.1177/0956797610364762

Nosek, B. A. (2005). Moderators of the relationship between implicit and explicit evaluation. *Journal of Experimental Psychology: General, 134*, 565–584. http://doi.org/10.1037/0096-3445.134.4.565

Nosek, B. A., & Banaji, M. R. (2001). The go/no-go association task. *Social Cognition, 19*, 625–666. http://doi.org/10.1521/soco.19.6.625.20886

Nosek, B. A., Greenwald, A. G., & Banaji, M. R. (2005). Understanding and using the Implicit Association Test: II. Method variables and construct validity. *Personality and Social Psychology Bulletin, 31*, 166–180. http://doi.org/10.1177/0146167204271418

Nosek, B. A., & Hansen, J. J. (2008). The associations in our heads belong to us: Searching for attitudes and knowledge in implicit evaluation. *Cognition and Emotion, 22*, 553–594. http://doi.org/10.1080/02699930701438186

Nosek, B. A., Hawkins, C. B., & Frazier, R. S. (2011). Implicit social cognition: From measures to mechanisms. *Trends in Cognitive Sciences, 15*, 152–159. http://doi.org/10.1016/j.tics.2011.01.005

Olson, M. A., Crawford, M. T., & Devlin, W. (2009). Evidence for the underestimation of implicit ingroup favoritism among low-status groups. *Journal of Experimental Social Psychology, 45*, 1111–1116. http://doi.org/10.1016/j.jesp.2009.06.021

Olson, M. A., & Fazio, R. H. (2004). Reducing the influence of extrapersonal associations on the Implicit Association Test: Personalizing the IAT. *Journal of Personality and Social Psychology, 86*, 653–667. http://doi.org/10.1037/0022-3514.86.5.653

Oswald, F. L., Mitchell, G., Blanton, H., Jaccard, J., & Tetlock, P. E. (2013). Predicting ethnic and racial discrimination: A meta-analysis of IAT criterion studies. *Journal of Personality and Social Psychology, 105*, 171–192. http://doi.org/10.1037/a0032734

Pasek, J., Tahk, A., Lelkes, Y., Krosnick, J. A., Payne, B. K., Akhtar, O., & Tompson, T. (2009). Determinants of turnout and candidate choice in the 2008 US presidential election illuminating the impact of racial prejudice and other considerations. *Public Opinion Quarterly, 73*, 943–994. http://doi.org/10.1093/poq/nfp079

Pavlović, M. D., & Žeželj, I. L. (2013). Brief Implicit Association Test: Validity and utility in prediction of voting behavior. *Psihologija, 46*, 261–278. http://doi.org/10.2298/PSI130606004P

Paulhus, D. L. (1991). Measurement and control of response bias. In J. P. Robinson, P. R. Shaver, & L. S. Wrightsman (Eds.), *Measures of personality and social psychological attitudes* (pp. 17–59). San Diego, CA: Academic Press.

Payne, B. K., Brown-Iannuzzi, J., Burkley, M., Arbuckle, N. L., Cooley, E., Cameron, C. D., & Lundberg, K. B. (2013). Intention Invention and the Affect Misattribution Procedure: Reply to Bar-Anan and Nosek (2012). *Personality and Social Psychology Bulletin, 39*, 375–386. http://doi.org/10.1177/0146167212475225

Payne, B. K., Burkley, M. A., & Stokes, M. B. (2008). Why do implicit and explicit attitude tests diverge? The role of structural fit. *Journal of Personality and Social Psychology, 94*, 16–31. http://doi.org/10.1037/0022-3514.94.1.16

Payne, B. K., Cheng, C. M., Govorun, O., & Stewart, B. D. (2005). An inkblot for attitudes: Affect misattribution as implicit measurement. *Journal of Personality and Social Psychology, 89*, 277–293. http://doi.org/10.1037/0022-3514.89.3.277

Payne, B. K., Govorun, O., & Arbuckle, N. L. (2008). Automatic attitudes and alcohol: Does implicit liking predict drinking? *Cognition & Emotion, 22*, 238–271. http://doi.org/10.1080/02699930701357394

Payne, B. K., Krosnick, J. A., Pasek, J., Lelkes, Y., Akhtar, O., & Tompson, T. (2010). Implicit and explicit prejudice in the 2008 American presidential election. *Journal of Experimental Social Psychology, 46*, 367–374. http://doi.org/10.1016/j.jesp.2009.11.001

Payne, B. K., McClernon, F. J., & Dobbins, I. G. (2007). Automatic affective responses to smoking cues. *Experimental and Clinical Psychopharmacology, 15*, 400–409. http://doi.org/10.1037/1064-1297.15.4.400

Petty, R. E., Fazio, R. H., & Briñol, P. (2009). The new implicit measures: An overview. In R. E. Petty, R. H. Fazio, & P. Briñol (Eds.), *Attitudes: Insights from the new implicit measures* (pp. 3–18). New York, NY: Psychology Press.

Power, P. M., Barnes-Holmes, D., Barnes-Holmes, Y., & Stewart, I. (2009). The Implicit Relational Assessment Procedure (IRAP) as a measure of implicit relative preferences: A first study. *The Psychological Record, 59*, 621–640.

Ranganath, K. A., Smith, C. T., & Nosek, B. A. (2008). Distinguishing automatic and controlled components of attitudes from direct and indirect measurement methods. *Journal of Experimental Social Psychology, 44*, 386–396. http://doi.org/10.1016/j.jesp.2006.12.008

Roddy, S., Stewart, I., & Barnes-Holmes, D. (2010). Anti-fat, pro-slim, or both? Using two reaction-time based measures to assess implicit attitudes to the slim and overweight. *Journal of Health Psychology, 15*, 416–425. http://doi.org/10.1177/1359105309350232

Rothermund, K., Teige-Mocigemba, S., Gast, A., & Wentura, D. (2009). Minimizing the influence of recoding in the Implicit Association Test: The Recoding-Free Implicit Association Test (IAT-RF). *The Quarterly Journal of Experimental Psychology, 62*, 84–98. http://doi.org/10.1080/17470210701822975

Rothermund, K., & Wentura, D. (2010). It's brief but is it better? An evaluation of the Brief Implicit Association Test. *Experimental Psychology, 57*, 233–237. http://doi.org/10.1027/1618-3169/a000060

Rothermund, K., Wentura, D., & De Houwer, J. (2005). Validity of the salience asymmetry account of the IAT: Reply to Greenwald, Nosek, Banaji, and Klauer (2005). *Journal of Experimental Psychology: General, 134*, 426–430. http://doi.org/10.1037/0096-3445.134.3.426

Sava, F. A., Maricutoiu, L. P., Rusu, S., Macsinga, I., Vîrg , D., Cheng, C. M., & Payne, B. K. (2012). An Inkblot for the Implicit Assessment of Personality: The Semantic Misattribution Procedure. *European Journal of Personality, 26*, 613–628. http://doi.org/10.1002/per.1861

Schwarz, N. (1999). Self-reports: How the questions shape the answer. *American Psychologist, 54*, 93–105. http://doi.org/10.1037/0003-066X.54.2.93

Sherman, J. W., Stroessner, S. J., Conrey, F. R., & Azam, O. A. (2005). Prejudice and stereotype maintenance processes: Attention, attribution, and individuation. *Journal of Personality and Social Psychology, 89*, 607–622. http://doi.org/10.1037/0022-3514.89.4.607

Smith, C. T., De Houwer, J., & Nosek, B. A. (2013). Consider the source: Persuasion of implicit evaluations is moderated by manipulations of source credibility. *Personality and Social Psychology Bulletin, 39*, 193–205. http://doi.org/10.1177/0146167212472374

Smith, C. T., & Nosek, B. A. (2011). Affective focus increases the concordance between implicit and explicit attitudes. *Social Psychology, 42*, 300–313. http://doi.org/10.1027/1864-9335/a000072

Spence, A., & Townsend, E. (2007). Predicting behaviour towards genetically modified food using implicit and explicit attitudes. *British Journal of Social Psychology, 46*, 437–457. http://doi.org/10.1348/014466606X152261

Sriram, N., & Greenwald, A. G. (2009). The brief implicit association test. *Experimental Psychology, 56*, 283–294. http://doi.org/10.1027/1618-3169.56.4.283

Steffans, M. C. (2004). Is the Implicit Association Test immune to faking? *Experimental Psychology, 51*, 165–179. http://doi.org/10.1027/1618-3169.51.3.165

Stieger, S., Göritz, A. S., Hergovich, A., & Voracek, M. (2011). Intentional faking of the Single Category Implicit Association Test and the Implicit Association Test. *Psychological Reports, 109*, 219–230. http://doi.org/10.2466/03.09.22.28.PR0.109.4.219-230

Teige-Mocigemba, S., & Klauer, K. C. (2008). 'Automatic' evaluation? Strategic effects on affective priming. *Journal of Experimental Social Psychology, 44*, 1414–1417. http://doi.org/10.1016/j.jesp.2008.04.004

Teige-Mocigemba, S., Klauer, K. C., & Rothermund, K. (2008). Minimizing method-specific variance in the IAT. *European Journal of Psychological Assessment, 24*, 237–245. http://doi.org/10.1027/1015-5759.24.4.237

Truelove, H. B., Greenberg, M. R., & Powers, C. W. (2013). Are implicit associations with nuclear energy related to policy support? Evidence from the Brief Implicit Association Test. *Environment and Behavior, 46*, 898–923. http://doi.org/10.1177/0013916513480861

Uhlmann, E. L., Leavitt, K., Menges, J. I., Koopman, J., Howe, M., & Johnson, R. E. (2012). Getting explicit about the implicit: A taxonomy of implicit measures and guide for their use in organizational research. *Organizational Research Methods, 15*, 553–601. http://doi.org/10.1177/1094428112442750

Uhlmann, E. L., Poehlman, T. A., & Nosek, B. A. (2012). Automatic associations: Personal attitudes or cultural knowledge? In J. Hanson (Ed.), *Ideology, psychology, and law* (pp. 228–260). Oxford, UK: Oxford University Press.

Vahey, N. A., Barnes-Holmes, D., Barnes-Holmes, Y., & Stewart, I. (2009). A first test of the Implicit Relational Assessment Procedure as a measure of self-esteem: Irish prisoner groups and university students. *The Psychological Record, 59*, 371–388.

Vianello, M., & Robusto, E. (2010). The Rasch models in the analysis of the Go/No Go Association Task. *Behavior Research Methods, 42*, 944–956. http://doi.org/10.3758/BRM.42.4.944

Wentura, D., & Rothermund, K. (2007). Paradigms we live by. A plea for more basic research on the IAT. In B. Wittenbrink & N. Schwarz (Eds.), *Implicit measures of attitudes* (pp. 195–215). New York, NY: Guilford Press.

Williams, B. J., & Kaufmann, L. M. (2012). Reliability of the Go/No-Go Association Task. *Journal of Experimental Social Psychology, 48*, 879–891. http://doi.org/10.1016/j.jesp.2012.03.001

Wittenbrink, B. (2007). Measuring attitudes through priming. In B. Wittenbrink & N. Schwarz (Eds.), *Implicit measures of attitudes* (pp. 17–58). New York, NY: Guilford Press.

Chapter 9
Objective Personality Tests

Tuulia M. Ortner[1] and René T. Proyer[2]

[1]Department of Psychology, University of Salzburg, Austria
[2]Department of Psychology, University of Zurich, Switzerland

This chapter aims to provide an overview of current developments and research on so-called objective personality tests (OPTs). After a short introductory overview of their history, the specifications and definitions of OPTs are discussed. We further present a system that aims to distinguish between three different categories of OPTs. We then outline the state of research on the psychometric properties of OPTs, especially with regard to findings on their reliability and validity. Finally, we make suggestions for future research and comment on the application of OPTs in practice.

A Short Overview of the History of OPTs in Psychological Assessment

The practice of obtaining information about personality from sources that go beyond self-reports by including samples of test takers' overt behavior has a history in psychological measurement as long as psychological testing itself. In fact, some initial concepts of OPTs were introduced in the late 19th century by the pioneer James McKeen Cattell as *mental tests*. In 1890, he proposed a series of 10 tests based on "experiment and measurement," thus aspiring to apply the exactness of the physical sciences. His battery contained heterogeneous tasks, including measures of personality. For example, the Dynamometer Pressure Test assessed a person's maximum possible squeeze of the hand and was supposed to measure effort and volitional aspects beyond mere physiological power.

Decades later, documentation on psychological testing during the Second World War indicated the use of objective personality testing-like procedures. For example, tests of perceptual abilities were employed in the German military in order to tap aspects of "character and personality structure" (see Fitts, 1946). During that time, the Office of American Strategic Services (OSS) also reported that emotional stability and tolerance for frustration were assessed via observation in standardized problem solving tasks (OSS Assessment Staff, 1948).

The current concepts of OPTs can be traced back to a more recent history of OPTs that began in the second half of the 20th century. These can be divided into two periods: Tests of the *first* generation were a result of Raymond Bernard Cattell's comprehensive theoretical approach that was based on the idea that a complete investigation of personality requires the inclusion of heterogeneous data based on three sources of information. In addition to self-reports (Q-data) and biographical data (L-data; Cattell, 1946; Cattell & Kline, 1977), he described tests (T-data) as one of the three sources of information in personality assessment. In order to allow for the assessment of T-data, Cattell and his collaborators developed the first generation of OPTs with the aim of designing Cursive Miniature Situations (Cattell, 1941, 1944) that simulate the behavioral expression of personality while meeting common standards of psychological tests. Within his prolific and decades-long period of test development, Cattell had already proposed no fewer than 500 tests by the mid-1960s. These were characterized by great variation with reference to materials and scoring methods (e.g., Cattell, 1968; Schuerger, 2008). In order to assess T-data, he included behavior samples, physical performance checks, and psychophysiological data as well as so-called projective techniques and creative design tasks. At the beginning of his research, the variables he included were related to Eysenck's research on personality as well as Thurstone's work in the domain of intelligence and perceptual variables (see Hundleby, Pawlik, & Cattell, 1965; Schmidt, 2006). In his research, he also incorporated questionnaire-like tests that were supposed to be able to hide what was being measured. He investigated the relations between these measures as well as the common structure that supported them (Cattell, 1948). Efforts by Cattell and his colleagues also led to the publication of the well-known Objective-Analytic Test Battery (Cattell & Schuerger, 1976, 1978); for an overview, see Kline and Cooper (1984) and Schuerger (2008).

Tests labeled as the *second* generation of OPTs emerged in the 1990s. They benefitted from the development of computer technologies that can provide highly flexible methods of item presentation and precise registration of a person's behavior (Ortner et al., 2007). Tests of the first generation were mostly designed in a *bottom–up* approach that aimed to provide additional information within a holistic approach and referred to personality factors according to empirical analyses in line with Cattell's theoretical framework. Tests of the second generation, by contrast, addressed specific personality-related concepts, such as achievement motivation, reflexivity vs. impulsivity, the ability to work under pressure, or vocational interests (for an overview, see Ortner et al., 2007). New technologies and opportunities in the measurement domain also allowed for broader varieties of task presentations, variables incorporated as scores, and interpretation. Examples include the use of tachistoscopically presented stimuli (e.g., Proyer, 2007; Proyer & Häusler, 2007), viewing times, reaction times (e.g., Proyer, 2007), reaction speed (Schmidt-Atzert, 2007), or other variables related to test performance (e.g., orientation of a figure in a maze; Ortner, Kubinger, Schrott, Radinger, & Litzenberger, 2006). In line with these technical advances, contemporary OPTs are characterized by greater user-friendliness compared with earlier approaches. Furthermore, new OPTs have overcome the criticism that examiners had to put forth enormous effort and face certain challenges during the administration of at least some tests. This second generation of OPTs is prevalent across many European countries.

Specification and Definitions of Objective Personality Tests

Several names and definitions for the group of tests addressed as OPTs have been proposed. Objective-analytic tests (Cattell, 1955) or simply objective tests (e.g., Cattell, 1946) are well-known terms and were suggested in a framework that also assigned standardized ability and achievement tests to this group. Performance tests of personality (Cronbach, 1970) was also suggested as a name. More recently, Kubinger (2009) introduced the term experiment-based assessment for measures that infer characteristics of personal style from observable behavior on "experimentally varied performance tasks." However, the term experiment is not meant to imply that OPTs are experiments in a narrow sense since the measurement procedure has to fulfill common psychometric standards.

R. B. Cattell (1968) distinguished the following two forms of objectivity in order to clarify the meaning of *objective* in OPTs: In the domain of psychological assessment, this term is used to indicate whether the result obtained by a test has been influenced by external conditions such as the setting, testing environment, testing materials, and examiners (see Pawlik, 2006). Cattell (1968) introduced a second, new *higher degree of objectivity* to specify the characteristics of OPTs:

> Observations on personality made by measuring actual behavior in a miniature situation – a test. The person reacts to a standard stimulus situation, and his behavior is measured in ways of which he may not be aware and with interpretations of which he will certainly not be cognizant. (p. 165)

Cattell wrote about the test taker, "[...] even when he wished to, he cannot know himself objectively enough to give a true picture" (Cattell, 1968, p. 53). In line with this reasoning, OPTs were designed to eliminate distortion through poor self-knowledge or impression management by assessing observable behavior as opposed to the self-reported behavior or attitudes assessed by questionnaires. As an additional potential benefit of OPTs, Cattell stated that a dependence on features related to language is present to a lesser extent in OPTs compared with questionnaires. "Only when experimental measurement is made in terms of behavioral response on exactly reproducible test situations can one have confidence in that replication of results, in different countries" (Cattell & Warburton, 1967, p. 4). Yet, there are no known newer studies that have compared the cultural sensitivity of scores on OPTs with the sensitivity of scores derived from questionnaires.

The common feature of OPTs is therefore the principle of deducing characteristics related to personality from observable behavior on performance tasks or other highly standardized miniature situations (Cattell & Warburton, 1967). People's individual characteristics are inferred from their overt behavior in such a standardized setting that lacks face validity (see Cattell, 1968; Schmidt, 1975). This is done through the application of achievement-oriented tasks or particular scoring methods (see Cattell & Kline, 1977).[1]

In conclusion, definitions of OPTs postulate several features: OPTs deduce information about a person's characteristics by assessing their behavior in a highly standardized miniature situation. OPT scores are not based on self-estimation or self-ratings of the construct of interest. Furthermore, the aims of OPTs are masked and, compared with self-report measures, OPTs have in fact shown a lower susceptibility to the manipulation and distortion of information, including faking and self-deception (Elliot, Lawty-Jones, & Jackson, 1996; Ziegler, Schmidt-Atzert, Bühner, & Krumm, 2007).

---

1 Taking the achievement-task-based definition into account, one could argue that Implicit Association Tests (IATs; Greenwald, McGhee, & Schwartz, 1998) and some other indirect measures presented in this volume may be representative of OPTs. IATs were developed to assess individual differences in the strength of associations between cognitive representations of at least two concepts (see Chapter 2 in this volume). Although this method has primarily been designed to measure interindividual differences in attitudes toward objects (e.g., Banse, Seise, & Zerbes, 2001), there was also a rather quick emergence of IATs that allowed the assessment of attitudes toward the self (self-esteem) as well as the self-concept of personality, such as anxiety (e.g., Egloff & Schmukle, 2002; Greenwald & Farnham, 2000). Achievement on an IAT-like reaction-time task serving as an indicator of self-esteem as one example (e.g., Rudolph, Schröder-Abé, Schütz, Gregg, & Sedikides, 2008) would fit the definition of OPTs given earlier. However, the IAT and other indirect measures that capture representations of the self are distinguished from OPTs in this chapter even if this distinction may not be very sharp: OPTs are defined as tests that do not address (implicit) representations but rather provide samples of realistic behavior. Information assessed by OPTs is not dependent on any mental representation, for example, the representation of the self as an achievement-motivated person (Pawlik, 2006) because OPTs directly assess the behavior associated with the construct of interest. Thus, objective and indirect tests will be viewed as different measurement approaches in this chapter.

Categories of Objective Personality Tests

As mentioned in the introduction, OPTs have been characterized by great variation from the very beginning (Cattell, 1968), and several attempts have been made to group these heterogeneous tests. Several decades ago, Hundleby (1973) proposed a categorization that differentiated between four groups of tests: (a) The assessment of expressive movements (e.g., characteristic movements of hand and body, allowing only a reduced assessment of very specific aspects of human personality); (b) simulated real-life data (i.e., the assessment of behavior in situations that resemble a target situation as much as possible); (c) physiological variables; and (d) motor-perceptual and performance tests (including measures of preference, response styles, responses to interference when performing an assigned task, and responses to suggestion) with the last group including most of the tests during this time.

Although current and newly developed OPTs still display great variability in task concepts, materials, and scoring methods, contemporary OPTs do not represent as great a variety of approaches as proposed by Cattell (e.g., projective tests are considered to be distinct today). In the following section, we propose a categorization of OPTs in the light of current narrower developments and definitions.

OPTs Masked as Achievement Tasks

In this category of tests, test takers are required to solve an achievement task as accurately and/or as quickly as possible without knowing what is actually being measured or how the instrument is being scored. As a characteristic of this group of tests, the task is not embedded in a simulated or imagined/suggested real-life context or real-life situation. Typically, test takers cannot distinguish these tests from classic (cognitive) performance tests. In most tests in this category, higher construct scores are associated with a more accurate or faster performance on the task. This indicates that an OPT-scoring procedure may even be independent from the task presented in the test itself. In earlier approaches, this was operationalized, for example, by asking participants to compare the lengths of 42 pairs of lines and to indicate whether (a) the one on the left or (b) the one on the right side is longer or whether (c) both are of equal length. The analysis is based on the number of comparisons made within a given time span (i.e., 30 s for Part I of the test). This is one of eight subtests for the measurement for Exvia vs. Invia (i.e., T45 in Cattell & Schuerger, 1976, 1978).

The Emotional Stroop Task (e.g., Dawkins & Furnham, 1989) can be understood as an earlier example of such an OPT in this category. Test takers are instructed to name the colors in which words are printed, whereas the words vary in their relevance to potential emotional topics. The lower the interference of the emotional stimuli, the faster and more accurately the colors will be named. Another example from this group is the Objective Achievement Motivation Test (OAT; Schmidt-Atzert, 2007): Test takers are instructed to pass fields on the screen colored in either red or green. Fields are passed by quickly clicking on matching (red or green) buttons (see Figure 9.1). The number of fields passed in a given time serves as an indicator of achievement motivation. A further example is given by Subtest 1 of the computerized Working Styles battery (Kubinger & Ebenhöh, 1996). The test is based on the T62 test Hesitancy by Cattell and Warburton (1967). Test takers see two figures on the screen and are instructed to select the larger one; after a decision has been made, a new pair of figures appears on the screen. The figures differ by only about 10% of their total size but are rotated to different angles. The number of decisions made within a given time is interpreted as an indicator of reflexivity (or impulsivity).

Another computerized battery of six tests was designed to measure stress resistance, which occurs when performance is not impaired by typical occupational short-term stressors (BAcO; see Kubinger, 2009; Ortner, 2012; Ortner, Kubinger, et al., 2006). The tasks assess aspects of successful problem-solving behavior in (simulated) stressful situations. The *time pressure task* instructs test takers to assign letters to symbols according to a given coding scheme as quickly and accurately as possible by dragging and dropping. The time available for assigning letters displayed on the screen is gradually reduced in the second part of the test. The given time-per-task screen is displayed in the middle of the screen by a digital clock, which counts back to zero. The scores assess whether test takers increase or decrease their coding speed and accuracy (Ortner, Kubinger, et al., 2006). The potential confounding of achievement and personality components creates a challenge when the accuracy and speed scores are computed.

Some tests postulate only minor effects of ability on test scores as a result of item selection (e.g., very easy items) and/or exercise trials in order to minimize advancing certain individuals due to preexisting experiences or ability (Schmidt-Atzert, 2007). Potential confounding can also be overcome by additionally assessing people's baseline performance, which can be included in item response theory models that are able to separate these aspects (e.g., Häusler, 2004).

OPTs That Aim to Represent Real-Life Simulations

In this category of OPTs, test takers are required to solve a less or more complex task embedded in a real-life situation or setting. Tests of this kind have not been developed or presented as pure achievement tasks, although participants work toward such a goal. The trait or state measured is usually not made transparent; however, the particular behavior shown in this situation is evaluated as an indicator of the test takers' expression of a specific personality characteristic.

A group of tests that were published during the last few years assigned to this category are experimental games, including, for example, the Balloon Analogue Risk Task (BART; Lejuez et al., 2002), the Betting Dice Test, or the Roulette Test (for both, see Rubio, Hernández, Zaldivar, Marquez, & Santacreu, 2010). All of these aim to measure constructs related to risk propensity by putting test takers into a gambling situation and scoring their behavior in the simulated environment. Test takers can maximize their gains by making less or more risky choices, where more risky choices are usually associated with higher gains. Another test that is aimed at assessing risk propensity is the Crossing the Street Test (Rubio et al., 2010; Santacreu, Rubio, & Hernández, 2006), which simulates a traffic situation. Test takers are instructed to navigate a pedestrian as quickly but also as safely as possible to reach the other side of the road through different traffic situations. Test takers are asked to make a decision about the position on the street from which a pedestrian should cross from one sidewalk to another. Safer positions are related to more walking effort, more time, and lower scores.

A series of OPTs allowing for the assessment of vocational interests based on so-called objective interest indices proposed by Cattell (Cattell, 1950, 1957) were developed by Proyer and were combined in the Multidimensional Objective Interest Battery (MOI; (Proyer, 2006; Proyer & Häusler, 2008). OPT approaches in this domain have a long tradition (Fryer, 1931; Super & Roper, 1941). One of the subtests of the MOI (Distribution of Money) asks participants to imagine having the responsibility to distribute €100,000 of their company's money to various organizations, clubs, other companies, or innovative project proposals. Test takers are informed that they have the final word in deciding who will receive the money. The concept is based on the assumption that decisions are based on personal interests – each of the organizations, clubs, companies, or innovative proposals is assigned to one of the six dimensions of vocational interest proposed by Holland (1997). A total score can be computed for money assigned to each of the six dimensions, and larger amounts of assigned money are indicators of greater interest in this domain.

A challenge for test development and the application of tests in this category lies in a stronger transparency (in comparison with other OPTs) that may also depend on the test administration context. If tests are, for example, employed within an occupational selection procedure, OPTs that are aimed at representing real-life situations may not elicit typical behavior but may be expected to produce socially desirable behavior. In line with more theoretical approaches, this would especially be the case if the OPTs in question activate more controlled than spontaneous behavior (see Chapter 3 in this volume). However, test concepts in this domain can still be scored in a way that is not transparent. For example, a test taker who is not familiar with Holland's classification scheme will not be able to correctly recognize or assign the organizations to the interest dimensions. On the other hand, a person applying for a job as a bus driver may be able to deduce from the aptitude assessment situation that a gambling task is being presented not just as a simple game but represents a relevant situation that is related to the vocational activity at hand. The question of whether the measurement aim can be uncovered and the test performance can be influenced in a specific direction by the test taker also seem to depend on the test situation itself. Furthermore, the question arises as to whether simulated situations better represent and predict real-life situations and behavior.

Questionnaire-Type OPTs That Ask for Evaluations or Decisions

In this category of OPTs, test takers are instructed to answer items that are similar to questionnaire items or to make other forms of evaluative decisions. Although these tests appear to exist in the twilight zone between objective tests and questionnaires, tests included as OPTs assess – unlike classic self-report questionnaires – different constructs than suggested by the item content; and therefore, they should also lack face validity.

Examples of such OPTs are given in Cattell's OA-TB (Cattell & Schuerger, 1976, 1978). For example, the T239 test (Decision Speed on Social Problems) asks test takers to solve specific problems by suggesting a solution (e.g., "You are a mile away from the nearest station when the car breaks down. What would you do? If you know, make a checkmark"). Rather than the answer, the speed with which a decision is made is scored as a sign of assertiveness and confidence. A different example is the T261 test (Attainability of Aims), which requires test takers to estimate their probability of achieving specific unlikely aims, such as dating a famous film star. The higher the probability estimate of the occurrence of this event, the more optimistic the person is evaluated on this test. Test T328 (Word Classification) requires test takers to classify words (e.g., honesty), as personal, emotional, exciting, or neutral. The words that are included were chosen as the items that had revealed the highest variability in terms of evaluation in pilot studies. It is assumed that highly anxious persons classify fewer words as neutral (see Cattell & Warburton, 1967). A new approach in this category is the Objective Heuristic Thinking Test (OHTT; Jasper & Ortner, 2014) that aims to assess thinking biases. Items of the Representativeness Scale demand estimations of the probability that a described person belongs to a certain group by given base rates for the membership. The Availability Scale requires the estimation of the probability that a particular person or a group of persons would encounter an unlikely event (e.g., plane crash). The Anchoring Scale consists of items including a short statement (e.g., "Imagine you have a bicycle with 7 gears") and a loosely related question (e.g., "How many grams does the bicycle's shifter weigh?"). Items were designed such that a reasonable answer to the question would be either much lower or much higher than the actual anchor value.

In sum, these questionnaire-type OPTs, like estimative items, are typically associated with the first generation of objective personality tests. New technologies allow for more adaptations and new variations in item material or mode of presentation than merely varying the scoring procedure. Thus, future successful developments that are based on these early Cattellian ideas should be expected (see Horn, 2006).

Validity of Objective Personality Tests

With regard to the early systematic empirical studies on the psychometric properties and construct validity of OPTs, Cattell expected to find that all three postulated sources that are necessary to build a complete picture of personality (Q-, L-, and T-data) would point to a common underlying structure of personality represented by so-called source traits (Cattell, 1957). However, his own extensive research program did not support this assumption: The T-data and Q-data sets showed only low convergence. With respect to the construct validity of OPTs, this lack of convergence led to formulation of the *method-trait problem*. It was concluded that different methods assess different aspects of the underlying traits and that OPTs and self-report questionnaires may thus systematically assess different aspects of personality (Hundleby et al., 1965). Similar results of nonconvergence were replicated by other authors (Häcker, Schmidt, Schwenkmezger, & Utz, 1975; Häcker, Schwenkmezger, & Utz, 1979; Skinner & Howarth, 1973). Most certainly, it cannot be argued that low or zero correlations of an objective test with Q-data support the validity of the OPT but rather that validation strategies need to go beyond simple correlations between a newly developed OPT with a questionnaire that measures the same underlying construct (see Ortner, Proyer, & Kubinger, 2006).

At that point, systematic empirical large-scale studies to investigate the construct validity of second-generation OPTs similar to the ones carried out in the early period of OPTs had not yet been conducted. In addition, most of these measures had been developed without referring explicitly to a unifying framework like the one that existed in Cattell's tradition. Furthermore, much less research has been published on OPTs in comparison with the large amount of research published in recent years on indirect measures, most notably on the Implicit Association Tests (IATs; see Chapter 2 in this volume). Nevertheless, a large number of studies employing new OPTs also revealed low correlations or a lack of convergence with self-report measures. For example, studies using the OAT (Schmidt-Atzert, 2004) revealed zero correlations with the achievement striving scale of the NEO-PI-R ($r = .02$; Ziegler, Schmukle, Egloff, & Bühner, 2010). Analyses of composite scores for conventional (questionnaire, nonverbal test) and seven OPTs from the initial version of the MOI (Proyer, 2006; Proyer & Häusler, 2008) for the assessment of vocational interests revealed correlations between –.20 (enterprising interests) and .41 (artistic interests) between corresponding scales (see Proyer, 2007). Dislich, Zinkernagel, Ortner, and Schmitt (2010) revealed a lack of convergence in the risk propensity domain between the Domain-Specific Risk-Taking (DOSPERT) Scale (Blais & Weber, 2001) and the BART ($r = –.17$). However, at least a medium convergence was found between the self-reported frequency of using rational calculation strategies and less risky choices in the Game of Dice task ($r = .45$; Brand, Heinze, Labudda, & Markowitsch, 2008).

The lack of convergence with established self-report measures has currently stimulated studies including new indirect measures, such as IAT, as well as studies on the relation between different OPTs that are aimed at assessing the same construct (Dislich et al., 2010; Ortner, Gerstenberg, Zinkernagel, & Schmitt, 2014). Thus, in line with dual-process theories (e.g., Gawronski & Bodenhausen, 2006; Strack & Deutsch, 2004); Schmitt et al. (Chapter 3 in this volume) argue that different OPTs may tap structurally more spontaneous or reflective aspects of a construct and may therefore converge better with indirect measures or questionnaires. Some OPTs may assess more associative, automatic, and spontaneous dispositions and may consequently show higher convergence with indirect measures than with direct measures (and vice versa). These considerations may serve as a way to resolve the so-called method-trait problem that troubled research in the first generation of OPTs (Pawlik, 2006). The issue of convergence may be addressed more comprehensively in combination with such new theories. In addition, the traditional multitrait-multimethod (MTMM; Campbell & Fiske, 1959) approach, in which several methods are employed for each trait and several tests are used to represent each group of methods (objective, indirect, direct), may represent a future approach for addressing questions of the construct validity of OPTs (see also Ortner & Schmitt, 2014).

Research on indirect measures has revealed that the correlation of IAT scores and direct measures depend on the degree of conceptual correspondence between the instruments (Hofmann, Gawronski, Gschwendner, Le, & Schmitt, 2005). This information may also serve as a starting point for future analyses involving OPTs. For example, with regard to different anxiety measures, Gschwendner, Hofmann, and Schmitt (2008) demonstrated that convergence was highest for measures that captured the same anxiety content (speech, spider, general) and the same specificity level (specific anxiety, general anxiety). Systematic approaches manipulating specificity similarity and content similarity may also help us to understand the processes underlying OPTs.

Furthermore, a lack of convergence between OPTs and other measures may also be caused by different structural properties of the assessed disposition – the degree to which objective personality tests measure more situation-specific states than stable traits. To further explore this possibility, latent state-trait theory (LST theory; Steyer, Schmitt, & Eid, 1999) can be employed. Recent research indicates that data obtained by using experimental games as OPTs show systematic person variance comparable to that of self-report measures of specific personality dispositions (Baumert, Schlösser, & Schmitt, 2014).

Another recent approach investigated conscientiousness OPTs and their convergence with data obtained by a questionnaire and a Single-Category IAT by employing a multi-method latent state-trait (MM-LST) model proposed by Courvoisier, Nussbeck, Eid, and Cole (2008). This allowed different sources of variance to be separated: stable and momentary trait influences, stable and momentary method influences, and measurement error influences. Based on data from 367 students assessed on three different measurement occasions, results indicated generally low convergence of the OPTs used with data obtained through other approaches. Furthermore, analyses revealed that the OPTs that were used assess stable rather than momentary components of the constructs. Substantial amounts of trait-method specificity revealed that different methods assess trait components that are not shared between OPTs and other measures (Koch, Ortner, Eid, Caspers, & Schmitt, 2014).

Initial results indicate that additional *moderators* of convergence may serve as a starting point from which to formulate more complex but also more successful hypotheses on the validity of OPTs (Dislich et al., 2010). Potential moderators of convergence are personality traits, situational characteristics, attributes of the construct, and attributes of the measurement procedure (see Chapter 3 in this volume). Some promising examples of criterion validity of frequently used OPTs are given in Table 9.1. Results on reliability and stability are also summarized for

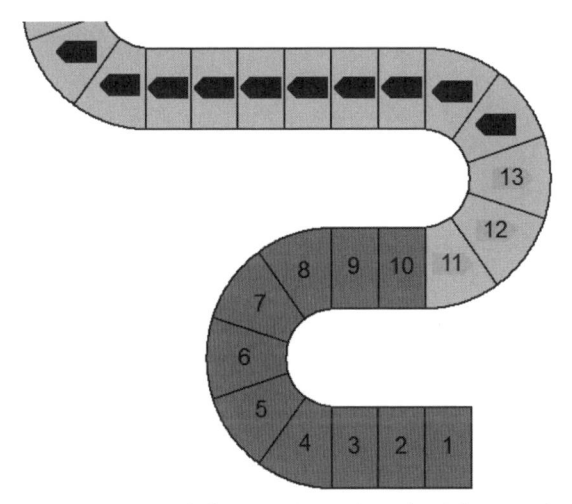

Figure 9.1. Instructional Item of the OAT. Reprinted with permisson from Schmidt-Atzert, L. (2007). *Objective Achievement Motivation Test.* Mödling, Austria: Dr. G. Schuhfried GmbH. ©Schuhfried GmbH.

the tests listed in the table. Results given in the table do not represent the heterogeneity of psychometric properties of available OPTs. For example, capturing measurement precision in terms of split-half correlations or internal consistency fails when only one score or item is available on a specific test. Further problems in interpreting retest correlations occur when test takers receive information during a test trial that influences his or her attitude or expectations toward forthcoming trials (Kubinger, 2009; Ortner et al., 2007).

With regard to transparency and test takers' opportunity to manipulate data provided by OPTs, several studies have indicated that answers are more difficult to fake on OPTs than on questionnaires. For example, this was shown for tests designed to assess impulsivity (Elliot et al., 1996; Hofmann & Kubinger, 2001), for a test of achievement motivation (Ziegler et al., 2010), and for a test of risk propensity in the context of driving behavior (Arendasy, Sommer, Herle, Schützhofer, & Inwanschitz, 2011). Overall, findings such as these lend support to the notion that OPTs can truly have advantages in terms of lower sensitivity to social desirability in comparison with questionnaires.

Concluding Remarks and Outlook

Reviewing the number of articles published on indirect measures within the last few years, especially with regard to the IAT, raises the question of why OPTs, especially of the second generation, have not yet garnered similar attention and popularity in research. One reason may be the large heterogeneity of tests in task concepts, scoring, and materials. In addition, experience has shown that results obtained for a specific measure cannot be transferred to other measures within this group, which is, to a lesser extent, also the case in research on IATs (see Chapter 2 in this volume).

With regard to the first generation of OPTs, Pawlik (2006) mentioned that researchers may tend to rely on questionnaires with a clear and often replicated factor structure (e.g., DeRaad, Perugini, & Szirmak, 1997; McCrae, Costa, Del Pilar, Rolland, & Parker, 1998). This may have been viewed as an advantage compared with the factor structure and very complex picture of interindividual

Table 9.1. Selected objective personality tests (OPTs) and examples of results of some psychometric properties

	r_α (internal consistency)	r_{tt} (retest correlation)	Validity support
Risk propensity			
Balloon Analogue Risk Task (BART; Lejuez et al., 2002)	.71 (Lejuez et al., 2002)	.66–.78 (2 weeks; White, Lejuez, & de Wit, 2008)	Scores were found to be positively associated with self-reported risk-related behaviors such as smoking ($r = .36$), gambling ($r = .44$), drug and alcohol consumption (both $r = .28$), and risky sexual behaviors ($r = .25$; $n = 86$; Lejuez et al., 2003; Lejuez et al., 2002). Smoking undergraduates scored higher than nonsmoking undergraduates ($n = 60$; $p < .01$; Lejuez et al., 2003).
Crossing the Street Test (CtST; Santacreu, Rubio, & Hernández, 2006)	.96 (Santacreu et al., 2006)	—	Scores predicted guessing tendencies on a multiple-choice test (1,325 applicants) for an ab initio air-traffic control training program (Rubio et al., 2010).
Game of Dice Test (GDT; Brand et al., 2005)	.68 (Dislich et al., 2010)	—	More risky choices in patients with attention-deficit/hyperactivity disorder (ADHD) compared with a control group ($n = 31$; $p = -.01$; Matthies, Philipsen, & Svaldi, 2012). Excessive Internet gamers ($n = 19$) showed reduced decision-making ability compared with a control group ($n = 19$) (Pawlikowski & Brand, 2011).
Risk Behaviour Test (RBT; Guttmann & Bauer, 2004)	—	.70 (6 weeks; Guttmann & Bauer, 2004)	Car drivers who had been conspicuous about their alcohol consumption and a parallelized sample of inconspicuous drivers ($n = 214$) were correctly assigned at a rate of 77% to the two groups on the basis of their RBT scores (Guttmann & Bauer, 2004).
Roulette Test (RT; Santacreu, Rubio, & Hernández, 2006)	.83 (Santacreu et al., 2006)	.43 (1 year)	Scores predicted a tendency to guess on a multiple-choice test (1,325 applicants) for an ab initio air-traffic control training program (Rubio et al., 2010).
The Risk Propensity Task (PTR; Aguado, Rubio, & Lucía, 2011)	.94 (Aguado et al., 2011)	—	A significant correlation was found between the PTR and another OPT, the Betting Dice Test (Arend, Botella, Contreras, Hernández, & Santacreu, 2003; $r = .31$; $n = 59$). Scores were revealed to be positively associated with a composite score based on self-reported smoking behavior, drinking behavior, gambling.... (−.34; Aguado et al., 2011).

Table 9.1. continued

	r_α (internal consistency)	r_{tt} (retest correlation)	Validity support
Achievement motivation			
Objective Achievement Motivation Test (OAT; Subtest 1; (OAT, Subtest 1; Schmidt-Atzert, 2004)	.95–.97 (Schmidt-Atzert, 2007)	.85 (after 29 days; Schmidt-Atzert, 2007)	The OAT had relations of $r = .24$ with the intermediate examination grade point average ($n = 59$) and $r = .23$ with the school-leaving examination grade point average ($n = 100$; Schmidt-Atzert, 2004). Furthermore, OAT scores predicted students' spontaneous willingness to agree to voluntarily work on an additional achievement test after passing a battery of personality tests and questionnaires (Ortner, Gerstenberg, Zinkernagel, & Schmitt, 2014).
Working Styles (Subtest 3; Kubinger & Ebenhöh, 1996)	–	.32 (1 or 2 weeks; Ortner, Gerstenberg, Zinkernagel, & Schmitt, 2014)	–
Vocational interests			
Multidimensional Objective Interest Inventory (contains three objective tests; Distribution of Money; Distractibility; Ambiguous Pictures; Proyer & Häusler, 2008)	.64–.81 for Distribution; .87–.92 for Distractibility (Proyer & Häusler, 2008); .50–.78 for Pictures (Proyer, 2006)	–	Test scores showed correlations between .08 and .25 with a nonverbal interest test ($N = 269$; data from Proyer et al., 2012); correlations in the expected direction with intelligence measures (e.g., .33 between verbal intelligence and artistic interests, $N = 120$; Proyer, 2006); $r = .18$ between investigative interests and achievement motivation assessed via Working Styles Subtest 3 (Proyer, 2006).

differences obtained by including OPTs in early factor analytic work (Hundleby et al., 1965; Pawlik, 1968). In fact, as data on convergent validity indicate, there is still a need to investigate what OPTs measure and how they relate to other personality measures. As most psychological findings in the domain of psychological assessment and personality psychology are based on self-report questionnaires today, researchers working on OPTs are faced with the problem of having to surpass this gold standard. In particular, the larger temporal stability and stronger correlations with other personality measures are mentioned as arguments for using self-report questionnaires. However, the weaknesses of self-reports are widely acknowledged and have been mentioned; for example, information obtained through self-reports can easily be distorted so that the accuracy of self-reports can be questioned. Furthermore, Cattell indicated that self-reports are bound to be incomplete. Nevertheless, as indicated by the literature, at least some newer OPTs with convincing results on their psychometric properties have been frequently integrated into research and are currently gaining popularity, such as the BART (Cazzell, Li, Lin, Patel, & Liu, 2012; Fukunaga, Brown, & Bogg, 2012; Lahat et al., 2012; Parkinson, Phiri, & Simons, 2012).

To obtain a better understanding of the psychometric properties of OPTs in general, future research should involve large-scale approaches that include different methods, and as mentioned here, moderator variables should be considered in MTMM models. Research approaches modeling OPT data at different points in time should also provide insight into the different measures that are being used to assess latent trait and state components. These longitudinal approaches should also allow researchers to take a broader approach, such as the one provided by modern change models, which allow trait variance to be separated from both method variance and state variance (Courvoisier et al., 2008; Geiser, Eid, Nussbeck, Courvoisier, & Cole, 2010; Koch et al., 2014).

However, researchers as well as practitioners have to face the fact that not every construct can be addressed in a similar way by all methods, and in this case, by OPTs. Whereas interpersonal behavior and social variables (e.g., extraversion) explain a considerable amount of variance in Q-data, these domains are very difficult to implement and assess by using standardized OPTs (Pawlik, 2006). It is more difficult to convert a realistic social situation into a computerized miniature situation in contrast to a task requiring conscientiousness. Furthermore, in certain cases, social desirability or a tendency to answer in a socially desirable direction might be a part of the construct of interest. Cattell and Scheier (1963) make such an argument for the measurement of *anxiety*. They suggest that "reaction tendencies on a social desirability-undesirability continuum are […] an essential part of anxiety measurement and a questionnaire catches them well" (p. 6). Hence, in some cases, the use of a questionnaire can be helpful for uncovering such aspects – and may be further encouraged from the viewpoint of a multimethod approach in psychological assessment.

What about the use of OPTs in psychological practice? With regard to the earlier approaches, the low utilization rates of OPTs in practice has been explained by their lower usability compared with questionnaires (Schmidt & Schwenkmezger, 1994b) as well as the "enormous undertaking to develop, validate and standardize" them (Hundleby, 1973, p. 84). The extensive effort required by examiners to present and score OPTs and even to construct them is nowadays less of a problem as considerable progress has been made by the availability of flexible software packages. Also, because OPTs of the second generation are almost exclusively administered in computerized settings, not only the administration itself but also the scoring has become much easier for the examiner.

Recent test developments have also inspired OPT use in practice (for an overview, see Ortner et al., 2007), and new developments have broadened their scope. Whereas clinical settings were one of the main fields in which OPTs were applied in earlier times (e.g., Cattell & Scheier, 1960; Kasielke, Hänsgen, & Strauss, 1985; Schmidt & Schwenkmezger, 1994a), the use of OPTs in the domains of human resources or selection seems to have gained importance in recent times (see, e.g., the examples of current uses in Ortner et al., 2006).

With regard to the use of OPTs, for example, in the domain of vocational interests in practice, Proyer (2006; Proyer & Häusler, 2008) proposed a multidimensional strategy with OPTs being one component of a larger test battery – along with a questionnaire and a nonverbal test (Proyer, 2007; Proyer, Sidler, Weber, & Ruch, 2012). Proyer argued that the application of OPTs for counseling is especially useful if (a) a person's differentiation of the profile(s) is low and/or (b) a person's vocational identity is diffuse. In these cases, nonverbal tests and OPTs were found to provide additional information beyond pure self-descriptions that may be distorted for different reasons (e.g., the expectations of others or a lack of knowledge in the domains that are covered by the conventional questionnaires for vocational interest). In the domain of vocational interests, this may help researchers to develop hypotheses about people's areas of interest that were previously hidden or less well-cultivated.

To summarize this chapter, research on OPTs has taken considerable steps forward in the past several years. There has been a transition from OPTs of the first generation to a second generation, making strong use of the possibilities offered by computerized assessment procedures. This has allowed researchers to develop new approaches in the design, presentation, as well as the scoring of the tests. Although there are efforts to further structure the field, OPTs still remain a rather heterogeneous group of tests. Although this heterogeneity is a disadvantage in terms of structure, it may offer the field benefits by providing a broad range of creative processes and ideas and the development of new assessment techniques. Recent studies give researchers reasons to be optimistic about the future role of OPTs in the standard repertoire of psychological assessment and their usefulness in both research and practice.

References

Aguado, D., Rubio, V. J., & Lucía, B. (2011). The Risk Propensity Task (PTR): A proposal for a behavioral performance-based computer test for assessing risk propensity. *Anales de Psicologia, 27*, 862–870.

Arend, I., Botella, J., Contreras, M. J., Hernández, J. M., & Santacreu, J. (2003). A betting dice test to study the interactive style of risk-taking behavior. *The Psychological Record, 53*, 217–230.

Arendasy, M., Sommer, M., Herle, M., Schützhofer, B., & Inwanschitz, D. (2011). Modeling effects of faking on an objective personality test. *Journal of Individual Differences, 32*, 210–218. http://doi.org/10.1027/1614-0001/a000053

Banse, R., Seise, J., & Zerbes, N. (2001). Implicit attitudes towards homosexuality: Reliability, validity, and controllability of the IAT. *Zeitschrift für Experimentelle Psychologie, 48*, 145–160.

Baumert, A., Schlösser, T., & Schmitt, M. (2014). Economic games: A performance-based assessment of fairness and altruism. *European Journal of Psychological Assessment, 30*, 178–192. http://doi.org/10.1027/1015-5759/a000183

Blais, A.-R., & Weber, E. U. (2001). A domain-specific risktaking (DOSPERT) scale for adult populations. *Judgement and Decision Making, 1*, 33–47.

Brand, M., Fujiwara, E., Borsutzky, S., Kalbe, E., Kessler, J., & Markowitsch, H. J. (2005). Decision-making deficits of Korsakoff patients in a new gambling task with explicit rules: Associations with executive functions. *Neuropsychology, 19*, 267–277. http://doi.org/10.1037/0894-4105.19.3.267

Brand, M., Heinze, K., Labudda, K., & Markowitsch, H. J. (2008). The role of strategies in deciding advantageously in ambiguous and risky situations. *Cognitive Processing, 9*, 159–173. http://doi.org/10.1007/s10339-008-0204-4

Campbell, D. T., & Fiske, D. W. (1959). Convergent and discriminant validation by the multitrait-multimethod matrix. *Psychological Bulletin, 56*, 81–105. http://doi.org/10.1037/h0046016

Cattell, J. M. (1890). Mental tests and measurements. *Mind, 15*, 373–381. http://doi.org/10.1093/mind/os-XV.59.373

Cattell, R. B. (1941). An objective test of character-temperatment I. *Journal of General Psychology, 25*, 59–73. http://doi.org/10.1080/00221309.1941.10544704

Cattell, R. B. (1944). An objective test of character-temperatment II. *Journal of Social Psychology, 19*, 99–114. http://doi.org/10.1080/00224545.1944.9918805

Cattell, R. B. (1946). *Description and measurement of personality*. New York, NY: World Book.

Cattell, R. B. (1948). Primary personality factors in the realm of objective tests. *Journal of Personality and Social Psychology, 16*, 459–487.

Cattell, R. B. (1950). The objective measurement of dynamic traits. *Educational and Psychological Measurement, 10*, 224–248. http://doi.org/10.1177/001316445001000204

Cattell, R. B. (1955). *Handbook for the Objective-Analytic Personality Test batteries: (including Adult and Child O-A Batteries)*. Savoy, IL: Institute for Personality and Ability Testing.

Cattell, R. B. (1957). *Personality and motivation – structure and measurement*. New York, NY: World Book Company.

Cattell, R. B. (1968). What is "objective" in "Objective Personality Tests"? In W. L. Barnette (Ed.), *Readings in Psychological Tests and Measurements* (pp. 163–168). Homewood, IL: Dorsey Press.

Cattell, R. B., & Kline, P. (1977). *The scientific analysis of personality and motivation*. London, UK: Academic Press.

Cattell, R. B., & Scheier, I. H. (1960). *Handbook for the Objective-Analytic (O-A) Anxiety Battery*. Champaign, IL: IPAT.

Cattell, R. B., & Scheier, I. H. (1963). *Handbook fort he IPAT Anxiety Scale Questionnaire (Self Analysis Form)*. Champaign, IL: IPAT.

Cattell, R. B., & Schuerger, J. M. (1976). *The Objective-Analytic (O-A) Test kit*. Champaign, IL: IPAT.

Cattell, R. B., & Schuerger, J. M. (1978). *Personality in action: Handbook for the Objective-Analytic (O-A) Test kit*. Champaign, IL: IPAT.

Cattell, R. B., & Warburton, F. W. (1967). *Objective Personality and Motivation Tests: A theoretical introduction and practical compendium*. Chicago, IL: University of Illinois Press.

Cazzell, M., Li, L., Lin, Z.-J., Patel, S. J., & Liu, H. (2012). Comparison of neural correlates of risk decision making between genders: An exploratory fNIRS study of the Balloon Analogue Risk Task (BART). *Neuroimage, 62*, 1896–1911. http://doi.org/10.1016/j.neuroimage.2012.05.030

Courvoisier, D. S., Nussbeck, F. W., Eid, M., & Cole, D. A. (2008). Analyzing the convergent and discriminant validity of states and traits: Development and applications of multimethod latent state-trait models. *Psychological Assessment, 20*, 270–280. http://doi.org/10.1037/a0012812

Cronbach, L. J. (1970). *Essentials of psychological testing*. New York, NY: Harper & Row.

Dawkins, K., & Furnham, A. (1989). The colour naming of emotional words. *British Journal of Psychology, 80*, 383–389. http://doi.org/10.1111/j.2044-8295.1989.tb02328.x

DeRaad, B., Perugini, M., & Szirmak, Z. (1997). In pursuit of a cross-lingual reference structure of personality traits: comparisons among five languages. *European Journal of Personality, 11*, 167–185. http://doi.org/10.1002/(SICI)1099-0984(199709)11:3<167::AID-PER286>3.0.CO;2-B

Dislich, F. X. R., Zinkernagel, A., Ortner, T. M., & Schmitt, M. (2010). Convergence of direct, indirect, and objective risk taking measures in the domain of gambling: The moderating role of impulsiveness and self-control. *Journal of Psychology, 218*, 20–27.

Egloff, B., & Schmukle, S. C. (2002). Predictive validity of an Implicit Association Test for assessing anxiety. *Journal of Personality and Social Psychology, 83*, 1441–1455. http://doi.org/10.1037/0022-3514.83.6.1441

Elliot, S., Lawty-Jones, M., & Jackson, C. (1996). Effects of dissimulation on self-report and objective measures of personality. *Personality and Individual Differences, 21*, 335–343. http://doi.org/10.1016/0191-8869(96)00080-3

Fitts, P. M. (1946). German applied psychology during World War II. *American Psychologist, 1*, 151–161. http://doi.org/10.1037/h0059674

Fryer, D. (1931). *The measurement of interests in relation to human adjustment*. New York, NY: Holt.

Fukunaga, R., Brown, J. W., & Bogg, T. (2012). Decision making in the Balloon Analogue Risk Task (BART): Anterior cingulate cortex signals loss aversion but not the infrequency of risky choices. *Cognitive Affective & Behavioral Neuroscience, 12*, 479–490. http://doi.org/10.3758/s13415-012-0102-1

Gawronski, B., & Bodenhausen, G. V. (2006). Associative and propositional processes in evaluation: An integrative review of implicit and explicit attitude change. [Review]. *Psychological Bulletin, 132*, 692–731. http://doi.org/10.1037/0033-2909.132.5.692

Geiser, C., Eid, M., Nussbeck, F. W., Courvoisier, D. S., & Cole, D. A. (2010). *Multitrait-multimethod change modelling. Asta-Advances in Statistical Analysis, 94*, 185–201. http://doi.org/10.1007/s10182-010-0127-0

Greenwald, A. G., & Farnham, S. D. (2000). Using the implicit association test to measure self-esteem and self-concept. *Journal of Personality and Social Psychology, 79*, 1022–1038. http://doi.org/10.1037/0022-3514.79.6.1022

Greenwald, A. G., McGhee, D. E., & Schwartz, J. K. L. (1998). Measuring individual differences in implicit cognition: the Implicit Association Test. *Journal of Personality and Social Psychology, 74*, 1464–1480. http://doi.org/10.1037/0022-3514.74.6.1464

Gschwendner, T., Hofmann, W., & Schmitt, M. (2008). Convergent and predictive validity of implicit and explicit anxiety measures as a function of specificity similarity and content similarity. *European Journal of Psychological Assessment, 24*, 254–262. http://doi.org/10.1027/1015-5759.24.4.254

Guttmann, G., & Bauer, H. (2004). *RISIKO – Risikoverhalten* [Risk behavior] [Software and manual]. Mödling, Austria: Schuhfried.

Häcker, H., Schmidt, L. R., Schwenkmezger, P., & Utz, H. E. (1975). Objektive Testbatterie, OA-TB 75 [Objective Test Battery, OA-TB 75]. Weinheim, Germany: Beltz.

Häcker, H., Schwenkmezger, P., & Utz, H. (1979). Über die Verfälschbarkeit von Persönlichkeitsfragebogen und Objektiven Persönlichkeitstests unter SD-Instruktion und in einer Auslesesituation [About fakeability of personality questionnaires and objective personality tests under SD-instruction and in a selection situation]. *Diagnostica, 25*, 7–23.

Häusler, J. (2004). An algorithm for the separation of skill and working style. *Psychology Science, 4*, 433–450.

Hofmann, K., & Kubinger, K. D. (2001). Herkömmliche Persönlichkeitsfragebogen und Objektive Persönlichkeitstests im „Wettstreit" um Unverfälschbarkeit [Personality questionnaires and objective personality tests in a non-fakeability contest]. *Report Psychologie, 26*, 298–304.

Hofmann, W., Gawronski, B., Gschwendner, T., Le, H., & Schmitt, M. (2005). A meta-analysis on the correlation between the implicit association test and explicit self-report measures. [Proceedings Paper]. *Personality and Social Psychology Bulletin, 31*, 1369–1385. http://doi.org/10.1177/0146167205275613

Holland, J. L. (1997). *Making vocational choices* (3rd ed.). Odessa, FL: Psychological Assessment Resources.

Horn, R. (2006). Die OA-TB 75: Neue Skizzen für die Gestaltung Objektiver Persönlichkeitstests [OA-TB 75: An outline for designing Objective Personality Tests]. In T. M. Ortner, R. T. Proyer & K. D. Kubinger (Eds.), *Theorie und Praxis objektiver Persönlichkeitstests* (pp. 102–111). Bern, Switzerland: Hans Huber.

Hundleby, J. D. (1973). The measurement of personality by objective tests. In P. Kline (Ed.), *New approaches in psychological measurement* (pp. 185–231). London, UK: Wiley.

Hundleby, J. D., Pawlik, K., & Cattell, R. B. (1965). *Personality factors in objective test devices*. San Diego, CA: Knapp.

Jasper, F., & Ortner, T. M. (2014). The tendency to fall for distracting information while making judgments: development and validation of the Objective Heuristic Thinking Test. *European Journal of Psychological Assessment, 30*, 193–207. http://doi.org/10.1027/1015-5759/a000214

Kasielke, E., Hänsgen, K.-D., & Strauss, E. (1985). Probleme und Möglichkeiten der Psychodiagnostik bei Patienten mit neurotischen Störungen und körperlichen Erkrankungen [Problems and possibilities of psychological testing of persons with neurological and somatic deseases]. *Zeitschrift für Differentielle und Diagnostische Psychologie, 6*, 89–105.

Kline, P., & Cooper, C. (1984). A construct validation oft he Objective-Analytic Test Battery (OATB). *Personality and Individual Differenes, 5*, 323–337. http://doi.org/10.1016/0191-8869(84)90071-0

Koch, T., Ortner, T. M., Eid, M., Caspers, J., & Schmitt, M. (2014). Evaluating the construct validity of objective personality tests using a multitrait-multimethod-multioccasion-(MTMM-MO) approach. *European Journal of Psychological Assessment, 30*, 209–230. http://doi.org/10.1027/1015-5759/a000212

Kubinger, K. D. (2009). The technique of objective personality-tests sensu R. B. Cattell nowadays: The Viennese pool of computerized tests aimed at experiment-based assessment of behavior. *Acta Psychologica Sinica, 41*, 1024–1036. http://doi.org/10.3724/SP.J.1041.2009.01024

Kubinger, K. D., & Ebenhöh, J. (1996). *Arbeitshaltungen – Kurze Testbatterie: Anspruchsniveau, Frustrationstoleranz, Leistungsmotivation, Impulsivität/Reflexivität* [Working Style – a short test-battery: Level of aspiration, achievement motivation, frustration tolerance, achievement motivastion, impulsiveness/reflexiveness] [Software and manual]. Frankfurt/M., Germany: Swets Test Services.

Lahat, A., Degnan, K. A., White, L. K., McDermott, J. M., Henderson, H. A., Lejuez, C. W., & Fox, N. A. (2012). Temperamental exuberance and executive function predict propensity for risk taking in childhood. *Development and Psychopathology, 24*, 847–856. http://doi.org/10.1017/S0954579412000405

Lejuez, C. W., Aklin, W. M., Jones, H. A., Richards, J. B., Strong, D. R., Kahler, C. W., & Read, J. P. (2003). The balloon analogue risk task (BART) differentiates smokers and nonsmokers. *Experimental and Clinical Psychopharmacology, 11*, 26–33. http://doi.org/10.1037/1064-1297.11.1.26

Lejuez, C. W., Read, J. P., Kahler, C. W., Richards, J. B., Ramsey, S. E., Stuart, G. L., . . . Brown, R. A. (2002). Evaluation of a behavioral measure of risk taking: The Balloon Analogue Risk Task (BART). *Journal of Experimental Psychology, 8*, 75–84.

Matthies, S., Philipsen, A., & Svaldi, J. (2012). Risky decision making in adults with ADHD. *Journal of Behavior Therapy and Experimental Psychiatry, 43*, 938–946. http://doi.org/10.1016/j.jbtep.2012.02.002

McCrae, R. R., Costa, P. T., Del Pilar, G. H., Rolland, J. P., & Parker, W. D. (1998). Cross-cultural assessment of the five-factor model – the revised NEO personality inventory. *Journal of Cross-Cultural Psychology, 29*, 171–188. http://doi.org/10.1177/0022022198291009

Ortner, T. M. (2012). Teachers' burnout is related to lowered speed and lowered quality for demanding short-term tasks. *Psychological Test and Assessment Modeling, 54*, 20–35.

Ortner, T. M., Gerstenberg, F. X., Zinkernagel, A., & Schmitt, M. (2014). *Convergence between Objective Personality Tests assessing achievement motivation and risk propensity with other measures.* Manuscript submitted for publication.

Ortner, T. M., Horn, R., Kersting, M., Krumm, S., Kubinger, K. D., Proyer, R. T., … Westhoff, K. (2007). Standortbestimmung und Zukunft Objektiver Persönlichkeitstests [Current state and future of Objective Personality Tests]. *Report Psychologie, 32*, 64–75.

Ortner, T. M., Kubinger, K. D., Schrott, A., Radinger, R., & Litzenberger, M. (2006). *Belastbarkeits-Assessment: Computerisierte Objektive Persönlichkeits-Testbatterie – Deutsch (BAcO-D)* [Stress resistance assessment: Computerized objective test battery – German version (BAcO-D)] [Software and manual]. Frankfurt/M., Germany: Harcourt Assessment.

Ortner, T. M., Proyer, R. T., & Kubinger, K. D. (Eds.). (2006). *Theorie und Praxis objektiver Persönlichkeitstests* [Theory and practice of objective personality tests]. Bern, Switzerland: Hans Huber.

Ortner, T. M., & Schmitt, M. (2014). Advances and continuing challenges in Objective Personality Testing. *European Journal of Psychological Assessment, 30*, 163–168. http://doi.org/10.1027/1015-5759/a000213

OSS Assessment Staff. (1948). *Assessment of men: Selection of personnel for the Office of Strategic Services*. New York, NY: Rinehart & Co.

Parkinson, B., Phiri, N., & Simons, G. (2012). Bursting with anxiety: Adult social referencing in an interpersonal Balloon Analogue Risk Task (BART). *Emotion, 12*, 817–826. http://doi.org/10.1037/a0026434

Pawlik, K. (1968). *Dimensionen des Verhaltens. Eine Einführung in Methodik und Ergebnisse faktorenanalytischer psychologischer Forschung* [Dimensions of Behavior: Introduction into method and results on the factor analytic approach in psychological research]. Bern, Switzerland: Huber.

Pawlik, K. (2006). Objektive Tests in der Persönlichkeitsforschung. In T. M. Ortner, R. T. Proyer & K. D. Kubinger (Eds.), *Theorie und Praxis objektiver Persönlichkeitstests* [Theory and practice of objective personality tests] (pp. 16–23). Bern, Switzerland: Hans Huber.

Pawlikowski, M., & Brand, M. (2011). Excessive Internet gaming and decision making: Do excessive World of Warcraft players have problems in decision making under risky conditions? *Psychiatry Research, 188*, 428–433. http://doi.org/10.1016/j.psychres.2011.05.017

Proyer, R. T. (2006). *Entwicklung Objektiver Persönlichkeitstests zur Erfassung des Interesses an beruflichen Tätigkeiten* [Development of objective personality tests for the assessment of vocational activities]. Landau, Germany: VEP.

Proyer, R. T. (2007). Convergence of conventional and behavior-based measures: Towards a multimethod approach in the assessment of vocational interests. *Psychology Science Quarterly, 49*, 168–183.

Proyer, R. T., & Häusler, J. (2007). Assessing behavior in standardized settings: The role of objective personality tests. *International Journal of Clinical and Health Psychology, 7*, 537–546.

Proyer, R. T., & Häusler, J. (2008). *Multimethodische Objektive Interessentestbatterie (MOI)* [Multimethod objective interest assessment battery]. Mödling, Austria: Schuhfried.

Proyer, R. T., Sidler, N., Weber, M., & Ruch, W. (2012). A multi-method approach to studying the relationship between character strengths and vocational interests in adolescents. *International Journal for Educational and Vocational Guidance, 12*, 141–157. http://doi.org/10.1007/s10775-012-9223-x

Rubio, V. J., Hernández, J. M., Zaldivar, F., Marquez, O., & Santacreu, J. (2010). Can we predict risk-taking behavior? Two behavioral tests for predicting guessing tendencies in a multiple-choice test. *European Journal of Psychological Assessment, 26*, 87–94. http://doi.org/10.1027/1015-5759/a000013

Rudolph, A., Schröder-Abé, M., Schütz, A., Gregg, A. P., & Sedikides, C. (2008). Through a glass, less darkly? Reassessing convergent and discriminant validity in measures of implicit self-esteem. *European Journal of Psychological Assessment, 24*, 273–281. http://doi.org/10.1027/1015-5759.24.4.273

Santacreu, J., Rubio, V. J., & Hernández, J. M. (2006). The objective assessment of personality: Cattells's T-data revisited and more. *Psychology Science, 48*, 53–68.

Schmidt, L. R. (1975). *Objektive Persönlichkeitsmessung in diagnostischer und klinischer Psychologie* [Objective assessment of personality in assessment and clinical psychology]. Weinheim, Germany: Beltz.

Schmidt, L. R. (2006). Objektive Persönlichkeitstests in der Tradition Cattells: Forschungslinien und Relativierungen [Objective personality tests in Cattells' tradition: Paths of reserach and limitations]. In T. M. Ortner, R. T. Proyer, & K. D. Kubinger (Eds.), *Theorie und Praxis objektiver Persönlichkeitstests* [Theory and practice of Objective Personality Tests] (pp. 24–37). Bern, Switzerland: Hans Huber.

Schmidt, L. R., & Schwenkmezger, P. (1994a). Differentialdiagnostische Untersuchungen mit Objektiven Persönlichkeitstests und Fragebogen im psychiatrischen Bereich: Neue empirische Ergebnisse [Psychological investigation using Objective Personality Tests and questionnaires in psychiatry: New empirical results]. *Diagnostica, 40*, 27–41.

Schmidt, L. R., & Schwenkmezger, P. (1994b). Objektive Persönlichkeitstests: Perspektiven für die Diagnostik [Objective personality tests: Perspectives for assessment]. In D. Bartussek & M. Amelang (Eds.), *Fortschritte der Differentiellen Psychologie und Psychologischen Diagnostik* [Advances in differential psychology and psychological assesment] (pp. 229–239). Göttingen, Germany: Hogrefe.

Schmidt-Atzert, L. (2004). *Objektiver Leistungsmotivations Test (OLMT)* [Objective Achievement Motivation Test] [Software and manual]. Mödling, Austria: Dr. G. Schuhfried GmbH.

Schmidt-Atzert, L. (2007). *Objektiver Leistungsmotivations Test (OLMT)* [Objective Achievement Motivation Test (OLMT)] [Software and manual]. Mödling, Austria: Dr. G. Schuhfried GmbH.

Schuerger, J. M. (2008). The Objective-Analytic Test Battery. In G. J. Boyle, G. Matthews & D. H. Saklofske (Eds.), *The SAGE handbook of personality theory and assessment* (Vol. 2, pp. 529–546). Los Angeles, CA: Sage.

Skinner, N. S. F., & Howarth, E. (1973). Cross-media independence of questionnaire and objective test personality factors. *Multivariate Behavioral Research, 8*, 23–40. http://doi.org/10.1207/s15327906mbr0801_2

Steyer, R., Schmitt, M., & Eid, M. (1999). Latent state-traittheory and research in personality and individual differences. *European Journal of Personality, 13*, 389–408. http://doi.org/10.1002/(SICI)1099-0984(199909/10)13:5<389::AID-PER361>3.0.CO;2-A

Strack, F., & Deutsch, R. (2004). Reflective and impulsive determinants of social behavior. *Personality and Social Psychology Review, 8*, 220–247. http://doi.org/10.1207/s15327957pspr0803_1

Super, D. E., & Roper, S. A. (1941). An objective technique for testing vocational interests. *Journal of Applied Psychology, 25*, 487–498. http://doi.org/10.1037/h0062004

White, T. L., Lejuez, C. W., & de Wit, H. (2008). Test-Retest characteristics of the Balloon Analogue Risk Task (BART). *Experimental and Clinical Psychopharmacology, 16*, 565–570. http://doi.org/10.1037/a0014083

Ziegler, M., Schmidt-Atzert, L., Bühner, M., & Krumm, S. (2007). Faking susceptibility of different measurement methods: Questionnaire, semi-projective, and objective. *Psychology Science, 49*, 291–307.

Ziegler, M., Schmukle, S., Egloff, B., & Bühner, M. (2010). Investigating measures of achievement motivation(s). *Journal of Individual Differences, 31*, 15–21. http://doi.org/10.1027/1614-0001/a000002

Part IV
Domains of Application

Chapter 10

Indirect Measures in the Domain of Health Psychology

Reinout W. Wiers[1], Katrijn Houben[2], Wilhelm Hofmann[3], and Alan W. Stacy[4]

[1]Department of Psychology, University of Amsterdam, The Netherlands
[2]Clinical Psychological Science, Maastricht University, The Netherlands
[3]Department of Psychology, University of Cologne, Germany
[4]School of Community and Global Health, Claremont Graduate University, CA, USA

This chapter aims to bridge the gap between contemporary theory and practice regarding behavioral assessment in the domain of health psychology. However, before summarizing the current state of affairs regarding measurement, it is crucial to first develop a motivation to invest time and effort into behavior-based assessment in this domain. What is the relevance? In order to answer that question, we use a famous quote in psychology: "There is nothing so practical as a good theory" (Lewin, 1951, p. 169). Why would a health psychologist invest time and effort into behavioral assessment, rather than simply asking people why they do what they do, with respect to health behaviors, as health psychologists have done for decades? Why do you smoke? Why do you drink? Why do you expose yourself to the burning sun for hours? Why do you engage in unsafe sex? Of course, you could ask more subtle facets about the behavior, like the expected pros and cons, their likelihood and value, and so on. You could ask for attitudes, beliefs, intentions and self-efficacy, and sure enough you would find that a significant portion of the variance in the behavior of interest is predicted by these variables. What research during the past decade has shown, however, is that you can predict behavior better if you also include so-called indirect measures. And that in some individuals the more traditional measures are better predictors, while in others these indirect measures are better predictors. Importantly, chances are these indirect measures are the better predictor among individuals with a relatively high risk for unhealthy behaviors, while the traditional measures do well in low-risk individuals (such as individuals from the easily accessible undergraduate student participant pool). Finally, recent evidence indicates that varieties of the newly developed assessment instruments can be used to modify some of the psychological processes implicated in health behaviors. Hence, there are good reasons to read further and to apply some of these methods. We begin with a brief introduction to underlying theory and then address methods, current issues, new developments, and future directions.

A Bit of Theory

The advance of indirect or implicit measures went hand in hand with the development of so-called dual-process models, in basic behavioral sciences (Evans, 2008; Gawronski & Bodenhausen, 2006; Kahneman, 2003; Smith & DeCoster, 2000; Strack & Deutsch, 2004), neuroscience (Bechara, 2005; Satpute & Lieberman, 2006), addiction (Stacy, Ames, & Knowlton, 2004; Wiers et al., 2007) and health psychology (Hofmann, Friese, & Wiers, 2008; Wiers, Houben, Roefs, Hofmann, & Stacy, 2010). The general idea behind these models is that human behavior is not only predicted by logical considerations and a rational weighing of pros and cons of behavioral options (reflective processes), but also to some extent by impulsive, associative processes that may be triggered outside of awareness. These impulsive processes are typically assessed with indirect measures, which indirectly infer the relevant cognitive-motivational processes underlying the behavior of interest from behavior (Hofmann, Friese, et al., 2008; see also Chapter 3 in this volume).

Theorists have emphasized that impulsive and reflective processes have different characteristics; impulsive processes have a large capacity, use associative mechanisms, and are independent of IQ, whereas reflective processes are fragile, use symbolic processing, and are related to IQ (Gawronski & Bodenhausen, 2006; Kahneman, 2003; Strack & Deutsch, 2004). This has important implications, directly related to the domain of health psychology: Placing something in the future or negating something requires symbolic thought (reflective processes). This has important implications for prevention, where negation is often used (e.g., "drinking alcohol does not make you feel relaxed"), which can result in the paradoxical effect that this expectancy is increased by the intervention (Krank, Ames, Grenard, Schoenfeld, & Stacy, 2010).

The strong version of this line of thinking (dual-systems theory) has been criticized (Keren & Schul, 2009; Kruglanski & Gigerenzer, 2011). The brain does not really consist of a separable impulsive and reflective system (although there is evidence for different memory systems; Squire, 2004). A more realistic perspective from a cognitive neuroscience perspective is that the brain creates a quick first impression of a motivationally relevant situation, and if resources permit, can engage in further processing that produces more reflective processing at the psychological level of description (Cunningham & Zelazo, 2007; Gladwin, Figner, Crone, & Wiers, 2011; Wiers, Gladwin, Hofmann, Salemink, & Ridderinkhof, 2013).

With this qualification in the back of our head, it is still important to capture some of these initial, impulsive reactions because in some people, in some situations, they may be the most important predictor of health behaviors. Dual process models predict that impulsive predictors are especially important when reflective processing capacity is weak. This can be either because of stable individual differences (trait) and/or because of momentary circumstances (state).

In a series of studies we tested individual differences in the prediction of health-related behaviors. The overall pattern of findings was that indirect measures were a better predictor of health-related behaviors in individuals with relatively weak executive control than in individuals with relatively strong executive control. These findings have been remarkably consistent, while different measures were used to assess the impulsive processes (e.g., open-ended memory associations or reaction time tests of associations), executive control (e.g., different tests of working memory, the classic Stroop test), both with young adult and with adolescent participants, across different countries (Germany, The Netherlands, US), and across different health-related behaviors, including eating candy despite being on a diet (Friese, Hofmann, & Wänke, 2008; Hofmann, Gschwendner, Friese, Wiers, & Schmitt, 2008), alcohol use and problems (Friese et al., 2008; Grenard et al., 2008; Houben & Wiers, 2009; Peeters et al., 2012, 2013; Thush et al., 2008), smoking (Grenard et al., 2008), sexual interest and aggression (Hofmann, Gschwendner, et al., 2008), HIV risk behavior (Ames, Grenard, & Stacy, 2013; Grenard, Ames, & Stacy, 2013), and aggression after alcohol (Wiers, Beckers, Houben, &

Hofmann, 2009). Note that in the last study not only the relevant associations were assessed (alcohol–power), but also control associations (alcohol–fun), and that only the alcohol–power associations predicted aggression after alcohol use in participants (young men) with relatively weak executive control capacity.

In all of these studies, the indirect measures were the stronger predictor of the relevant health behavior in the participants with relatively weak executive control capacity. Obviously, this group runs the highest risk regarding a variety of health-related outcomes. In some studies it was found that the explicit measure was the better predictor of the health behavior in individuals with relatively strong executive control capacity. However, this was not always found (Littlefield, Verges, McCarthy, & Sher, 2011). Hence, there is some evidence that the rational models of behavior are particularly well suited to predict behavior of low-risk groups, such as undergraduate students, who happen to be the most easily accessible participants for many researchers. However, when the goal is to predict health behaviors in high-risk groups, especially in groups with relatively weak executive control capacity, evidence indicates that it is a good idea to also include indirect measures. Most of these studies included behavioral measures to assess both the relevant impulsive processes and the relevant executive control capacity, but associations in memory may also be assessed with paper-and-pencil measures, as long as assessment procedures make sure that the assessment is a previously validated, indirect measure of memory (Grenard et al., 2008; Stacy, Ames, & Grenard, 2006). Further, an index of executive control (or the related concept of self-control) can be assessed with self-reports (Friese et al., 2008), although it is somewhat questionable to what extent this can be generalized to high-risk groups (Friese et al., 2008, assessed self-reported self-control in undergraduate students). Further, some may question whether such measures are simply a self-perception of problem behaviors that are being predicted (also a frequent construct validity problem for traditional direct measures of attitude, beliefs, expectancies, self-efficacy, and so on). Another alternative for populations with less optimal self-insight (e.g., children and adolescents with externalizing disorders) is the use of a rating scale filled out by the parents, such as the Behavior Rating Inventory of Executive Function (BRIEF; Toplak, Bucciarelli, Jain, & Tannock, 2008).

Second, the relative prediction of impulsive and reflective processes has been examined as a function of state manipulations. When people are depleted of control resources, stressed, or drunk, the relative influence of impulsive processes becomes stronger (for reviews, see Hofmann, Friese, & Strack, 2009; Hofmann, Friese, et al., 2008). For instance, when alcohol is used, the knife cuts on two sides: Impulsive processes are primed (for more alcohol, but also for other appetitive behaviors, including food, sex, and other substances) and reflective processes are impaired (Field, Wiers, Christiansen, Fillmore, & Verster, 2010; Hofmann & Friese, 2008; Wiers, Houben, et al., 2010). And of course, many health-related behaviors occur under the influence of alcohol. Hence, these effects offer additional reasons why indirect measures should be used in health psychology.

Assessing Impulsive Processes

There are different ways to measure relatively impulsive, spontaneous processes in health psychology. From a measurement perspective, the three most common procedures used in health research can be divided into three classes: open-ended assessments of memory associations (paper and pencil), reaction time tests (RT tests), and indirect physiological measures (e.g., eye movements, brain measures, etc.). For reasons of space, we only briefly discuss the last category. A different way to structure these measures is by which cognitive processes they attempt to measure, where often three classes of processes are distinguished: attentional bias, memory associations, and action tendencies. Since this chapter is primarily on measurement, we will focus on the first categorization, but mention the different constructs they attempt to measure.

Open-Ended Memory Measures

Tests of memory associations using word production in addiction have used various types of word association procedures, based on basic memory research (for a review, see Stacy et al., 2006). Common tests have used free word association, in which the participant mentions the first word that comes to mind in response to a cue word, phrase, or picture, or a variant termed controlled association, in which a category of some type (e.g., verb) is requested using similar *top of mind* instructions (e.g., Friday night, …..). When these tests do not directly inquire about the target concept (e.g., drug associations), then they are indirect and may have the capability of assessing implicit processes. Indeed, consistent evidence across diverse paradigms from basic research shows that word association tests are capable of detecting implicit conceptual memory, and associations uncovered in these tests predict the spontaneous activation of cognitions across a wide range of experimental procedures (see Stacy et al., 2006, for details).

As with any implicit assessment method, it is important to state the specific nature of the implicit process attributed to measurement outcomes (De Houwer, Teige-Mocigemba, Spruyt, & Moors, 2009). The meaning of implicit processes in the implicit memory literature focuses on memory in the absence of deliberate or conscious recollection of a previous event, not on unconscious activation of the content of associations. Thus, activation or retrieval of associations is spontaneous but association content must come to mind to detect the associations with these methods.

Addiction research began using word association methods comprehensively with the work of Szalay and colleagues (Szalay, Bovasso, Vilov, & Williams, 1992), who focused on an associative network approach without invoking implicit cognition concepts. These investigators found different associative structures in drug users vs. non-users and among participants entering vs. those successfully completing drug treatment. Most associative network approaches are quite different from prevailing (deliberative) cognitive theories of health behavior and suggest that associations operate on behavior spontaneously, without the need for reflection. Such networks not only involve associations between affect and behavior, but may include any type of association that can be represented in memory, for example, associations between situational cues and behavior and concept-to-concept associations. Cue–behavior associations may be more important than affective or outcome associations once habits have begun to be established.

Most work by Szalay and colleagues has used a variant of free word association classified as continuous association. Continuous association elicits repeated associations to the same cue. For example, *Friday night* is listed 10 times on a page and the participant responds with the first word each instance makes them think of, with the requirement that they try to think of a different response each time. Repeated responses to the same cue can sometimes yield more variation in responses and may more readily detect some clinically relevant associative responses. However, response chaining, in which the previous response rather than the cue influences subsequent responses, is a potential problem. Most of the addiction research using word association conducted after the groundbreaking work of Szalay has relied on more traditional word association, either using free word association or a form of controlled association termed *verb generation*; verb generation asks for the first action or behavior that comes to mind in response to the cue, which may be a word, picture, or other stimulus. The first use of this technique in health research was in a study of college students, who were asked to generate the first behavior that came to mind in response to a series of alcohol-related and neutral short phrases (Stacy, 1994). The alcohol-related phrases did not explicitly mention alcohol or its synonyms but were obtained from college student norms for likely (perceived) positive outcomes of alcohol use (e.g., having fun, feeling good). Strong correlations were found between the generation of alcohol responses (in response to normatively high frequency alcohol outcomes) and alcohol consumption, even though nothing was asked about alcohol until after the associations were elicited using this indirect assessment. A number of studies have replicated this finding but have also documented the importance of associations between cues and alcohol as well as other substances (see Ames, Franken, & Coronges, 2006; and Stacy et al., 2006, for reviews), and recent findings have demonstrated the utility of the approach in evaluating dual-process theories of HIV risk behavior (Ames et al., 2013; Grenard et al., 2013).

In a comprehensive meta-analysis of over 89 effect sizes from studies sampling nearly 20,000 participants, word association tasks demonstrated the best effect sizes/predictive effects among all indirect tests of alcohol or other drug-related associations studied to date (Rooke, Hine, & Thorsteinsson, 2008). Prospective prediction has also been demonstrated in a number of studies, also adjusting for some but not all possible confounders (e.g., Kelly, Haynes, & Marlatt, 2008; Kelly, Masterman, & Marlatt, 2005; Stacy, 1997).

Two interesting recent innovations deserve mentioning. The first is to use self-coding in paper-and-pencil tests. Krank and colleagues successfully used this method, which greatly reduces the research burden in large studies (having two people judge thousands of open-ended answers can be costly), and produced valid results (Frigon & Krank, 2009; Krank, Schoenfeld, & Frigon, 2010). Second, Woud and colleagues (Woud, Fitzgerald, Wiers, Rinck, & Becker, 2012) developed a method to use ambiguous stories to which participants give a spontaneous response. Similar methods have been used in anxiety research, to assess and to modify interpretation bias (e.g., Salemink & Wiers, 2011). Hence, this method may open up new ways to change interpretative biases in addiction as well (other forms of cognitive bias modification are briefly discussed later). Finally, non-RT varieties of affective priming procedures have been developed, but given their conceptual link to these RT procedures, we discuss them in the next section.

Reaction Time Measures

During the past decades, there has been an explosion in the use of RT measures to assess relatively implicit and spontaneous processes in (health) behaviors. We order them here with respect to the constructs they (attempt to) assess: attentional bias, memory associations, and action tendencies (see also Chapter 2 in this volume, for a further overview of RT measures used in this domain).

Regarding attentional bias, most studies have used either a variety of the addiction Stroop task or a variety of the visual probe task (for a review, see Field & Cox, 2008). In the addiction Stroop task, attentional bias is inferred from a slowing in RT when participants name the color of words referring to their substance of abuse, as compared with neutral words. In the visual probe task, two pictures or words are presented simultaneously for a brief period, one representing the substance of abuse and the other a matched neutral stimulus. This is followed by the presentation of a probe (e.g., an arrow pointing up or down), to which the participant has to react. Attentional bias is inferred if participants react faster to the probe when it replaces a representation of the substance, compared with when it replaces the neutral picture or word. Using these two measures, researchers have fairly consistently found that heavier substance use is related to a stronger attentional bias, both in student and in general population samples (see Cox, Fadardi, & Pothos, 2006; and Field & Cox, 2008, for reviews). However, reliability is limited, especially of the visual probe test, and the two tests correlate poorly (for a discussion, see Ataya et al., 2012a, 2012b; and Field & Christiansen, 2012). This implies that this type of test may be of use in an experimental design to assess group differences (especially after a manipulation), but is less suited for predicting later behavior of an individual.

Other measures have been developed as well, for example, a variety of the change detection paradigm, where it has been found that substance abusers detect quick changes in a complex visual scene faster when they occur in substance-related stimuli than when they occur in nonsubstance-related stimuli (Jones, Jones, Smith, & Copley, 2003), and an attentional blink paradigm has shown some promising effects, although reliability can still be improved (Tibboel, De Houwer, & Field, 2010). One advantage of the latter test is that a distinction can be made between different attentional processes: a fast engagement process and a slower disengagement process. For this reason, researchers have started to use methods to register eye movements as well (Field, Eastwood, Bradley, & Mogg, 2006; Schoenmakers, Wiers, & Field, 2008), and interestingly, attentional bias assessed with eye movements correlates higher with subjective craving than RT measures (Field, Munafo, & Franken, 2009).

The second class of RT measures attempts to assess memory associations, mostly affective associations, a purpose similar to non-RT memory association measures discussed earlier. The most often used RT test to assess associations is the Implicit Association Test (IAT), developed by Greenwald and colleagues (Greenwald, McGhee, & Schwartz, 1998). The IAT as well as recent varieties are explained in a separate chapter in this volume (Chapter 3). The IAT has a number of strengths, which explain its popularity: it is a flexible tool (different associations can be assessed), easy to use, and much more reliable than many other implicit measures, with test–retest correlations of around .70 (Hofmann, Gawronski, Gschwendner, Le, & Schmitt, 2005; Wiers, Van de Luitgaarden, Van den Wildenberg, & Smulders, 2005). Furthermore, the IAT can be assessed reliably over the Internet (Houben & Wiers, 2008, 2009; Houben, Nosek, & Wiers, 2010). However, questions have been raised regarding the validity of the test, with much ongoing debate (Blanton et al., 2009; De Houwer et al., 2009; Greenwald, Nosek, Banaji, & Klauer, 2005; Nosek & Sriram, 2007; Rothermund & Wentura, 2004; Rothermund, Wentura, & De Houwer, 2005). Most importantly, the predictive validity of the test has been well established in over a hundred studies now, including many in health psychology domains (for a meta-analysis, see Greenwald, Poehlman, Uhlmann, & Banaji, 2009). In the domain of addictive behaviors, dozens of studies have demonstrated that the IAT predicts unique variance in the addictive behavior after controlling for explicit predictors (Greenwald et al., 2009; Rooke et al., 2008; Wiers, Houben, et al., 2010). Finally, research using mathematical modeling has demonstrated that the IAT does assess associative processes, but scores are also influenced by control processes (Conrey, Sherman, Gawronski, Hugenberg, & Groom, 2005; Sherman et al., 2008).

We discuss some of the main findings now. First, evidence from studies using bipolar IATs did not support the hypothesis that substance users have positive implicit attitudes toward addictive substances. Bipolar IATs contrasting alcohol with soft drinks as positive have repeatedly shown stronger negative associations with alcohol than with soft drinks (e.g., De Houwer, Crombez, Koster, & De Beul, 2004; Houben et al., 2010; Houben & Wiers, 2006a, 2006b;

Wiers, Van Woerden, Smulders, & De Jong, 2002). Similarly, smokers also demonstrated negative rather than positive implicit attitudes toward smoking on bipolar IATs (Huijding, De Jong, Wiers, & Verkooijen, 2005; Sherman, Presson, Chassin, Rose, & Koch, 2003; Swanson, Rudman, & Greenwald, 2001). Importantly, however, implicit attitudes did predict behavior in the expected direction, as less negative implicit attitudes on the bipolar IAT consistently show a positive relationship with drinking behavior (De Houwer et al., 2004; Houben et al., 2010) and with smoking (De Houwer, Custers, & De Clercq, 2006; Swanson et al., 2001). Hence, the absolute score on an IAT should not be over-interpreted (this person or group has positive or negative implicit attitudes toward category X), because the IAT is a relative measure and the absolute score is influenced by other factors, such as attention-grabbing properties of the categories (compare to Rothermund & Wentura, 2004). What is interesting is a reliable difference between groups on the same variety of the IAT, for example, smokers scoring relatively more positive than nonsmokers or heavy drinkers scoring relatively more positive than light drinkers (see also Roefs et al., 2011).

The observed unexpected negative implicit substance attitudes may be partly explained by extrapersonal associations or cultural knowledge that may not reflect one's personal attitudes, which is known to influence IAT scores (Olson & Fazio, 2004). Olson and Fazio (2004) argued that implicit attitudes might best be captured using a personalized IAT that is less affected by cultural knowledge and therefore more closely reflects personal attitudes. In line with this idea, studies that have examined implicit substance-related attitudes with a personalized version of the bipolar IAT have demonstrated positive implicit attitudes toward alcohol (Houben & Wiers, 2007) and toward smoking (De Houwer et al., 2006) that were positively correlated with substance use. In addition, figure–ground asymmetries may play a role (one category grabbing more attention than the other category; Rothermund & Wentura, 2004). Hence, the overall negative implicit attitudes assessed with bipolar IATs should not be interpreted as demonstrating that participants really have a negative attitude toward X. However, these measures predict unique variance in addictive behaviors, as well as other health behaviors, such as condom use (Marsh, Johnson, & Scott-Sheldon, 2001).

Bipolar IATs, however, can only be used to measure whether a substance is associated more strongly with positive or negative affect. While one would expect substances to be more strongly associated with positive affect, reflecting the incentive value of substances, from the dual-process perspective, one could also argue that substance users might at the same time hold negative associations with substances. Given that substance users probably experience negative consequences from their substance use and receive negative information about substance use (i.e., cultural knowledge), such negative information may eventually crystallize into negative implicit associations in the impulsive system. Therefore, perhaps a better way to examine implicit substance attitudes is to separate the positive/negative dimension into positive–neutral and negative–neutral so that positive and negative associations can be assessed separately.

Studies using such unipolar IATs or unipolar single-category IATs (Karpinski & Steinman, 2006), in which the comparison category (e.g., soft drinks, nonsmoking) is also omitted, have shown that alcohol (Houben et al., 2010; Houben & Wiers, 2006a, 2006b; Jajodia & Earleywine, 2003; McCarthy & Thompsen, 2006) as well as smoking (McCarthy & Thompsen, 2006) are associated with both positive and negative affect, but that elevated substance use is related only to the strength of positive implicit substance associations. Negative implicit associations, although sometimes stronger than positive associations, are typically unrelated to substance use. Findings with other varieties of the test, as well as with other RT measures, such as the Extrinsic Affective Simon Test (De Houwer, 2003b), found less strong negative associations, and generally, relatively positive associations are related to drinking (De Houwer & De Bruycker, 2007a). However, given the modest reliability of the EAST, the IAT is probably a better measure of individual differences in associations (De Houwer & De Bruycker, 2007b).

Note that in substance use, not only associations in the positive–negative dimension appear relevant, there are also indications that (positive) arousal associations are specifically strong in heavy users (De Houwer et al., 2004; Houben & Wiers, 2006a, 2006b; Wiers et al., 2005; Wiers et al., 2002). In addition, associations between alcohol and approach have also been related to heavy drinking (Ostafin & Palfai, 2006; Palfai & Ostafin, 2003). The latter associations are conceptually related to the third class of processes discussed here: action tendencies.

Two recent studies employed another variety of the IAT in alcohol research: the Alcohol Identity IAT, which attempts to measure the extent to which the participant identifies with being a drinker, as a defining characteristic of the self (Gray, LaPlante, Bannon, Ambady, & Shaffer, 2011). Gray and colleagues found that this variety of the IAT predicted risky drinking practices in college students, and in another recent study it was found that among six different IAT varieties, the Alcohol Identity IAT best correlated with alcohol use and problems in college students (Lindgren, Neighbors, Teachman, Wiers, Greenwald, 2013). Hence, the Drinker Identity IAT appears to be a particularly promising instrument among American college students. It is an interesting question to what extent this will also be the case in cultures where drinking is more normative, as in Western Europe.

Researchers have also recently used an IAT to assess automatically activated coping motives (Lindgren, Hendershot, Neighbors, Blayney, & Otto, 2011), which correlated with genetic risk factors (Hendershot, Lindgren, Liang, & Hutchison, 2012). This is relatively difficult because the IAT uses single terms and coping motives reflect a *change* in affect: Alcohol or other substances are used in order to alleviate negative affect (Comeau, Stewart, & Loba, 2001; Cooper, Frone, Russell, & Mudar, 1995; Wiers, 2008; Wiers, Houben, Smulders, Conrod, & Jones, 2006). In English there are single terms representing this uplifting change in affect, which may be more difficult to represent in other languages (e.g., in Dutch).

In order to assess relatively automatic processes underlying negative reinforcement (Baker, Piper, McCarthy, Majeskie, & Fiore, 2004), priming measures may be most optimally suited, because they include a temporal structure (Wiers et al., 2006). In this way it can be investigated to what extent negative affect activates alcohol (or other substances) or the other way around. Using a semantic priming measure in problem drinkers low or high on psychiatric distress, Zack and colleagues found that the activation of alcohol concepts by negative cues correlated with intensity of psychiatric distress and with a tendency to drink in negative states (Zack, Toneatto, & MacLeod, 1999), with similar findings for young problem drinkers (Zack, Poulos, Fragopoulos, Woodford, & MacLeod, 2006). However, a recent large study did not find automatically activated coping motives in alcoholic patients (Woud et al., 2013). One issue with priming measures is their modest reliability, compared with the IAT, but there are ways to increase this reliability, such as using a limited response window (Cunningham, Preacher, & Banaji, 2001). Hence, currently it is still unclear whether coping motives are automatically activated: We have trouble assessing it (compare to Wiers et al., 2006) and coping motives may be the result of a more reflective process (Wiers, 2008). Finally, the aforementioned ambiguous stories may also be used to assess automatically activated motivational processes to drink in order to cope with negative feelings (Woud et al., 2012).

Another recently developed method to study implicit cognition is the Implicit Relational Assessment Procedure (IRAP; Barnes-Holmes et al., 2006), with first applications to health psychology in adolescent smoking (Vahey, Boles, & Barnes-Holmes, 2010), implicit attitudes toward obesity (Roddy, Stewart, & Barnes-Holmes, 2012), and implicit attitudes toward cocaine in cocaine-dependent patients (Carpenter, Martinez, Vadhan, Barnes-Holmes, & Nunes, in press). A problem of the method is that it is rather challenging and typically a stringent response criterion is introduced, which could result in a lack of measurement in the most vulnerable individuals (who lack sufficient cognitive control to reach the stringent criterion). However, preliminary evidence suggests that the procedure may be adjusted for use with adolescents (Vahey et al., 2010) and addicted individuals (Carpenter et al., 2012).

The third class of RT measures used in addiction research in the past decade attempts to assess relatively automatic action tendencies of approach or avoidance. This has been done with yet another variety of the flexible IAT (Ostafin & Palfai, 2006; Palfai & Ostafin, 2003). It was found that heavy drinkers associate drinking more strongly with approach than with avoidance, and this was related to cue-induced craving. Some other paradigms have been developed to assess action tendencies. The first is a paradigm, sometimes referred to with the overly general label *stimulus–response compatibility* (SRC), in which participants are instructed in one block to move a manikin (little man) toward pictures of the substance and away from other pictures (approach substance block), and in another block to move the manikin away from the substance and toward other pictures (avoid substance block). Substance use and misuse (alcohol, cigarettes, marijuana) have all been found to be related to relatively fast approach movements in this task (Field et al., 2006; Field, Kiernan, Eastwood, & Child, 2008; Mogg, Bradley, Field, & De Houwer, 2003). In a recent functional magnetic resonance imaging study using a variety of this task, it was found that brain activity during this task predicted escalation of marijuana use 6 months later (Cousijn et al., 2012). Other approach–avoidance tasks have been developed, which use a joystick that is pulled (approach) or pushed (avoid). In one successful variety a zooming mechanism has been incorporated: When the joystick is pulled, the picture size increases on the computer screen, and when it is pushed, it decreases (Rinck & Becker, 2007). When heavy drinkers were instructed to pull or push in response to the format of the picture (irrespective of the contents), they were found to be faster in pulling than in pushing alcohol pictures, a difference not found for general positive or negative pictures (Wiers, Rinck, Dictus, & Van den Wildenberg, 2009). Note that this measure is more indirect than the SRC and IAT, which both instruct participants to categorize stimuli with respect to a relevant dimension (here combining alcohol and approach in one block and alcohol and avoid in another block), whereas in the approach-avoidance task (AAT), participants react to an aspect of the stimulus that is unrelated to the contents, such as the format of the picture (De Houwer, 2003a). In this way the AAT is structurally similar to the Extrinsic Affective Simon Task (De Houwer, 2003b; compare to Huijding & De Jong, 2005). One major advantage of this more indirect type of task is that it can be changed into a modification task (Wiers, Eberl, Rinck, Becker, & Lindenmeyer, 2011; Wiers, Rinck, Kordts, Houben, & Strack, 2010), discussed later. One disadvantage is that these tasks usually have a more modest reliability. One direct comparison of the SRC and AAT indeed found that the SRC outperformed the AAT as a measurement instrument (Field, Caren, Fernie, & De Houwer, 2011). However, two other recent studies found that while the AAT did not correlate with substance use at the moment of assessment, it was the best predictor of subsequent escalation of cannabis use (Cousijn, Goudriaan, & Wiers, 2011) and alcohol use in adolescents with weak executive control (Peeters et al., 2013). In the cannabis study, very carefully selected pictures along with nicely matched control pictures were used, and reliability of the AAT was adequate (.6). In addition, there are recent attempts to assess approach and avoidance tendencies separately, in a unipolar way, similar to what has been developed for the IAT (Sharbanee et al., 2013).

In summary, there are many RT measures to assess attentional bias, memory associations, and action tendencies. There appears to be a trade-off indicating that the more indirect a measure is, the lower the reliability. The more reliable measures make participants explicitly categorize stimuli (IAT, SRC, IRAP). However, more indirect measures are still interesting, because they may predict prospectively and may be changed into modification tasks. Finally, it should be noted that although the literature on implicit or indirect measures is strongly dominated by RT measures, some processes may be better assessed using different techniques, such as physiological indices (e.g., eye movements to assess attentional bias) and open-ended measures (to assess spontaneous memory associations).

How to Measure Reflective Processes

Given the limited space and the focus of this volume, we do not extensively discuss the assessment of reflective processes. However, we do like to emphasize that at least two aspects should be assessed: explicit motivation to control impulsive tendencies as well as ability to do so (Fazio, 1990; Hofmann, Friese, et al., 2008; Wiers et al., 2007). In the first category, one can assess expected outcomes, beliefs, motives, attitudes, norms, motivation to change behavior, etc. Again, we do not want to leave the reader with the impression that these measures are not important: Like more indirect measures, they predict unique variance in (health) behavior, as meta-analyses have demonstrated (Greenwald et al., 2009; Rooke et al., 2008). In addition, there are indications that these measures are in fact the best predictors in individuals with relatively strong executive control abilities (Hofmann, Gschwendner, et al., 2008; Thush et al., 2008), although in many instances we do not know if good prediction is the result of the cognitions ascribed to the construct or a self-reflection and alternative measure of the habit being predicted (criterion contamination). Another relevant perspective is the goal-pursuit perspective; careful consideration of the goals an individual holds may make seemingly irrational (health-related) behaviors become better understandable, and there is ample evidence of automatic goal-activation (for a recent review and perspective, see Köpetz, Lejuez, Wiers, & Kruglanski, 2013; see also Chapter 7 in this volume, for the assessment of implicit motives).

This brings us to the second class of reflective measures that one should assess: individual difference measures in executive control or working memory. Studies demonstrating that implicit processes are particularly strong predictors of health behaviors in individuals with relatively poor executive control have used broad measures, such as the classic Stroop Color–Word Interference Test (Houben & Wiers, 2009; Peeters et al., 2012, 2013; Wiers, Beckers, et al., 2009), the Self-Ordered Pointing Test that can be used in children and adolescents (Grenard et al., 2008; Thush et al., 2008), the Iowa Gambling Task to measure affective decision making (a form of "hot" executive control; Ames et al., 2013), and complex-span tasks, ideal for use in adults (Friese, Bargas-Avila, Hofmann, & Wiers, 2010; Grenard et al., 2013; Hofmann, Gschwendner, et al., 2008). In addition, there is preliminary evidence that different tests of different aspects of executive control (executive attention, inhibitory control, and affect regulation) each interact with implicit processes to predict health behavior (Hofmann, Friese, & Roefs, 2009). Hence, motivation to control, as well as ability (or abilities) to control, should be assessed.

How to Measure Individual Differences in Related Traits

We would like to briefly note that in addition to tests of implicit or associative processes, motivation, and ability to control, it could be helpful to assess more general aspects of personality (e.g., impulsivity, sensation seeking) related to health behaviors. However, the aforementioned moderation effects of executive control on the prediction of addictive behaviors by implicit tests were not reduced after controlling for these traits (Wiers, Ames, Hofmann, Krank, & Stacy, 2010). Hence, we strongly believe that in addition to general measures of personality and executive abilities, it is important to assess behavior-specific impulsive processes. In addition, general personality facets related to health behaviors may also be assessed using behavioral tests. For example, there are interesting tests of sensation seeking and risk taking (Lejuez et al., 2007), reward and punishment sensitivity (Frank & Claus, 2006; Robbins, 2007), and decision making in cold vs. hot situations (Figner, Mackinlay, Wilkening, & Weber, 2009). We refer the reader to Chapter 3 in this volume.

Current Issues, New Developments

Before ending, we touch upon some current issues and recent developments. First, impulsive processes can be primed, which might provide a better assessment. For example, after a prime dose of alcohol, an attentional bias for alcohol gets stronger and more strongly correlated with an approach bias for alcohol in heavy drinkers (Schoenmakers et al., 2008). Alcohol can also make other appetitive biases more salient, such as for cigarettes (Field, Mogg, & Bradley, 2005), food (Hofmann & Friese, 2008), and (unsafe) sex (MacDonald, MacDonald, Zanna, & Fong, 2000; MacDonald, Zanna, & Fong, 1996); for further reviews, see Field et al. (2010) and Wiers, Houben, et al. (2010). It is an interesting question to what extent alcohol-primed assessment (or assessment of impulsive processes in a hot situation) is a better predictor of actual health behaviors. To the best of our knowledge this has not been tested. Relatedly, assessment after triggering a relevant mood may provide better assessment of the relevant cognitive motivational processes involved, as has been demonstrated for stress (Field & Powell, 2007; Field & Quigley, 2009; Sinha et al., 2009) and for anxious and depressed feelings in coping drinkers and a positive mood in enhancement drinkers (Birch et al., 2008; Grant & Stewart, 2007; Grant, Stewart, & Mohr, 2009; Stewart, Hall, Wilkie, & Birch, 2002).

Second, as mentioned earlier, a new branch of experimental psychopathology research has emerged that does not only try to measure cognitive processes involved in psychopathology, but also tries to directly change them, by using modified versions of the assessment instruments used. Two strategies can be used: train the general capacity to control, such as working memory training (often used in ADHD; for a review, see Klingberg, 2010), with first studies in addiction (Bickel, Yi, Landes, Hill, & Baxter, 2011; Houben, Wiers & Jansen, 2011), or change the more spontaneous impulsive processes involved in the behavior (for a review, see Wiers et al., 2013).

MacLeod and colleagues first developed a re-training procedure targeting an attentional bias for threat-related stimuli in the domain of anxiety (MacLeod, Rutherford, Campbell, Ebsworthy, & Holker, 2002). They modified an assessment instrument (visual probe test) with the goal of manipulating the underlying process. In this test, two pictures appear simultaneously on the computer screen (one disorder-related, one control), followed by a probe to which people react (e.g., an arrow pointing up or down). In an assessment variety of the test, the probe appears equally often in the location previously occupied by the threat stimulus and in the location previously occupied by the control stimulus. In a modified version of the task, a contingency is introduced, with the probe appearing more often on the location occupied by the threat stimulus (to strengthen the bias) or more often on the location occupied by the neutral stimulus (to reduce the bias). Results indicated that the attentional bias modification had been successful, as assessed with different stimuli in the same task (close generalization), and further generalization was found in a subsequent stress-inducing task, with participants in the attend-threat condition showing greater distress than participants in the attend-neutral condition. Subsequent research in this domain investigated clinical applications, typically with multiple training sessions, with recent successful studies in clinically anxious patient groups (Amir, Beard, Burns, & Bomyea, 2009; Schmidt, Richey, Buckner, & Timpano, 2009) and in targeted prevention (See, MacLeod, & Bridle, 2009).

Similar procedures have been applied to addictive behaviors, to re-train an attentional bias for a substance. These studies involved a single session of cognitive bias modification, assessing close generalization (different stimuli in same task) and further generalization (different tasks, craving, choice of drink). These studies showed a very similar pattern: An attentional bias for alcohol (Field et al., 2007; Field & Eastwood, 2005; Schoenmakers, Wiers, Jones, Bruce, & Jansen, 2007) and smoking (Attwood, O'Sullivan, Leonards, Mackintosh, & Munafo, 2008; Field, Duka, Tyler, & Schoenmakers, 2009) could be modified in both directions. However, no evidence for generalization was found after a single session of re-training (Field et al., 2007; Field, Duka, et al., 2009; Schoenmakers et al., 2007). More encouragingly, the first two studies using *repeated* attentional re-training in problem drinkers (Fadardi & Cox, 2009) and alcohol-dependent patients in treatment (Schoenmakers et al., 2010) both found generalized positive effects. In addition, Wiers and colleagues modified the approach–avoidance test to re-train an approach bias in students and found generalized effects on the bias and on subsequent drinking behavior in a taste test (Wiers, Rinck, et al., 2010), and re-training alcoholic patients helped them to stay abstinent a year after treatment discharge (Wiers et al., 2011). In a recent replication study, it was found that the clinical effect replicated and was mediated by the change in approach bias (Eberl et al., 2013). Further, patients with a strong alcohol-approach bias profited most from the training (moderation).

This brings us back to the issue of measurement: Ideally one would want to train only individuals with a strong cognitive bias. However, in order to allocate individuals to conditions, a very reliable measurement is needed. And as mentioned earlier, the assessment instruments modified for re-training are typically very indirect (visual probe test for attentional re-training, AAT for approach-bias retraining) and typically have a poor to modest reliability. They are therefore not suitable for individual decisions regarding suitability of the modification training. One option could be to use another, more reliable test to assess the same construct (e.g., the emotional Stroop task for an attentional bias, or the SRC or IAT for an approach bias), but these measures typically correlate very weakly (Ataya et al., 2012a, 2012b; Field et al., 2011) and in some cases even give opposite results. Indeed, in a recent study using the SRC to predict relapse, it was found that patients with a stronger avoidance bias showed an increased risk for relapse (Spruyt et al., 2012), while another (larger) recent study found that patients with a strong alcohol-approach bias, as assessed with the AAT, profited most from approach-bias re-training (Eberl et al., 2013; see Wiers, Gladwin & Rinck, 2013, for further discussion). Hence, it is clear that this area can profit from a further development of reliable assessment instruments.

Conclusion

From our review it should be clear that much can be gained by including indirect measures in the domain of health psychology and the related domains of clinical psychology. Different, relatively spontaneous implicit processes can be assessed (attentional bias, memory bias, action tendencies), and many studies have now demonstrated that these measures predict unique variance in these behaviors over self-report assessment alone. Second, research has demonstrated that these measures are particularly powerful in predicting health behaviors in individuals with relatively poor executive control functions, typically individuals with increased risk for health problems. Third, research is emerging that demonstrates that some of these processes can be directly interfered with, with relevant effects on health behaviors. Clearly, this is a promising area of research.

At the same time, further improvement in the measurement of implicit or relatively spontaneous cognitive-motivational processes in health psychology is needed. Hence, more research on optimizing these measures is needed in this area, to predict health behaviors and ultimately to make informed decisions on which intervention would be most suited for a specific individual.

References

Ames, S. L., Franken, I. H. A., & Coronges, K. (2006). Implicit cognition and drugs of abuse. In R. W. Wiers & A. W. Stacy (Eds.), *Handbook of implicit cognition and addiction* (pp. 363–378). Thousand Oaks, CA: Sage.

Ames, S. L., Grenard, J. L., & Stacy, A. W. (2013). Dual process interaction model of HIV-risk behaviors among drug offenders. *Aids and Behavior, 17*, 914–925. http://doi.org/10.1007/s10461-012-0140-2

Amir, N., Beard, C., Burns, M., & Bomyea, J. (2009). Attention modification program in individuals with generalized anxiety disorder. *Journal of Abnormal Psychology, 118*, 28–33. http://doi.org/10.1037/a0012589

Ataya, A. F., Adams, S., Mullings, E., Cooper, R. M., Attwood, A. S., & Munafo, M. R. (2012a). Internal reliability of measures of substance-related cognitive bias. *Drug and Alcohol Dependence, 121*, 148–151. http://doi.org/10.1016/j.drugalcdep.2011.08.023

Ataya, A. F., Adams, S., Mullings, E., Cooper, R. M., Attwood, A. S., & Munafo, M. R. (2012b). Methodological considerations in cognitive bias research: The next steps. *Drug and Alcohol Dependence, 124*, 191–192. http://doi.org/10.1016/j.drugalcdep.2012.02.008

Attwood, A. S., O'Sullivan, H., Leonards, U., Mackintosh, B., & Munafo, M. R. (2008). Attentional bias training and cue reactivity in cigarette smokers. *Addiction, 103*, 1875–1882. http://doi.org/10.1111/j.1360-0443.2008.02335.x

Baker, T. B., Piper, M. E., McCarthy, D. E., Majeskie, M. R., & Fiore, M. C. (2004). Addiction motivation reformulated: An affective processing model of negative reinforcement. *Psychological Review, 111*, 33–51. http://doi.org/10.1037/0033-295X.111.1.33

Barnes-Holmes, D., Barnes-Holmes, Y., Power, P., Hayden, E., Milne, R., & Stewart, I. (2006). Do you really know what you believe? Developing the Implicit Relational Assessment Procedure (IRAP) as a direct measure of implicit beliefs. *The Irish Psychologist, 32*, 169–177.

Bechara, A. (2005). Decision making, impulse control and loss of willpower to resist drugs: A neurocognitive perspective. *Nature Neuroscience, 8*, 1458–1463. http://doi.org/10.1038/nn1584

Bickel, W. K., Yi, R., Landes, R. D., Hill, P. F., & Baxter, C. (2011). Remember the future: Working memory training decreases delay discounting among stimulant addicts. *Biological Psychiatry, 69*, 260–265. http://doi.org/10.1016/j.biopsych.2010.08.017

Birch, C. D., Stewart, S. H., Wiers, R. W., Klein, R. M., Maclean, A. D., & Berish, M. J. (2008). The mood-induced activation of implicit alcohol cognition in enhancement and coping motivated drinkers. *Addictive Behaviors, 33*, 565–581. http://doi.org/10.1016/j.addbeh.2007.11.004

Blanton, H., Jaccard, J., Klick, J., Mellers, B., Mitchell, G., & Tetlock, P. E. (2009). Strong claims and weak evidence: Reassessing the predictive validity of the IAT. *Journal of Applied Psychology, 94*, 567–582; discussion 583–603.

Carpenter, K. M., Martinez, D., Vadhan, N. L., Barnes-Holmes, D., & Nunes, V. E. (2012). Measures of attentional bias and relational responding are associated with behavioral treatment outcome for cocaine dependence. *The American Journal of Drug and Alcohol Abuse, 38*, 146–154. http://doi.org/10.3109/00952990.2011.643986

Comeau, N., Stewart, S. H., & Loba, P. (2001). The relations of trait anxiety, anxiety sensitivity, and sensation seeking to adolescents' motivations for alcohol, cigarette, and marijuana use. *Addictive Behaviors, 26*, 803–825. http://doi.org/10.1016/S0306-4603(01)00238-6

Conrey, F. R., Sherman, J. W., Gawronski, B., Hugenberg, K., & Groom, C. J. (2005). Separating multiple processes in implicit social cognition: The quad model of implicit task performance. *Journal of Personality and Social Psychology, 89*, 469–487. http://doi.org/10.1037/0022-3514.89.4.469

Cooper, M. L., Frone, M. R., Russell, M., & Mudar, P. (1995). Drinking to regulate positive and negative emotions: A motivational model of alcohol use. *Journal of Personality and Social Psychology, 69*, 990–1005. http://doi.org/10.1037/0022-3514.69.5.990

Cousijn, J., Goudriaan, A. E., Ridderinkhof, K. R., Van den Brink, W., Veltman, D. J., & Wiers, R. W. (2012). Approach-bias predicts development of cannabis problem severity in heavy cannabis users: Results from a prospective FMRI study. *PLoS One, 7*, e42394. http://doi.org/10.1371/journal.pone.0042394

Cousijn, J., Goudriaan, A. E., & Wiers, R. W. (2011). Reaching out towards cannabis: Approach-bias in heavy cannabis users predicts changes in cannabis use. *Addiction, 106*, 1667–1674. http://doi.org/10.1111/j.1360-0443.2011.03475.x

Cox, W. M., Fadardi, J. S., & Pothos, E. M. (2006). The addiction-Stroop test: Theoretical considerations and procedural recommendations. *Psychological Bulletin, 132*, 443–476. http://doi.org/10.1037/0033-2909.132.3.443

Cunningham, W. A., Preacher, K. J., & Banaji, M. R. (2001). Implicit attitude measures: Consistency, stability, and convergent validity. *Psychological Science, 12*, 163–170. http://doi.org/10.1111/1467-9280.00328

Cunningham, W. A., & Zelazo, P. D. (2007). Attitudes and evaluations: A social cognitive neuroscience perspective. *Trends in Cognitive Sciences, 11*, 97–104. http://doi.org/10.1016/j.tics.2006.12.005

De Houwer, J. (2003a). A structural analysis of indirect measures of attitudes. In J. Musch & K. C. Klauer (Eds.), *The psychology of evaluation: Affective processes in cognition and emotion* (pp. 219–244). Mahwah, NJ: Lawrence Erlbaum.

De Houwer, J. (2003b). The Extrinsic Affective Simon Task. *Experimental Psychology, 50*, 77–85. http://doi.org/10.1026//1618-3169.50.2.77

De Houwer, J., Crombez, G., Koster, E. H. W., & De Beul, N. (2004). Implicit alcohol-related cognitions in a clinical sample of heavy drinkers. *Journal of Behavior Therapy and Experimental Psychiatry, 35*, 275–286. http://doi.org/10.1016/j.jbtep.2004.05.001

De Houwer, J., Custers, R., & De Clercq, A. (2006). Do smokers have a negative implicit attitude towards smoking? *Cognition and Emotion, 20*, 1274–1284. http://doi.org/10.1080/02699930500484506

De Houwer, J., & De Bruycker, E. (2007a). The identification-EAST as a valid measure of implicit attitudes toward alcohol-related stimuli. *Journal of Behavior Therapy and Experimental Psychiatry, 38*, 133–143. http://doi.org/10.1016/j.jbtep.2006.10.004

De Houwer, J., & De Bruycker, E. (2007b). The implicit association test outperforms the extrinsic affective Simon task as an implicit measure of inter-individual differences in attitudes. *British Journal of Social Psychology, 46*, 401–421. http://doi.org/10.1348/014466606X130346

De Houwer, J., Teige-Mocigemba, S., Spruyt, A., & Moors, A. (2009). Implicit measures: A normative analysis and review. *Psychological Bulletin, 135*, 347–368. http://doi.org/10.1037/a0014211

Eberl, C., Wiers, R. W., Pawelczack, S., Rinck, M., Becker, E. S., & Lindenmeyer, J. (2013). Approach bias modification in alcohol dependence: Do clinical effects replicate and for whom does it work best? *Developmental Cognitive Neuroscience, 4*, 38–51. http://doi.org/10.1016/j.dcn.2012.11.002

Evans, J. S. B. T. (2008). Dual-processing accounts of reasoning, judgment, and social cognition. *Annual Review of Psychology, 59*, 255–278. http://doi.org/10.1146/annurev.psych.59.103006.093629

Fadardi, J. S., & Cox, W. M. (2009). Reversing the sequence: Reducing alcohol consumption by overcoming alcohol attentional bias. *Drug and Alcohol Dependence, 101*, 137–145. http://doi.org/10.1016/j.drugalcdep.2008.11.015

Fazio, R. H. (1990). The MODE model as an integrative framework. *Advances in Experimental Social Psychology, 23*, 75–109. http://doi.org/10.1016/S0065-2601(08)60318-4

Field, M., Caren, R., Fernie, G., & De Houwer, J. (2011). Alcohol approach tendencies in heavy drinkers: Comparison of effects in a Relevant Stimulus-Response Compatibility task and an approach/avoidance Simon task. *Psychology of Addictive Behaviors, 25*, 697–701. http://doi.org/10.1037/a0023285

Field, M., & Christiansen, P. (2012). Commentary on 'Internal reliability of measures of substance-related cognitive bias'. *Drug and Alcohol Dependence, 124*, 189–190. http://doi.org/10.1016/j.drugalcdep.2012.02.009

Field, M., & Cox, W. M. (2008). Attentional bias in addictive behaviors: A review of its development, causes, and consequences. *Drug and Alcohol Dependence, 97*, 1–20. http://doi.org/10.1016/j.drugalcdep.2008.03.030

Field, M., Duka, T., Eastwood, B., Child, R., Santarcangelo, M., & Gayton, M. (2007). Experimental manipulation of attentional biases in heavy drinkers: Do the effects generalise? *Psychopharmacology, 192*, 593–608. http://doi.org/10.1007/s00213-007-0760-9

Field, M., Duka, T., Tyler, E., & Schoenmakers, T. (2009). Attentional bias modification in tobacco smokers. *Nicotine and Tobacco Research, 11*, 812–822. http://doi.org/10.1093/ntr/ntp067

Field, M., & Eastwood, B. (2005). Experimental manipulation of attentional bias increases the motivation to drink alcohol. *Psychopharmacology, 183*, 350–357. http://doi.org/10.1007/s00213-005-0202-5

Field, M., Eastwood, B., Bradley, B. P., & Mogg, K. (2006). Selective processing of cannabis cues in regular cannabis users. *Drug and Alcohol Dependence, 85*, 75–82. http://doi.org/10.1016/j.drugalcdep.2006.03.018

Field, M., Kiernan, A., Eastwood, B., & Child, R. (2008). Rapid approach responses to alcohol cues in heavy drinkers. *Journal of Behavior Therapy and Experimental Psychiatry, 39*, 209–218. http://doi.org/10.1016/j.jbtep.2007.06.001

Field, M., Mogg, K., & Bradley, B. P. (2005). Alcohol increases cognitive biases for smoking cues in smokers. *Psychopharmacology, 180*, 63–72. http://doi.org/10.1007/s00213-005-2251-1

Field, M., Munafo, M. R., & Franken, I. H. A. (2009). A meta-analytic investigation of the relationship between attentional bias and subjective craving in substance abuse. *Psychological Bulletin, 135*, 589–607. http://doi.org/10.1037/a0015843

Field, M., & Powell, H. (2007). Stress increases attentional bias for alcohol cues in social drinkers who drink to cope. *Alcohol and Alcoholism, 42*, 560–566. http://doi.org/10.1093/alcalc/agm064

Field, M., & Quigley, M. (2009). Mild stress increases attentional bias in social drinkers who drink to cope: A replication and extension. *Experimental and Clinical Psychopharmacology, 17*, 312–319. http://doi.org/10.1037/a0017090

Field, M., Wiers, R. W., Christiansen, P., Fillmore, M. T., & Verster, J. C. (2010). Acute alcohol effects on inhibitory control and implicit cognition: Implications for loss of control over drinking. *Alcoholism: Clinical and Experimental Research, 34*, 1346–1352.

Figner, B., Mackinlay, R. J., Wilkening, F., & Weber, E. U. (2009). Affective and deliberative processes in risky choice: Age differences in risk taking in the Columbia Card Task. *Journal of Experimental Psychology: Learning Memory Cognition, 35*, 709–730.

Frank, M. J., & Claus, E. D. (2006). Anatomy of a decision: Striato-orbitofrontal interactions in reinforcement learning, decision making, and reversal. *Psychological Review, 113*, 300–326. http://doi.org/10.1037/0033-295X.113.2.300

Friese, M., Bargas-Avila, J., Hofmann, W., & Wiers, R. W. (2010). Here's looking at you, bud: Alcohol-related memory structures predict eye movements for social drinkers with low executive control. *Social Psychological and Personality Science, 1*, 143–151.

Friese, M., Hofmann, W., & Wänke, M. (2008). When impulses take over: Moderated predictive validity of explicit and implicit attitude measures in predicting food choice and consumption behaviour. *British Journal of Social Psychology, 47*, 397–419. http://doi.org/10.1348/014466607X241540

Frigon, A. P., & Krank, M. D. (2009). Self-coded indirect memory associations in a brief school-based intervention for substance use suspensions. *Psychology of Addictive Behaviors, 23*, 736–742. http://doi.org/10.1037/a0017125

Gawronski, B., & Bodenhausen, G. V. (2006). Associative and propositional processes in evaluation: An integrative review of implicit and explicit attitude change. *Psychological Bulletin, 132*, 692–731. http://doi.org/10.1037/0033-2909.132.5.692

Gladwin, T. E., Figner, B., Crone, E. A., & Wiers, R. W. (2011). Addiction, adolescence, and the integration of control and motivation. *Developmental Cognitive Neuroscience, 1*, 364–376. http://doi.org/10.1016/j.dcn.2011.06.008

Grant, V. V., & Stewart, S. H. (2007). Impact of experimentally induced positive and anxious mood on alcohol expectancy strength in internally motivated drinkers. *Cognitive Behaviour Therapy, 36*, 102–111. http://doi.org/10.1080/16506070701223289

Grant, V. V., Stewart, S. H., & Mohr, C. D. (2009). Coping-anxiety and coping-depression motives predict different daily mood-drinking relationships. *Psychology of Addictive Behaviors, 23*, 226–237. http://doi.org/10.1037/a0015006

Gray, H. M., LaPlante, D. A., Bannon, B. L., Ambady, N., & Shaffer, H. J. (2011). Development and validation of the Alcohol Identity Implicit Associations Test (AI-IAT). *Addictive Behaviors, 36*, 919–926. http://doi.org/10.1016/j.addbeh.2011.05.003

Greenwald, A. G., McGhee, D. E., & Schwartz, J. L. K. (1998). Measuring individual differences in implicit cognition: The Implicit Association Test. *Journal of Personality and Social Psychology, 74*, 1464–1480. http://doi.org/10.1037/0022-3514.74.6.1464

Greenwald, A. G., Nosek, B. A., Banaji, M. R., & Klauer, K. C. (2005). Validity of the salience asymmetry interpretation of the Implicit Association Test: Comment on Rothermund and Wentura (2004). *Journal of Experimental Psychology: General, 134*, 420. http://doi.org/10.1037/0096-3445.134.3.420

Greenwald, A. G., Poehlman, T. A., Uhlmann, E. L., & Banaji, M. R. (2009). Understanding and using the Implicit Association Test: III. Meta-analysis of predictive validity. *Journal of Personality and Social Psychology, 97*, 17–41. http://doi.org/10.1037/a0015575

Grenard, J. G., Ames, S. L., & Stacy, A. W. (2013). Deliberative and spontaneous cognitive processes associated with HIV risk behavior. *Journal of Behavioral Medicine, 36*, 95–107. http://doi.org/10.1007/s10865-012-9404-6

Grenard, J. L., Ames, S. L., Wiers, R. W., Thush, C., Sussman, S., & Stacy, A. W. (2008). Working memory capacity moderates the predictive effects of drug-related associations on substance use. *Psychology of Addictive Behaviors, 22*, 426–432. http://doi.org/10.1037/0893-164X.22.3.426

Hendershot, C. S., Lindgren, K. P., Liang, T., & Hutchison, K. E. (2012). COMT and ALDH2 polymorphisms moderate associations of implicit drinking motives with alcohol use. *Addiction Biology, 17*, 192–201. http://doi.org/10.1111/j.1369-1600.2010.00286.x

Hofmann, W., & Friese, M. (2008). Impulses got the better of me: Alcohol moderates the influence of implicit attitudes toward food cues on eating behavior. *Journal of Abnormal Psychology, 117*, 420–427. http://doi.org/10.1037/0021-843X.117.2.420

Hofmann, W., Friese, M., & Roefs, A. (2009). Three ways to resist temptation: The independent contributions of executive attention, inhibitory control, and affect regulation to the impulse control of eating behavior. *Journal of Experimental Social Psychology, 45*, 431–435. http://doi.org/10.1016/j.jesp.2008.09.013

Hofmann, W., Friese, M., & Strack, F. (2009). Impulse and self-control from a dual-systems perspective. *Perspectives on Psychological Science, 4*, 162–176. http://doi.org/10.1111/j.1745-6924.2009.01116.x

Hofmann, W., Friese, M., & Wiers, R. W. (2008). Impulsive versus reflective influences on health behavior: A theoretical framework and empirical review. *Health Psychology Review, 2*, 111–137. http://doi.org/10.1080/17437190802617668

Hofmann, W., Gawronski, B., Gschwendner, T., Le, H., & Schmitt, M. (2005). A meta-analysis on the correlation between the implicit association test and explicit self-report measures. *Personality and Social Psychology Bulletin, 31*, 1369–1385. http://doi.org/10.1177/0146167205275613

Hofmann, W., Gschwendner, T., Friese, M., Wiers, R. W., & Schmitt, M. (2008). Working memory capacity and self-regulatory behavior: Toward an individual differences perspective on behavior determination by automatic versus controlled processes. *Journal of Personality and Social Psychology, 95*, 962–977. http://doi.org/10.1037/a0012705

Houben, K., Nosek, B. A., & Wiers, R. W. (2010). Seeing the forest through the trees: A comparison of different IAT variants measuring implicit alcohol associations. *Drug and Alcohol Dependence, 106*, 204–211. http://doi.org/10.1016/j.drugalcdep.2009.08.016

Houben, K., & Wiers, R. W. (2006a). Assessing implicit alcohol associations with the Implicit Association Test: Fact or artifact? *Addictive Behaviors, 31*, 1346–1362. http://doi.org/10.1016/j.addbeh.2005.10.009

Houben, K., & Wiers, R. W. (2006b). A test of the salience asymmetry interpretation of the Alcohol-IAT. *Experimental Psychology, 53*, 292–300. http://doi.org/10.1027/1618-3169.53.4.292

Houben, K., & Wiers, R. W. (2007). Are drinkers implicitly positive about drinking alcohol? Personalizing the alcohol-IAT to reduce negative extrapersonal contamination. *Alcohol and Alcoholism, 42*, 301–307. http://doi.org/10.1093/alcalc/agm015

Houben, K., & Wiers, R. W. (2008). Measuring implicit alcohol associations via the Internet: Validation of Web-based Implicit Association Tests. *Behavior Research Methods, 40*, 1134–1143. http://doi.org/10.3758/BRM.40.4.1134

Houben, K., & Wiers, R. W. (2009). Response inhibition moderates the relationship between implicit associations and drinking behavior. *Alcoholism: Clinical and Experimental Research, 33*, 626–633. http://doi.org/10.1111/j.1530-0277.2008.00877.x

Houben, K., Wiers, R. W., Jansen, A. (2011). Getting a grip on drinking behavior: Training working memory to reduce alcohol abuse. *Psychological Science, 22*, 968–975.

Huijding, J., & De Jong, P. J. (2005). A pictorial version of the Extrinsic Affective Simon Task: Sensitivity to generally affective and phobia-relevant stimuli in high and low spider fearful individuals. *Experimental Psychology, 52*, 289–295. http://doi.org/10.1027/1618-3169.52.4.289

Huijding, J., De Jong, P. J., Wiers, R. W., & Verkooijen, K. (2005). Implicit and explicit attitudes towards smoking in a smoking and a non-smoking setting. *Addictive Behaviors, 30*, 949–961. http://doi.org/10.1016/j.addbeh.2004.09.014

Jajodia, A., & Earleywine, M. (2003). Measuring alcohol expectancies with the implicit association test. *Psychology of Addictive Behaviors, 17*, 126–133. http://doi.org/10.1037/0893-164X.17.2.126

Jones, B. T., Jones, B. C., Smith, H., & Copley, N. (2003). A flicker paradigm for inducing change blindness reveals alcohol and cannabis information processing biases in social users. *Addiction, 98*, 235–244. http://doi.org/10.1046/j.1360-0443.2003.00270.x

Kahneman, D. (2003). A perspective on judgment and choice: Mapping bounded rationality. *American Psychologist, 58*, 697–720. http://doi.org/10.1037/0003-066X.58.9.697

Karpinski, A., & Steinman, R. B. (2006). The single category implicit association test as a measure of implicit social cognition. *Journal of Personality and Social Psychology, 91*, 16–32. http://doi.org/10.1037/0022-3514.91.1.16

Kelly, A. B., Haynes, M. A., & Marlatt, G. A. (2008). The impact of adolescent tobacco-related associative memory on smoking trajectory: An application of negative binomial regression to highly skewed longitudinal data. *Addictive Behaviors, 33*, 640–650. http://doi.org/10.1016/j.addbeh.2007.11.008

Kelly, A. B., Masterman, P. W., & Marlatt, G. A. (2005). Alcohol-related associative strength and drinking behaviours: concurrent and prospective relationships. *Drug and Alcohol Review, 24*, 489–498. http://doi.org/10.1080/09595230500337675

Keren, G., & Schul, Y. (2009). Two is not always better than one. A critical evaluation of two-system theories. *Perspectives on Psychological Science, 4*, 533–550. http://doi.org/10.1111/j.1745-6924.2009.01164.x

Klingberg, T. (2010). Training and plasticity of working memory. *Trends in Cognitive Sciences, 14*, 317–324. http://doi.org/10.1016/j.tics.2010.05.002

Köpetz, C. E., Lejuez, C. W., Wiers, R. W., & Kruglanski, A. W. (2013). Motivation and self-regulation in addiction: A call for convergence. *Perspectives on Psychological Science, 8*, 3–24. http://doi.org/10.1177/1745691612457575

Krank, M. D., Ames, S. L., Grenard, J. L., Schoenfeld, T., & Stacy, A. W. (2010). Paradoxical effects of alcohol information on alcohol outcome expectancies. *Alcoholism: Clinical and Experimental Research, 34*, 1193–1200.

Krank, M. D., Schoenfeld, T., & Frigon, A. P. (2010). Self-coded indirect memory associations and alcohol and marijuana use in college students. *Behavioral Research Methods, 42*, 733–738. http://doi.org/10.3758/BRM.42.3.733

Kruglanski, A. W., & Gigerenzer, G. (2011). Intuitive and deliberate judgments are based on common principles. *Psychological Review, 118*, 97–109. http://doi.org/10.1037/a0020762

Lejuez, C. W., Aklin, W., Daughters, S., Zvolensky, M., Kahler, C., & Gwadz, M. (2007). Reliability and validity of the youth version of the Balloon Analogue Risk Task (BART-Y) in the assessment of risk-taking behavior among inner-city adolescents. *Journal of Clinical Child and Adolescent Psychology, 36*, 106–111. http://doi.org/10.1080/15374410709336573

Lewin, K. (1951). *Field theory in social science; selected theoretical papers*. New York, NY: Harper & Row.

Lindgren, K. P., Hendershot, C. S., Neighbors, C., Blayney, J. A., & Otto, J. M. (2011). Implicit coping and enhancement motives predict unique variance in drinking in Asian Americans. *Motivation and Emotion, 35*, 435–443. http://doi.org/10.1007/s11031-011-9223-z

Lindgren, K. P., Neighbors, C., Teachman, B. A., Wiers, R. W., Greenwald, A. G. (2013). I drink therefore I am: Validating alcohol-related implicit association tests. *Psychology of Addictive Behaviors, 27*, 1–13. http://doi.org/10.1037/a0027640

Littlefield, A. K., Verges, A., McCarthy, D. M., & Sher, K. J. (2011). Interactions between self-reported alcohol outcome expectancies and cognitive functioning in the prediction of alcohol use and associated problems: A further examination. *Psychology of Addictive Behaviors, 25*, 542–546. http://doi.org/10.1037/a0022090

MacDonald, T. K., MacDonald, G., Zanna, M. P., & Fong, G. T. (2000). Alcohol, sexual arousal, and intentions to use condoms in young men: Applying alcohol myopia theory to risky sexual behavior. *Health Psychology, 19*, 290–298. http://doi.org/10.1037/0278-6133.19.3.290

MacDonald, T. K., Zanna, M. P., & Fong, G. T. (1996). Why common sense goes out of the window: Effects of alcohol on intentions to use condoms. *Personality and Social Psychology Bulletin, 22*, 763–775. http://doi.org/10.1177/0146167296228001

MacLeod, C., Rutherford, E., Campbell, L., Ebsworthy, C., & Holker, L. (2002). Selective attention and emotional vulnerability: Assessing the causal basis of their association through the experimental manipulation of attentional bias. *Journal of Abnormal Psychology, 111*, 107–123. http://doi.org/10.1037/0021-843X.111.1.107

Marsh, K. L., Johnson, B. T., & Scott-Sheldon, L. A. (2001). Heart versus reason in condom use: Implicit versus explicit attitudinal predictors of sexual behavior. *Zeitschrift für Experimentelle Psychologie, 48*, 161–175.

McCarthy, D. M., & Thompsen, D. M. (2006). Implicit and explicit measures of alcohol and smoking cognitions. *Psychology of Addictive Behaviors, 20*, 436–444. http://doi.org/10.1037/0893-164X.20.4.436

Mogg, K., Bradley, B. P., Field, M., & De Houwer, J. (2003). Eye movements to smoking-related pictures in smokers: Relationship between attentional biases and implicit and explicit measures of stimulus valence. *Addiction, 98*, 825–836. http://doi.org/10.1046/j.1360-0443.2003.00392.x

Nosek, B. A., & Sriram, N. (2007). Faulty assumptions: A comment on Blanton, Jaccard, Gonzales, and Christie (2006). *Journal of Experimental Social Psychology, 43*, 393–398. http://doi.org/10.1016/j.jesp.2006.10.018

Olson, M. A., & Fazio, R. H. (2004). Reducing the influence of extrapersonal associations on the Implicit Association Test: Personalizing the IAT. *Journal of Personality and Social Psychology, 86*, 653–667. http://doi.org/10.1037/0022-3514.86.5.653

Ostafin, B. D., & Palfai, T. P. (2006). Compelled to consume: The Implicit Association Test and automatic alcohol motivation. *Psychology of Adddictive Behaviors, 20*, 322–327. http://doi.org/10.1037/0893-164X.20.3.322

Palfai, T. P., & Ostafin, B. D. (2003). Alcohol-related motivational tendencies in hazardous drinkers: Assessing implicit response tendencies using the modified-IAT. *Behaviour Research and Therapy, 41*, 1149–1162. http://doi.org/10.1016/S0005-7967(03)00018-4

Peeters, M., Monshouwer, K., Schoot, R. A., Janssen, T., Vollebergh, W. A., & Wiers, R. W. (2013). Automatic processes and the drinking behavior in early adolescence: A prospective study. *Alcoholism: Clinical and Experimental Research, 37*, 1737–1744.

Peeters, M., Wiers, R. W., Monshouwer, K., Van de Schoot, R., Janssen, T., & Vollebergh, W. A. (2012). Automatic processes in at-risk adolescents: The role of alcohol-approach tendencies and response inhibition in drinking behavior. *Addiction, 107*, 1939–1946. http://doi.org/10.1111/j.1360-0443.2012.03948.x

Rinck, M., & Becker, E. S. (2007). Approach and avoidance in fear of spiders. *Journal of Behavior Therapy and Experimental Psychiatry, 38*, 105–120. http://doi.org/10.1016/j.jbtep.2006.10.001

Robbins, T. W. (2007). Shifting and stopping: Fronto-striatal substrates, neurochemical modulation and clinical implications. *Philosophical Transactions of the Royal Society of London, B Biological Sciences, 362*, 917–932. http://doi.org/10.1098/rstb.2007.2097

Roddy, S., Stewart, I., & Barnes-Holmes, D. (in press). Facial reactions reveal that slim is good but fat is not bad: Implicit and explicit measures of body-size bias. *European Journal of Social Psychology, 41*, 688–694. http://doi.org/10.1002/ejsp.839

Roefs, A., Huijding, J., Smulders, F. T. Y., MacLeod, C. M., De Jong, P., Wiers, R. W., & Jansen, A. T. M. (2011). Implicit measures of association in psychopathology research. *Psychological Bulletin, 137*, 149–193. http://doi.org/10.1037/a0021729

Rooke, S. E., Hine, D. W., & Thorsteinsson, E. B. (2008). Implicit cognition and substance use: A meta-analysis. *Addictive Behaviors, 33*, 1314–1328. http://doi.org/10.1016/j.addbeh.2008.06.009

Rothermund, K., & Wentura, D. (2004). Underlying processes in the Implicit Association Test (IAT): Dissociating salience from associations. *Journal of Experimental Psychology: General, 133*, 139–165. http://doi.org/10.1037/0096-3445.133.2.139

Rothermund, K., Wentura, D., & De Houwer, J. (2005). Validity of the salience asymmetry account of the Implicit Association Test: Reply to Greenwald, Nosek, Banaji, and Klauer (2005). *Journal of Experimental Psychology: General, 134*, 426. http://doi.org/10.1037/0096-3445.134.3.426

Salemink, E., & Wiers, R. W. (2011). Modifying threat-related interpretive bias in adolescents. *Journal of Abnormal Child Psychology, 39*, 967–976. http://doi.org/10.1007/s10802-011-9523-5

Satpute, A. B., & Lieberman, M. D. (2006). Integrating automatic and controlled processes into neurocognitive models of social cognition. *Brain Research, 1079*, 86–97. http://doi.org/10.1016/j.brainres.2006.01.005

Schoenmakers, T., De Bruin, M., Lux, I. F., Goertz, A. G., Van Kerkhof, D. H., & Wiers, R. W. (2010). Clinical effectiveness of attentional bias modification training in abstinent alcoholic patients. *Drug and Alcohol Dependence, 109*, 30–36. http://doi.org/10.1016/j.drugalcdep.2009.11.022

Schoenmakers, T., Wiers, R. W., & Field, M. (2008). Effects of a low dose of alcohol on cognitive biases and craving in heavy drinkers. *Psychopharmacology, 197*, 169–178. http://doi.org/10.1007/s00213-007-1023-5

Schoenmakers, T., Wiers, R. W., Jones, B. T., Bruce, G., & Jansen, A. T. M. (2007). Attentional re-training decreases attentional bias in heavy drinkers without generalization. *Addiction, 102*, 399–405. http://doi.org/10.1111/j.1360-0443.2006.01718.x

Schmidt, N. B., Richey, J. A., Buckner, J. D., & Timpano, K. R. (2009). Attention training for generalized social anxiety disorder. *Journal of Abnormal Psychology, 118*, 5–14. http://doi.org/10.1037/a0013643

See, J., MacLeod, C., & Bridle, R. (2009). The reduction of anxiety vulnerability through the modification of attentional bias: A real-world study using a home-based cognitive bias modification procedure. *Journal of Abnormal Psychology, 118*, 65–75. http://doi.org/10.1037/a0014377

Sharbanee, J. S., Stritzke, W. G. K., Wiers, R. W., Young, P., Rinck, M., & MacLeod, C. (2013). The interaction of approach-alcohol action tendencies, working memory capacity, and current task goals predicts the inability to regulate drinking behaviour. *Psychology of Adddictive Behaviors, 27*, 649–661. http://doi.org/10.1037/a0029982

Sherman, J. W., Gawronski, B., Gonsalkorale, K., Hugenberg, K., Allen, T. J., & Groom, C. J. (2008). The self-regulation of automatic associations and behavioral impulses. *Psychological Review, 115*, 314–335. http://doi.org/10.1037/0033-295X.115.2.314

Sherman, S. J., Presson, C. C., Chassin, L., Rose, J. S., & Koch, K. (2003). Implicit and explicit attitudes toward cigarette smoking: The effects of context and motivation. *Journal of Social and Clinical Psychology, 22*, 13–39. http://doi.org/10.1521/jscp.22.1.13.22766

Sinha, R., Fox, H. C., Hong, K. A., Bergquist, K., Bhagwagar, Z., & Siedlarz, K. M. (2009). Enhanced negative emotion and alcohol craving, and altered physiological responses following stress and cue exposure in alcohol dependent individuals. *Neuropsychopharmacology, 34*, 1198–1208. http://doi.org/10.1038/npp.2008.78

Smith, E. C., & DeCoster, J. (2000). Dual-process models in social and cognitive psychology: Conceptual integration and links to underlying memory systems. *Personality and Social Psychology Review, 4*, 108–131. http://doi.org/10.1207/S15327957PSPR0402_01

Spruyt, A., De Houwer, J., Tibboel, H., Verschuere, B., Crombez, G., Verbanck, P., ... Noël, X. (2012). On the predictive validity of automatically activated approach/avoidance tendencies in abstaining alcohol-dependent patients. *Drug and Alcohol Dependence, 127*, 81–86. http://doi.org/10.1016/j.drugalcdep.2012.06.019

Squire, L. R. (2004). Memory systems of the brain: A brief history and current perspective. *Neurobiology of Learning and Memory, 82*, 171–177. http://doi.org/10.1016/j.nlm.2004.06.005

Stacy, A. W. (1994, June). *Evidence of implicit memory activation of alcohol concepts: Toward parallel memory models of addiction*. Paper presented at the Annual Meeting of the Research Society on Alcoholism, Maui, HI.

Stacy, A. W. (1997). Memory activation and expectancy as prospective predictors of alcohol and marijuana use. *Journal of Abnormal Psychology, 106*, 61–73. http://doi.org/10.1037/0021-843X.106.1.61

Stacy, A. W., Ames, S. L., & Grenard, J. (2006). Word association tests of associative memory and implicit processes: theoretical and assessment issues. In R. W. Wiers & A. W. Stacy (Eds.), *Handbook of implicit cognition and addiction* (pp. 75–90). Thousand Oaks, CA: Sage.

Stacy, A. W., Ames, S. L., & Knowlton, B. (2004). Neurologically plausible distinctions in cognition relevant to drug use etiology and prevention. *Substance Use and Misuse, 39*, 1571–1623. http://doi.org/10.1081/JA-200033204

Stewart, S. H., Hall, E., Wilkie, H., & Birch, C. D. (2002). Affective priming of alcohol schema in coping and enhancement motivated drinkers. *Cognitive and Behavior Therapy, 31*, 68–80. http://doi.org/10.1080/16506070252959508

Strack, F., & Deutsch, R. (2004). Reflective and impulsive determinants of social behavior. *Personality and Social Psychology Review, 8*, 220–247. http://doi.org/10.1207/s15327957pspr0803_1

Swanson, J. E., Rudman, L. A., & Greenwald, A. G. (2001). Using the implicit association test to investigate attitude-behaviour consistency for stigmatised behaviour. *Cognition and Emotion, 15*, 207–230. http://doi.org/10.1080/0269993004200060

Szalay, L., Bovasso, G., Vilov, S., & Williams, R. E. (1992). Assessing treatment effects through changes in perceptions and cognitive organization. *American Journal of Drug and Alcohol Abuse, 18*, 407–428. http://doi.org/10.3109/00952999209051039

Thush, C., Wiers, R. W., Ames, S. L., Grenard, J. L., Sussman, S., & Stacy, A. W. (2008). Interactions between implicit and explicit cognition and working memory capacity in the prediction of alcohol use in at-risk adolescents. *Drug and Alcohol Dependence, 94*, 116–124. http://doi.org/10.1016/j.drugalcdep.2007.10.019

Tibboel, H., De Houwer, J., & Field, M. (2010). Reduced attentional blink for alcohol-related stimuli in heavy social drinkers. *Journal of Psychopharmacology, 24*, 1349–1356. http://doi.org/10.1177/0269881109106977

Toplak, M. E., Bucciarelli, S. M., Jain, U., & Tannock, R. (2008). Executive functions: performance-based measures and the behavior rating inventory of executive function (BRIEF) in adolescents with attention deficit/hyperactivity disorder (ADHD). *Child Neuropsychology, 15*, 53–72. http://doi.org/10.1080/09297040802070929

Vahey, N., Boles, S., & Barnes-Holmes, D. (2010). Measuring adolescents' smoking-related social identity preferences with the Implicit Relational Assessment Procedure (IRAP) for the first time: A starting point that explains later IRAP evolutions. *International Journal of Psychology and Psychological Therapy, 10*, 453–474.

Wiers, R. W. (2008). Alcohol and drug expectancies as anticipated changes in affect: Negative reinforcement is not sedation. *Substance Use Misuse, 43*, 429–444. http://doi.org/10.1080/10826080701203021

Wiers, R. W., Ames, S. L., Hofmann, W., Krank, M., & Stacy, A. W. (2010). Impulsivity, impulsive and reflective processes and the development of alcohol use and misuse in adolescents and young adults. *Frontiers in Psychology, 1*, 1–12. http://doi.org/10.3389/fpsyg.2010.00144

Wiers, R. W., Bartholow, B. D., Van den Wildenberg, E., Thush, C., Engels, R. C., Sher, K. J., … Stacy, A. W. (2007). Automatic and controlled processes and the development of addictive behaviors in adolescents: A review and a model. *Pharmacology Biochemistry and Behavior, 86*, 263–283. http://doi.org/10.1016/j.pbb.2006.09.021

Wiers, R. W., Beckers, L., Houben, K., & Hofmann, W. (2009). A short fuse after alcohol: Implicit power associations predict aggressiveness after alcohol consumption in young heavy drinkers with limited executive control. *Pharmacology Biochemistry and Behavior, 93*, 300–305. http://doi.org/10.1016/j.pbb.2009.02.003

Wiers, R. W., Eberl, C., Rinck, M., Becker, E., & Lindenmeyer, J. (2011). Re-training automatic action tendencies changes alcoholic patients' approach bias for alcohol and improves treatment outcome. *Psychological Science, 22*, 490–497. http://doi.org/10.1177/0956797611400615

Wiers, R. W., Gladwin, T. E., Hofmann, W. Salemink, E., & Ridderinkhof, K. R. (2013). Cognitive bias modification and control training in addiction and related psychopathology: Mechanisms, clinical perspectives and ways forward. *Clinical Psychological Science, 1*, 192–212. http://doi.org/10.1177/2167702612466547

Wiers, R. W., Gladwin, T. E., & Rinck, M. (2013). Should we train alcohol-dependent patients to avoid alcohol? Commentary on Spruyt et al "On the predictive validity of automatically activated approach/avoidance tendencies in abstaining alcohol-dependent patients". *Frontiers in Psychiatry, 4*, 33.

Wiers, R. W., Houben, K., Roefs, A., Hofmann, W., & Stacy, A. W. (2010). Implicit cognition in health psychology: Why common sense goes out of the window. In B. Gawronski & B. K. Payne (Eds.), *Handbook of implicit social cognition* (pp. 463–488). New York, NY: Guilford.

Wiers, R. W., Houben, K., Smulders, F. T. Y., Conrod, P. J., & Jones, B. T. (2006). To drink or not to drink: The role of automatic and controlled cognitive processes in the etiology of alcohol-related problems. In R. W. Wiers & A. W. Stacy (Eds.), *Handbook of implicit cognition and addiction* (pp. 339–361). Thousand Oaks, CA: Sage.

Wiers, R. W., Rinck, M., Dictus, M., & van den Wildenberg, E. (2009). Relatively strong automatic appetitive action-tendencies in male carriers of the OPRM1 G-allele. *Genes, Brain, and Behavior, 8*, 101–106. http://doi.org/10.1111/j.1601-183X.2008.00454.x

Wiers, R. W., Rinck, M., Kordts, R., Houben, K., & Strack, F. (2010). Retraining automatic action-tendencies to approach alcohol in hazardous drinkers. *Addiction, 105*, 279–287. http://doi.org/10.1111/j.1360-0443.2009.02775.x

Wiers, R. W., Van de Luitgaarden, J., Van den Wildenberg, E., & Smulders, F. T. Y. (2005). Challenging implicit and explicit alcohol-related cognitions in young heavy drinkers. *Addiction, 100*, 806–819. http://doi.org/10.1111/j.1360-0443.2005.01064.x

Wiers, R. W., Van Woerden, N., Smulders, F. T. Y., & de Jong, P. J. (2002). Implicit and explicit alcohol-related cognitions in heavy and light drinkers. *Journal of Abnormal Psychology, 111*, 648–658. http://doi.org/10.1037/0021-843X.111.4.648

Woud, M. L., Fitzgerald, D., Wiers, R. W., Rinck, M., & Becker, E. (2012). Getting into the spirit: Alcohol-related interpretation bias in heavy drinking students. *Psychology of Adddictive Behaviors, 26*, 627–632. http://doi.org/10.1037/a0029025

Woud, M. L., Wiers, R. W., Pawelzcak, S., Becker, E. S., Lindenmeyer, J., & Rinck, M. (2013). Does negative affect prime alcohol in alcohol-dependent inpatients? A large-scale clinical investigation of the moderating role of depression and executive control. *Experimental Psychopathology, 4*, 279–290. http://doi.org/10.5127/jep.031012

Zack, M., Poulos, C. X., Fragopoulos, F., Woodford, T. M., & MacLeod, C. M. (2006). Negative affect words prime beer consumption in young drinkers. *Addictive Behaviors, 31*, 169–173. http://doi.org/10.1016/j.addbeh.2005.04.016

Zack, M., Toneatto, T., & MacLeod, C. M. (1999). Implicit activation of alcohol concepts by negative affective cues distinguishes between problem drinkers with high and low psychiatric distress. *Journal of Abnormal Psychology, 108*, 518–531. http://doi.org/10.1037/0021-843X.108.3.518

Chapter 11

Indirect Measures in Forensic Contexts

Alexander F. Schmidt[1,2], Rainer Banse[2], and Roland Imhoff[3]

[1]Institute for Health and Behaviour, Health Promotion and Aggression Prevention, University of Luxembourg, Luxembourg
[2]Institute of Psychology, Social & Legal Psychology, University of Bonn, Germany
[3]Social Cognition, University of Cologne, Germany

Whenever psychologists try to diagnose a condition or disposition, psychometrically precise assessment procedures are of paramount importance. This general need is amplified in applied forensic contexts where diagnostic decisions may collide with individual and societal rights and needs. Assessment outcomes have as far-reaching consequences for the respondent (e.g., restraint of individual freedom) as for members of society as a whole (e.g., risk of future victimization). These conflicting interests underscore the need for valid measures. However, classic self-report assessment procedures such as questionnaires and interviews are inherently transparent and can easily be faked by respondents who are aware of the personal consequences of the assessment outcome.

Another problem of (forensic) assessment based on self-reports is the high demand imposed on respondents' introspective abilities. Some forensically relevant constructs may lack introspective accessibility per se, such as situation-specific impulses and implicit offence-facilitating theories (cognitive distortions). Other constructs may in principle be open to introspection but the quality of self-report depends on certain cognitive skills that are not common among prototypical forensic populations, who usually have relatively low education levels and weak verbal skills. Due to these crucial validity threats, researchers and practitioners alike question the usefulness of self-report techniques (but see Grieger, Hosser, & Schmidt, 2012; Walters, 2006). Therefore, specifically in forensic contexts, there is a strong need for reliable and valid measurement paradigms. Ideally, these should not rely on explicit self-report and introspection and should be less transparent as well as less deliberately controllable.

What Are Direct/Indirect Versus Explicit/Implicit Measures?

The search for a solution to the drawbacks of self-report approaches has led to an increasing research interest in *implicit* and/or *indirect* measures. This measurement approach has shown remarkable predictive validity across different psychological subdisciplines (e.g., Friese, Hofmann, & Schmitt, 2008; Perugini, Richetin, & Zogmaister, 2010), including the forensic domain (Snowden & Gray, 2010). The success of indirect measures has been attributed to the fact that these approaches benefit from being (a) inherently less transparent than self-report measures (due to the indirect character of the measurement procedure) and (b) able to tap into automatic attitudes and behavioral dispositions (because of the implicitness of the constructs to be measured). However, despite the immense popularity of these measures, the precise terminological differences between the theoretical attributes indirect and implicit do not always seem to be unequivocal as these terms are often used interchangeably.

For the remainder of the chapter we will rely on the terminological distinction proposed by De Houwer (2006). Accordingly, we have to distinguish between two different uses of the term *measure*, which either refers to the measurement outcome or the measurement process. The term *implicit* is reserved for various functional properties of the measurement outcome. These properties describe typical criteria of automaticity that specify the particular sense in which a measure is implicit (e.g., respondents' lack of awareness of the relationship between the assessed construct and the measurement outcome, lack of conscious access to the relevant construct, lack of voluntarily control over the assessment outcome). These properties do not necessarily co-occur and have to be demonstrated empirically rather than being mere presumptions. The term *indirect* refers to the procedural properties of the measurement that are always based on an explicit set of rules of how the measurement score is derived from the assessment (otherwise, it would not qualify as a measure in a scientific sense). Whereas direct measures rely on introspective self-descriptions or ratings of indicators (e.g., questionnaire items) of the relevant construct, *indirect* assessment procedures use the behavior exhibited in response to a stimulus (e.g., response latencies while categorizing images) to draw indirect inferences on the construct in question. Notably, the measurement outcome of an indirect measure is not necessarily implicit (De Houwer, 2006), as, for example, individuals might be fully aware of the purpose of the assessment (which is true for most indirect measures utilized in forensic psychology).

In line with De Houwer's (2006) aforementioned terminological distinction, in the remainder of this chapter we focus on forensically relevant measures that draw their diagnostic inferences indirectly from task behavior (i.e., response latencies[1]). A wide range of forensically relevant, latency-based indirect measures have been introduced to tap into various domains of individual differences (Snowden & Gray, 2010). By far the most research utilizing indirect measures, however, has focused on deviant sexual interests (DSI) in children[2] (for recent overviews, see Snowden, Craig, & Gray, 2011; Thornton & Laws, 2009a). Indirect latency-based measures of DSI are often referred to as *attention-based measures* (Gress & Laws, 2009; Kalmus & Beech, 2005; Ó Ciardha, 2011), postulating that the underlying processes rely on the differential allocation of attentional resources. However, for most of these measures this remains hypothetical, as only a small body of empirical research into their procedural underpinnings exists. Also, empirical demonstrations of relevant implicitness criteria are missing. As a consequence, in focusing on the nature of the dependent variable we prefer to use *latency-based indirect measures* as the theoretically most parsimonious umbrella term.

---

1   Due to space restrictions we will exclude indirect assessment paradigms that capitalize on physiological reactions such as polygraphy in the field of deception detection (for a critical overview, see National Research Council, Committee to Review the Scientific Evidence on the Polygraph, 2003; but see Verschuere, Ben-Shakar, & Meijer, 2011) or penile plethysmography/phallometry (for an overview, see Kalmus & Beech, 2005).

2   Throughout this chapter the term *deviant* refers to sexual interest in prepubescent children (irrespective of other paraphilic or otherwise atypical sexual interests) as indicated by corresponding fantasies or behavior.

Latency-Based Indirect Measures of Deviant Sexual Interests

An overview of latency-based indirect measures of DSI utilizing samples involving male sexual offenders against children is reported in Table 11.1 in the appendix. All of these measures capitalize on individual differences in (sexual) information processing and, as a result, also get framed as cognitive approaches to the assessment of DSI (Thornton & Laws, 2009a).

An important distinction is whether indirect measures assess DSI or deviant sexual preferences (DSP). *Interest* refers to the absolute level of sexual interest in a specific target category (e.g., prepubescent children) irrespective of interest in other categories (e.g., postpubescent individuals), whereas *preference* denotes relative sexual preference for one target category over another target category and is usually based on a difference index of a target category minus a comparison category (e.g., prepubescent over postpubescent individuals). Notably, although representing two different conceptualizations, interest and preference are often used interchangeably in the literature. Several indirect measures – the most prominent example being the Implicit Association Test (IAT; see Chapter 2 in this volume) – are inherently conceptualized as DSP measures because they are calculated from latency differences based on sexually relevant vs. sexually irrelevant trials. DSP measures do not convey diagnostic information about the absolute level of DSI, because the baseline level of DSI gets eliminated in the computation. Thus, a person with strong interest in both children and adults will have DSP scores comparable to a person with weak interest in both target categories.

In addition to the DSI/DSP distinction, latency-based indirect measures of DSI can be grouped into two distinct measurement approaches: task-relevant and task-irrelevant paradigms (Rönspies et al., 2015). Task-relevant indirect DSI/DSP measures involve the explicit categorization of sexual target categories – either as sexually relevant themselves or in combination with classification trials of sexual attributes. Due to the explicit task requirement to process sexual relevance, it is fairly transparent to the respondent that DSI is the diagnostic construct of interest. However, as respondents are not usually informed that response latencies are the central dependent variable and the underlying rationale of the diagnostic inference is unknown to them, these measures qualify as indirect. Task-irrelevant measures are based on the detection of sexually irrelevant characteristics (e.g., location, color, semantic meaning) of target stimuli that are presented together with distracting sexually relevant vs. irrelevant background stimuli (e.g., adults, children). The underlying rationale is that sexually relevant background stimuli interfere with the primary detection task due to attentional capture resulting in increased response latencies.

Task-Relevant Indirect Measures of Deviant Sexual Interests

Viewing Time Tasks

Viewing times (VTs) were the first ever latency-based indirect measure of sexual interest (Rosenzweig, 1942). In the standard VT procedure, participants are asked to evaluate pictures of target individuals on a graded scale of sexual attractiveness/arousal. The response latency of this judgment is unobtrusively measured. It is a robust finding that this response latency is longer for sexually attractive as compared with sexually unattractive targets and, in turn, VT measures can be used to discriminate between participants with respect to sexual preference (e.g., Imhoff et al., 2010).

The underlying processes driving the robust effects of longer response latencies for sexually attractive targets are not entirely clear. Three mechanisms have been frequently proposed: (a) deliberate delay due to the hedonic quality of sexually preferred targets, (b) automatic attentional adhesion, (c) slowing down of decision-making processes after the presentation of explicit erotic stimuli (sexual content-induced delay; Geer & Bellard, 1996). We conducted a series of experiments providing the first causal tests of VT processes (Imhoff et al., 2010). Deliberate delay to keep pleasant stimuli in sight longer was ruled out because prolonged response latencies also emerged for relevant sexual attractiveness ratings in the absence of target pictures that had been presented beforehand for a fixed amount of time. Additionally, VT effects emerged when restricted response windows of 1,000 ms were utilized. Furthermore, attentional adhesion to sexually attractive stimuli also could not fully explain VT effects: If sexually attractive stimuli lead to longer response latencies because the stimuli automatically capture participants' attention and distract them from the rating task, VT effects should vanish when the sexually attractive stimuli are taken away from the participants prior to rating sexual attractiveness. However, as described before, this was not the case. Finally, VT effects still emerged for stimuli depicting target stimuli's heads without any further indications of erotic content, thereby ruling out sexual content-induced delay as a causal explanation. These results raise the question of whether the term *viewing time* is a misnomer, as participants saw all stimuli for the same amount of time under restricted viewing conditions but still differed in their response latencies. Accordingly, standard VT effects should be described as prolonged decision latencies for sexually attractive targets (Imhoff et al., 2010).

As a consequence, two further mechanisms remained as plausible explanations for VT effects even in absence of a stimulus while responding: (a) automatic time-consuming schematic processes triggered by sexually attractive stimuli (stimulus-specific effects) and (b) cognitive demands associated with the task of rating sexual attractiveness (task-specific effects). Imhoff, Schmidt, Weiß, Young, and Banse (2012) disentangled stimulus- and task-specific effects by manipulating the sexual orientation perspective under which male participants responded to standard VT tasks. It was shown that VT effects were predominantly a function of the assigned perspective (task-specific account) and not dependent on participants' sexual orientation (stimulus-specific account). In other words, sexual attractiveness ratings from a vicarious (e.g., heterosexual) perspective took longest when the targets were adult females, regardless of participants' actual hetero- or homosexual orientation. This is at odds with the notion that VT measures primarily tap into hot automatic processes elicited by sexually attractive stimuli rather than task-dependent response strategies (e.g., scrutinizing whether the stimulus exhibits the right age, sex, and/or attractiveness for being a sexually exciting stimulus). The latter process is based on the assumption that the more criteria for endorsing sexual attraction have to be affirmed, the longer the scrutinizing takes (i.e., VTs increase), whereas rejection of any criterion allows the process to stop immediately (i.e., VTs decrease). In line with this account of task- vs. stimuli-specific effects, Glasgow (2009) reported that neither perceived sexual competition of female mate rivals nor filial affection to children in heterosexual women – both stimulus characteristics hypothesized to increase VTs for sexually irrelevant categories – conflated standard VT effects while rating sexual attractiveness.

Since the first demonstrations of VT effects for child sexual offenders (Harris, Rice, Quinsey, & Chaplin, 1996), there have been numerous independent forensic replications (for an overview of VT studies on DSI, see Table 11.1 in the appendix). VT tasks have been shown to distinguish between child sexual offenders and nonoffending controls (Glasgow, 2009; Harris et al., 1996; *d*

= 1.61 and 1.00, respectively), mixed community and offender controls (Banse, Schmidt, & Clarbour, 2010; Fromberger et al., 2012; $d = 0.76–0.82$), as well as varying offender control groups such as nonsexual offenders (Babchishin, Nunes, & Kessous, 2014; Banse et al., 2010; $d = 0.86–1.84$) and adult sexual offenders (Abel et al., 2004; Gress, 2005; Worling, 2006; $d = 0.51–1.08$). They also differentiated between different subtypes of child sexual offenders (e.g., child sexual offenders who victimized boys or boys and girls vs. only girls; Gress, 2005; Schmidt, Gykiere, Vanhoeck, Mann, & Banse, 2014; $d = 0.84–1.65$).

Reports of internal consistency on raw latencies (Cronbach's α) for forensic VT measures generally ranged between 0.72 and 0.93 (with only two notable exceptions of 0.60 [male child stimuli; Letourneau, 2002] and 0.62 [male adolescent stimuli; Worling, 2006]; see Table 11.1 in the appendix). Sets of African American stimuli were tested in two studies (Abel, Huffman, Warberg, & Holland, 1998; Letourneau, 2002), but only the latter author reported origin-specific analyses (internal consistency of the African American categories was comparable to the Caucasian stimulus set with α values ranging from 0.72 to 0.87). These generally satisfying to good coefficients might overestimate the reliability of VT measures as the calculations might be confounded with general executive functioning (i.e., reaction speed). However, general classification speed as assessed by a different task was found to be unrelated to VT DSI/DSP measures (Schmidt et al., 2014). At present, no data on retest reliability are available for VT DSI measures.

VT DSI measures oftentimes converge with corresponding self-report measures (e.g., Abel et al., 1998; Babchishin, et al., 2014; Banse et al., 2010; Glasgow, 2009; Harris et al., 1996; Worling, 2006) as well as DSP Implicit Association Tests (Babchishin, Nunes, & Hermann, 2013; Banse et al., 2010). However, particularly in light of problems with self-reports, comparing VT with other nonself-reported measures seems advisable. A prime candidate for this is penile plethysmography (PPG), often regarded as the most valid measure of DSI (Seto, 2008; regarding methodological shortcomings, see, e.g., Kalmus & Beech, 2005). Two studies that concurrently utilized VT and PPG measures of DSI/DSP confirmed their convergent validity (Letourneau, 2002; Stinson & Becker, 2008; r values between .28 and .61). However, another study reported a negative association between VT and PPG indexes ($r = -.47$; Babchishin et al., 2014), rendering the findings on convergence of VT with PPG assessments inconclusive. The Screening Scale for Pedophilic Interests (Seto & Lalumière, 2001) is another indicator of pedophilic interest based on an index of offending behavior. It is phallometrically validated and also associated with recidivism risk (Seto, Harris, Rice, & Barbaree, 2004). VT measures were reported to converge with the Screening Scale for Pedophilic Interests (Banse et al., 2010; Schmidt et al., 2014). Additionally, Schmidt et al. (2014) reported preliminary support for positive correlations of VT DSI/DSP measures with recidivism risk as assessed by standard actuarial risk indicators (Static-99R; Helmus, Thornton, Hanson, & Babchishin, 2012).

At present, no data have been published on the fakeability of VT paradigms when used in forensic contexts (as this would risk informing at least a number of offenders of the underlying scoring procedures). Obviously, VT tasks are easy to fake once the measurement rationale is known. In line with this, naïvely dissimulating pedophiles were significantly less accurately classified than nondissimulating pedophilic child sexual offenders (Gray & Plaud, 2005; $d = -2.13$). This finding can be criticized in terms of its post hoc classification algorithms for the dissimulators and its strong sample selection effects (Sachsenmaier & Gress, 2009). Opposing evidence stems from another study: VT tasks did not show differences between noninformed deniers vs. admitters of child sexual offending such that both deniers and admitters could be discriminated from nonsexual offender controls (Babchishin et al., 2014; $d = 1.22$ and 1.32, respectively). The results from Babchishin et al. (2014) thus provide the first evidence of the robustness of VT tasks against noninformed dissimulation, although this finding awaits replication.

In summary, VT tasks can be regarded as among the most frequently researched latency-based measures of DSI. There have been numerous reports from different laboratories demonstrating that VT measures are satisfactorily reliable and valid indicators of DSI in forensic contexts. The VT effect has been regarded as so robust that there are commercially distributed VT paradigms (e.g., Abel, 1995). However, from a scientific perspective data based on Abel's VT routines have to be treated with some caution as crucial methodological details have not been published (for a critical overview, see Sachsenmaier & Gress, 2009). Furthermore, VT tasks have been shown to be robust against deniers (Babchishin et al., 2014) uninformed about successful faking strategies.

On the other hand, the predominantly task-driven nature of VT effects is a potential threat to the diagnostic validity of VT paradigms (Imhoff et al., 2012). The task-dependency also cautions against the interpretation of VT effects as caused by automatic processes elicited by sexually attractive stimuli and outside of conscious control (i.e., attentional adhesion; Imhoff et al., 2010). Thus, participants' compliance in completing the secondary rating task from their own self-relevant perspective is crucial. VT measures result in good differentiations of sexually deviant from nondeviant samples only as long as participants comply with the instructions to rate how subjectively sexually attractive targets are. However, when participants (naïvely or knowingly) complete the task from a perspective other than their own (Imhoff et al., 2012) or with a completely different task (e.g., rating age of the target; Imhoff, Petruschke, Dierkes, Banse, & Weber, 2015), latency patterns in standard VT paradigms will most likely be nondiagnostic.

Implicit Association Tests

The Implicit Association Test (IAT) introduced by Greenwald, McGhee, and Schwartz (1998) is another prominently researched latency-based indirect measure. In forensic contexts, the prototypical Children/Adults DSP IAT is based on two double discrimination tasks – the so-called critical blocks – assessing associative strengths between target categories (e.g., *children* vs. *adults*) and attribute categories (e.g., *sexually exciting* vs. *sexually unexciting*), both arranged on bipolar dimensions (for a detailed description of the assessment procedure and underlying processes, see Chapter 2 in this volume). Classic IATs are usually scored by calculating the difference between the mean response latencies of compatible and incompatible critical blocks, divided by the pooled standard deviation of the response latencies (Greenwald, Nosek, & Banaji, 2003). Given that this calculation depends on a standardized difference index, DSP IATs are inherently effect size measures (analogous to Cohen's d) of relative DSP (as opposed to absolute DSI measures such as raw VTs).

There have been several independent reports of DSP IAT effects in forensic populations (for an overview, see Table 11.1). DSP IATs differentiated between child sexual offenders and nonoffending controls (Mihailides, Devilly, & Ward, 2004; Nunes, Firestone, Baldwin, 2007; d = 0.71 and 0.92, respectively), mixed community and offender controls (Banse et al., 2010; d = 0.43–0.82), as well as varying offender control groups such as nonsexual offenders (Brown, Gray, & Snowden, 2009; Mihailides et al., 2004; d = 0.92 and 0.95, respectively) or adult sexual offenders (Gray, Brown, MacCulloch, Smith, & Snowden, 2005; d = 0.84). Furthermore, DSP IATs distinguished between child sexual offenders who victimized either only boys or boys and girls vs. only girls (Schmidt et al., 2014; d = 0.64–0.72) and child sexual offenders whose victims were under 12 years of age vs. 12 years and older (Brown et al., 2009; $d = 0.77$). Van Leeuwen et al. (2013) reported strong DSP IAT differences between self-identified community pedophiles and nonoffending controls ($d = 1.74$). DSP IATs were not confounded by general classification speed abilities (Schmidt et al., 2014). In a meta-analysis, Babchishin et al. (2013) reported a mean DSP IAT effect of $d = 0.63$ between child molesters and nonmolesters. As expected, group differences were largest for comparisons of child sexual offenders with nonoffenders ($d = 0.96$), followed by comparisons with nonsexual offenders ($d = 0.58$) and with rapists ($d = 0.48$). Notably, treatment participation was a significant moderator of IAT effects: DSP IATs showed larger effects for child sexual offenders who had not undergone treatment than for treated child sexual abusers when compared with control groups. These findings corroborate either treatment effects on indirectly assessed DSP or confounds associated with child sexual offender treatment (e.g., group selection effects on behalf of suspected lower DSI levels).

Retest reliability was tested only once for DSP IATs ($r_{tt} = .63$; Brown et al., 2009). Reports of internal consistency (Cronbach's α) for DSP IATs comparing sexual interest in children vs. adults ranged between 0.72 and 0.83 (Table 11.1 in the appendix), thereby corroborating the satisfactory reliability of these measures. However, the only two studies using sex-specific DSP IATs (Banse et al., 2010; Schmidt et al., 2014) reported lower α values for *Boys/Men* (0.61 and 0.65, respectively) in comparison with Girls/Women IATs (0.79 and 0.82). This difference might be attributed to variance restrictions in typical forensic samples: Homosexual orientation is usually overrepresented in randomly selected child sexual offender samples. This results in less clearly differentiated DSP patterns for Boys/Men IATs between child sexual offender and control groups: Homosexually oriented child sexual abusers show less DSP as they are likely to be interested in both boys and men, whereas heterosexual controls are interested in neither boys nor men and thus show less DSP as well (Banse et al., 2010; Schmidt et al., 2014). Whether the underlying rationale of sex-specific DSP IATs to disentangle sexual orientation from sexual maturity preferences is a viable option to increase criterion validity is an open empirical question as sex-differentiated IATs produced smaller DSP effects than generic Children/Adults IATs (Babchishin et al., 2013).

Convergent validity with other DSP measures was shown meta-analytically (Babchishin et al., 2013): DSP IATs converged with moderate effect sizes with self-report, VT, and offence-behavioral measures of DSI (Screening Scale for Pedophilic Interests) as well as with actuarial estimates of recidivism risk ($r = .27$). Reported DSP IAT associations with corresponding PPG indexes have not been convincing so far.

Although the IAT has been considered resistant to deliberate faking attempts, it has repeatedly been shown to be fakeable when respondents are informed about successful faking strategies (e.g., slowing of latencies in consistent blocks), are experienced with the paradigm, and/or are strongly motivated to fake results (Teige-Mocigemba, Klauer, & Sherman, 2010). Nevertheless, there is preliminary evidence (Brown et al., 2009) that DSP IATs can distinguish between denying child sexual offenders and nonsexual offending control groups ($d = 1.01$) but not between denying and admitting child sexual offenders ($d = 0.27$; nonsignificant). On the other hand, Babchishin et al. (2014) failed to show any differentiation between either deniers or admitters vs. nonsexual offender controls, respectively.

In summary, in addition to VT tasks, IATs have emerged as a second robust paradigm for indirectly assessing DSI/DSP. Multiple studies from independent laboratories as well as a first meta-analysis (Babchishin et al., 2013) demonstrated that IATs are reliable and valid indicators of DSP for children over adults in forensic contexts. Still, some issues need further research. First, given that the interference effects that drive DSP IATs are based on the associative strength between concepts such as *children* and *sexual excitement,* where these associations originate from is an interesting question (Snowden et al., 2011). Is an association of children and sex a valid indicator of genuine DSP or an indicator of childhood experiences of sexual abuse – a condition quite prevalent among child sexual abusers (Seto, 2008)? Second, IATs have repeatedly been proven fakeable. Attempts to develop methodological strategies to detect and even correct deliberate manipulations of IAT results in forensic populations (Cvencek, Greenwald, Brown, Gray, & Snowden, 2010) need to be viewed with some caution. Statistics on the discriminatory power of detection algorithms are based on group means, which may have limited validity in single case diagnostics (i.e., relative group differences used to classify dissimulation are not available in single case assessments and are based on sample characteristics that might not be relevant to the actual case in question). Also, as these statistics are based on comparisons with response-latencies in consistent blocks of an uncritical baseline IAT (e.g., Gender/Self IAT; Cvencek et al., 2010), respondents who know this could easily start to fake the baseline IAT as well (by slowing latencies in the consistent block of the baseline IAT). It seems somewhat of a paradox to derive faking-resistant countermeasures from a measure that is fakeable in itself.

Implicit Relational Assessment Procedure

A fairly recent, task-relevant indirect measure is the Implicit Relational Assessment Procedure (IRAP) introduced by Dawson, Barnes-Holmes, Gresswell, Hart, and Gore (2009). In the IRAP, target categories (children vs. adults) and target words representing sexual vs. nonsexual attributes are presented in either consistent (in accordance with the respondent's individual associations) or inconsistent (at odds with the respondent's associations) pairings. During the task, participants are forced to categorize the presented pairings as either true or false according to predetermined contingencies: During one type of blocks (consistent for nondeviant individuals), participants are required to categorize adults as sexual (e.g., *Adult – Sexual – True; Adult –Nonsexual – False*) and children as nonsexual (e.g., *Child – Nonsexual – True; Child – Sexual – False*) as opposed to (inconsistent) blocks during which the feedback contingencies were reversed, and participants were required to categorize adults as nonsexual (e.g., *Adult – Sexual – False; Adult – Nonsexual – True*) and children as sexual (e.g., *Child – Sexual – True; Child – Nonsexual – False*). The rationale of the IRAP is that it takes less time to respond positively to pairings that are consistent with beliefs than to pairings inconsistent with beliefs, because during consistent trials answer keys and initial responses are matched, whereas in inconsistent trials the initial response has to be inhibited and overcome with an alternative response that is incompatible with automatic individual associations. Similar to the IAT, the IRAP DSP index is calculated as a *d*-measure from the difference of response latencies in consistent vs. inconsistent blocks (Dawson et al., 2009). Dawson et al. (2009) were able to differentiate between child sexual abusers and nonoffender controls ($d = 0.91$) and the IRAP DSP index was unrelated to years of education in their sample. No further psychometric properties were reported. Hence, the IRAP has to be regarded as among the least researched indirect measures of DSI/DSP with only preliminary findings concerning its validity.

Eye Movement Tracking Task

Fromberger et al. (2012) recently demonstrated the potential of assessing eye movements as another indirect measure of DSP. In a paired comparison task, pictures of girls vs. women and boys vs. men had to be classified according to which of the stimuli was more sexually attractive. Initial fixation latencies as well as relative fixation times aggregated into DSP indexes differentiated between pedophilic child sexual abusers and nonpedophilic (healthy and forensic non-child sexual offending) controls ($d = 1.84$ and 1.34, respectively). Initial fixation latencies showed good diagnostic accuracy in terms of sensitivity and specificity. This preliminary finding holds promise for forensic purposes because initial fixation latencies are deemed quite robust against faking attempts as they are regarded as an indicator of automatic bottom–up information processing. However, average mean initial fixation latencies in the study by Fromberger et al. (2012) were roughly 1 s, which cannot be regarded as indicating initial automatic information processing. Clearly, more research is needed on the reliability of these eye movement measures as well as their potential to distinguish deniers and nondeniers from relevant control groups.

Task-Irrelevant Indirect Measures of Deviant Sexual Interests

Emotional Stroop Tasks

The classic Stroop interference paradigm (Stroop, 1935) has been among the first to be adapted to an indirect measure of DSP in forensic populations (for an overview, see Price, Beech, Mitchell, & Humphreys, in press). Initially, Emotional Stroop Task variants in which participants had to classify the print color of *sexual* vs. *neutral* word stimuli were utilized. Sexual words are hypothesized to produce longer response latencies compared with neutral words due to increased emotional salience that interferes with the color classification task. In an initial study, Smith and Waterman (2004) found no such effect between child sexual offenders and rapists for sexual words representing child molesting and rape themes (only five offenders in each group). On the other hand, Price and Hanson (2007) were able to discriminate child sexual offenders from nonoffending controls ($d = 0.82$) utilizing the same stimulus words as Smith and Waterman (2004) but failed to show any effects with an alternative, more offence-specific stimulus set. Another Emotional Stroop Task variant utilizing differently colored pictorial stimuli of children vs. adults did not distinguish between child sexual offenders and nonoffending control groups (Ó Ciardha & Gormley, 2012). Van Leeuwen et al. (2013) introduced a picture–word Stroop variant during which words superimposed on pictures of children vs. adults had to be classified as either sexual or neutral. Notably, contrary to the classic Emotional Stroop Task variants, sexually relevant pictures in this picture–word Stroop test were presumed to facilitate classifications of sexual words. Self-identified pedophiles' response latencies were shown to differ from those of nonoffending controls on this DSP index in the expected directions ($d = 1.41$). As Van Leeuwen et al. (2013) provide evidence for a facilitatory (as opposed to the traditional inhibitory) effect of sexually relevant images, it remains unclear whether the heterogeneity of these effects (Price et al., 2012) are due to methodological factors (e.g., differing stimulus sets and Stroop variants) or to sample characteristics (e.g., intra- vs. extrafamilial child sexual abusers). In summary, there is inconclusive evidence for DSP Stroop paradigms as valid indicators of individual differences in forensic contexts.

Attentional Blink

Based on the attentional blink phenomenon (Raymond, Shapiro, & Arnell, 1992), Beech et al. (2008) introduced the Rapid Serial Visual Presentation Task (RSVP). This paradigm capitalizes on the fact that if the first target presented is sexually relevant, it interferes with the perception of the second target when the targets are presented in rapid succession. Beech and his colleagues showed that intra- and extrafamilial child molesters in contrast to nonsexual offender controls made more errors in reporting a second target when they were presented target pictures of children vs. pictures of animals ($d = 1.00$ and 1.28, respectively) in an RSVP task. However, Crooks, Rostill-Brookes, Beech, & Bickley (2009) did not replicate these findings in a sample of adolescent child molesters, leaving open the question of whether the findings might be explained by sample differences (i.e., adolescent child sexual offenders are deemed to exhibit lower DSI levels than adult child molesters) or by a lack of task validity.

Choice Reaction Time Task

In the prototypical Choice Reaction Time Task (Wright & Adams, 1994), individuals have to detect target probes (e.g., dots) that are superimposed on either sexually relevant or irrelevant pictorial stimuli (e.g., pictures of adults vs. children). It has been shown twice that a DSP index of mean response latencies for infants vs. adults discriminated between child sexual offenders and nonsex-offending controls (Mokros, Dombert, Osterheider, Zappalà, & Santtila, 2010; Pöppl et al., 2011; $d = 1.41$ and 0.99, respectively) without further psychometric properties being reported.

In summary, attention-based/task-irrelevant paradigms have been quite successfully used in clinical populations where avoidance of threat or negative valence is claimed to be the source of the attentional bias (Cisler, Bacon, & Williams, 2009). Yet, corresponding DSI/DSP tasks lack a consistent pattern of effects congruent with the supposed rationale of selective attention. This might result from the fact that in the case of DSI/DSP positive valence and approach behavior associated with sexual interest might facilitate rather than divert attention allocation. Additionally, most attention-based paradigms cannot disentangle initial attentional capture and subsequent difficulties in disengagement from the relevant stimuli (Fox, Derakshan, & Standage, 2011). This leads to theoretical problems in predetermining the directedness of the hypothesized attention biases in research with sexually relevant stimuli (Prause, Janssen, & Hetrick, 2008), leaving it unclear whether potential group differences represent sexual interest or other sources of attention biases (e.g., phobic avoidance). More elaborate theoretical frameworks that clarify the relationship between attention biases and DSI are needed. Importantly, data on reliability – a common problem with attention-based measures of individual differences (Cisler et al., 2009) – are generally missing for task-irrelevant measures. Hence, it is fair to conclude that task-irrelevant approaches are currently the least developed indirect DSI measures.

What Goes Up Must Come Down – Implicit Assumptions About Implicit Measures

New developments often foster excessive and to some degree illusory expectations. This is certainly true for indirect/implicit measures (Perugini & Banse, 2007). It is thus necessary to thoroughly examine the empirical foundations of the implicit assumptions about implicit measures (for an overview, see Gawronski, 2009). Probably the most common beliefs about implicit measures are that they assess subconscious associations not accessible through introspection, and, relatedly, that they are therefore not fakeable. Likewise, it is often claimed that implicit measures circumvent problems of social desirability because respondents are supposedly not able to adjust their responses on indirect measures. But lack of introspective access does not necessarily imply that the associations are subconscious (De Houwer, 2006). In fact, empirical results point to quite the contrary (e.g., Gawronski, Hofmann, & Wilbur, 2006). Furthermore, although indirect measures are obviously not as easy to fake as self-report measures, both VTs and IATs are fakeable under specific boundary conditions as laid out in the previous sections (see http://www.innocentdads.org/abel.htm for detailed instruction on how to fake VT DSI measures; Cvencek et al., 2010). Ultimately, it is likely that no scientific, psychological measure will ever be completely immune to faking attempts, although resistance across measures will vary along a continuum and indirect measures are obviously situated on the more resistant end. Paradigms that tap into early levels of bottom–up/stimulus-driven processes such as startle probe reflex (Hecker, King, & Scoular, 2009) or anti-saccade tasks (Fox et al., 2011) seem to be promising future options as they might be even more resilient against faking attempts and deliberative top–down regulation.

Another interesting conundrum concerns the idea of the *true value* or the *true self*. All the issues concerning social desirability and fakeability imply that indirect/implicit measures are able to tap into individuals' genuine attitudes, opinions, or sexual interests that the respondent in forensic contexts is motivated to conceal from self-reports. However, this is dependent on what one would psychologically regard as the true self. On the one hand, it might be assumed that the true self is revealed under circumstances of failing deliberate control (e.g., disinhibition from alcohol consumption giving rise to the true self). On the other hand, it might be hypothesized that the true self can be inferred from what a person deliberately does and explicitly chooses in a controlled mode (Gawronski, 2009). Theoretically, from a dual-systems perspective it can be claimed that indirect measures should predict spontaneous behaviors whereas explicit measures should be related to deliberate behaviors. However, there is a whole set of situational and personal moderators of these relationships (Friese et al., 2008; Perugini et al., 2010; see Chapter 3 in this volume) underscoring that especially in applied forensic diagnostics one has to be cautious not to draw diagnostic inferences from single direct or indirect measures. All these sources of measurement error conflate criterion/predictive validity and thus it is questionable to interpret any single measure as an absolute index of a specific psychological attribute. Diagnostic conclusions are much safer if they are derived from multiple valid, convergent, and conceptually different measures that tap into unique parts of criterion variance. Corroborating this, combining direct and indirect measures into test batteries has been proven as incrementally valid over and above single (direct and indirect) DSI indicators in child sexual abuser populations (Babchishin et al., 2014; Banse et al., 2010; Schmidt, Mokros, & Banse, 2013). Therefore, in forensic contexts the pressing question remains when and under what boundary conditions are implicit/indirect measures incrementally valid predictors of specific behaviors above and beyond explicit measures.

What Should We Aim For? A Research Outlook

Important steps on the way to developing DSI measurement tasks have been made (Thornton & Laws, 2009b). The current state of research suggests that VTs and IATs are the most promising and best validated indirect measures of DSI/DSP. Several replications have been successfully conducted with independent samples and by different research laboratories. Preliminary work on the effects of various moderators on task performance (e.g., general reaction speed; Schmidt et al., 2014; denial; Babchishin et al., 2014; Brown et al., 2009) has been undertaken.

Methodological Aims

In terms of methodology, future research should aim to increase the reliability of indirect DSI/DSP measures and routinely report relevant coefficients that are based on corresponding test subsets (e.g., split-half coefficients, Cronbach's α). An effective strategy to optimize reliability is to use a sufficient number of trials. Additionally, in order to maximize differences between individuals (as opposed to experimental conditions), a fixed random stimulus order identical for all participants should be used because a fully randomized stimuli order adds unnecessary portions of random error to the measure.

More research focusing on convergent and discriminant validity with other established measures of DSI is needed. Each single validation criterion is plagued with its own set of problems. Self-reported DSI is regarded as amenable to various impression management influences. Sexual delinquent behavior such as child molesting represents a criminological/judicial category rather than a specific indication of a psychological construct such as DSI/DSP (empirically only up to 50% of child sexual offenders exhibit pedophilic DSP; Seto, 2008; taking indirect latency-based measures into account prevalences even decrease as shown by Schmidt and colleagues, 2013). Clinical pedophilia diagnoses suffer from low reliability and/or validity as these are usually based on inferences from offence behavior rendering them tautological. Thus, future research should preferably focus on behavioral measures based on PPG or sexual behavior on the Internet. Assessing these additional behaviors might be the only way to solve the paradox of not having a directly accessible validation criterion for DSI.

Standardization is another important aim. Phallometric assessments have been extensively criticized for a lack of standardization of stimuli, assessment procedures, and scoring (e.g., Kalmus & Beech, 2005). This critique has been routinely named as one of the main reasons for the development of indirect DSI measures. However, at present indirect measures of DSI are far from being standardized, too – neither in terms of stimuli nor scoring algorithms. Such idiosyncrasies constitute barriers against comparing results and undermine knowledge accumulation. An easily accomplished way of standardizing latency-based measures might be to use an analog to the d-measure of the IAT (Greenwald et al., 2003) based on the standardized mean differences of the relevant sexual interest categories as most measures rely on a DSP difference index comparing responses to child vs. adult stimuli.

Theoretical Aims

Future research needs to address questions pertaining to why and how indirect DSI/DSP measures differentiate between offender subgroups, as well as the boundary conditions affecting their validity. Therefore, it is highly advisable to control for factors such as intra- vs. extrafamilial child sexual offending, antisociality/psychopathy, pre- vs. postpubescent victims, victim sex, sexual orientation, and/or risk levels to disentangle the influence of sample characteristics from methodological issues. Apart from these issues, there is need for theoretical clarification of exactly what indirect measures assess and how implicit/indirect sexual interest indicators relate to sexual behavior when behavior contradicts explicit sexual interests. The exact relationship between latency-based DSI measures and actual (e.g., physiologically assessed) sexual arousal is as of yet unclear (Ó Ciardha, 2011). Since latency-based sexual interest indications cannot be regarded as the same as physiological sexual arousal, the relation between these two observational levels should be clarified for each latency-based measure and indirect measures as a whole.

Clinical Aims

Ultimately, a desirable goal would be not only to methodologically improve and theoretically better understand measures of DSI/DSP, but to make them more accessible to clinical usage. As one example of an approach toward applied usability, Banse et al. (2010) have created the Explicit and Implicit Sexual Interest Profile (EISIP) – a user-friendly test battery that produces profile outputs that can be interpreted by clinicians outside of research laboratory settings immediately after the assessment. Additionally, future work might focus on the development of norms for relevant offender and nonoffender populations. Finally, data on predictive validity, the most relevant piece of the puzzle for applied purposes, are still missing for most indirect latency-based measures (but see Gray et al., 2013 for VT measures and prospective recidivism). Nevertheless, as phallometrically assessed DSI has been proven to be among the best predictors of sexual reoffending (Mann, Hanson, & Thornton, 2010), high hopes might be put into VTs and IATs – the most valid DSI/DSP measures – as less costly and laborious adjuncts to PPG assessments. Preliminary cross-sectional reports of correlations with actuarial risk assessment instruments (Schmidt et al., 2012) and convergence of VT with PPG measures (Letourneau, 2002; Stinson & Becker, 2008) corroborate that this long-term research effort is worthwhile to pursue.

References

Abel, G. G. (1995). *The Abel Assessment for Sexual Interest–2 (AASI–2)*. Atlanta, GA: Abel Screening.

Abel, G. G., Huffman, J., Warberg, B., & Holland, C. L. (1998). Visual reaction time and plethysmography as measures of sexual interest in child molesters. *Sexual Abuse: A Journal of Research and Treatment, 10*, 81–95.

Abel, G. G., Jordan, A., Rouleau, J. L., Emerick, R., Barboza-Whitehead, S., & Osborn, C. (2004). Use of visual reaction time to assess male adolescents who molest children. *Sexual Abuse: A Journal of Research and Treatment, 16*, 255–265.

Babchishin, K. M., Nunes, K. L., & Hermann, C. A. (2013). The validity of Implicit Association Test (IAT) measures of sexual attraction to children: A meta-analysis. *Archives of Sexual Behavior, 42*, 487–499. http://doi.org/10.1007/s10508-012-0022-8

Babchishin, K. M., Nunes, K. L., & Kessous, N. (2014). A multimodal examination of sexual interest in children: A comparison of sex offenders and non-sex offenders. *Sexual Abuse: A Journal of Research and Treatment, 26*, 343–374. http://doi.org/10.1177/1079063213492343

Banse, R., Schmidt, A. F., & Clarbour, J. (2010). Indirect measures of sexual interest in child sex offenders: A multi-method approach. *Criminal Justice and Behavior, 37*, 319–335. http://doi.org/10.1177/0093854809357598

Beech, A. R., Kalmus, E., Tipper, S. P., Baudouin, J. Y., Flak, V., & Humphreys, G. W. (2008). Children induce an enhanced attentional blink in child molesters. *Psychological Assessment, 20*, 397–402. http://doi.org/10.1037/a0013587

Brown, A. S., Gray, N. S., & Snowden, R. J. (2009). Implicit measurement of sexual associations in child sex abusers: Role of victim type and denial. *Sexual Abuse: A Journal of Research and Treatment, 21*, 166–180.

Cisler, J. M., Bacon, A. K., Williams, N. L. (2009). Phenomenological characteristics of attentional biases towards threat: A critical review. *Cognitive Therapy and Research, 33*, 221–234. http://doi.org/10.1007/s10608-007-9161-y

Crooks, V. L., Rostill-Brookes, H., Beech, A. R., & Bickley, J. A. (2009). Applying Rapid Serial Visual Presentation to adolescent sexual offenders: Attentional bias as a measure of deviant sexual interest? *Sexual Abuse: A Journal of Research and Treatment, 21*, 135–148.

Cvencek, D., Greenwald, A. G., Brown, A. S., Gray, N. S., & Snowden, R. J. (2010). Faking of the Implicit Association Test is statistically detectable and partly correctable. *Basic and Applied Social Psychology, 32*, 302–314. http://doi.org/10.1080/01973533.2010.519236

Dawson, D. L., Barnes-Holmes, D., Gresswell, D. M., Hart, A. J. P., & Gore, N. J. (2009). Assessing the implicit beliefs of sexual offenders using the Implicit Relational Assessment Procedure: A first study. *Sexual Abuse: A Journal of Research and Treatment, 21*, 57–75.

De Houwer, J. (2006). What are implicit measures and why are we using them. In R. W. Wiers & A. W. Stacy (Eds.), *The handbook of implicit cognition and addiction* (pp. 11–28). Thousand Oaks, CA: Sage.

Friese, M., Hofmann, W., & Schmitt, M. (2008). When and why do implicit measures predict behaviour?: Empirical evidence for the moderating role of opportunity, motivation, and process reliance. *European Review of Social Psychology, 19*, 285–338. http://doi.org/10.1080/10463280802556958

Fox, E., Derakshan, N., & Standage, H. (2011). The assessment of human attention. In K. C. Klauer, A. Voss, & C. Stahl (Eds.), *Cognitive methods in social psychology* (pp. 15–47). New York, NY: Wiley.

Fromberger, P., Jordan, K., Steinkrauss, H., von Herder, J., Witzel, J., Stolpmann, G., ... Müller, J. L. (2012). Diagnostic accuracy of eye movements in assessing pedophilia. *Journal of Sexual Medicine, 9*, 1868–1882. http://doi.org/10.1111/j.1743-6109.2012.02754.x

Gawronski, B. (2009). Ten frequently asked questions about implicit measures and their frequently supposed, but not entirely correct answers. *Canadian Psychology, 50*, 141–150. http://doi.org/10.1037/a0013848

Gawronski, B., Hofmann, W., & Wilbur, C. J. (2006). Are "implicit" attitudes unconscious? *Consciousness and Cognition, 15*, 485–499. http://doi.org/10.1016/j.concog.2005.11.007

Geer, J. H., & Bellard, H. S. (1996). Sexual content induced delays in unprimed lexical decisions: Gender and context effects. *Archives of Sexual Behavior, 25*, 91–107.

Glasgow, D. V. (2009). Affinity: The development of a self-report assessment of paedophile sexual interest incorporating a viewing time validity measure. In D. Thornton & D. R. Laws (Eds.), *Cognitive approaches to the assessment of sexual interest in sexual offenders* (pp. 59–84). Chichester, UK: Wiley-Blackwell.

Gray, S. R., Abel, G. G., Jordan, A., Garby, T., Wiegel, M., & Harlow, N. (2013). Visual Reaction Time™ as a predictor of sexual offense recidivism. *Sexual Abuse: A Journal of Research and Treatment*. Advance online publication.

Gray, N. S., Brown, A. S., MacCulloch, M. J., Smith, J., & Snowden, R. J. (2005). An implicit test of the associations between children and sex in pedophiles. *Journal of Abnormal Psychology, 114*, 304–308. http://doi.org/10.1037/0021-843X.114.2.304

Gray, S. R., & Plaud, J. J. (2005). A comparison of the Abel Assessment for Sexual Interest and penile plethysmography in an outpatient sample of sexual offenders. *Journal of Sexual Offender Commitment: Science and the Law, 1*, 1–10.

Grieger, L., Hosser, D., & Schmidt, A. F. (2012). Predictive validity of self-reported self-control for different forms of recidivism. *Journal of Criminal Psychology, 2*, 80–95. http://doi.org/10.1108/20093821211264405

Greenwald, A. G., McGhee, D. E., & Schwartz, J. L. K. (1998). Measuring individual differences in implicit cognition: The Implicit Association Test. *Journal of Personality and Social Psychology, 74*, 1464–1480. http://doi.org/10.1037/0022-3514.74.6.1464

Greenwald, A. G., Nosek, B. A., & Banaji, M. R. (2003). Understanding and using the Implicit Association Test: I. An improved scoring algorithm. *Journal of Personality and Social Psychology, 85*, 197–216. http://doi.org/10.1037/h0087889

Gress, C. L. Z. (2005). Viewing time measures and sexual interest: Another piece of the puzzle. *Journal of Sexual Aggression, 11*, 117–125. http://doi.org/10.1080/13552600500063666

Gress, C. L. Z., & Laws, R. D. (2009). Measuring sexual deviance: Attention-based measures. In A. R. Beech, L. A. Craig, & K. D. Browne (Eds.), *Assessment and treatment of sex offenders: A handbook* (pp. 109–128). New York, NY: Wiley-Blackwell.

Harris, G. T., Rice, M. E., Quinsey, V. L., & Chaplin, T. C. (1996). Viewing time as a measure of sexual interest among child molesters and normal heterosexual men. *Behaviour Research and Therapy, 34*, 389–394. http://doi.org/10.1016/0005-7967(95)00070-4

Hecker, J. E., King, M. W., & Scoular, R. J. (2009). The startle probe reflex: An alternative approach to the measurement of sexual interest. In D. Thornton & D. R. Laws (Eds.), *Cognitive approaches to the assessment of sexual interest in sexual offenders* (pp. 59–84). Chichester, UK: Wiley-Blackwell.

Helmus, L., Thornton, D., Hanson, R. K., & Babchishin, K. M. (2012). Improving the predictive accuracy of Static-99 and Static-2002 with older sex offenders: Revised age weights. *Sexual Abuse: A Journal of Research and Treatment, 24*, 64–101.

Imhoff, R., Petruschke, P., Dierkes, R., Banse, R., & Weber, B. (2015). *Neuronal responses to sexually attractive stimuli as goal-driven top-down or stimulus-driven bottom up effects.* Manuscript in preparation.

Imhoff, R., Schmidt, A. F., Nordsiek, U., Luzar, C., Young, A. W., & Banse, R. (2010). Viewing time effects revisited: Prolonged response latencies for sexually attractive targets under restricted task conditions. *Archives of Sexual Behavior, 39,* 1275–1288. http://doi.org/10.1007/s10508-009-9595-2

Imhoff, R., Schmidt, A. F., Weiß, S., Young, A. W., & Banse, R. (2012). Vicarious Viewing Time: Prolonged response latencies for sexually attractive targets as a function of task- or stimulus-specific processing. *Archives of Sexual Behavior, 41,* 1389–1401. http://doi.org/10.1007/s10508-011-9879-1

Kalmus, E., & Beech, A. R. (2005). Forensic assessment of sexual interest: A review. *Aggression and Violent Behavior, 10,* 193–218. http://doi.org/10.1016/j.avb.2003.12.002

Letourneau, E. J. (2002). A comparison of objective measures of sexual arousal and interest: Visual reaction time and penile plethysmography. *Sexual Abuse: A Journal of Research and Treatment, 14,* 207–223.

Mann, R. E., Hanson, K. R., & Thornton, D. (2010). Assessing risk for sexual recidivism: Some proposals on the nature of psychologically meaningful risk factors. *Sexual Abuse: A Journal of Research and Treatment, 22,* 191–217.

Mihailides, S., Devilly, G. J., & Ward, T. (2004). Implicit cognitive distortions and sexual offending. *Sexual Abuse: A Journal of Research and Treatment, 16,* 333–350.

Mokros, A., Dombert, B., Osterheider, M., Zappalà, A., & Santtila, P. (2010). Assessment of pedophilic sexual interest with an attentional choice reaction time task. *Archives of Sexual Behavior, 39,* 1081–1090. http://doi.org/10.1007/s10508-009-9530-6

National Research Council, Committee to Review the Scientific Evidence on the Polygraph. (2003). *The polygraph and lie detection.* Washington, DC: National Academy Press.

Nunes, K. L., Firestone, P., & Baldwin, M. W. (2007). Indirect assessment of cognitions of child sexual abusers with the Implicit Association Test. *Criminal Justice and Behavior, 34,* 454–475. http://doi.org/10.1177/0093854806291703

Ó Ciardha, C. (2011). A theoretical framework for understanding deviant sexual interest and cognitive distortions as overlapping constructs contributing to sexual offending against children. *Aggression and Violent Behavior, 16,* 493–502. http://doi.org/10.1016/j.avb.2011.05.001

Ó Ciardha, C., & Gormley, M. (2012). Using a pictorial-modified Stroop Task to explore the sexual interests of sexual offenders against children. *Sexual Abuse: A Journal of Research and Treatment, 24,* 175–197.

Perugini, M., & Banse, R. (2007). Editorial: Personality, implicit self-concept and automaticity. *European Journal of Personality, 21,* 257–261. http://doi.org/10.1002/per.637

Perugini, M., Richetin, J., & Zogmaister, C. (2010). Prediction of behavior. In B. Gawronski & B. K. Payne (Eds.), *Handbook of social cognition – measurement, theory, and applications* (pp. 255–277). New York, NY: Guilford.

Pöppl, T. A., Nitschke, J., Dombert, B., Santtila, P., Greenlee, M. W., Osterheider, M., & Mokros, A. (2011). Functional cortical and subcortical abnormalities in pedophilia: A combined study using a choice reaction time task and fMRI. *Journal of Sexual Medicine, 8,* 1660–1674. http://doi.org/10.1111/j.1743-6109.2011.02248.x

Prause, N., Janssen, E., & Hetrick, W. P. (2008). Attention and emotional responses to sexual stimuli and their relationship to sexual desire. *Archives of Sexual Behavior, 37,* 934–949. http://doi.org/10.1007/s10508-007-9236-6

Price, S. A., Beech, A. R., Mitchell, I. J., & Humphreys, G. W. (2012). The promises and perils of the emotional Stroop task: A general review and considerations for use with forensic samples. *Journal of Sexual Aggression, 18,* 253–268. http://doi.org/10.1080/13552600.2010.545149

Price, S. A., & Hanson, R. K. (2007). A modified Stroop task with sexual offenders: Replication of a study. *Journal of Sexual Aggression, 13,* 203–216. http://doi.org/10.1080/13552600701785505

Raymond, J. E., Shapiro, K. L., & Arnell, K. A. (1992). Temporary suppression of visual processing in an RSVP task: An attentional blink? *Journal of Experimental Psychology: Human Perception and Performance, 18,* 849–860.

Rönspies, J., Schmidt, A. F., Melnikova, A., Krumova, R., Zolfagari, A. & Banse, R. (2015). Indirect measurement of sexual orientation – comparison of the implicit relational assessment procedure, viewing time, and choice reaction time tasks. *Archives of Sexual Behavior.* Advance online publication.

Rosenzweig, S. (1942). The photoscope as an objective device for evaluating sexual interest. *Psychosomatic Medicine, 4*, 150–157. http://doi.org/10.1097/00006842-194204000-00004

Sachsenmaier, S. J., & Gress, C. L. Z. (2009). The Abel Assessment for Sexual Interests-2: A critical review. In D. Thornton & D. R. Laws (Eds.), *Cognitive approaches to the assessment of sexual interest in sexual offenders* (pp. 31–57). Chichester, UK: Wiley-Blackwell.

Seto, M. C. (2008). *Pedophilia and sexual offending against children: Theory, assessment and intervention*. Washington, DC: APA. http://doi.org/10.1037/11639-000

Seto, M. C., Harris, G. T, Rice, M. E., & Barbaree, H. E. (2004). The Screening Scale for Pedophilic Interests predicts recidivism among adult sex offenders with child victims. *Archives of Sexual Behavior, 33*, 455–466. http://doi.org/10.1023/B:ASEB.0000037426.55935.9c

Seto, M. C., & Lalumière, M. L. (2001). A brief screening scale to identify pedophilic interests among child molesters. *Sexual Abuse: A Journal of Research and Treatment, 13*, 15–25.

Snowden, R. J., Craig, R. L., Gray, N. S. (2011). Indirect behavioral measures of cognition among sexual offenders. *Journal of Sex Research, 48*, 192–217. http://doi.org/10.1080/00224499.2011.557750

Snowden, R. J., & Gray, N., S. (2010). Implicit social cognition in forensic settings. In B. Gawronski & B. K. Payne (Eds.), *Handbook of implicit social cognition – measurement, theory, and applications* (pp. 522–534). New York, NY: Guilford.

Schmidt, A. F., Gykiere, K., Vanhoeck, K., Mann, R. E., & Banse, R. (2014). Direct and indirect measures of sexual maturity preferences differentiate subtypes of child sexual abusers. *Sexual Abuse: A Journal of Research and Treatment, 26*, 107–126. http://doi.org/10.1177/1079063213480817

Schmidt, A. F., Mokros, A., & Banse, R. (2013). Is pedophilic sexual preference continuous? A taxometric analysis based on direct and indirect measures. *Psychological Assessment, 25*, 1146–1153. http://doi.org/10.1037/a0033326

Smith, P., & Waterman, M. (2004). Processing bias for sexual material: The Emotional Stroop and sexual offenders. *Sexual Abuse: A Journal of Research and Treatment, 16*, 163–171.

Stinson, J. D., & Becker, J. V. (2008). Assessing sexual deviance: A comparison of physiological, historical, and self-report measures. *Journal of Psychiatric Practice, 14*, 379–388. http://doi.org/10.1097/01.pra.0000341892.51124.85

Stroop, J. R. (1935). Studies of interference in serial verbal reactions. *Journal of Experimental Psychology, 18*, 643–662. http://doi.org/10.1037/h0054651

Teige-Mocigemba, S., Klauer, K. C., & Sherman, J. W. (2010). A practical guide to Implicit Association Tests and related tasks. In B. Gawronski & B. K. Payne (Eds.), *Handbook of social cognition – measurement, theory, and applications* (pp. 117–139). New York, NY: Guilford.

Thornton, D., & Laws, D. R. (2009a). *Cognitive approaches to the assessment of sexual interest in sexual offenders*. Chichester, UK: Wiley-Blackwell. http://doi.org/10.1002/9780470747551

Thornton, D., & Laws, D. R. (2009b). Postscript: Steps towards effective assessment of sexual interest. In D. Thornton & D. R. Laws (Eds.), *Cognitive approaches to the assessment of sexual interest in sexual offenders* (pp. 59–84). Chichester, UK: Wiley-Blackwell.

van Leeuwen, M. L., van Baaren, R. B., Chakhssi, F., Loonen, M. G. M., Lippmann, M., & Dikjksterhuis, A. (2013). Assessment of implicit sexual associations in non-incarcerated pedophiles. *Archives of Sexual Behavior, 42*, 1501–1507. http://doi.org/10.1007/s10508-013-0094-0

Verschuere, B., Ben-Shakar, G., & Meijer, E. (2011). *Memory detection: Theory and application of the Concealed Information Test*. Cambridge, UK: Cambridge University Press. http://doi.org/10.1017/CBO9780511975196

Walters, G. D. (2006). Risk-appraisal versus self-report in the prediction of criminal justice outcomes. *Criminal Justice and Behavior, 33*, 279–304. http://doi.org/10.1177/0093854805284409

Worling, J. R. (2006). Assessing sexual arousal with adolescent males who have offended sexually: Self-report and unobtrusively measured viewing time. *Sexual Abuse: A Journal of Research and Treatment, 18*, 383–400.

Wright, L. W., & Adams, H. E. (1994). Assessment of sexual preference using a choice reaction time task. *Journal of Psychopathology and Behavioral Assessment, 16*, 221–231. http://doi.org/10.1007/BF02229209

Appendix

Table 11.1. Overview of psychometric results from studies on latency-based indirect measures of deviant sexual interest in children

Measure	Categories	Reliability	Validity — Group comparison (n)	Effect-size reported	Cohen's d equivalent
Viewing Time (VT)					
Harris, Rice, Quinsey, & Chaplin (1996)	Adult–Child	n/a	CSO vs. NOC	$d = 1.00**$	1.00
			Girls-only CSO vs. NOC	$r = -.60***$	1.50
Abel, Huffmann, Warberg, & Holland (1998)	Adult male	$\alpha = 0.88$			
	Adolescent male	$\alpha = 0.89$			
	Young male	$\alpha = 0.87$			
	Adult female	$\alpha = 0.86$			
	Adolescent female	$\alpha = 0.84$			
	Young female	$\alpha = 0.90$			
Letourneau (2002)	Male children (age 2–4)	$\alpha = 0.60$			
	Male children (age 8–10)	$\alpha = 0.75$			
	Male adolescents (age 14–17)	$\alpha = 0.90$			
	Male adults (age 22 and over)	$\alpha = 0.90$			
	Male children (age 0–10)	n/a	CSO with boy victims (10) vs. SO (47)	$r = .69**$	2.51
	Female children (age 2–4)	$\alpha = 0.87$			
	Female children (age 8–10)	$\alpha = 0.86$			
	Female adolescents (age 14–17)	$\alpha = 0.85$			
	Female adults (age 22 and over)	$\alpha = 0.80$			
	Female children (0–10)	n/a	CSO with girl victims (34) vs. SO (23)	$r = .08$	0.16
Abel et al. (2004)	Children–adults	n/a	Adolescent CSO (1170) vs. Adolescent AC (534)	$AUC = .64^{snr}$	0.51
Gress (2005)	Children–adults	n/a	CSO (19) vs. rapists (7)	Frequency table	1.08*
			CSO with male or mixed victims (9) vs. CSO with female victims (17)	Frequency table	1.65*

Table 11.1. continued

Measure	Categories	Reliability	Validity Group comparison (n)	Effect-size reported	Cohen's d equivalent
Gray & Plaud (2005)		n/a	Dissimulating pedophilic CSO (11) vs. Pedophilic CSO (28)	Frequency table	−2.13*
			VT (39) vs. PPG (39)	Frequency table	0.43
Worling (2006)	Prepubescent/postpubescent[b]	n/a	CSO (52) vs. sexual offenders with peer or adolescent victims (26)	AUC^b = .61	0.40
	Male toddlers	α = 0.82			
	Male preadolescents	α = 0.79	CSO with two or more victims vs. SO	AUC^b = .60	0.36
	Male adolescents	α = 0.62	CSO with any male victims vs. SO	AUC^b = .69**	0.70
	Male adults	α = 0.72	CSO with only male victims vs. SO	AUC^b = .73**	0.87
	Female toddlers	α = 0.73	CSO with any female victims vs. SO	AUC^b = .42	−0.29
	Female preadolescents	α = 0.82	CSO with only female victims vs. SO	AUC^b = .43	−0.25
	Female adolescents	α = 0.77			
	Female adults	α = 0.77			
Glasgow (2009)	Male child	α = 0.93			
	Male preadolescent	α = 0.8			
	Male adolescent	α = 0.9			
	Male adult	α = 0.89			
	Female child	α = 0.92			
	Female preadolescent	α = 0.87			
	Female adolescent	α = 0.89			
	Female adult	α = 0.93			
	Adult–child	n/a	CSO (31) vs. NOC (31)	AUC = .87[snr]	1.59
Banse, Schmidt, & Clarbour (2010)	Postpubescent males	α = 0.85	CSO (38) vs. NSOC (37)/NOC (38)	AUC = .82*	1.29
	Postpubescent females	α = 0.86		AUC = .56	0.21

Table 11.1. continued

Measure	Categories	Reliability	Validity Group comparison (n)	Effect-size reported	Cohen's d equivalent
	Prepubescent males	α = 0.85		AUC = .80*	1.19
	Prepubescent females	α = 0.77		AUC = .76*	1.00
	Children–adults	n/a		AUC = .51	0.04
	Postpubescent males		CSO with boy victims only (14) vs. NSOC (37)	AUC = .89*	1.73
	Postpubescent females			AUC = .63	0.47
	Prepubescent males			AUC = .90*	1.81
	Prepubescent females			AUC = .81*	1.24
	Children–adults			AUC = .33	−0.62
	Postpubescent males		CSO with girl victims only (16) vs. NSOC (37)	AUC = .78*	1.09
	Postpubescent females			AUC = .74*	0.91
	Prepubescent males			AUC = .86*	1.53
	Prepubescent females			AUC = .73*	0.87
	Children–adults			AUC = .46	−0.14
Schmidt, Gykiere, Vanhoeck, Mann, & Banse (2014)	Postpubescent males	α = 0.90	CSO with male or mixed victims (18) vs. girls-only CSO (36)	r = .47**	1.13
	Postpubescent females	α = 0.90		r = −.37**	−0.84
	Prepubescent males	α = 0.95		r = .47*	1.13
	Prepubescent females	α = 0.93		r = .00	0.00
	Children–adults	n/a		r = .42**	0.98
Babchishin, Nunes, & Kessous (2014)	Child–adult	n/a	CSO (35) vs. NSOC (21)	d = 1.15*	1.15
			Admitting CSO (20) vs. NSOC (20)	d = 1.32*	1.32
			Denying CSO (12) vs. NSOC (20)	d = 1.22*	1.22
Fromberger et al. (2012)	Children–adults	n/a	Pedophilic CSO (19) vs. AC (7)/NOC (48)	AUC = 0.76***	1.00

Table 11.1. continued

Measure	Categories	Reliability	Validity — Group comparison (n)	Effect-size reported	Cohen's d equivalent
Implicit Association Test (IAT)					
Mihailides, Devilly, & Ward (2004)	Children–not children/sexual–not sexual	n/a	CSO (25) vs. NSOC (25)	$t = 3.15**$	0.63
Gray, Brown, MacCulloch, Smith, & Snowden (2005)	Children–adults/sex–nonsex	n/a	CSO (25) vs. NOC (25)	$t = 4.76***$	0.95
			CSO (18) vs. AC (60)	$d = 0.84*$	0.84
Nunes, Firestone, & Baldwin (2007)	Children–adults/sexy–not sexy	n/a	CSO (24) vs. NOC (29)	$r = .33*$	0.70
	Children–adults/pleasant–unpleasant	n/a	CSO (27) vs. NOC (29)	$r = .21$	0.43
Brown, Gray, & Snowden (2009)	Children–adults/sex–nonsex	$\alpha = 0.80$ $r_{tt} = .63$	CSO with victims < 12 years of age (54) vs. CSO with victims > 12 years of age (21)	$d = 0.77**$	0.77
			CSO (54) vs. NSOC (49)	$d = 0.92***$	0.92
			Admitting CSO (20) vs. NSOC (49)	$d = 0.75*$	0.75
			Denying CSO (55) vs. NSOC (49)	$d = 1.01**$	1.01
			Denying (55) vs. Admitting CSO (20)	$d = 0.27$	0.27
Banse, Schmidt, & Clarbour (2010)	1. Boys–men/sexually exciting–sexually unexciting	$\alpha = 0.65$	CSO (38) vs. NSOC (37)/NOC (38)	$AUC = .62*$	0.43
	2. Girls–women/sexually exciting–sexually unexciting	$\alpha = 0.79$		$AUC = .72*$	0.82
	3. Children–adults/sexually exciting–sexually unexciting	n/a		$AUC = .71*$	0.78
	1.		CSO with boy victims only (14) vs. NSOC (37)	$AUC = .60$	0.36
	2.			$AUC = .67$	0.62
	3.			$AUC = .71*$	0.78
	1.		CSO with girl victims only (16) vs. NSOC (37)	$AUC = .57$	0.25
	2.			$AUC = .56$	0.21
	3.			$AUC = .60$	0.36

Table 11.1. continued

Measure	Categories	Reliability	Validity Group comparison (n)	Effect-size reported	Cohen's d equivalent
Babchishin, Nunes, & Kessous (2014)	Children–adults/sexy–not sexy	n/a	CSO (35) vs. NSOC (21)	d = 0.44	0.44
			Admitting CSO (22) vs. NSOC (21)	d = 0.35	0.35
			Denying CSO (13) vs. NSOC (21)	d = 0.51	0.51
Schmidt, Gykiere, Vanhoeck, Mann, & Banse (2014)	Boys–men/sexually exciting–sexually unexciting	α = 0.61	CSO with male or mixed victims (18) vs. Girls-only CSO (36)	r = .29*	0.64
	Girls–women/sexually exciting–sexually unexciting	α = 0.82		r = .23	0.50
	Children–adults/sexually exciting–sexually unexciting	n/a		r = .32*	0.72
Van Leeuwen et al. (2013)	Children–adults/sex-related–neutral	n/a	SCP (20) vs. NOC (20)	AUC = .89^{snr}	1.73
Implicit Relational Assessment Procedure (IRAP)					
Dawson, Barnes-Holmes, Gresswell, Hart, & Gore (2009)	Children–adults	n/a	CSO (16) vs. NOC (16)	χ² = 5.489*	0.91
Eye Movement Tracking					
Fromberger et al. (2012)	Children–adults (initial fixation latency)	n/a	Pedophilic CSO (20) vs.	AUC = 0.90***	1.81
	Children–adults (relative fixation time)	n/a	SO with adult victims (7)/NOC (48)	AUC = 0.83***	1.35
Choice Reaction Task (CRT)					
Mokros, Dombert, Osterheider, Zappalà, & Santtila (2010)	Infants–adults	n/a	CSO (21) vs. NSOC (21)	AUC = 0.84**	1.41
Pöppl et al. (2011)	Infants–adults	n/a	CSO (9) vs. NSOC (11)	d = 0.99*	0.99
Stroop Variants					
Smith & Waterman (2004; Emotional Stroop)	Sexual–neutral	n/a	CSO (5) vs. rapists (5)	t = 0.831	0.53

Table 11.1. continued

Measure	Categories	Reliability	Validity Group comparison (n)	Effect-size reported	Cohen's d equivalent
Price & Hanson (2007; Emotional Stroop)	Sexual–neutral	n/a	CSO (15) vs. rapists (15)	n/a	−0.45
			CSO (15) vs. violent NSOC (15)	n/a	−0.03
			CSO (15) vs. nonviolent NSOC (15)	n/a	0.14
			CSO (15) vs. NOC (15)	n/a	0.82*
	Child molesting–neutral		CSO (15) vs. rapists (15)	n/a	−0.28
			CSO (15) vs. violent NSOC (15)	n/a	0.26
			CSO (15) vs. nonviolent NSOC (15)	n/a	0.07
			CSO (15) vs. NOC (15)	n/a	0.58
Ó Ciardha & Gormley (2012; Picture Stroop)	Rape–neutral	n/a	CSO (15) vs. rapists (15)	n/a	0.19
	Children–adults	n/a	CSO (24) vs. NOC (24)	AUC = .56	0.21
			Highly deviant CSO (15) vs. NOC (24)	AUC = .59	0.32
Van Leeuwen et al. (2013; Picture–Word Stroop)	Children–adults	n/a	SCP (20) vs. NOC (20)	AUC = .84^{snr}	1.41
Rapid Serial Visual Presentation (RSVP)					
Beech et al. (2008)	T1 Child–T1 animal	n/a	Intrafamilial CSO (16) vs. NSOC (17)	r = .45**	1.00
			Extrafamilial CSO (18) vs NSOC (17)	r = .54***	1.28
Crooks, Rostill-Brookes, Beech, & Bickley (2009)	T1 Child–T1 animal	n/a	Adolescent CSO (20) vs. Adolescent NSOC (26)	n/a	—

Notes. All comparisons with male participants and based on uncorrected, raw data. n/a = Not available; CSO = child sexual offenders; NSOC = nonsexual offenders; NOC = nonoffender controls; AC = nonchild sexual offending controls; SO = sexual offenders with adult and/or child victims; SCP = self-identified community pedophiles; PPG = penile plethysmography; VT = Viewing Time.
[a]No differences reported for all discriminant analyses in Abel et al. (1998). [b]All comparisons/effect sizes reported in Worling (2006) are based on the Prepubescent/Postpubescent Deviance Index. snr = significance level not reported.
* p < .05; ** p < .01; *** p < .001.

Chapter 12
Implicit Measures in Consumer Psychology

Malte Friese[1] and Andrew Perkins[2]

[1]Department of Psychology, Saarland University, Saarbrücken, Germany
[2]Carson College of Business, Washington State University, WA, USA

Implicit measures have been everywhere in psychology in the last 15 years or so. Researchers have employed implicit measures to investigate spider phobia and suicidal ideation in clinical psychology (Glashouwer et al., 2010; Huijding & De Jong, 2006), job attitudes and biases in personnel selection in organizational psychology (Agerstrom & Rooth, 2011; Leavitt, Fong, & Greenwald, 2011; Rooth, 2010), proneness to exercise in sport psychology (Bluemke, Brand, Schweizer, & Kahlert, 2010; Conroy, Hyde, Doerksen, & Ribeiro, 2010), or the prediction of voting behavior in political psychology (Arcuri, Castelli, Galdi, Zogmaister, & Amadori, 2008; Friese, Smith, Plischke, Bluemke, & Nosek, 2012; Galdi, Arcuri, & Gawronski, 2008). Implicit measures have been scrutinized by researchers in cognitive psychology (Mierke & Klauer, 2003; Rothermund & Wentura, 2004; Siegel, Dougherty, & Huber, 2012) and received particularly great attention in social psychology in the investigation of, for example, stereotypes, prejudice, and attitude change (Dovidio, Kawakami, Johnson, & Johnson, 1997; Fazio, Jackson, Dunton, & Williams, 1995; Gawronski & Bodenhausen, 2006; Rydell & McConnell, 2006). Somewhat surprisingly, implicit measures also received great interest in consumer psychology, although at first glance consumer attitudes seem to deliver few reasons for the implementation of implicit measures in consumer psychology research: Many consumers know the products that are important for them for a long time and have evolved elaborated brand and product attitudes. They neither have difficulty with reporting them, nor do social desirability or impression management concerns exert strong influences as in other domains such as stereotyping or intergroup behavior. Put differently, when a consumer likes a certain soft drink, there is little reason to assume the consumer is not aware of her or his liking and even less reason to assume that the consumer would be unwilling to report her or his preference. In addition, many brands and products do not seem to be prone to triggering highly inconsistent and conflicting attitudes. In sum, these are all factors that would seem to align implicit and explicit cognition, leading to high implicit–explicit correspondence (Nosek, 2005), and hence to leave little room for implicit measures to excel in comparison to explicit self-report measures in consumer psychology.

Despite all this, research employing implicit measures is prospering in consumer psychology, as is documented not only by the increasing number of original research articles featuring implicit measures published in the consumer domain, but also by special issues (Nevid, 2010), review articles (Gregg & Klymowsky, 2013), and book chapters such as the present one (see also Friese, Hofmann, & Wänke, 2009; Perkins & Forehand, 2010). Quite obviously, researchers believe that implicit measures can contribute in a meaningful way to the investigation of various concepts and processes of importance in consumer psychology such as the formation, change, and consequences of consumer attitudes, the self-concept, consumer decisions, and consumption behavior. Although the structural differences between consumer psychology and more obvious fields of investigation for implicit measures such as stereotyping and intergroup behavior exist, researchers have collected broad evidence for the usefulness of implicit measures in consumer-related contexts. Some reasons to rely on implicit measures were similar to those in other subdisciplines in psychology: the fear of distortions through self-presentation and impression management tendencies that could influence the measurement of explicit self-report, assumed lack of awareness of the processes that are captured with implicit measures and the belief that these processes can be better captured with implicit than explicit measures, or the observation that explicit self-report measures showed unsatisfactory predictive validity in some contexts in which implicit measures were assumed to fare better.

The present chapter seeks to give an overview of this research literature. First, we look at some precursors of implicit measures in consumer psychology. In the main part of this chapter, we provide an overview of empirical studies employing implicit measures in the consumer context. This overview is divided into two subsections. The first subsection primarily reviews research in which implicit measures have been used as dependent variables to show effects of some (quasi-)experimental manipulations. The second subsection primarily reviews research in which implicit measures have been used as independent variables or predictors of consumer-related behavior. Finally, we provide an outlook and discuss some challenges for future research using implicit measures in the consumer domain.

What Are Implicit Measures?

Implicit measures are used to assess spontaneous, gut-level responses that are often affectively toned (Smith & Nosek, 2011) and not necessarily endorsed by the person if asked directly about the respective topic and given appropriate time to think about an answer. They are believed to tap into an associative network in memory and therefore capture predominantly associative processes and to a lesser extent propositional processes (Gawronski & Bodenhausen, 2006; Strack & Deutsch, 2004). Associative processes can influence deliberate judgments by serving as their basis, but they can also be rejected as such and replaced by reflective or propositional thoughts. Depending on several boundary conditions, associative and propositional processes may align or dissociate, and – again depending on boundary conditions – they may influence behavior similarly or in different ways under different circumstances (Friese, Hofmann, & Schmitt, 2008; Hofmann, Gschwendner, Nosek, & Schmitt, 2005; see also Chapter 3 in this volume).

Many implicit measures rely on response latencies and even if they do not, the measurement procedure usually requires speeded responding that prevents well thought-out responses (Fazio & Olson, 2003; Payne, Cheng, Govorun, & Stewart, 2005). The last two decades has seen a surge of implicit measures and researchers continue to introduce new measures and modifications of established ones. The most prominent measures are evaluative priming (Fazio et al., 1995), the Implicit Association Test (IAT; Greenwald, McGhee, & Schwartz, 1998), the Single-Category Implicit Association Test (SC-IAT; Karpinski & Steinman, 2006), and the Affect Misattribution Procedure (AMP; Payne et al., 2005; for an overview, see Nosek, Hawkings, & Frazier, 2011). As in other fields, the dominance of these measures is also reflected in the consumer domain. Other chapters in this volume have extensively reviewed these measures (especially Chapters 2, 4, and 9 in this volume; see also Gawronski & Payne, 2010).

Precursors of Implicit Measures in Consumer Psychology

Using indirect measures to gain insights into consumers' attitudes (or other constructs) or to measure and predict impulsive behavior is not new. Long before the wave of implicit (and usually indirect) measures was introduced, researchers had recognized the reactivity of explicit self-report measures and invented measures that would be called indirect or even implicit today (Webb, Campbell, Schwartz, & Sechrest, 1966). A prominent example is Haire's shopping list procedure (Haire, 1950). When instant coffee was introduced in 1949, sales were disappointing. To the surprise of marketing researchers, consumers reported disliking the taste, although in previously conducted blind taste tests consumers had not noticed a difference between instant and regular coffee. Haire (1950) had the idea of preparing fake shopping lists and handing them out to consumers. In one condition the shopping list contained instant coffee and in a different condition it contained regular drip coffee. Then Haire asked participants to describe the person who had allegedly written the list. Consumers described the instant coffee buyer as lazy and an inadequate mother and housewife, suggesting that in contrast to what they claimed overtly, poor taste was probably not the reason that kept consumers from buying instant coffee.

Another early attempt at getting at possibly different aspects of consumers' attitudes than reported in traditional questionnaires is the error-choice technique by Hammond (1948). It rests on the assumption that people have more positive associations toward objects they like than toward objects they dislike, and that these attitudes influence consumer behavior. The task is described as a knowledge test in which respondents choose between two alternative answers to a question about a certain product. Both of the answers given are in fact wrong. One is biased in favor of the product in question; the other is biased in the other direction. The method rests on the assumption that attitudes toward the product will influence the answers to the questions. For example, one glass of a certain fruit drink may contain 20% of the suggested daily dose of vitamin C. In the error-choice method, consumers could be asked "What do you think, how much of the daily dose of vitamin C does one glass of this fruit drink contain?" with response options "15%" and "25%." A more positive attitude toward the fruit drink would be assumed if respondents chose the higher percentage, because a high vitamin C content is usually regarded as something positive.

A final example is the swift-selection platform that seeks to simulate impulsive consumer choices (Salcher, 1995). The reasoning here is that impulsive consumer choices may be driven by forces that may be difficult to verbalize and therefore difficult to predict based on self-reports. Several products are hidden on a platform behind a curtain or a lid. The curtain opens for only a few seconds and participants are instructed to choose one of the products. This procedure is intended to impede reflective thinking and promote impulsive choices. Although it is questionable how many (if any) consumer choices are actually made with such little reflection (apart from habitual responses that are not choices in the same sense anymore), the swift-selection platform is certainly a valuable indicator of the spontaneous attraction of the presented products.

The measures presented in this section prevent deliberate, reflective thinking about the attribute researchers want to measure in different ways. Haire's shopping list procedure is reminiscent of projective methods (and the associated reliability problems), Hammond's error-choice method is indirect and builds on unrecognized influences of attitudes on judgments, and the swift-selection platform puts individuals under time pressure when simulating a consumer choice. Different from these measures, nowadays implicit measures rely on modern computer technology to present large amounts of stimuli in highly standardized fashion in order to achieve a more nuanced picture of the target construct and acceptable reliability that allows for the assessment of individual differences.

Implicit Measures as Dependent Variables

In the early stages of research using implicit measures in consumer psychology, researchers sought to establish construct validity of the new measures, often by investigating the relation between an implicit and an explicit measurement of the same construct. For example, Brunel, Tietje, and Greenwald (2004) used implicit measures in two different contexts, one in which they expected a high correspondence between implicit and explicit measures, and one in which they expected a dissociation. Implicitly (IAT; Greenwald et al., 1998) and explicitly (differential scales) measured attitudes correlated highly in a study on attitudes toward computers (PC vs. Mac). Participants with favorable explicit attitudes toward PCs, who owned a PC, and who used a PC more often than a Mac also showed stronger implicitly measured attitudes for PCs as compared with Macs. This pattern was reversed and more pronounced for Mac loyalists than for PC loyalists. Mac loyalists also associated Mac computers more strongly with the self than PC loyalists associated PCs with the self, suggesting that owning and using a Mac is more central to the self for Mac users than owning and using a PC is for PC users (see also Maison, Greenwald, & Bruin, 2001, 2004). In a second study in the realm of stereotyping and prejudice, implicitly and explicitly measured attitudes toward advertisements featuring African American vs. Caucasian spokespeople were dissociated, as expected. Overall, participants reported no explicit preference for a particular type of advertisement, but the IAT effect suggested that on average advertisements featuring Caucasian spokespeople were implicitly preferred to advertisements featuring African American spokespeople. This effect was particularly pronounced for Caucasian participants. African American participants showed an explicit preference for advertisements featuring black spokespeople, but no difference in the IAT.

Another dissociation between implicitly and explicitly measured attitudes emerged in a study investigating attitudes toward genetically modified food using the Go/No-Go Association Task (GNAT; Nosek & Banaji, 2001) as implicit and semantic differential scales as explicit measures (Spence & Townsend, 2006). Effects of the implicit measure suggested that participants held – to the surprise of the authors – neutral to positive implicit evaluations of genetically modified food (depending on context variations in the Go/No-Go Association Task).

Attitude Change

Several researchers employed implicit measures to capture changes in attitudes toward products and brands that are due to the activation or formation of associations that may not be easily captured by explicit measures, or that trigger cognitive processes that are differentially captured by implicit and explicit measures. In these cases, including both implicit and explicit measures will deliver a more comprehensive picture and discover effects that may go unnoticed in the absence of one of those measures.

In an intriguing set of studies, Dimofte and Yalch (2007a, 2007b) investigated the effects of brand slogans that are ambiguous in the sense that they have another meaning in addition to the one intended by the marketer (polysemous brand slogans). For example, the slogan *Raising the bar* can be understood as a promotion for unreached quality and service of a product. A secondary meaning, however, may hint "at the difficulty one has in qualifying for the service or meeting the requirements (e.g., credit score and contract length) implied by such an elite service" (Dimofte & Yalch, 2007a, p. 518). The authors showed that polysemous brand slogans led to implicit associations of negative secondary meanings with the brand, particularly for participants with good automatic access to secondary meanings (assessed with a specific measure akin to an executive control task). Implicit associations were assessed with IATs. The changes in implicit associations were not always paralleled by changes in explicitly measured attitudes, suggesting that in these cases implicit measures captured something unique. The authors argue that real marketing claims often bear secondary meanings that may have unintended effects on implicit associations with yet unknown but potentially powerful implications on behavior.

In a related vein, Forehand and Perkins (2005) presented their participants advertisements that featured voiceovers of celebrities. Implicitly measured attitudes toward these celebrities (IAT, measured several weeks earlier) correlated positively with implicitly measured attitudes toward the advertised brand, irrespective of whether or not the participants had correctly identified the celebrity in the advertisement. By contrast, explicitly measured celebrity attitudes correlated positively with explicitly measured attitude change toward the brand only for participants who were unable to correctly identify the celebrity. For those who had correctly identified the brand, this relationship was negative, suggesting an overcorrection of this rationally irrelevant potential influence of the celebrity on brand liking.

Implicitly measured attitudes may also transfer from one product to another. Using IATs, Ratliff, Swinkels, Klerx, and Nosek (2012) showed that implicitly measured attitudes toward one product (body lotions) automatically transferred to a different product of the same brand even if consumers knew nothing about this other product (deodorants). In a second study, consumers received relevant information about new products (orange juices). When evaluating these new products, they were able to ignore the largely irrelevant information about the previously seen products of the same brand (apple juices) and built their explicit evaluations based on only this relevant information. However, on an implicit level, there was still attitude transfer in the sense that the previously received information about the apple juices influenced the implicit evaluation of the new products (orange juices), even though rationally it would have been irrelevant for the evaluation. Presumably, the previously seen information about the other product generated associations to this product and the brand more generally that transferred to the subsequently presented product of the same brand. These transferred associations later influenced performance on the IAT.

Going a step further, Horcajo, Brinol, and Petty (2010) showed that associations toward even much less related concepts than two products of the same brand as in the studies by Ratliff and colleagues (2012) are sufficient to produce changes in one as a function of thinking about the other. Consumers pondered a persuasive message in favor of using the color green as the future institutional color for the local university, thereby fostering positive implicit associations to the beer brand Heineken, which is closely associated with the color green, as indicated by an IAT. Apparently, the elaboration of arguments in favor of the color green led to changes in its evaluation that spread to related concepts such as Heineken (see also Dimofte & Yalch, 2011; Strick, Van Baaren, Holland, & Van Knippenberg, 2009).

In one study using a more blatant persuasion attempt, participants watched antitobacco or antimarijuana TV spots (Czyzewska & Ginsburg, 2007). The spots had no effect on explicitly measured attitudes toward tobacco. Unexpectedly, explicitly measured attitudes toward marijuana even became more positive after watching the antimarijuana spot. By contrast, implicitly measured attitudes (IAT) toward tobacco were more negative after viewing an antitobacco spot and implicitly measured attitudes toward marijuana were more negative after viewing an antimarijuana spot. To explain the unexpected finding, the authors speculate about a reactance effect such that the teenage participants may have spontaneously generated counter-arguments against the antimarijuana (but not the antitobacco) spot, which led them to show an inverse persuasion effect on an explicit level for the antimarijuana spot.

One powerful way to change implicit evaluations is to associate the respective object with the self. Gawronski, Bodenhausen, and Becker (2007) showed that merely choosing a product creates associations between the self and the product (as indicated by an affective priming task, Fazio et al., 1995). Postdecisional changes of implicit evaluations of the chosen product were mediated by an associative transfer of implicit self-evaluations to the chosen object (Koole, Dijksterhuis, & Van Knippenberg, 2001; Nuttin, 1985). Choosing a product enhanced implicit evaluations of the product for consumers with high, but not low implicit self-esteem. Explicit evaluations were not collected.

Building on these findings, different groups of researchers used IAT-like procedures (Ebert, Steffens, Von Stulpnagel, & Jelenec, 2009) in which they consistently paired self-related stimuli with a certain product and other-related stimuli with a different product (Perkins & Forehand, 2012; Prestwich, Perugini, Hurling, & Richetin, 2010). Different implicit measures such as an IAT or an AMP (Payne et al., 2005) revealed preferences for the products that had previously been associated with the self, particularly for those participants with high implicit self-esteem. While the results of both groups of researchers were quite similar on the implicit level, Prestwich and colleagues (2010) did not find them to generalize to explicit attitude measures whereas they did generalize to explicit attitude measures and purchase intentions in the studies by Perkins and Forehand (2012).

Evaluative Conditioning

The prototypical way to change associative structures that implicit measures are believed to tap into is evaluative conditioning (EC; De Houwer, Thomas, & Baeyens, 2001; Gawronski & Bodenhausen, 2006). In typical EC procedures, valenced unconditioned stimuli are paired with a priori (largely) neutral stimuli with the aim of transferring valence of the unconditioned stimulus to the conditioned stimulus. This valence transfer is assumed to occur on an associative basis with little to no propositional processing involved (but this assumption has been challenged, e.g., Pleyers, Corneille, Luminet, & Yzerbyt, 2007).

In one study based on an EC procedure, consumers saw pictures of snack foods that were paired with pictures of negatively valenced female body shapes (Lebens et al., 2011). Pictures of fruit were paired with pictures of positively valenced body shapes. This procedure reduced positive and enhanced negative associations to high-fat foods as indicated by SC-IATs. However, no effects of the EC procedure were found in a behavioral choice task in a virtual supermarket. A similar study used pictures of adverse health consequences of eating too much snack food as unconditioned stimuli (Hollands, Prestwich, & Marteau, 2011). This EC changed implicit evaluations of snack foods particularly for those participants who were implicitly positive about snack foods at baseline. In this study, consumers were more likely to choose fruit over chocolate in a behavioral choice task and this effect was mediated by changes in implicit evaluations. Note that neither of these studies established conditions that are known to foster predictive validity of implicit measures for consumer choice behavior, namely, conditions that promote the reliance on associative processes such as time pressure or reduced cognitive capacity (Friese, Hofmann, & Schmitt, 2008; Strack & Deutsch, 2004, see next section). Such a manipulation may have strengthened the results relating to the behavioral consequences of the changes in implicitly measured attitudes.

An earlier study took into account these boundary conditions of the predictive validity of implicit measures: Gibson (2008) showed that it is even possible to condition implicitly (but not explicitly) measured attitudes toward established brands of soft drinks (at least for those consumers who hold a priori neutral attitudes toward these brands). The conditioned implicitly measured attitudes predicted brand choice in a subsequent choice task, but only for those participants who were forced to rely on more efficient associative processes because their cognitive resources were taxed by a demanding secondary task.

The same stimulus can even serve as a positive or negative unconditioned stimulus depending on individual preferences. In one study (Redker & Gibson, 2009), a piece of country music served as the unconditioned stimulus as background music in a commercial for an unfamiliar brand of root beer. For participants who liked country music, implicitly and explicitly measured attitudes were more positive after the conditioning procedure than for participants who disliked country music. In addition, implicit attitudes had incremental validity over the explicit measure in a choice task between two unfamiliar root beers, one of them being the beer presented in the commercial earlier.

Summary

A number of studies have used implicit measures as dependent measures and found known-group differences or changes in implicit evaluations due to experimental manipulations. These studies provide initial evidence for validity of implicit measures in the consumer domain. However, for most studies it remains unknown how long lasting the effects were and if, when, and how they influenced subsequent consumer behavior. Future research should therefore incorporate more longitudinal designs and include behavioral dependent measures to address these questions that are relevant from both a basic research and an applied perspective.

Many of the presented studies were decidedly explorative in nature. While a certain lack of strong theoretical predictions is normal in a new field, future research should more rigorously rely on contemporary theories and models (e.g., Gawronski & Bodenhausen, 2006; Strack & Deutsch, 2004) to design studies that are able to test specific hypotheses. From our perspective, those findings that did not occur in parallel with explicit measures are those that provide a particularly good opportunity to learn more about the properties, usefulness, and applicability of implicit measures. These are also the studies that are especially valuable for the development of a theoretical understanding that allows predictions to be made about when and when not implicit and explicit measures will show analogous effects (Gawronski & Bodenhausen, 2006) – a question that is further complicated by the fact that different implicit measures can also react differently to experimental manipulations, depending on their specific task characteristics (Deutsch & Gawronski, 2009).

Implicit Measures as Predictors of Behavior

Predictive validity is seen by many as the gold standard for evaluating the usefulness of a measurement instrument. Predicting judgments and behavior over and beyond what is predicted by established measures suggests that a new measure can contribute to a more comprehensive understanding and add unique value also in applied contexts.

Perugini (2005; Perugini, Richetin, & Zogmaister, 2010) suggested three general models of predictive validity of implicit and explicit attitudes. The additive model suggests that implicit and explicit attitudes jointly predict behavior with both kinds of attitudes explaining unique portions of variance. The multiplicative model assumes that implicit and explicit attitudes interact in influencing behavior. Depending on the type of interaction, aligned implicit and explicit attitudes can facilitate behavior execution while conflicting kinds of attitudes may impede a fluent behavior execution (compare to Strack & Deutsch, 2004). Finally, the double-dissociation model postulates implicit attitudes to predict spontaneous, mindless, largely uncontrolled behavior while explicit attitudes should predict reflective, deliberate, largely controlled behavior (see Chapters 2 and 3 in this volume). The literature in general includes studies supporting each of these three models and their variants (for a review, see Perugini et al., 2010) and this is also true for the subset of studies relevant for consumer psychology. The amount of published research exceeds by far what we can discuss in detail in the present chapter. We therefore highlight only a few exemplary studies.

The additive model has received support in a study in which an IAT about fair trade vs. conventional products had incremental validity over explicit attitude measures in the prediction of self-reported buying behavior of fair trade products (Vantomme, Geuens, De Houwer, & De Pelsmacker, 2005). An AMP related to alcohol explained unique variance in several self-reported indices of drinking behavior beyond explicit measures (Payne, Govorun, & Arbuckle, 2008). In the same study, an IAT and an evaluative priming measure were less strongly related to these behavioral criteria and did not exhibit incremental validity beyond explicit measures.

Several researchers have used implicit measures to predict food choice (the favorite choice set up by various researchers being the choice between healthy fruit and unhealthy snacks). Results have been mixed with some studies finding no support for predictive validity of the implicit measure (Ayres, Conner, Prestwich, & Smith, 2012; Karpinski & Hilton, 2001), or support for some (picture–picture naming task) but not other implicit measures (evaluative priming; Spruyt, Hermans, De Houwer, Vandekerckhove, & Eelen, 2007). Richetin, Perugini, Prestwich, and O'Gorman (2007) analyzed consumer choices across several studies together and found good support for the predictive validity of the employed IATs (see also Perugini, 2005). Recent evidence suggests that these results generalize to actual buying behavior of these products (Prestwich, Hurling, & Baker, 2011).

In a study using implicitly (GNAT) and explicitly (semantic differentials) measured attitudes toward genetically modified food, Spence and Townsend (2007) employed a structural equation modeling approach to test all three models of predictive validity with respect to three different behavioral criteria varying in spontaneity (vignettes, a choice task with ample time to choose, and an equivalent gain lottery task). The additive model fitted the data best.

Less evidence corroborates the multiplicative model. In one study (Steinman & Karpinski, 2008), an SC-IAT predicted the intention to visit and buy something at a particular fashion store interactively with explicitly measured attitudes (semantic differentials) such that the behavioral prediction was particularly good when implicitly and explicitly measured attitudes toward the brand of the store went hand in hand (see also Perugini, 2005).

In consumer psychology, implicitly and explicitly measured attitudes are often highly correlated, reducing the potential for incremental validity of implicit over explicit measures (Greenwald, Poehlman, Uhlmann, & Banaji, 2009). In terms of predicting behavior, those contexts in which implicit and explicit attitudes are not strongly aligned are particularly interesting, because in these contexts implicit and explicit measures are more likely to predict different shares of the behavioral variance. Thus, from this perspective it is not necessarily most interesting to maximize implicit–behavior relations per se, but to maximize incremental validity beyond explicit measures.

A prominent approach to predictive validity of implicit measures is the assumption that implicit measures primarily predict spontaneous, impulsive, less controlled behavior while explicit measures predict primarily deliberate, reflective, largely controlled behavior (double-dissociation pattern; Perugini, 2005; Perugini et al., 2010). Applied to consumer behavior, this perspective suggests that implicit measures should be particularly successful in predicting (a) low involvement and impulsive purchases that are prone to occur without much reflection or (b) choice and consumption behavior that occurs under processing constraints such as time pressure or distraction that prevents a consumer from careful information processing during those behaviors. All of these behaviors have been argued to be prevalent in real-life consumer behavior (Faber & Vohs, 2011; Hoyer, 1984; Laaksonen, 1994).

To test these assumptions, researchers have established conditions that should foster the predictive validity of implicit measures by increasing the reliance on associative processes and decreasing the reliance on propositional processes. In many studies, additional explicit measures were employed that were expected to show the opposite pattern as compared with implicit measures: better predictive validity under conditions that increase the reliance on propositional processes. Several studies found support for these predictions. In a prototypical study, participants chose five items out of a variety of small chocolate bars and various fruit (Friese, Hofmann, & Wänke, 2008). Half of the participants could devote their full cognitive capacity to the task while the other half was strongly distracted by memorizing an eight-digit number in parallel. This manipulation was intended to impede reflective processing and foster the reliance on associative processes. As expected, an IAT relating to chocolate vs. fruit predicted the choice behavior for distracted, but not undistracted participants. By contrast, a parallel explicit attitude measure predicted choice behavior for undistracted, but not distracted participants (see Figure 12.1). In addition to cognitive capacity (see also Gibson, 2008; for conflicting evidence, see Scarabis, Florack, & Gosejohann, 2006), several other experimental manipulations have revealed functionally equivalent effects in that they differentially impacted the predictive validity of implicit and explicit measures. Although these manipulations were established in the laboratory, they induced mental states that are common in everyday life and can thus claim some ecological validity. Conditions that have been shown to foster the predictive validity of implicit measures and reduce the predictive validity of explicit measures include time pressure (Beattie & Sale, 2011; Friese, Wänke, & Plessner, 2006), reduced self-regulatory resources (Friese, Hofmann, & Wänke, 2008; Hofmann, Rauch, & Gawronski, 2007), moderate alcohol intoxication (Hofmann & Friese, 2008), positive mood (Holland, de Vries, Hermsen, & van Knippenberg, 2012), a promotion focus (Florack, Friese, & Scarabis, 2010), and salience of death-related thoughts (Friese & Hofmann, 2008). The respective contrasting experimental groups regularly fostered the predictive validity of explicit measures, with implicit measures contributing marginal amounts of incremental validity (e.g., being sober, being in a bad mood).

In addition to experimental manipulations, researchers have identified several individual difference variables that similarly foster the reliance on associative processes and are therefore associated with better predictive validity of implicit measures. These include low working memory capacity (Friese & Hofmann, 2012; Hofmann, Gschwendner, Friese, Wiers, & Schmitt, 2008), low trait self-control (Friese & Hofmann, 2009), high impulsivity (Friese & Hofmann, 2009), low inhibitory control (Hofmann, Friese, & Roefs, 2009), preference for intuition (Richetin, Perugini, Adjali, & Hurling, 2007), and habitualness of the investigated behavior (Conner,

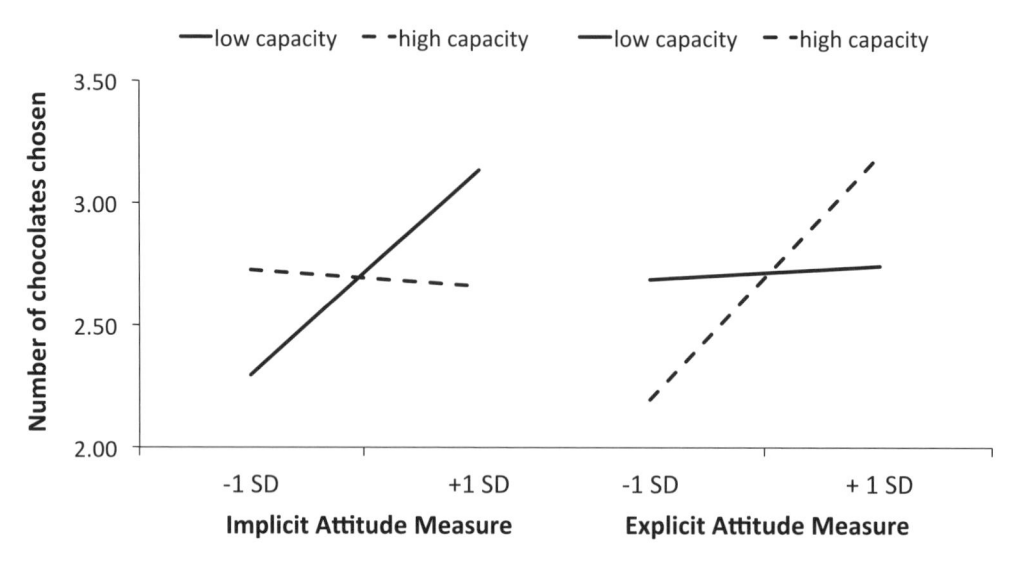

Figure 12.1. Number of chocolates chosen as a function of attitude measure (implicit vs. explicit) and cognitive capacity manipulation (low vs. high). Data from Friese, Hofmann, & Wänke (2008, Study 1). Reproduced with permission from the British Journal of Social Psychology, ©The British Psychological Society.

Perugini, O'Gorman, Ayres, & Prestwich, 2007). In these studies, researchers investigated diverse self-reported and observed consumer behaviors such as choosing (e.g., Holland et al., 2012), eating (e.g., Hofmann et al., 2007), drinking (e.g., Friese & Hofmann, 2009), and use of media (e.g., Friese & Hofmann, 2012; for overviews, see Friese, Hofmann, & Schmitt, 2008, as well as Chapter 3 in this volume).

Summary

All three models of predictive validity of implicit measures (Perugini et al., 2010) have received support in the literature on consumer behavior, albeit to different extents. Few studies were specifically set up to test the multiplicative model, and of these only a subset supported this model. The additive model received more support, especially in those studies that investigated the predictive validity of implicit and explicit measures without taking into account further conditions that may foster or impede the predictive validity of implicit and explicit measures. Some of these studies were explorative without commitment to any theoretical stance; some specifically tested the additive model. The double-dissociation model received most attention and most support in terms of number of supporting studies. Interestingly, extending earlier conceptions, this research revealed that implicit and explicit measures do not necessarily predict different kinds of behavior. Instead, they can also predict the same behavior (e.g., product choice), but under different circumstances. Implicit measures tend to predict behavior better when conditions foster the reliance on associative processes (e.g., low cognitive capacity, low working memory capacity), and explicit measures tend to be more successful when conditions foster the reliance on propositional processes (e.g., full cognitive capacity, high working memory capacity). However, the comparatively large number of studies supporting the double-dissociation model may primarily reflect that researchers were particularly interested in this model of predictive validity. It does not imply that in the long term the evidence will support this model more than the other two models. Future research should more systematically clarify the conditions under which each model will most likely be supported.

Future Challenges and Outlook

In the past decades, many researchers employing implicit measures in their research were interested in showing the value these measures can have for psychological science. As a consequence, knowledge about these measures has accumulated at an enormous pace. From our perspective, now is the time to devote equal attention to explicit measures in order to more comprehensively harness these measures, for example, by using affectively toned explicit measures that aim to tap into similar structures implicit measures do (Ayres et al., 2012). This will have two advantages: First, under most circumstances explicit measures are easier and quicker to assess without technical equipment. They may therefore save costs should they provide similar information as implicit measures. Second, any incremental value that implicit measures show beyond a comprehensive explicit assessment is even more convincing than evidence that did not fully harness the potential of explicit measures. Embedding research designs even more than in the past in models and theories that make clear predictions about when and why implicit measures should make a useful addition to the researchers' toolbox will help to reach this aim.

From a measurement perspective, it will be important for consumer psychologists to more intensively clarify the contributions different implicit measures can make. While in theory they are all intended to tap into concepts underlying the associative structure such as implicit attitudes or the implicit self-concept, in practice different implicit measures rely on different mechanisms with which they try to tap into the constructs of interest (De Houwer & Moors, 2010). As a consequence, studies employing more than one implicit measure often end up with diverging results (e.g., Payne et al., 2008; Spruyt et al., 2007). In addition, reliabilities for many implicit measures are low, which further contributes to low correlations among implicit measures and difficulties to replicate findings (LeBel & Paunonen, 2011). We therefore deem it important to investigate the boundary conditions under which different implicit measures will excel and why.

For a discipline with significant applied interests such as consumer psychology, it is of particular importance to bring its acquired knowledge to a real-life test. Will the effects and relations between variables that have been observed under controlled circumstances in the laboratory generalize to outside the laboratory, using real and diverse stimuli and products, participants with diverse backgrounds, in environments that are much more messy and complex than in the laboratory? If they do, how enduring are these effects? Answering these kinds of questions will reveal how *practically* significant the contributions really are that implicit measures can make. The last 15 years have provided ample evidence that implicit measures can help to shed light on many phenomena in psychology, many of them grounded in basic research (Gawronski & Payne, 2010). Consumer psychology can be among the first to seriously explore the applied implications of this knowledge in real-world settings.

Acknowledgments

Preparation of this chapter was supported by a grant from the Voluntary Academic Society Basel to Malte Friese. This chapter was written in July 2012 and is based on the literature available at that time.

References

Agerstrom, J., & Rooth, D. O. (2011). The role of automatic obesity stereotypes in real hiring discrimination. *Journal of Applied Psychology, 96*, 790–805. http://doi.org/10.1037/a0021594

Arcuri, L., Castelli, L., Galdi, S., Zogmaister, C., & Amadori, A. (2008). Predicting the vote: Implicit attitudes as predictors of the future behavior of decided and undecided voters. *Political Psychology, 29*, 369–387. http://doi.org/10.1111/j.1467-9221.2008.00635.x

Ayres, K., Conner, M. T., Prestwich, A., & Smith, P. (2012). Do implicit measures of attitudes incrementally predict snacking behaviour over explicit affect-related measures? *Appetite, 58*, 835–841. http://doi.org/10.1016/j.appet.2012.01.019

Beattie, G., & Sale, L. (2011). Shopping to save the planet? Implicit rather than explicit attitudes predict low carbon footprint consumer choice. *The International Journal of Environmental, Cultural, Economic and Social Sustainability, 7*, 211–232.

Bluemke, M., Brand, R., Schweizer, G., & Kahlert, D. (2010). Exercise might be good for me, but I don't feel good about it: Do automatic associations predict exercise behavior? *Journal of Sport & Exercise Psychology, 32*, 137–153.

Brunel, F. D. R. F., Tietje, B. C., & Greenwald, A. G. (2004). Is the implicit association test a valid and valuable measure of implicit consumer social cognition? *Journal of Consumer Psychology, 14*, 385. http://doi.org/10.1207/s15327663jcp1404_8

Conner, M., Perugini, M., O'Gorman, R., Ayres, K., & Prestwich, A. (2007). Relations between implicit and explicit measures of attitudes and measures of behavior: Evidence of moderation by individual difference variables. *Personality and Social Psychology Bulletin, 33*, 1727–1740. http://doi.org/10.1177/0146167207309194

Conroy, D. E., Hyde, A. L., Doerksen, S. E., & Ribeiro, N. F. (2010). Implicit attitudes and explicit motivation prospectively predict physical activity. *Annals of Behavioral Medicine, 39*, 112–118. http://doi.org/10.1007/s12160-010-9161-0

Czyzewska, M., & Ginsburg, H. J. (2007). Explicit and implicit effects of anti-marijuana and anti-tobacco TV advertisements. *Addictive Behaviors, 32*, 114–127. http://doi.org/10.1016/j.addbeh.2006.03.025

De Houwer, J., & Moors, A. (2010). Implicit measures: Similarities and differences. In B. Gawronski & B. K. Payne (Eds.), *Handbook of implicit social cognition* (pp. 176–193). New York, NY: Guilford Press.

De Houwer, J., Thomas, S., & Baeyens, F. (2001). Association learning of likes and dislikes: A review of 25 years of research on human evaluative conditioning. *Psychological Bulletin, 127*, 853–869. http://doi.org/10.1037/0033-2909.127.6.853

Deutsch, R., & Gawronski, B. (2009). When the method makes a difference: Antagonistic effects on "automatic evaluations" as a function of task characteristics of the measure. *Journal of Experimental Social Psychology, 45*, 101–114. http://doi.org/10.1016/j.jesp.2008.09.001

Dimofte, C. V., & Yalch, R. F. (2007a). Consumer response to polysemous brand slogans. *Journal of Consumer Research, 33*, 515–522. http://doi.org/10.1086/510225

Dimofte, C. V., & Yalch, R. F. (2007b). The SMAART scale: A measure of individuals' automatic access to secondary meanings in polysemous statements. *Journal of Consumer Psychology, 17*, 49–58. http://doi.org/10.1207/s15327663jcp1701_8

Dimofte, C. V., & Yalch, R. F. (2011). The mere association effect and brand evaluations. *Journal of Consumer Psychology, 21*, 24–37. http://doi.org/10.1016/j.jcps.2010.09.005

Dovidio, J. F., Kawakami, K., Johnson, C., & Johnson, B. (1997). On the nature of prejudice: Automatic and controlled processes. *Journal of Experimental Social Psychology, 33*, 510–540. http://doi.org/10.1006/jesp.1997.1331

Ebert, I. D., Steffens, M. C., Von Stulpnagel, R., & Jelenec, P. (2009). How to like yourself better, or chocolate less: Changing implicit attitudes with one IAT task. *Journal of Experimental Social Psychology, 45*, 1098–1104. http://doi.org/10.1016/j.jesp.2009.06.008

Faber, R. J., & Vohs, K. D. (2011). Self-regulation and spending: Evidence from impulsive and compulsive buying. In K. D. Vohs & R. F. Baumeister (Eds.), *Handbook of self-regulation: Research, theory, and applications* (2nd ed., pp. 537–550). New York, NY: Guilford Press.

Fazio, R. H., Jackson, J. R., Dunton, B. C., & Williams, C. J. (1995). Variability in automatic activation as an unobtrusive measure of racial attitudes: A bona fide pipeline? *Journal of Personality and Social Psychology, 69*, 1013–1027. http://doi.org/10.1037/0022-3514.69.6.1013

Fazio, R. H., & Olson, M. A. (2003). Implicit measures in social cognition research: Their meaning and uses. *Annual Review of Psychology, 54*, 297–327. http://doi.org/10.1146/annurev.psych.54.101601.145225

Florack, A., Friese, M., & Scarabis, M. (2010). Regulatory focus and reliance on implicit preferences in consumption contexts. *Journal of Consumer Psychology, 20*, 193–204. http://doi.org/10.1016/j.jcps.2010.02.001

Forehand, M. R., & Perkins, A. (2005). Implicit assimilation and explicit contrast: A set/reset model of response to celebrity voice-overs. *Journal of Consumer Research, 32*, 435–441. http://doi.org/10.1086/497555

Friese, M., & Hofmann, W. (2008). What would you have as a last supper? Thoughts about death influence evaluation and consumption of food products. *Journal of Experimental Social Psychology, 44*, 1388–1394. http://doi.org/10.1016/j.jesp.2008.06.003

Friese, M., & Hofmann, W. (2009). Control me or I will control you: Impulse, trait self-control, and the guidance of behavior. *Journal of Research in Personality, 43*, 795–805. http://doi.org/10.1016/j.jrp.2009.07.004

Friese, M., & Hofmann, W. (2012). Just a little bit longer: Viewing time of erotic material from a self-control perspective. *Applied Cognitive Psychology, 26*, 489–496. http://doi.org/10.1002/acp.2831

Friese, M., Hofmann, W., & Schmitt, M. (2008). When and why do implicit reaction time measures predict behavior? Empirical evidence for the moderating role of motivation, opportunity, and process reliance. *European Review of Social Psychology, 19*, 285–338. http://doi.org/10.1080/10463280802556958

Friese, M., Hofmann, W., & Wänke, M. (2008). When impulses take over: Moderated predictive validity of explicit and implicit attitude measures in predicting food choice and consumption behaviour. *British Journal of Social Psychology, 47*, 397–419. http://doi.org/10.1348/014466607X241540

Friese, M., Hofmann, W., & Wänke, M. (2009). The impulsive consumer: Predicting consumer behavior with implicit reaction time measures. In M. Wänke (Ed.), *Frontiers in social psychology: Social psychology of consumer behavior* (pp. 335–364). New York, NY: Psychology Press.

Friese, M., Smith, C. T., Plischke, T., Bluemke, M., & Nosek, B. A. (2012). Do implicit attitudes predict actual voting behavior particularly for undecided voters? *Plos One, 7*, e44130. http://doi.org/10.1371/journal.pone.0044130

Friese, M., Wänke, M., & Plessner, H. (2006). Implicit consumer preferences and their influence on product choice. *Psychology and Marketing, 23*, 727–740. http://doi.org/10.1002/mar.20126

Galdi, S., Arcuri, L., & Gawronski, B. (2008). Automatic mental associations predict future choices of undecided decision-makers. *Science, 321*, 1100–1102. http://doi.org/10.1126/science.1160769

Gawronski, B., & Bodenhausen, G. V. (2006). Associative and propositional processes in evaluation: An integrative review of implicit and explicit attitude change. *Psychological Bulletin, 132*, 692–731. http://doi.org/10.1037/0033-2909.132.5.692

Gawronski, B., Bodenhausen, G. V., & Becker, A. P. (2007). I like it, because I like myself: Associative self-anchoring and post-decisional change of implicit evaluations. *Journal of Experimental Social Psychology, 43*, 221–232. http://doi.org/10.1016/j.jesp.2006.04.001

Gawronski, B., & Payne, B. K. (2010). *Handbook of implicit social cognition*. New York, NY: Guilford Press.

Gibson, B. (2008). Can evaluative conditioning change attitudes toward mature brands? New evidence from the Implicit Association Test. *Journal of Consumer Research, 35*, 178–188. http://doi.org/10.1086/527341

Glashouwer, K. A., De Jong, P. J., Penninx, B., Kerkhof, A., Van Dyck, R., & Ormel, J. (2010). Do automatic self-associations relate to suicidal ideation? *Journal of Psychopathology and Behavioral Assessment, 32*, 428–437. http://doi.org/10.1007/s10862-009-9156-y

Greenwald, A. G., McGhee, D. E., & Schwartz, J. L. K. (1998). Measuring individual differences in implicit cognition: The Implicit Association Test. *Journal of Personality and Social Psychology, 74*, 1464–1480. http://doi.org/10.1037/0022-3514.74.6.1464

Greenwald, A. G., Poehlman, T. A., Uhlmann, E. L., & Banaji, M. R. (2009). Understanding and using the implicit association test: III. Meta-analysis of predictive validity. *Journal of Personality and Social Psychology, 97*, 17–41. http://doi.org/10.1037/a0015575

Gregg, A. P., & Klymowsky, J. (2013). The Implicit Association Test in market research: Potentials and pitfalls. *Psychology & Marketing, 30*, 588–601. http://doi.org/10.1002/mar.20630

Haire, M. (1950). Projective techniques in marketing research. *Journal of Marketing, 14*, 649–656. http://doi.org/10.2307/1246942

Hammond, K. R. (1948). Measuring attitudes by error-choice: An indirect method. *The Journal of Abnormal and Social Psychology, 43*, 38–48. http://doi.org/10.1037/h0059576

Hofmann, W., & Friese, M. (2008). Impulses got the better of me: Alcohol moderates the influence of implicit attitudes toward food cues on eating behavior. *Journal of Abnormal Psychology, 117*, 420–427. http://doi.org/10.1037/0021-843X.117.2.420

Hofmann, W., Friese, M., & Roefs, A. (2009). Three ways to resist temptation: The independent contributions of executive attention, inhibitory control, and affect regulation to the impulse control of eating behavior. *Journal of Experimental Social Psychology, 45*, 431–435. http://doi.org/10.1016/j.jesp.2008.09.013

Hofmann, W., Gschwendner, T., Friese, M., Wiers, R. W., & Schmitt, M. (2008). Working memory capacity and self-regulatory behavior: Toward an individual differences perspective on behavior determination by automatic versus controlled processes. *Journal of Personality and Social Psychology, 95*, 962–977. http://doi.org/10.1037/a0012705

Hofmann, W., Gschwendner, T., Nosek, B. A., & Schmitt, M. (2005). What moderates implicit-explicit consistency? *European Review of Social Psychology, 16*, 335–390. http://doi.org/10.1080/10463280500443228

Hofmann, W., Rauch, W., & Gawronski, B. (2007). And deplete us not into temptation: Automatic attitudes, dietary restraint, and self-regulatory resources as determinants of eating behavior. *Journal of Experimental Social Psychology, 43*, 497–504. http://doi.org/10.1016/j.jesp.2006.05.004

Holland, R. W., de Vries, M., Hermsen, B., & van Knippenberg, A. (2012). Mood and the attitude-behavior link: The happy act on impulse, the sad think twice. *Social Psychological and Personality Science, 3*, 356–364. http://doi.org/10.1177/1948550611421635

Hollands, G. J., Prestwich, A., & Marteau, T. M. (2011). Using aversive images to enhance healthy food choices and implicit attitudes: An experimental test of evaluative conditioning. *Health Psychology, 30*, 195–203. http://doi.org/10.1037/a0022261

Horcajo, J., Brinol, P., & Petty, R. E. (2010). Consumer persuasion: Indirect change and implicit balance. *Psychology & Marketing, 27*, 938–963. http://doi.org/10.1002/mar.20367

Hoyer, W. D. (1984). An examination of consumer decision-making for a common repeat purchase product. *Journal of Consumer Research, 11*, 822–829. http://doi.org/10.1086/209017

Huijding, J., & De Jong, P. J. (2006). Specific predictive power of automatic spider-related affective associations for controllable and uncontrollable fear responses toward spiders. *Behaviour Research and Therapy, 44*, 161–176. http://doi.org/10.1016/j.brat.2005.01.007

Karpinski, A., & Hilton, J. L. (2001). Attitudes and the Implicit Association Test. *Journal of Personality and Social Psychology, 81*, 774–788. http://doi.org/10.1037/0022-3514.81.5.774

Karpinski, A., & Steinman, R. B. (2006). The single category implicit association test as a measure of implicit social cognition. *Journal of Personality and Social Psychology, 91*, 16–32. http://doi.org/10.1037/0022-3514.91.1.16

Koole, S. L., Dijksterhuis, A., & van Knippenberg, A. (2001). What's in a name: Implicit self-esteem and the automatic self. *Journal of Personality and Social Psychology, 80*, 669–685. http://doi.org/10.1037/0022-3514.80.4.669

Laaksonen, P. (1994). *Consumer involvement: Concepts and research*. London, UK: Routledge.

Leavitt, K., Fong, C. T., & Greenwald, A. G. (2011). Asking about well-being gets you half an answer: Intra-individual processes of implicit and explicit job attitudes. *Journal of Organizational Behavior, 32*, 672–687. http://doi.org/10.1002/job.746

LeBel, E. P., & Paunonen, S. V. (2011). Sexy but often unreliable: The impact of unreliability on the replicability of experimental findings with implicit measures. *Personality and Social Psychology Bulletin, 37*, 570–583. http://doi.org/10.1177/0146167211400619

Lebens, H., Roefs, A., Martijn, C., Houben, K., Nederkoorn, C., & Jansen, A. (2011). Making implicit measures of associations with snack foods more negative through evaluative conditioning. *Eating Behaviors, 12*, 249–253. http://doi.org/10.1016/j.eatbeh.2011.07.001

Maison, D., Greenwald, A. G., & Bruin, R. (2001). The Implicit Association Test as a measure of implicit consumer attitudes. *Polish Psychological Bulletin, 32*, 61–69.

Maison, D., Greenwald, A. G., & Bruin, R. H. (2004). Predictive validity of the Implicit Association Test in studies of brands, consumer attitudes, and behavior. *Journal of Consumer Psychology, 14*, 405. http://doi.org/10.1207/s15327663jcp1404_9

Mierke, J., & Klauer, K. C. (2003). Method-specific variance in the Implicit Association Test. *Journal of Personality and Social Psychology, 85*, 1180–1192. http://doi.org/10.1037/0022-3514.85.6.1180

Nevid, J. S. (2010). Introduction to the special issue: Implicit measures of consumer response – the search for the holy grail of marketing research. *Psychology & Marketing, 27*, 913–920. http://doi.org/10.1002/mar.20365

Nosek, B. A. (2005). Moderators of the relationship between implicit and explicit evaluation. *Journal of Experimental Psychology: General, 134*, 565–584. http://doi.org/10.1037/0096-3445.134.4.565

Nosek, B. A., & Banaji, M. R. (2001). The Go/No-go Association Task. *Social Cognition, 19*, 625–666. http://doi.org/10.1521/soco.19.6.625.20886

Nosek, B. A., Hawkins, C. B., & Frazier, R. S. (2011). Implicit social cognition: From measures to mechanisms. *Trends in Cognitive Sciences, 15*, 152–159. http://doi.org/10.1016/j.tics.2011.01.005

Nuttin, J. M. (1985). Narcissism beyond gestalt and awareness: The name letter effect. *European Journal of Social Psychology, 15*, 353–361. http://doi.org/10.1002/ejsp.2420150309

Payne, B. K., Cheng, C. M., Govorun, O., & Stewart, B. D. (2005). An inkblot for attitudes: Affect misattribution as implicit measurement. *Journal of Personality and Social Psychology, 89*, 277–293. http://doi.org/10.1037/0022-3514.89.3.277

Payne, B. K., Govorun, O., & Arbuckle, N. L. (2008). Automatic attitudes and alcohol: Does implicit liking predict drinking? *Cognition and Emotion, 22*, 238–271. http://doi.org/10.1080/02699930701357394

Perkins, A. W., & Forehand, M. (2010). Implicit social cgnition and indirect measures in consumer behavior. In B. Gawronski & B. K. Payne (Eds.), *Handbook of implicit social cognition: Measurement, theory, and applications* (pp. 535–547). New York, NY: Guilford Press.

Perkins, A. W., & Forehand, M. R. (2012). Implicit self-referencing: The effect of nonvolitional self-association on brand and product attitude. *Journal of Consumer Research, 39*, 142–156. http://doi.org/10.1086/662069

Perugini, M. (2005). Predictive models of implicit and explicit attitudes. *British Journal of Social Psychology, 44*, 29–45. http://doi.org/10.1348/014466604X23491

Perugini, M., Richetin, J., & Zogmaister, C. (2010). Prediction of behavior. In B. Gawronski & B. K. Payne (Eds.), *Handbook of implicit social cognition* (pp. 255–278). New York, NY: Guilford Press.

Pleyers, G., Corneille, O., Luminet, O., & Yzerbyt, V. (2007). Aware and (dis)liking: Item-based analyses reveal that valence acquisition via evaluative conditioning emerges only when there is contingency awareness. *Journal of Experimental Psychology: Learning, Memory, and Cognition, 33*, 130–144.

Prestwich, A., Hurling, R., & Baker, S. (2011). Implicit shopping: Attitudinal determinants of the purchasing of healthy and unhealthy foods. *Psychology & Health, 26*, 875–885. http://doi.org/10.1080/08870446.2010.509797

Prestwich, A., Perugini, M., Hurling, R., & Richetin, J. (2010). Using the self to change implicit attitudes. *European Journal of Social Psychology, 40*, 61–71. http://doi.org/10.1002/ejsp.610

Ratliff, K. A., Swinkels, B. A. P., Klerx, K., & Nosek, B. A. (2012). Does one bad apple(juice) spoil the bunch? Implicit attitudes toward one product transfer to other products by the same brand. *Psychology & Marketing, 29*, 531–540. http://doi.org/10.1002/mar.20540

Redker, C. M., & Gibson, B. (2009). Music as an unconditioned stimulus: Positive and negative effects of country music on implicit attitudes, explicit attitudes, and brand choice. *Journal of Applied Social Psychology, 39*, 2689–2705. http://doi.org/10.1111/j.1559-1816.2009.00544.x

Richetin, J., Perugini, M., Adjali, I., & Hurling, R. (2007). The moderator role of intuitive versus deliberative decision making for the predictive validity of implicit and explicit measures. *European Journal of Personality, 21*, 529–546. http://doi.org/10.1002/per.625

Richetin, J., Perugini, M., Prestwich, A., & O'Gorman, R. (2007). The IAT as a predictor of food choice: The case of fruits versus snacks. *International Journal of Psychology, 42*, 166–173. http://doi.org/10.1080/00207590601067078

Rooth, D. O. (2010). Automatic associations and discrimination in hiring: Real world evidence. *Labour Economics, 17*, 523–534. http://doi.org/10.1016/j.labeco.2009.04.005

Rothermund, K., & Wentura, D. (2004). Underlying processes in the Implicit Association Test (IAT): Dissociating salience from associations. *Journal of Experimental Psychology: General, 133*, 139–165. http://doi.org/10.1037/0096-3445.133.2.139

Rydell, R. J., & McConnell, A. R. (2006). Understanding implicit and explicit attitude change: A systems of reasoning analysis. *Journal of Personality and Social Psychology, 91*, 995–1008. http://doi.org/10.1037/0022-3514.91.6.995

Salcher, E. F. (1995). *Psychologische Marktforschung* [Psychological market research]. Berlin, Germany: Walter de Gruyter. http://doi.org/10.1515/9783110893168

Scarabis, M., Florack, A., & Gosejohann, S. (2006). When consumers follow their feelings: The impact of affective or cognitive focus on the basis of consumers' choice. *Psychology & Marketing, 23*, 1015–1034. http://doi.org/10.1002/mar.20144

Siegel, E. F., Dougherty, M. R., & Huber, D. E. (2012). Manipulating the role of cognitive control while taking the implicit association test. *Journal of Experimental Social Psychology, 48*, 1057–1068. http://doi.org/10.1016/j.jesp.2012.04.011

Smith, C. T., & Nosek, B. A. (2011). Affective focus increases the concordance between implicit and explicit attitudes. *Social Psychology, 42*, 300–313. http://doi.org/10.1027/1864-9335/a000072

Spence, A., & Townsend, E. (2006). Implicit attitudes towards genetically modified (GM) foods: A comparison of context-free and context-dependent evaluations. *Appetite, 46*, 67–74. http://doi.org/10.1016/j.appet.2005.09.003

Spence, A., & Townsend, E. (2007). Predicting behaviour towards genetically modified food using implicit and explicit attitudes. *British Journal of Social Psychology, 46*, 437–457. http://doi.org/10.1348/014466606X152261

Spruyt, A., Hermans, D., De Houwer, J., Vandekerckhove, J., & Eelen, P. (2007). On the predictive validity of indirect attitude measures: Prediction of consumer choice behavior on the basis of affective priming in the picture-picture naming task. *Journal of Experimental Social Psychology, 43*, 599–610. http://doi.org/10.1016/j.jesp.2006.06.009

Steinman, R. B., & Karpinski, A. (2008). The Single Category Implicit Association Test (SC-IAT) as a measure of implicit consumer attitudes. *European Journal of Social Sciences, 7*, 32–42.

Strack, F., & Deutsch, R. (2004). Reflective and impulsive determinants of social behavior. *Personality and Social Psychology Review, 8*, 220–247. http://doi.org/10.1207/s15327957pspr0803_1

Strick, M., Van Baaren, R. B., Holland, R. W., & Van Knippenberg, A. (2009). Humor in advertisements enhances product liking by mere association. *Journal of Experimental Psychology-Applied, 15*, 35–45. http://doi.org/10.1037/a0014812

Vantomme, D., Geuens, M., De Houwer, J., & De Pelsmacker, P. (2005). Implicit attitudes toward green consumer behaviour. *Psychologica Belgica, 45*, 217–239. http://doi.org/10.5334/pb-45-4-217

Webb, E. J., Campbell, D. T., Schwartz, R. D., & Sechrest, L. (1966). *Unobtrusive measures: Nonreactive research in the social sciences*. Chicago, IL: Rand McNally.

Chapter 13

Observation of Intra- and Interpersonal Processes

Axel Schölmerich and Julia Jäkel

Department of Developmental Psychology, Ruhr-University Bochum, Germany

Observation of Intra- and Interpersonal Processes

Many of the underlying constructs in personality are a combination of internal states and externally observable behaviors, and assessment varies due to biases of observers, situational factors, and instrument formats (Kammeyer-Mueller, Steel, & Rubenstein, 2010). Scientific or systematic observation consists of elicitation and recording (e.g., video, in vivo coding, and in writing) of human behavior. Observation differs from perception in that it is purposeful, focuses on predefined categories, serves precise objectives, and preferably includes criteria for the assessment of validity, reliability, and objectivity. Historically, behavior observation has played a prominent role particularly in developmental psychology, with influences arising from ethology as well as biology. With the technological availability of recording through film and video, the use of observational methods has gained wide acceptance.

Psychological constructs like *extraversion* cannot be observed directly, and observable behavior is context-sensitive. Observational procedures tend to introduce context (e.g., the observer or technical artifacts). For comparative purposes, some degree of standardization of the setting to be observed is required, limiting the cross-situational validity of the observation for the construct. This poses a particular challenge for personality assessment, since the very definition of *personality* involves cross-situational, context-free dimensions such as extraversion or dominance (Carver & Scheier, 2004). Obviously, it is much easier to construct a comprehensive questionnaire with items covering a wide variety of contexts than to sample behavior in a similar way.

It is well known that questionnaires, objective tests, and behavior observation measures of personality yield different results (Skinner & Howarth, 1973) and different trait structures (Dyson, Olino, Durbin, Goldsmith, & Klein, 2012).

One reason to use observational methods (OM) for assessment of intra- and interpersonal processes is their presumed better validity, reliability, and objectivity in comparison with questionnaires. For example, when administering questionnaires, different informants (parents, teachers, self-report) judge individuals differently (Anderson, Doyle, & the Victorian Infant Collaborative Study Group, 2003; Shum, Neulinger, O'Callaghan, & Mohay, 2008), whereas OM include observer agreement checks. An additional reason to use OM in assessment of children is to overcome their limitations to respond to self-report questions. However, the use of OM requires that the behavior under question is selected to represent significant aspects of the construct we are interested in. Particularly in work contexts, this is frequently the case. Abilities such as working in a team, taking responsibility, and making decisions under stress can be elicited and observed and are, for example, used in assessment centers for personnel selection purposes (Eurich, Krause, Cigularov, & Thornton, 2009).

Observational procedures can be classified on a number of dimensions. In the context of personality assessment, the most important ones are:
1. Naturalistic vs. experimental,
2. Rating vs. micro-analytical,
3. Aiming at intrapersonal vs. interpersonal constructs.

We briefly explain those distinctions. First, a naturalistic observation uses a context, which occurs in the natural environment of the person(s) observed, for example, a feeding situation or the confrontation with a stranger. The instruction usually includes a reference to behave "as you usually do." Well-known examples are the Feeding Scale by Chatoor et al. (1997) and the various play and interaction scales for observation of parent–child dyadic behavior (Bornstein, Toda, Azuma, Tamislemonda, & Ogino, 1990). A widely used example of a more experimental approach is the Still-Face Paradigm (Tronick, Als, Adamson, Wise, & Brazelton, 1978), which starts with a more or less natural interaction between caregiver and baby, followed by the instruction to freeze the face upon auditory prompt. Crucial for this assessment are the attempts of the infant to reengage the adult, and these are recorded.

Second, in addition to variations in the situational setting, observational methods differ in the fidelity of recording. Global ratings can summarize large amounts of information in a single index score, verbal descriptions of events are a compromise between integration and detail, and precise micro-analytical procedures can allow sophisticated statistical analysis including sequential or process parameters. Diaries are a structured form of a verbal protocol, introduced by pioneers like Darwin and Preyer, who observed their own children and produced extensive records (Magai & McFadden, 1995). Other popular methods define critical events, like an act of aggression in a kindergarten setting, and then switch to verbal protocols or video records to follow that instance. Microanalytic observations rely on an explicit system of codes representing defined behaviors. These can be exclusive (only one of a set of behaviors can be active at any time; e.g., [a] baby has body contact, [b] is within arms' reach, [c] further away) but also concurrent (several categories can overlap in time; e.g., [a] mother smiles, [b] mother vocalizes, [c] mother touches baby). Those alternatives have far-reaching implications for possible analytical approaches (Schölmerich, 2011).

Third, several published behavioral observation schemes share many features even though they aim at vastly different constructs. Behavioral inhibition (Kagan, Reznick, Snidman, Gibbons, & Johnson, 1988) is an intrapersonal concept, much like temperament, maternal sensitivity, or personality, while attachment is by definition an interpersonal construct, describing a relationship between a child and his or her caregiver. Both observational protocols include confrontation with stress, novel play objects, a stranger, and have the child's mother in the room. Typically, intrapersonal observation schemes should contain detailed information on the setting including scripts for the behavior of others, and interpersonal schemes need to contain codes for the behavior of the interactional partner; however, this is frequently not the case.

Examples of Behavioral Observation Instruments

Assessment of Attachment and Dyadic Parent–Child Behavior

One of the most popular observation schemes aiming at interpersonal constructs is the Strange Situation (Ainsworth, Blehar, Waters, & Wall, 1978). Since its publication the validity and predictive value of this procedure have been critically debated (Lamb, Thompson, Gardner, Charnov, & Estes, 1984). The Strange Situation was initially designed to capture the relationship between a 1-year-old child and his or her primary caretaker, usually the mother, to predict the quality of attachment. Ainsworth used extensive home observations during the first year of life (approximately 72 hr of home visits per child, and 22 behaviorally anchored ratings later condensed into four scales, with maternal sensitivity the most important one). The sample was relatively small (< 40 mother–infant dyads). She found systematic variation of attachment security in the Strange Situation and maternal behavior during the first year of life of the child, with roughly 60% of children classified as secure. Subsequent use of the Strange Situation worldwide has basically confirmed the general distribution initially suggested by Ainsworth et al. (1978), although some cultural variation exists (Van IJzendoorn & Kroonenberg, 1988). The Strange Situation consists of eight episodes lasting 3 min each, during which mother and infant are placed in an unfamiliar room with attractive toys. A stranger (unfamiliar adult) enters the room, after which the mother leaves to return in the next episode. Next, the child is left alone in the room, then the unfamiliar person enters and tries to engage the child. Finally, the mother comes back. For the purpose of attachment classification, the child's behavior is analyzed during the reunification episodes to evaluate the child's effective use of the mother as a source of security. The amount of distress or negative emotions displayed by the child is irrelevant for the classification into attachment categories. The coding of Strange Situation behavior is quite complex and specific trainings and reliability checks are necessary. Moreover, a semicommercial coding of recorded child behavior through established laboratories as well as training for the laboratory procedure is available (e.g., at the University of Minnesota: http://attachment-training.com/at/). The Strange Situation mainly serves research purposes, even though some studies have also used it for evaluation of intervention (e.g., home visiting programs, effects of out-of-home care). Using Strange Situation behavior as a diagnostic instrument in individual cases (e.g., custody issues) is generally discouraged, mainly for reasons of lack of proven validity. In addition, the Strange Situation is only applicable during a relatively brief age period from 12 to about 18 months of age.

An alternative measure of attachment is the Attachment-Q-Set (AQS; Waters, 1987). The procedure is usually applied in the home of children; however, it can also be adapted for use in day-care settings (De Schipper, Tavecchio, & Van IJzendoorn, 2008). It consists of 90 behaviorally defined items, which need to be sorted primarily in high, middle, and low stacks of approximately 30 items according to how much they describe the child in question. The set was translated into several languages and the attention to detail in the behavioral descriptions requires familiarity with the items, thus making trained observers desirable. However, it can also be used with mothers as observers (Schölmerich, Fracasso, Lamb, & Broberg, 1995; Teti & McGourty, 1996). Valid results can be expected if sufficient observation time is available and the applicable age range is between 1 and 5 years. The Q-sort methodology has the advantage that response tendencies can be avoided since each item is sorted relative to other items. Attachment security is subsequently judged against an existing criterion sort, which was derived from expert judgments describing an "ideally secure" child. A correlation coefficient over all items between the child-related sort and the criterion sort is the degree of security for that particular child.

Numerous instruments are available to assess dyadic parent–child behavior. For example, the Revised Family Observation Schedule (FOS-R-III; Boyle et al., 2010; Sanders, Waugh, Tully, & Hynes, 1996) was developed in order to evaluate the effectiveness of a standardized parent training program (Triple P). The FOS-R-III assesses both positive and negative parent and child behaviors across a number of different situations at home with sessions coded in 10-s time intervals. Behavior is judged by trained observers and then measured by calculating the percentage of intervals in which the parent or child displays behaviors such as praise and responsiveness (positive parent behavior), appropriate verbal or nonverbal interactions and affection toward parents (positive child behavior), angry or hostile facial expression (parent aversive behavior), and noncompliance or physical attacks (child disruptive behavior). Studies have reported satisfactory to good interobserver reliability scores (κ = .74–.88; Hahlweg, Heinrichs, Kuschel, Bertram, & Naumann, 2010) and 81–96% of agreement (Boyle et al., 2010), respectively.

The Assessment of Mother–Child Interactions with the Etch-a-Sketch (AMCIES; Jäkel, Wolke, & Chernova, 2012; Wolke, Rios, & Unzer, 1995) has been developed as a standardized coding system for dyadic mother–child interactions in a task that simulates a homework situation. The AMCIES has been administered to preschoolers and primary school children (6 and 8 years of age) but the level of task difficulty may be adjusted for younger or older children. Mothers and children are observed during a standardized play situation using an Etch-a-Sketch, a toy that allows one to draw pictures by means of two buttons, one for horizontal and one for vertical lines. The instruction is that the mother should use one button and the child the other button, thus both have to work together to copy a simple template (i.e., a picture of a house). The behavior rating may be done directly (in vivo) or afterward (evaluating videotaped interactions). For the video rating, the AMCIES consists of six subscales for the mother, five subscales for the child, and two subscales for mother–child joint behavior that are combined into the following index scales: Maternal Sensitivity, Verbal Control, Harmony, Child Task Persistence (a measure of attention span), Child Social Interactions with the mother, and overall Physical Activity. Interrater reliabilities are available; for example, κ scores range between .76 and .89 (Schneider et al., 2009) and intraclass correlation coefficients (ICCs) for single scores range from .74 to .92 for maternal behavior, from .69 to .75 for child behavior, and from .72 to .86 for joint behavior scales, respectively (Jäkel et al., 2012). For the in vivo rating, only four subscales are considered and combined into an index scale of Maternal Sensitivity. These in vivo ratings are in agreement with the video-rated scores (in vivo and video-rated Maternal Sensitivity scales correlate with r = .65; ICC = .76) and thus present a resource-effective alternative to video ratings of maternal behavior.

The Feeding Scale (Chatoor et al., 1997) aims to measure intrapersonal constructs based on a rating of 46 behaviors of mother and infant in a naturalistic setting, with ratings on a 4-point Likert scale. It can be applied to dyads including children up to 3 years of age. There are five subscales: Dyadic Reciprocity, Dyadic Conflict, Talk and Distraction, Struggle for Control, and Maternal Non-Contingency. The feeding situation can be performed in a laboratory or clinical practice and mothers are asked to bring the food items they usually feed their children. The Feeding Scale is mainly useful for infants with feeding disorders, but the authors claim that the feeding situation offers a good window into the dyadic relationship and is therefore suitable as a context for a broader assessment of the mother–infant relationship. The scale is based on previous versions and has been validated to distinguish infants with nonorganic failure to thrive (NOFTT) from healthy controls, as well as subgroups of NOFTT from each other.

The scale revealed good interrater reliability (ICC = .82–.92) as well as moderate test–retest reliability (r = .46–.72) for a 2-week period (Chatoor et al., 1997).

Assessment of Temperament and Self-Regulation

The concept of infant temperament calls for a more personality-oriented approach than the relationship-focused procedures described previously. Infant temperament has traditionally been studied using home and laboratory observations as well as parent reports, with each method entailing its own strengths and caveats (Rothbart & Goldsmith, 1985). The majority of studies on the structure of temperament in young children have relied on parent-report measures. A notable exception is the Laboratory Temperament Assessment Battery (LAB-TAB) by Goldsmith and Rothbart (1999), a laboratory observational measure available in three different versions according to the developmental status of the child (prelocomotor, locomotor, and preschool). The prelocomotor and the locomotor version consist of 20 defined episodes, organized around five central dimensions of temperament (fear, anger/frustration, joy/pleasure, interest/persistence, and activity level). The preschool version contains 32 episodes in seven dimensions (fear, distress, exuberance, interest/persistence, activity level, inhibitory control, and contentment). The manuals specify the situation, procedure, equipment, data analysis, and rules for video recording.

For coding, possible infant responses are considered as either absent or present and parameters of the response are recorded, such as latency, duration, and intensity (Goldsmith & Rothbart, 1999, p. 1). For the prelocomotor version, only six to eight of the 20 episodes can be carried out during one visit to the laboratory; a recommendation is to start with a pleasure/interest episode, have the fear and anger episodes interspersed, and use the activity level episode as free play somewhat in the middle. The application of the procedure needs two or three experimenters, one of whom should be trained to interact in a standard way with infant and mother. Gagne, Van Hulle, Aksan, Essex, and Goldsmith (2011) report good internal consistencies (α between 0.50 and 0.94 with only one score below 0.73) and substantial item–total correlations (.30 < r < .94) for the composites derived from LAB-TAB episodes in a home-based version for the preschool age group.

In a recent study, the structure of temperament in preschoolers was assessed with the LAB-TAB to apply the Five Factor model of personality to young children (Dyson et al., 2012). Episodes were videotaped and coded later by trained raters who were unaware of the study variables. Confirmatory factor analyses suggested five independent dimensions: sociability, positive affect / interest, dysphoria, fear / inhibition, and constraint vs. impulsivity. Interrater reliabilities were obtained for 35 tapes with two-way random, absolute agreement ICCs and internal consistency of the scales with Cronbach's α coefficients for the entire sample of 559 3-year-old children. Overall, reliability scores varied from just acceptable to excellent with ICCs ranging from .51 to .98 and Cronbach's α from 0.50 to 0.87 across all subscales. As is typical for laboratory measures, the external validity of these findings is limited: Child behavior and emotions may be situation-specific and based on a predefined number of contexts that did not include peer interactions.

The ability to self-regulate attention and behavior during a challenging test situation is assessed with the Tester's Rating of Child Behavior (TRCB; Wolke & Meyer, 1999). The procedure is applied while another standardized test (e.g., the K-ABC; Kaufman & Kaufman, 1983) is administered and is thus highly cost- and time-effective. The TRCB consists of thirteen 9-point rating scales, which are combined into three index scales: Task Orientation, Behavior

Regulation, and Activity. Interrater reliabilities (ICC) of the TRCB index scales have been reported to range from .63 to .97 (Jäkel, Wolke, & Bartmann, 2012).

In a similar way, child attention across an assessment day may be evaluated as a consensus rating by a whole research team (i.e., psychologists, psychometricians, and pediatricians) with the TEAM index scale of attention (Jäkel et al., 2012). Due to the conceptualization of this instrument as a consensus rating combining several informants' input, interrater reliability information is not available; however, the TEAM rating provides a comprehensive, highly valid, reliable, and objective multi-informant assessment of a child's attention-regulation abilities. Behavior ratings such as the TRCB and TEAM that are administered during standard testing have the advantage of effectively observing children's self-regulation across challenging situations that are similar to the demands of the classroom environment in school.

Assessment of Emotions

The observation and coding of emotions, that is, coding systems for facial expression (Ekman & Friesen, 1978) have been of particular relevance for psychology and its neighboring disciplines. The Facial Action Coding System (FACS) has been refined over the years (Ekman & Rosenberg, 2005) and applied to manifold purposes. For example, the FACS has been utilized to develop the Japanese and Caucasian Brief Affect Recognition Test (JACBART; Matsumoto et al., 2000), which measures adults' emotion-recognition abilities. The JACBART has been reported to offer good internal reliability, convergent validity, and test–retest correlations; however, its ecological validity has been questioned (Matsumoto et al., 2000).

In addition to applying the FACS to adults, the Baby FACS has been developed as a tool to measure facial expressions in infants (Camras, Campos, Oster, Miyake, & Bradshaw, 1992; Rosenstein & Oster, 1988). The Baby FACS is a comprehensive, anatomically based coding system for discrete, minimally distinguishable actions of the facial muscles (termed action units). Using videotapes, these action units are identified and defined by trained coders. Cross-cultural validity of the Baby FACS has been demonstrated (Camras et al., 2007; Segal et al., 1995) and interrater reliabilities of $\kappa > .62$ are satisfactory (Camras et al., 2007).

Assessment of Personality

The various dimensions underlying intra- and interpersonal behavior in different contexts may be best described as an individual's personality. Recently, a near consensus has been found on the structure by which differently conceptualized personality traits can be arranged, which is in favor of the Big Five (Dyson et al., 2012; Prinzie, Stams, Dekovic, Reijntjes, & Belsky, 2009). With regards to content, the Big Five may be a valid option for capturing different personality traits; however, although multi-informant assessments are the gold standard, they are traditionally only measured via questionnaires.

This is not the case for the interpersonal circumplex model, which states that interpersonal behavior may be rated in terms of two orthogonal dimensions: dominance and affiliation (Wiggins, 1982) or, respectively, agency and communion (Wiggins & Broughton, 1991). The latter two have been measured in a sample of 99 young adults by video rating 17 standardized dyadic role-play situations with a short version of the Minimum Redundancy Scales (MRS-30; Leising & Bleidorn, 2011). Situations were videotaped and then rated by female students who were blind to the study objectives with a standardized procedure using 35 pairs of adjectives. Interrater reliabilities were computed with Cronbach's α and ranged from 0.13 to 0.87 for single situations and from 0.58 to 0.90 for agreement averaged across situations. Additional analyses suggested good to excellent replicability of the factors across observers as well as stability across situations (Leising & Bleidorn, 2011).

In a similar manner, gender differences in dominance and affiliation were measured with molecular behavioral observations in a real-life situation (i.e., in an executive job selection assessment center; Luxen, 2005). Participants' behavior was videotaped and coded by trained observers. Interrater reliabilities were excellent, with ICCs ranging from .91 to .97 (Luxen, 2005) and compared with laboratory assessments the approach has the advantage of very high ecological validity.

Cross-Cultural Assessment of Interpersonal Behavior

According to a cross-cultural model of development and behavior classification, individuals may be positioned in a matrix along the two orthogonal dimensions of agency (autonomy vs. heteronomy) and interpersonal distance (relatedness vs. separateness; Kagitcibasi, 2005, 2012). These dimensions have predominantly been assessed with semistructured interviews such as the Socialization Goals Inventory (SGI; Harwood, Schölmerich, Schulze, & Gonzalez, 1999), Q-sort instruments (Durgel, Leyendecker, Yagmurlu, & Harwood, 2009), and self-report questionnaires, although cross-cultural research has a long tradition of behavior observation as the method of choice.

Conclusion

For psychological research and diagnostic assessment of intra- and interpersonal processes through observation there are many established procedures available. However, the majority of those we have presented here are developed and used in research settings (i.e., for group-based data analysis) and they lack the discriminant validity necessary for individual diagnostic purposes. Validation studies and efforts to develop standardization references need to be addressed in future research in order to achieve availability of gold standard assessment tools and to make individual study findings comparable. Unfortunately, our literature search suggested that the tendency to develop new instruments may be particularly prevalent among researchers using observation methods, thus hampering the replicability and comparability across studies and the long-needed development of established standards. However, considering the caveats of alternative assessment approaches (e.g., self-report questionnaires), observation procedures offer excellent validity and objectivity to answer manifold questions. Ultimately it may be advisable to combine behavior observation methods with other techniques of assessment to validate findings until established instrument standards become available.

References

Ainsworth, M. D. S., Blehar, M. C., Waters, E., & Wall, S. (1978). *Patterns of attachment*. Hillsdale, NJ: Lawrence Erlbaum Associates.

Anderson, P., Doyle, L. W., & the Victorian Infant Collaborative Study Group. (2003). Neurobehavioral outcomes of school-age children born extremely low birth weight or very preterm in the 1990s. *JAMA, 289*, 3264–3272. http://doi.org/10.1001/jama.289.24.3264

Bornstein, M. H., Toda, S., Azuma, H., Tamislemonda, C., & Ogino, M. (1990). Mother and infant activity and interaction in Japan and in the United States: A comparative microanalysis of naturalistic exchanges focused on the organization of infant attention. *International Journal of Behavioral Development, 13*, 289–308. http://doi.org/10.1177/016502549001300302

Boyle, C. L., Sanders, M. R., Lutzker, J. R., Prinz, R. J., Shapiro, C., & Whitaker, D. J. (2010). An analysis of training, generalization, and maintenance effects of Primary Care Triple P for parents of preschool-aged children with disruptive behavior. *Child Psychiatry & Human Development, 41*, 114–131. http://doi.org/10.1007/s10578-009-0156-7

Camras, L. A., Campos, J. J., Oster, H., Miyake, K., & Bradshaw, D. (1992). Japanese and American infants' responses to arm restraint. *Developmental Psychology, 28*, 578–583. http://doi.org/10.1037/0012-1649.28.4.578

Camras, L. A., Oster, H., Bakeman, R., Meng, Z., Ujiie, T., & Campos, J. J. (2007). Do infants show distinct negative facial expressions for fear and anger? Emotional expression in 11-month-old European American, Chinese, and Japanese infants. *Infancy, 11*, 131–155. http://doi.org/10.1111/j.1532-7078.2007.tb00219.x

Carver, C. S., & Scheier, M. F. (2004). *Perspectives on personality* (5th ed.). New York, NY: Allyn & Bacon.

Chatoor, I., Getson, P., Menvielle, E., Brasseaux, C., Odonnell, R., Rivera, Y., & Mrazek, D. A. (1997). A feeding scale for research and clinical practice to assess mother-infant interactions in the first three years of life. *Infant Mental Health Journal, 18*, 76–91. http://doi.org/10.1002/(SICI)1097-0355(199721)18:1<76::AID-IMHJ6>3.0.CO;2-Z

De Schipper, J. C., Tavecchio, L. W. C., & Van IJzendoorn, M. H. (2008). Children's attachment relationships with day care caregivers: Associations with positive caregiving and the child's temperament. *Social Development, 17*, 455–470. http://doi.org/10.1111/j.1467-9507.2007.00448.x

Durgel, E. S., Leyendecker, B., Yagmurlu, B., & Harwood, R. (2009). Sociocultural influences on German and Turkish immigrant mothers' long-term socialization goals. *Journal of Cross-Cultural Psychology, 40*, 834–852. http://doi.org/10.1177/0022022109339210

Dyson, M. W., Olino, T. M., Durbin, C. E., Goldsmith, H. H., & Klein, D. N. (2012). The structure of temperament in preschoolers: A two-stage factor analytic approach. *Emotion, 12*, 44–57. http://doi.org/10.1037/a0025023

Ekman, P., & Friesen, W. V. (1978). *The facial action coding system*. Palo Alto, CA: Consulting Psychologist's Press.

Ekman, P., & Rosenberg, E. (2005). *What the face reveals. Basic and applied studies of spontaneous expression using the facial action coding system (FACS)*. Oxford, UK: University Press. http://doi.org/10.1093/acprof:oso/9780195179644.001.0001

Eurich, T. L., Krause, D. E., Cigularov, K., & Thornton, G. C. (2009). Assessment centers: Current practices in the United States. *Journal of Business and Psychology, 24*, 387–407. http://doi.org/10.1007/s10869-009-9123-3

Gagne, J. R., Van Hulle, C. A., Aksan, N., Essex, M. J., & Goldsmith, H. H. (2011). Deriving childhood temperament measures from emotion-eliciting. Behavioral episodes: Scale construction and initial validation. *Psychological Assessment, 23*, 337–353. http://doi.org/10.1037/a0021746

Goldsmith, H. H., & Rothbart, M. K. (1999). *The Laboratory Temperament Assessment Battery: Description of procedures. Locomotor version*. Unpublished manuscript.

Hahlweg, K., Heinrichs, N., Kuschel, A., Bertram, H., & Naumann, S. (2010). Long-term outcome of a randomized controlled universal prevention trial through a positive parenting program: Is it worth the effort? *Child and Adolescent Psychiatry and Mental Health, 4*, 14. http://doi.org/10.1186/1753-2000-4-14

Harwood, R. L., Schölmerich, A., Schulze, P. A., & Gonzalez, Z. (1999). Cultural differences in maternal beliefs and behaviors: A study of middle-class Anglo and Puerto Rican mother-infant pairs in four everyday situations. *Child Development, 70*, 1005–1016. http://doi.org/10.1111/1467-8624.00073

Jäkel, J., Wolke, D., & Bartmann, P. (2012). Poor attention rather than hyperactivity/impulsivity predicts academic achievement in very preterm and fullterm adolescents. *Psychological Medicine, 43*, 183–196. http://doi.org/10.1017/S0033291712001031

Jäkel, J., Wolke, D., & Chernova, J. (2012). Mother and child behaviour in very preterm and term dyads at 6 and 8 years. *Developmental Medicine & Child Neurology, 54*, 716–723. http://doi.org/10.1111/j.1469-8749.2012.04323.x

Kagan, J., Reznick, J. S., Snidman, N., Gibbons, J., & Johnson, M. O. (1988). Childhood derivatives of inhibition and lack of inhibition to the unfamiliar. *Child Development, 59*, 1580–1589. http://doi.org/10.2307/1130672

Kagitcibasi, C. (2005). Autonomy and relatedness in cultural context – implications for self and family. *Journal of Cross-Cultural Psychology, 36*, 403–422. http://doi.org/10.1177/0022022105275959

Kagitcibasi, C. (2012). Sociocultural change and integrative syntheses in human development: Autonomous-related self and social–cognitive competence. *Child Development Perspectives, 6*, 5–11. http://doi.org/10.1111/j.1750-8606.2011.00173.x

Kammeyer-Mueller, J., Steel, P. D. G., & Rubenstein, A. (2010). The other side of method bias: The perils of distinct source research designs. *Multivariate Behavioral Research, 45*, 294–321. http://doi.org/10.1080/00273171003680278

Kaufman, A. S., & Kaufman, N. (1983). *Kaufman assessment battery for children*. Circle Pines, MN: American Guidance Service.

Lamb, M. E., Thompson, R. M., Gardner, W., Charnov, E. L., & Estes, D. (1984). Security of infantile attachment as assessed in the Strange Situation – its study and biological interpretation. *Behavioral and Brain Sciences, 7*, 127–147. http://doi.org/10.1017/S0140525X00026522

Leising, D., & Bleidorn, W. (2011). Which are the basic meaning dimensions of observable interpersonal behavior? *Personality and Individual Differences, 51*, 986–990. http://doi.org/10.1016/j.paid.2011.08.003

Luxen, M. F. (2005). Gender differences in dominance and affiliation during a demanding interaction. *Journal of Psychology, 139*, 331–347. http://doi.org/10.3200/JRLP.139.4.331-347

Magai, C., & McFadden, S. H. (1995). *The role of emotions in social and personality development: History, theory and research*. New York, NY: Springer.

Matsumoto, D., LeRoux, J., Wilson-Cohn, C., Raroque, J., Kooken, K., Ekman, P., … Goh, A. (2000). A new test to measure emotion recognition ability: Matsumoto and Ekman's Japanese and Caucasian Brief Affect Recognition Test (JACBART). *Journal of Nonverbal Behavior, 24*, 179–209. http://doi.org/10.1023/A:1006668120583

Prinzie, P., Stams, G. J. J. M., Dekovic, M., Reijntjes, A. H. A., & Belsky, J. (2009). The relations between parents' Big Five personality factors and parenting: A meta-analytic review. *Journal of Personality and Social Psychology, 97*, 351–362. http://doi.org/10.1037/a0015823

Rosenstein, D., & Oster, H. (1988). Differential facial responses to 4 basic tastes in newborns. *Child Development, 59*, 1555–1568. http://doi.org/10.2307/1130670

Rothbart, M. K., & Goldsmith, H. H. (1985). Three approaches to the study of infant temperament. *Developmental Review, 5*, 237–260. http://doi.org/10.1016/0273-2297(85)90012-7

Sanders, M. R., Waugh, L., Tully, L., & Hynes, K. (1996). *The revised family observation schedule* (3rd ed.). Brisbane, Australia: Parenting and Family Support Centre, The University of Queensland.

Schneider, S., Houweling, J. E. G., Gommlich-Schneider, S., Klein, C., Nündel, B., & Wolke, D. (2009). Effect of maternal panic disorder on mother-child interaction and relation to child anxiety and child self-efficacy. *Archives of Women's Mental Health, 12*, 251–259. http://doi.org/10.1007/s00737-009-0072-7

Schölmerich, A. (2011). Verhaltensbeobachtung. In H. Keller (Ed.), *Handbuch der Kleinkindforschung* (4th ed., pp. 768–791). Bern, Switzerland: Huber.

Schölmerich, A., Fracasso, M. P., Lamb, M. E., & Broberg, A. G. (1995). Interactional harmony at 7 and 10 months of age predicts security of attachment as measured by Q-sort ratings. *Social Development, 4*, 62–74. http://doi.org/10.1111/j.1467-9507.1995.tb00051.x

Segal, L. B., Oster, H., Cohen, M., Caspi, B., Myers, M., & Brown, D. (1995). Smiling and fussing in seven-month-old preterm and full-term black infants in the still-face situation. *Child Development, 66*, 1829–1843. http://doi.org/10.2307/1131913

Shum, D., Neulinger, K., O'Callaghan, M., & Mohay, H. (2008). Attentional problems in children born very preterm or with extremely low birth weight at 7-9 years. *Archives of Clinical Neuropsychology, 23*, 103–112. http://doi.org/10.1016/j.acn.2007.08.006

Skinner, N. S. J. F., & Howarth, E. (1973). Cross-media independence of questionnaire and objective-test personality factors. *Multivariate Behavioral Research, 8*, 23–40. http://doi.org/10.1207/s15327906mbr0801_2

Teti, D. M., & McGourty, S. (1996). Using mothers versus trained observers in assessing children's secure base behavior: Theoretical and methodological considerations. *Child Development, 67*, 597–605. http://doi.org/10.2307/1131834

Tronick, E., Als, H., Adamson, L., Wise, S., & Brazelton, T. B. (1978). The infant's response to entrapment between contradictory messages in face-to-face interaction. *Journal of the American Academy of Child Psychiatry, 17*, 1–13. http://doi.org/10.1016/S0002-7138(09)62273-1

Van IJzendoorn, M. H., & Kroonenberg, P. M. (1988). Cross-cultural patterns of attachment: A meta-analysis of the Strange Situation. *Child Development, 59*, 147–156. http://doi.org/10.1111/j.1467-8624.1988.tb03202.x

Waters, E. (1987). *The Attachment-Q-Set (Version 3)*. Retrieved from http://www.psychology.sunysb.edu/attachment/measures/content/aqs_items.pdf

Wiggins, J. S. (1982). Circumplex models of interpersonal behavior in clinical psychology. In P. C. Kendall & J. N. Butcher (Eds.), *Handbook of research methods in clinical psychology* (pp. 183–222). New York, NY: John Wiley.

Wiggins, J. S., & Broughton, R. (1991). A geometric taxonomy of personality-scales. *European Journal of Personality, 5*, 343–365. http://doi.org/10.1002/per.2410050503

Wolke, D., & Meyer, R. (1999). Ergebnisse der Bayerischen Entwicklungsstudie: Implikationen für Theorie und Praxis [Findings of the Bavarian Developmental Study: Implications for theory and praxis]. *Kindheit und Entwicklung, 8*, 24–36.

Wolke, D., Rios, P., & Unzer, A. (1995). *AMCIES evaluation of mother-child interaction with the Etch-A-Sketch*. Unpublished manuscript, University of Hertfordshire, Hertfordshire, UK.

Contributors

Rainer Banse
Social & Legal Psychology
Institute for Psychology
University of Bonn
Kaiser-Karl-Ring 9
53111 Bonn
Germany
E-mail rbanse@uni-bonn.de

Nicola Baumann
Department of Psychology
University of Trier
54286 Trier
Germany
E-mail nicola.baumann@uni-trier.de

Michael Bender
School of Social and Behavioral Sciences
Department of Social Psychology
Babylon, Center for the Study of the Multi-cultural Society
Tilburg University
P.O. Box 90153
5000 LE Tilburg
The Netherlands
E-mail m.bender@tilburguniversity.edu

Robert F. Bornstein
Derner Institute of Advanced Psychological Studies
212 Blodgett Hall
Adelphi University
Garden City, NY 11530
USA
E-mail bornstein@adelphi.edu

Athanasios Chasiotis
Tilburg University
School of Social and Behavioral Sciences
Department of Social Psychology
Babylon, Center for the Study of the Multi-cultural Society
P.O. Box 90153
5000 LE Tilburg
The Netherlands
E-mail a.chasiotis@tilburguniversity.edu

Giulio Costantini
Department of Psychology
University of Milan-Bicocca
Piazza dell'Ateneo Nuovo, 1
20126 Milan
Italy
E-mail giulio.costantini@unimib.it

Malte Friese
Department of Psychology
Saarland University
P.O. Box 15 11 50
66041 Saarbruecken
Germany
E-mail malte.friese@uni-saarland.de

Friederike Gerstenberg
Kreisdiakonieverband Esslingen
Psychologische Beratungsstelle
Berliner Str. 27
73728 Esslingen
Germany
E-mail fgerstenberg@me.com

Tobias Gschwendner
Lebensberatung Trier
Kochstr. 2
54290 Trier
Germany
E-mail tobias.gschwendner-lukas@gmx.de

Wilhelm Hofmann
Social and Economic Cognition I
Department of Psychology
University of Cologne
Richard-Strauss-Str. 2
50931 Cologne
Germany
E-mail wilhelm.hofmann@uni-koeln.de

Katrijn Houben
Clinical Psychological Science
Maastricht University
P.O. Box 616,
6200 MD Maastricht
The Netherlands
E-mail k.houben@maastrichtuniversity.nl

Roland Imhoff
Social Cognition
University of Cologne
Richard-Strauss-Str. 2
50931 Cologne
Germany
E-mail roland.koeln@uni-koeln.de

Julia Jaekel
Department of Developmental Psychology
Faculty of Psychology
Ruhr-University Bochum
44780 Bochum
Germany
E-mail julia.jaekel@ruhr-uni-bochum.de

Martina Kaufmann
Department of Psychology
University of Trier
Universitätsring 15
54286 Trier
Germany
E-mail martina.kaufmann@uni-trier.de

Tuulia M. Ortner
Department of Psychology
University of Salzburg
Hellbrunnerstrasse 34
5020 Salzburg
Austria
E-mail tuulia.ortner@sbg.ac.at

Marco Perugini
Department of Psychology
University of Milan-Bicocca
Piazza dell'Ateneo Nuovo, 1
20126 Milan
Italy
E-mail marco.perugini@unimib.it

Andrew Perkins
Associate Professor, Marketing
Washington State University
Carson College of Buisness
Pullman, WA 99164
USA
E-mail a.perkins@wsu.edu

René Proyer
Department of Psychology
University of Zurich
Personality and Assessment
Binzmühlestr. 14/Box 7
Zürich
Switzerland
E-mail r.proyer@psychologie.uzh.ch

Kate A. Ratliff
Department of Psychology
University of Florida
945 Center Drive Gainesville
FL 32611
USA
E-mail ratliff@ufl.edu

Juliette Richetin
Department of Psychology
University of Milan-Bicocca
Piazza dell'Ateneo Nuovo, 1
20126 Milan
Italy
E-mail juliette.richetin@unimib.it

Alexander Schmidt
Institute for Health and Behaviour
Health Promotion and Aggression Prevention
University of Luxembourg
Route de Diekirch
7201 Walferdange
Luxembourg
E-mail alexander.schmidt@uni.lu

Manfred Schmitt
Department of Psychology
University of Koblenz-Landau
Fortstr. 7
76829 Landau
Germany
E-mail schmittm@uni-landau.de

Axel Schölmerich
Department of Developmental Psychology
Faculty of Psychology
Ruhr-University Bochum
44780 Bochum
Germany
E-mail axel.schoelmerich@rub.de

Colin Tucker Smith
Department of Psychology
University of Florida
945 Center Drive
Gainesville, FL 32611
USA
E-mail colinsmith@ufl.edu

Alan W. Stacy
School of Community and Global Health
Claremont Graduate University
675 West Foothill Boulevard, Suite 310
Claremont, CA 91711-3475
USA
E-mail alan.stacy@cgu.edu

Fons J. R. van de Vijver
Department of Culture Studies
Babylon, Center for the Study of
the Mulicultural Society
Tilburg University
P.O. Box 90153
5000 LE Tilburg
The Netherlands
E-mail fons.vandevijver@uvt.nl

Reinout W. Wiers
Addiction Development and Psychopathology (ADAPT) Lab
Department of Psychology
University of Amsterdam
Weesperplein 4
1018 XA Amsterdam
The Netherlands
E-mail r.w.wiers@gmail.com

Axel Zinkernagel
Department of Psychology
University of Koblenz-Landau
Fortstr. 7
76829 Landau
Germany
E-mail zinkernagel@uni-landau.de

Cristina Zogmaister
Department of Psychology
University of Milan-Bicocca
Piazza dell'Ateneo Nuovo, 1
20126 Milan
Italy
E-mail cristina.zogmaister@unimib.it

Subject Index

A

abilities, introspective 31, 34, 69, 81, 105, 113, 173, 183
abilitiy to work under pressure (tests of) 134
achievement 101, 102
 – (tests of) 29, 134, 143
achievement motivation 47, 134, 136, 141, 143
 – (tests of) 134, 136, 139, 141, 143
action tendency 156, 157, 160, 161
addiction 156, 158, 161, 163
administration bias (cross-cultural) 87
affect 4, 6, 8, 18, 41, 68, 69, 70, 71, 72, 81, 83, 88, 89, 91, 97–108, 115, 121, 123, 124, 156, 157, 159, 160, 162, 196, 214, 215
affective misattribution procedure (AMP; affect misattribution procedure) 98
affect misattribution procedure (AMP) 100, 123, 124, 196
 – moral behavior (attitude toward) 124
 – smoking (attitude toward) 124
 – voting behavior (prediction of) 118, 124
affiliation 101, 102
 – motive, see need for affiliation-intimacy
age groups (attitude toward) 125
agentic 54
 – needs 51
 – self-focus 49
aggression 154, 155
alcohol 116, 122–124, 142, 154, 157–161, 163, 164
 – Alcohol Identity (IAD) 160
 – attitude toward 116, 122–124, 157–161, 163, 164
 – use 116, 122–124, 142, 154, 157–161, 163, 164
ambiguous stories 83, 86, 88, 160
ambivalence 107
anxiety (measures of) 37, 38, 140, 144
anxious worrying 40
approach 104, 140
approach behavior 101, 102, 182
approach-oriented behaviors, see approach behavior

approach-avoidance task (AAT) 161
assertiveness (test of) 144
assessment
 – Assessment of Mother–Child Interactions with the Etch-a-Sketch (AMCIES) 214
 – cross-cultural 217
 – of attachment and dyadic parent-child behavior 213
 – of children 19, 52, 56, 57, 91, 103, 162, 174, 213, 214, 216
 – of emotions 216
 – of personality 216
associative
 – network 70, 156, 196
 – processes 196, 203, 204
attachment 55, 212, 213
Attachment-Q-Set (AQS) 213
attentional bias 156–158, 162–164
attitude
 – change 105, 198, 199
 – implicit 25, 38, 113, 158, 159, 161, 201, 202, 205
 – importance 37
attitudes
 – explicit 38, 115–117, 120, 121, 123, 198, 200, 202, 203
 – implicit 25, 38, 113, 158, 159, 161, 201, 202, 205
autobiographical 52
 – Autobiographical Memory Test (AMT) 53, 54
 – narratives 50, 51
 – specificity 53
automated 49, 54, 58
 – assessment, see automated structural coding
 – structural coding 48, 49, 54, 58
automatic affective reactions 18
automaticity 32, 174
autosuggestion 33
avoidance behavior 101, 104
Axis II diagnoses 71

B

Balloon Analogue Risk Task (BART) 137, 139, 142

ball-tossing task 119
behavior
– observation 4, 6, 7, 16, 97, 104, 113, 211–213, 217
– observation systems 6
behavioral
– consistency, see consistency: cross-situational
– inhibition 180, 212
– intentions 5, 8, 32–35, 200
– observation 4, 6, 7, 16, 97, 104, 113, 211–213, 217
– plans 5, 8, 32, 33
– schemata 5, 8, 31–33, 35, 36, 56, 212
– script 5, 8, 31–33, 35, 56, 212
– trait measures 29, 30
behavior-based assessment 3, 5, 6, 8, 9, 153
Behavior Rating Inventory of Executive Function (BRIEF) 155
Belastbarkeits-Assessment: computerisierte Objektive Persönlichkeits-Testbatterie (BAcO) 137
Betting Dice Test 137, 142
Big Five 216
Big Three 82
biographical data 133
blatant prejudice 38
– explicit prejudice 121
blink
– attentional 182
bodily expressions 104

C

card pull 69
category
– labels 114, 116
– systems (behavior observation) 4
causal links (in narrative) 51
change
– detection paradigm 158
– models 144
Choice Reaction Time Task 182
circadian cortisol 101
clinical predictions 69
coda (element of narrative structure) 48
coder-based thematic coding 49
coding
– accuracy 137
– manual 47, 48, 51, 84, 86, 89
– speed 137
– system 47, 49, 52, 83, 91, 214, 216
coding/counting rules 49
cognitive
– complexity 51, 52
– control processes 18, 158
– dissonance 34
– load effects 20
– performance tests 136
collectivism 47
collectivistic values 47
communal needs 51, 54
complex-span tasks 162
conceptual correspondence 30, 140
confidence (test of) 138
congruent context 35
conscious control 105, 178
consistency, cross-situational 29
consistency
– internal 84, 89
construct
– bias (cross-cultural) 87
– validity 23, 24, 67, 72
– -related components 21, 73, 140
consumer
– attitudes 116, 121, 123, 195–199, 201, 202
– decisions 196
– goods (attitude toward) 116, 123
– -related behavior 196
consumption behavior 115
content
– analysis 46, 91, 92
– similarity (of measures) 38, 140
content coding 45–63
– manuals, see coding: -manual, -system
– methods 4, 5, 83
– procedures 51, 58
– structural 46, 49
– techniques 49, 57
– thematic 47, 48, 49, 56, 57
context effects 25, 53
contextual factors 113
continuous associations 156
controlled processes 35
convergence (of multiple methods) 5, 8, 23, 29–31, 36, 70, 89, 115, 139, 140, 177, 185
coping
– motive 160
– style 65, 72

corrugator muscle 104
cortisol response 101
creative design tasks 134
criterion validity 140
Crossing the Street Test (CtST) 142
cultural
– appropriateness 55, 89
– knowledge 115
– sensitivity 135
Cursive Miniature Situations 134

D

decision making 30, 162, 163, 176
deliberate
– behavior 23, 183, 202, 203
– goal-directed responding 68
– self-presentation 23
deliberation 34, 35
dependent personality disorder (PD) 71
depression 53
derogation of outgroup 19
deviant sexual interests (DSI) 174, 175
deviant sexual preferences (DSP) 175
diaries 212
diary sampling method 68
differentiation (in narrative) 51, 52
diffusion-model analysis 21
discrimination task 178
disgust sensitivity 39
display rules 39
Domain-Specific Risk-Taking Scale (DOSPERT) 139
d-prime (GNAT) 120
dual-process models 153
dual-process theories 140
dual-systems theory 154, 183
dynamics of action theory (DOA) 84
Dynamometer Pressure Test 133

E

ecological validity 50, 52, 57
effect, facilitatory 181
Ego Impairment Index 73
elaborated integration (in narrative) 51
elaborative style of reminiscing 56
eliciting conditions (of a narrative) 50
emotion 216
– expression 38, 48, 57, 104
– regulation 106
– -specific associations 100

emotional stability 133
endocrinological processes 82
error-choice technique 197
evaluative conditioning 200
evaluative priming (EP) task 119, 120, 196
– reliability 120
examiners (effects of) 135
executive control 154
experience-sampling procedures 71
experiment-based assessment 134
explicit
– affect 8, 32, 97
– Explicit and Implicit Sexual Interest Profile (EISIP) 185
– goals and values 82
– motivational system 82
– motives 5, 81–84
– risk propensity 39
– self-knowledge 33, 34, 36, 38
expressive movements 136
external conditions (effects of) 135
extremity ratings 88
Extrinsic Affective Simon Task (EAST) 121, 122
– identification 122
– interindividual differences 122
– percentage of errors 121
– spiders (attitude toward) 122
eye movement 180
eyewitness accuracy 16, 52, 53

F

facial
– electromyography (EMG) 104
– expression 39
– expressions 104
– muscl activity 104
– muscle activity 105
Facial Action Coding System (FACS) 104, 216
Facial Action Coding System (FACS) - Baby FACS 216
faking 105, 115, 117, 125, 181
family interaction models 88
Family System Test (FAST) 103
fantasy-based methods 82
Features-of-Events (FOE) checklists 52
Feeding Scale 214
figure–ground recoding strategy 20
figure placement techniques 100, 103

flow 103
forensic 6, 7, 52, 70–72, 173, 174, 176–181, 183
fragile self-concept 40
free-response test 65
frequency 54, 57
  – of words 45
  – fundamental, see measure: vocal pitch
functionality (of words) 45, 49

G

Game of Dice task (GDT) 139
gatekeeper model (of priming) 24
Go/No-Go Association Task (GNAT) 120, 121
  – gender (attitude toward) 121
  – genetically modified food (attitude toward) 121
  – reliability 121
  – sexuality (attitude toward) 121
goal 25, 30, 33, 35, 38, 47, 50, 66, 68, 69, 81–83, 86, 90, 137, 155, 162, 163, 185, 217
  – anticipation 83
  – discrepancy 35
  – -directed behavior 81
  – -directed responding, see deliberate behavior 68
grid technique (Mulit-Motive Grid, MMG) 82
grounded theory 47, 52
group-level biases 116, 126

H

Haire's shopping list procedure 197
Hand Test 65
help-seeking 68, 71
heteroscedasticity 21
histrionic personality disorder 70, 71
HIV risk behavior 154, 157
Hotzman inkblot technique 65, 68
homogeneity of variance 21
human resources 145

I

idiographic methods 57
implementation strategy (of motive) 89, 101, 102
implicit 71, 72
  – dependency strivings 70, 71
  – measures 113–126, 173, 174, 182, 183, 195
  – motives 5, 47, 48, 58, 81–92
implicit affect 97, 98, 100, 106
Implicit Association Test, Brief (BIAT) 118
  – focal categories 118
  – order effects 119
  – reliability 118
Implicit Association Test (IAT) 8, 15–26, 30, 38, 40, 82, 98, 99, 114–116, 118, 119, 135, 140, 158–161, 178–180, 183, 192, 196, 202
  – accuracy 17, 20
  – activation of association 21
  – attitude (assessing) 8, 115
  – attribute dimension 17–19
  – bipolar 158, 159
  – categories 114
  – children/adults (DSP) 178–180, 183
  – compatible block 17, 18, 20
  – construct-specific variance 21
  – consumption behavior (predicted) 115
  – context of measurement 22, 25
  – contrast category 25, 26, 98, 99
  – convergent validity 21–23, 30
  – critical block 17, 18, 20, 114
  – D score 20, 21
  – differential drift rate (IATv) 21, 24
  – discriminant validity 22
  – double categorization 17, 19
  – effect 114
  – flexible 158, 161, 183
  – general-anxiety (assessing) 38
  – incompatible block 17, 18
  – incremental validity 23, 202
  – internal consistency 20, 22, 98
  – outlier criterion 20
  – paper and pencil 19
  – predictive validity 23, 89, 115
  – race 114, 115
  – recoding 116
  – reliability 15, 19, 21, 22, 23, 115
  – romantic relationships (predicting duration) 115
  – score 17–20, 24, 98, 115, 116, 140, 159, 178
  – self-concept (assessing) 22, 40, 135
  – speech anxiety (assessing) 38
  – spider-anxiety (assessing) 38
  – split-half reliability 22

- spontaneous variability 20
- stimulus category 98
- suicidal behavior (predicts) 115
- test–retest correlation 22, 158
- training phase 118
- unipolar 159
- voting behavior (prediction of) 115

Implicit Association Test, personalized IAT (PIAT) 115, 116
- smoking (attitude toward) 116
- stigmatized groups (attitude toward) 116

Implicit Association Test, Recoding-Free (IAT-RF) 116

Implicit Association Test, Single-Block (SB-IAT) 98, 116

Implicit Association Test, SingleAttribute-IAT 98

Implicit Association Test, Single-Block-Single-Target (SB-ST-IAT) 98

Implicit Association Test, Single-Category (SC-IAT) 98, 117, 196

Implicit Association Test, Single-Target (ST-IAT) 117
- nuclear power (attitudes toward) 117

implicit-explicit 30–32, 37–41, 195
- consistency 31, 37–40
- convergence 30, 32
- self-esteem discrepancie 40

Implicit Positive and Negative Affect Test (IPANAT) 100, 101
- discriminant validity 100

Implicit Relational Assessment Procedure (IRAP) 124, 125, 160, 180, 193
- food (attitude toward) 125
- nationalities (attitude toward) 125
- overweight people (attitude toward) 125

impression management 35, 135, 184, 195, 196
impulsive processes 155
impulsiveness 39
impulsivity 134, 136
- tests of 34, 72, 73, 136, 141, 163
index systems (behavior observation) 4
individual variability calibration 20, 21
individualism 47
information processing 51, 70, 175, 181, 203
- style 70

ingroup bias 19
inhibitory control 162, 203, 215
instrument bias (cross-cultural) 87, 88
integration (in narrative) 51, 52, 55, 212
intelligence tests 40
interpersonal 212
- circumplex model 216
- Interpersonal Dependency Inventory (IDI) 70, 71
- influences 70
- processes 211
- relatedness 81, 217
interracial interaction 119
intertextual analysis 49, 58
interview 7, 17, 38, 46, 68, 173, 217
intimacy 90, 102, 103
intrapersonal 212
- influences 70
- processes 211
introspective
- access 113
- limits 105
introspectively accessible 31
intuition 25, 31, 34, 35, 39, 203
Invia 136
iota coefficient 67
Iowa Gambling Task 162
IQ 154
item bias (cross-cultural) 87, 88
item response theory 84, 137

J

Japanese and Caucasian Brief Affect Recognition Test (JACBART) 216

K

kappa coefficient 67

L

Laboratory Temperament Assessment Battery (LAB-TAB) 215
latency-based 18, 20, 21, 103, 105, 120, 122, 123, 125, 174–185, 196, 215
latent
- factors 30, 32
- latent state-trait theory (LST theory) 140
- variable model 32
L-data, see self-reports
level of specification 38

life story 45, 55
linguistic
– analysis 58
– indicators 55, 56
– Linguistic Inquiry and Word Count (LIWC) 45, 48, 49, 54, 55, 57
locus of control 47
logarithmic transformation 21
log-transformation 20

M

manual for scoring motive imagery in running text 83
mathematical aptitude self-concept 40
meaning making 46, 48
measure(s)
– associative 100
– direct 15, 16, 21–25
– explicit 196, 198, 203
– implicit 113–126
– indirect 15–17, 22–25, 106, 108, 153, 173, 174, 182, 183
– objective, see objective measures
– psychophysiological 4
– physiological 155
– task irrelevant 6, 175, 181, 182
– task relevant 6, 175, 180
– vocal pitch 104
memory
– associations 156
– capacity, see working memory capacity
– talk 56
mental
– health 46, 53–55
– tests 133
method(s)
– bias (cross-cultural) 87
– nomothetic 57
– observational (OM) 6, 211, 212
– method–trait problem 139, 140
– variance 144
methodologies
– qualitative 45, 46, 58
  research techniques 50
– quantitative 45, 58
  research techniques 50
Minimum Redundancy Scales (MRS-30) 216
mixed-methods approaches 57
moderators of convergence 140

mood 115
mood state 97
moral
– behavior 29, 124
– dilemmas 124
mother–child reminiscence 56
motivation
– to control prejudiced reactions 37
motivational influences 105
motive(s) 31
– Motive Dictionary 91
– imagery 47, 83, 88, 89
– themes 101
motor-perceptual and performance tests 136
Multidimensional Objective Interest Battery (MOI) 137, 143
multi-method latent state-trait (MM-LST) 140
multimethod strategy assessment 41
multitrait-multimethod approach (MTMM, see multitrait-multimethod framework)
multitrait-multimethod framework 8, 140, 144

N

n Achievement, see need for achievement
n Affiliation, see need for affiliation-intimacy
n Power, see need for power
Name–Letter Task (NLT) 16, 17
narcissism 23, 68, 73
narrative coding system 7
narrative(s) 91
– job loss 54
– military deployment 54
– other/self ratio 57
need(s)
– for achievement 83, 84, 87
– for affiliation-intimacy 81–83, 88
– for closure 36, 39
– for consistency 36
– for power 83, 84, 88
– implicit 70
negative performance feedback 41
non-normal distribution 21

O

objective
– measures 1, 3, 5, 8, 134, 138, 143, 211
– Objective Achievement Motivation Test (OAT) 136, 139, 143

– Objective-Analytic Test Battery
  (OA-TB) 134, 138
– objective-analytic tests 134
– Objective Heuristic Thinking Test
  (OHTT) 138
– Objective Personality Test(s) (OPTs)
  6–8, 39, 133–142, 144, 145
– personality tests 4, 6, 7, 30, 32, 39,
  133, 134, 139
observation
– systematic 211
Omnibus Values Questionnaire 47
openness to experience 34
Operant Motive Test (OMT) 82, 87, 88, 91,
  92, 100, 101
orientation (element of narrative structure) 48
overgeneral memory (OGM) retrieval style 53

P

parent report 155, 211, 215
penile plethysmography (PPG) 174, 177
perceived distinctiveness 22
perceptual-cognitive style 64, 71
performance
– tests of personality 134
personality
– factors 31–34, 134
– measures 30, 144
– Personality Diagnostic Questionnaire-
  Revised (PDQ-R) 71
– differences 54
– tests, see objective personality tests
– traits (as moderators) 32, 34, 35, 140
– variables 7
personnel selection 30, 195, 212
person–situation interactions 29
phallometry 174, 185
Picture Story Exercise (PSE) 47, 82, 83, 84,
  87, 88, 89, 91, 92
placements of objects 105
polygraphy 174
polysemous brand slogans 198, 199
power 101, 102
practice blocks 114, 116, 118
predictive
– validity 117
prime 99, 123
priming
– affective 98
– evaluative 119, 120

– masked affective 100
– semantic 160
– subliminal affective 100
principal component analysis 25
private self-consciousness 36, 37
process pure 24
projective
– measures 4–7, 47, 64–66, 97, 100, 134,
  217
– method 64, 197
– techniques 4–7, 134
– tests 4, 7, 47, 65, 136
propositional processes 196, 204
PROTAN 91
PSE/TAT
– construct equivalence (cross-cultural)
  88
– cue ambiguity 87
– cue strength 86
– differential item functioning (cross-
  cultural) 88
– extensivity 87
– internal consistency 84
– local stochastic statistical independence
  84
– reactance 87
– sexual arousal (assessing) 87
– stimulus pull 86
– universality 85–88
PSE, test–retest reliability 84
psychology
– clinical 30, 65, 164, 195
– consumer 6, 7, 12, 195, 196, 198, 202,
  205
– developmental 211
– health 6, 7, 153–155, 158, 164, 165
punishment sensitivity 163

Q

Q-data, see self-report
Q-sort 213, 217
questionnaire(s) 3–8, 16, 17, 24, 25, 30,
  39, 47, 54, 68, 69, 71–73, 134, 135,
  138–140, 143–145, 173, 174, 197, 211,
  216, 217

R

race (attitude toward) 115, 118, 121, 124
racial prejudice 99
random walk model 18

rapid serial visual presentation (RSVP) 194
Rapid Serial Visual Presentation Task (RSVP) 182
reaction
 – speed 134, 177, 183
 – time measures 4, 98, 157
 – time test(s) (RT test[s]) 135, 154, 155, 158, 182
reduced autobiographical memory specificity (rAMS), see overgeneral memory retrieval style
reflective–impulsive model (RIM) 32
reflective processes 162
reflectiveness 39
reflexivity (tests of), see impulsivity
reproducible test situations 135
research
 – cross-cultural 87
 – narrative 45
resolutions (in narrative) 48
response
 – compatibility effect 17
 – conflicts 106
 – latency 120, 122, 123, 125
 – response-competition task 114
Revised Family Observation Schedule (FOS-R-III) 214
reward sensitivity 163
RIM Comprehensive System (CS)
 – Barrier and Penetration (BPS) Scoring System 66
 – concurrent validity 67, 68
 – content scoring 65
 – content variables, see thematic variables
 – defense style 65, 67
 – incremental validity 68, 73
 – interrater reliability 67
 – Lerner Defense Scale (LDS) 66
 – Mutuality of Autonomy (MOA) Scale 66
 – predictive validity 67
 – Primary Process (PriPro) Scoring 66
 – Rorschach Oral Dependency (ROD) Scale 66, 70, 71
 – Thought Disorder Index (TDI) 66
Risk Behaviour Test (RBT) 142
risk propensity 39
 – Risk Propensity Task 142
 – test of 137, 139, 141, 142

risk-taking 39, 63, 139
Rorschach inkblot method (RIM) 64, 65, 67, 68, 69, 70, 71, 72, 73, 100
Rorschach Performance Assessment System (R-PAS) 66, 68
Rorschach Prognostic Rating Scale (RPRS) 66
Roulette Test (RT) 142

S
sample bias (cross-cultural) 87
scholastic aptitude self-concept 40
school achievement 89
Screening Scale for Pedophilic Interests 177, 179
self (attitude toward) 125
self-concept 22, 25, 31, 33, 34, 36, 40, 41, 65, 135, 196
 – explicit 33, 40, 41
 – implicit 33, 40, 41, 196
self-control 34, 39, 155, 203
self-monitoring 36, 37, 105
self-observation theory 34
self-ordered pointing test 162
self-presentation 105
self-presentational concerns 113, 115
self-regulate 99, 102
 – attention 215
 – behavior 215
self-report(s) 68, 69, 70, 71, 72, 73, 97, 105, 108, 133, 139
 – L-Data 3, 133
 – measures 113, 116, 120, 124
 – Q-Data 30, 144
signal detection 120, 121
Simulated Real-Life 136
single case diagnostics 180
situational
 – characteristics (as moderators) 140
 – factors, see situational moderators
 – influences, see interpersonal influences
 – moderators 23, 35, 40, 69, 183
skewness 20, 21
smoking 116
 – interventions 54
social desirability 37, 113, 183
Socialization Goals Inventory (SGI) 217
sorting paired features task (SPF) 122, 123
specific emotions 104
specificity similarity 38, 140

speed–accuracy trade-off 20
spiders 122
spontaneous behavior 23, 68, 69, 71, 138, 183, 202, 203
standard actuarial risk indicators (Static-99R) 177
standard stimulus situation 135
startle probe reflex 183
state 31, 34, 57, 67, 69, 70, 83, 97, 108, 137, 140, 144, 154, 155, 160, 203, 211
– affect 101, 104
– variance 8, 144
still-face paradigm 212
stimulus
– attribution test 65
– stimulus–response compatibility (SRC) 161
– -specific effects 176
Strange Situation 213
stress resistance 137
Stroop Color-Interference Test 154
Stroop task(s)
– addiction 157
– emotional 181
structural
– analysis 5, 48, 49, 58
– fit 22, 23, 24, 25
– scoring 48, 49, 65
swift-selection platform 197
syntactic elements 46, 48
systematic-functional linguistics 49

T

task-specific effects 176
T-data, see objective personality tests
TEAM index scale of attention 216
terror management theory 102
test batteries 183
Tester's Rating of Child Behavior (TRCB) 215
testing materials (effects of) 135
thematic
– analysis, see content coding: thematic
– content-coding system, see content coding: thematic
– Thematic Apperception Test (TAT) 83, 87, 88, 92
– variables 69, 70
theory
– of mind 91
– of planned behavior 5, 32, 33

threshold 18
– criterion 18
– of awareness 100
trait 7, 29–35, 38, 39, 72, 97, 99, 104, 137, 139, 140, 144, 154, 162, 163, 203, 216
– affect 104
– variance 8, 144
transparency (of test) 138, 141
tolerance 133

U

unidimensional categorization
Units-of-Information (UOI) 52

V

validity 108
– cross-situational 211
– of OPTs 140
– predictive 81, 89, 115, 120, 125, 201
– three general models of predictive (additive model, multiplicative model, double-dissociation model) 202, 204
validity patterns 23
– additive 23, 202, 204
– double additive 23
– double dissociation 23, 202, 204
– interactive/mulitiplicative 23, 202, 204
– moderation 23
– partial dissociation 23
– simple association 23
value survey 47
viewing times (VT) 176, 177, 178, 183, 189
visual probe task 157
vocal characteristics 104
vocational interests (tests of) 134, 137, 139, 143, 145
voice markers 104

W

well-being (prediction of) 54, 55
word
– association test 156
– classification 81, 138
– count 46, 48, 49, 53, 54, 58
– count procedures, see word count
working memory capacity 23, 38, 203, 204
Working Styles battery 136, 143

Z

zygomatic muscle 104

European Journal of Psychological Assessment

Official Organ of the European Association of Psychological Assessment (EAPA)

Free online sample issue at
www.hogrefe.com/journals/ejpa

Editor-in-Chief
Matthias Ziegler, Berlin, Germany

Associate Editors
Martin Bäckström, Sweden
Gary N. Burns, USA
Laurence Claes, Belgium
David Gallardo-Pujol, Spain
Samuel Greiff, Luxembourg
Lena Lämmle, Germany
Carolyn MacCann, Australia
Sebastian Sauer, Germany
Marit Sijbrandij, The Netherlands

Impact factor of 1.250 for 2013!

ISSN 1015-5759,
ISSN-Print 1015-5759, ISSN-Online 2151-2426

4 issues per annum (= 1 volume)

Subscription rates (2015):
Libraries / Institutions: US $434.00 / € 319.00 / £ 256.00
Individuals: US $208.00 / € 152.00 / £ 121.00
+ postage and handling: US $16.00 / € 12.00 / £ 10.00

The main purpose of the EJPA is to present important articles which provide seminal information on both theoretical and applied developments in this field. Articles reporting the construction of new measures or an advancement of an existing measure are given priority.

The journal is directed to practitioners as well as to academicians: The conviction of its editors is that the discipline of psychological assessment should, necessarily and firmly, be attached to the roots of psychological science, while going deeply into all the consequences of its applied, practice-oriented development.

Psychological assessment is experiencing a period of renewal and expansion, attracting more and more attention from both academic and applied psychology, as well as from political, corporate, and social organizations. The journal presents clearly written original papers, reviews, and case studies in all domains of psychological assessment.

Electronic Full Text:
The full text of the European Journal of Psychological Assessment – current and past issues (from 1995 onward) – is available online at www.psyjournals.com and in PsycARTICLES (included in subscription price).

Abstracting Services:
The journal is abstracted/indexed in Current Contents / Social & Behavioral Sciences (CC/S&BS), Social Sciences Citation Index (SSCI), Social SciSearch, PsycINFO, Psychological Abstracts, PSYNDEX, ERIH, and Scopus.

Hogrefe Publishing
38 Chauncy Street, Suite 1002 · Boston, MA 02111 · USA
Tel: (866) 823-4726 · Fax: (617) 354-6875
E-Mail: customerservice@hogrefe.com

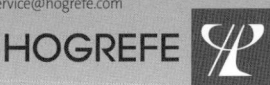

Hogrefe Publishing
Merkelstr. 3 · 37085 Göttingen · Germany
Tel: +49 551 999 500 · Fax: +49 551 999 50 111
E-Mail: customerservice@hogrefe.de

HOGREFE

Order online at **www.hogrefe.com**

PSYCHOLOGICAL ASSESSMENT – SCIENCE AND PRACTICE

New Book Series!

See details at www.hogrefe.com!

Yael Benyamini · Marie Johnston · Evangelos C. Karademas (Eds.)

Assessment in Health Psychology

2015, vi + 320 pp.
ISBN 978-0-88937-452-2
US $63.00 / £ 36.00 / € 44.95

This book presents and discusses the best and most appropriate assessment methods and instruments for all specific areas that are central for health psychologists. It also describes the conceptual and methodological bases for assessment in health psychology, as well the most important current issues and recent progress in methods. A unique feature of this book, which brings together leading authorities on health psychology assessment, is its emphasis on the bidirectional link between theory and practice.

Assessment in Health Psychology is addressed to masters and doctoral students in health psychology, to all those who teach health psychology, to researchers from other disciplines, including clinical psychology, health promotion, and public health, as well as to health policy makers and other healthcare practitioners.

This volume provides a thorough and authoritative record of the best available assessment tools and methods in health psychology.

From the Contents:

Part I: Introduction

Chapter 1: Introduction by E. C. Karademas, Y. Benyamini, and M. Johnston

Part II: Domains Assessed

Chapter 2: Social Cognitions in Health Behavior by M. Conner

Chapter 3: Self-Efficacy and Outcome Expectancies by R. Schwarzer and A. Luszczynska

Chapter 4: Illness Representations by L. D. Cameron, A. Durazo, and H. M. Rus

Chapter 5: Health Behavior by A. Luszczynska and M. Hagger

Chapter 6: Patient–Physician Communication and Patient Satisfaction by K. B. Haskard-Zolnierek and S. L. Williams

Chapter 7: Adherence to Medical Advice by J. A. Chambers and R. E. O'Carroll

[...]

Part III: Assessment Methods and Issues

Chapter 18: Ecological Momentary Assessment by Derek W. Johnston

Chapter 19: Reporting Behavior Change Interventions and Techniques by S. Michie and C. E. Wood

Chapter 20: Cultural Adaptation of Measures by S. López-Roig and M.-Á. Pastor

Chapter 21: Assessment in Children by D. Christie

[...]

Part IV: Conclusion

Chapter 23: Assessment: Moving Beyond Association to Explanation and Intervention by H. Leventhal, D. E. McCarthy, E. Roman, and E. A. Leventhal

Chapter 24: Measurement Issues in Health Psychology by M. Johnston, Y. Benyamini, and E. C. Karademas

---

Hogrefe Publishing
30 Amberwood Parkway · Ashland, OH 44805 · USA
Tel: (800) 228-3749 · Fax: (419) 281-6883
E-Mail: customerservice@hogrefe.com

Hogrefe Publishing
Merkelstr. 3· 37085 Göttingen · Germany
Tel: +49 551 999 500 · Fax: +49 551 999 50 111
E-Mail: customerservice@hogrefe.de

Hogrefe Publishing c/o Marston Book Services Ltd
160 Eastern Ave., Milton Park · Abingdon, OX14 4SB · UK
Tel: +44 1235 465577 · Fax +44 1235 465556
E-mail: direct.orders@marston.co.uk

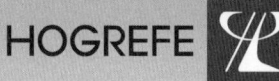

HOGREFE

Order online at **www.hogrefe.com**
or call toll-free **(800) 228-3749** (US only)